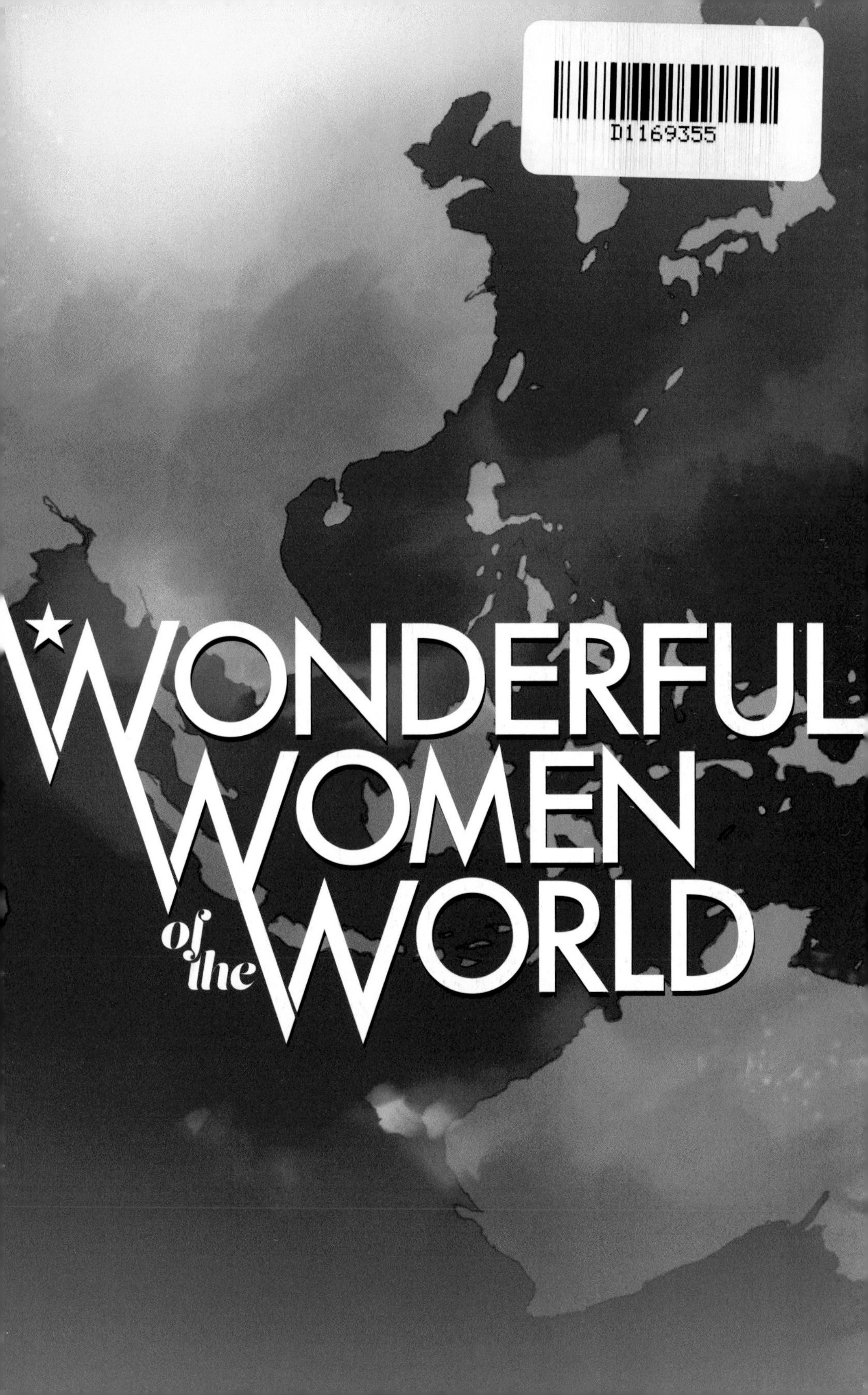

Wonderful Women of the World

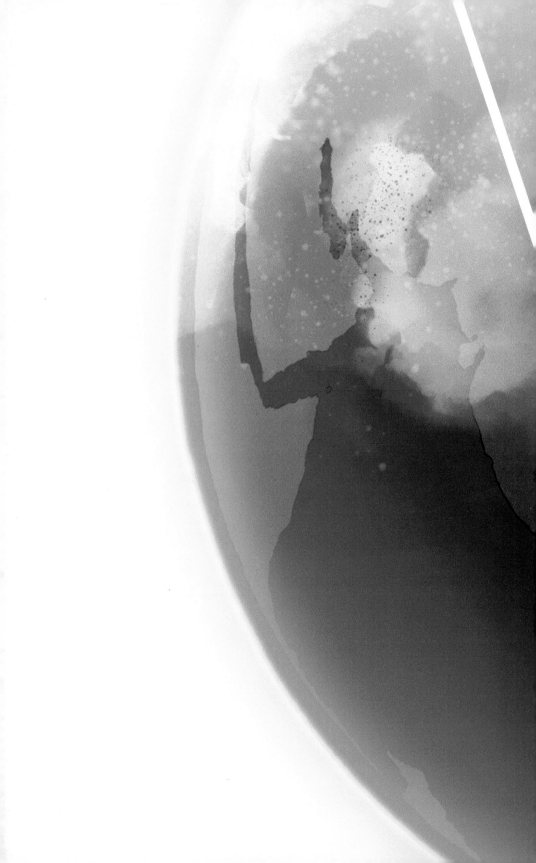

Wonderful Women of the World

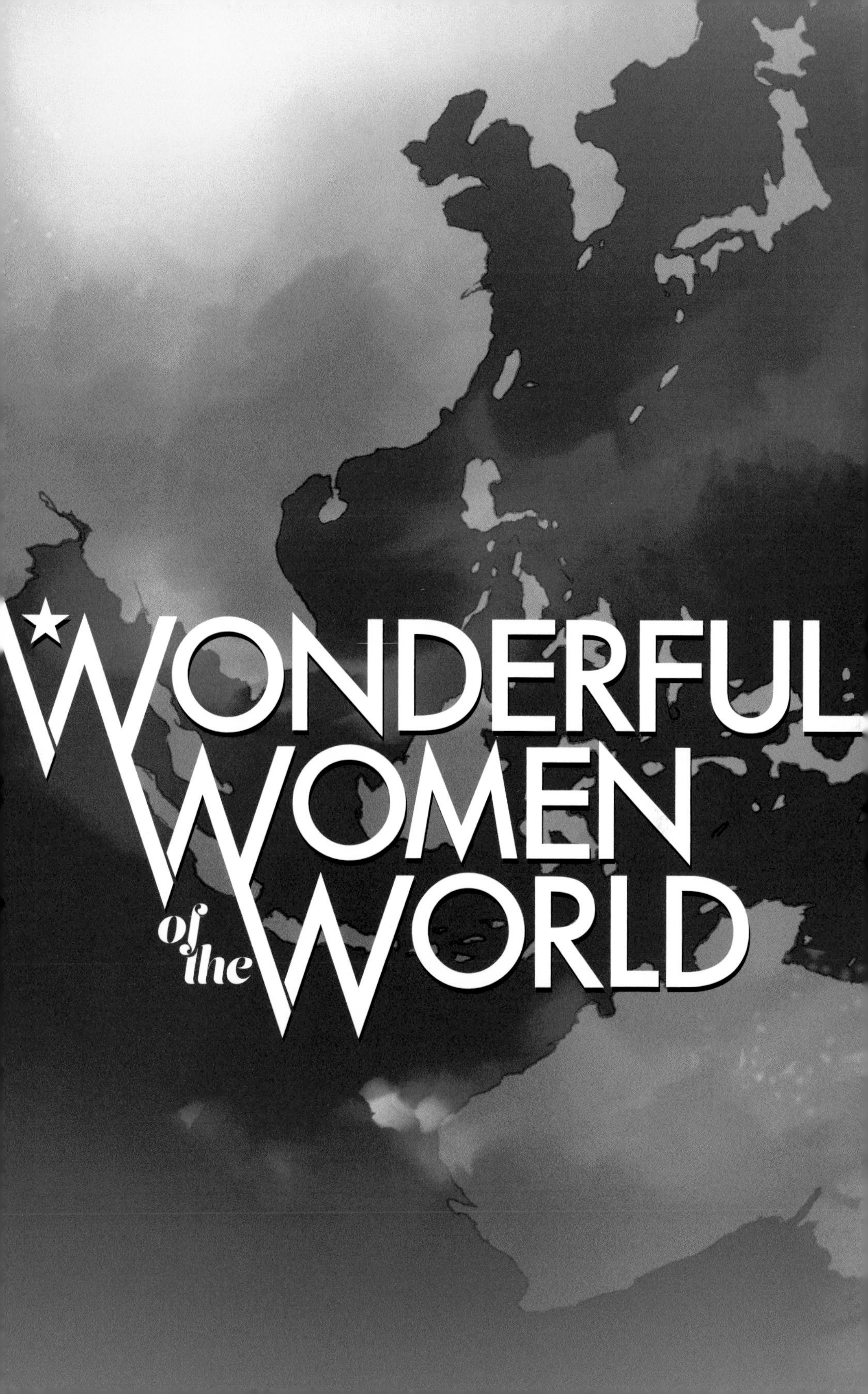

KRISTY QUINN EDITOR
COURTNEY JORDAN ASSISTANT EDITOR
STEVE COOK DESIGN DIRECTOR — BOOKS
AMIE BROCKWAY-METCALF PUBLICATION DESIGN
SANDY ALONZO PUBLICATION PRODUCTION

MARIE JAVINS EDITOR-IN-CHIEF, DC COMICS

DANIEL CHERRY III SENIOR VP — GENERAL MANAGER
JIM LEE PUBLISHER & CHIEF CREATIVE OFFICER
JOEN CHOE VP — GLOBAL BRAND & CREATIVE SERVICES
DON FALLETTI VP — MANUFACTURING OPERATIONS & WORKFLOW MANAGEMENT
LAWRENCE GANEM VP — TALENT SERVICES
ALISON GILL SENIOR VP — MANUFACTURING & OPERATIONS
NICK J. NAPOLITANO VP — MANUFACTURING ADMINISTRATION & DESIGN
NANCY SPEARS VP — REVENUE

WONDERFUL WOMEN OF THE WORLD

DC — a WarnerMedia Company.

DC Comics, 2900 West Alameda Ave., Burbank, CA 91505

Printed by LSC Communications, Crawfordsville, IN, USA.
8/20/21. First Printing.

ISBN: 978-1-77950-378-7

Library of Congress Control Number: 2020945273

CONTENTS

PART FIVE: EQUALITY

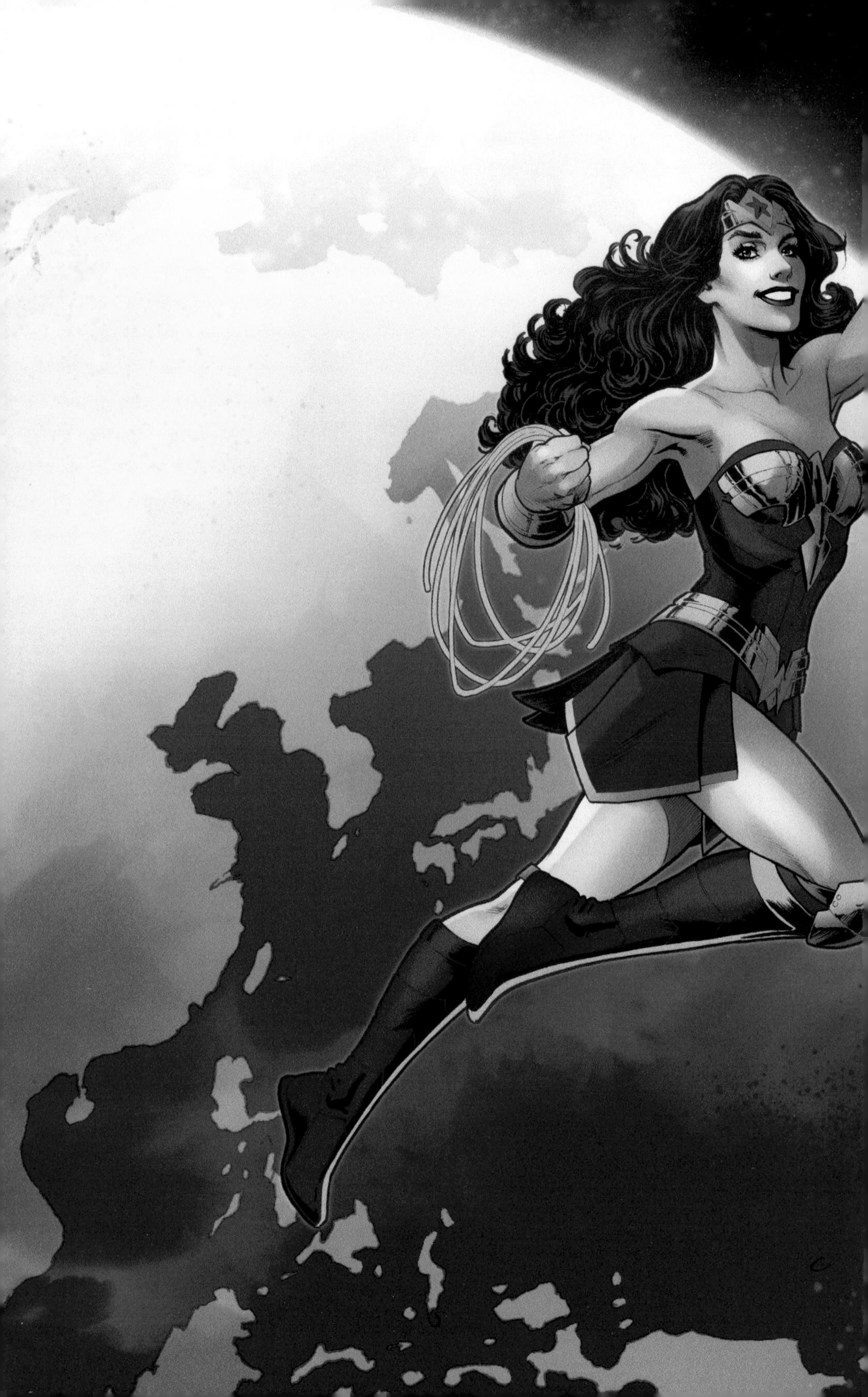

a GIRL with a HERO can do ANYTHING

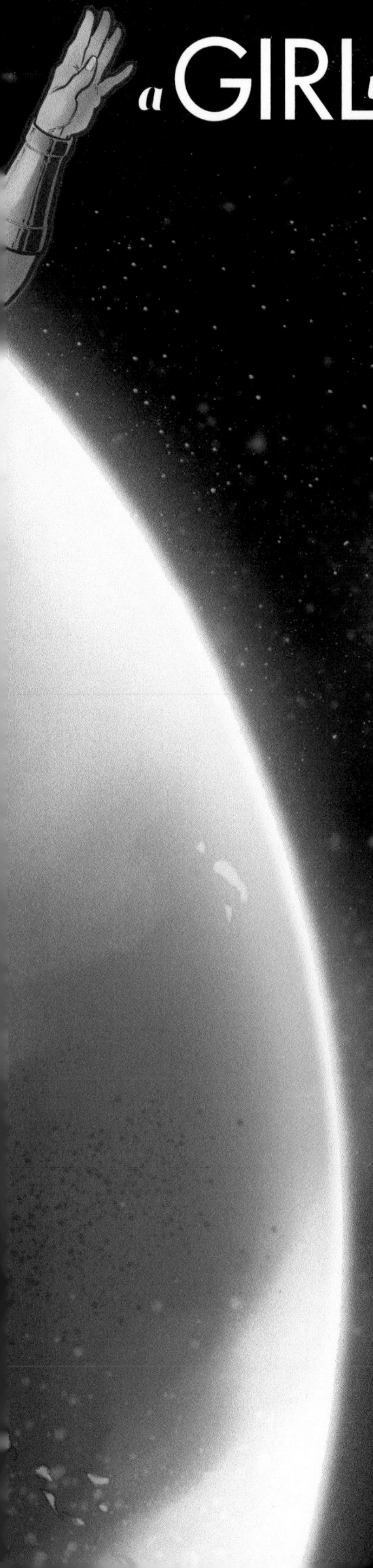

When I was a kid, I did a project for school about the different sections of the newspaper. I was confused by the Help Wanted ads—employment offers listed in long columns at the back of the paper. They were segregated into jobs offered to two genders: female and male. I asked my parents and teacher why there was a difference between jobs for women and jobs for men. (There was rarely discussion back then about nonbinary people, sadly.)

They explained that women were made to be mothers and to work only as secretaries, nurses, or teachers. Men got to do everything else. This was the first time I realized that adults were ridiculous. I could clearly see the injustice in the situation. Why couldn't they?

This all unfolded just as a groundbreaking television show appeared: *Wonder Woman*, starring Lynda Carter in the title role. This show changed my life. Diana/Wonder Woman showed me that women could be way more than the sliver of life seen in the want ads. Wonder Woman was strong, fast, tough, smart, funny, compassionate, and wore great boots. She wanted to fight evil and create justice. Much to my mother's dismay, Wonder Woman became *my* superhero.

I bought a life-size Wonder Woman poster and hung it on my closet door. Mom was suspicious about the growing second wave of feminism; she wanted me to conform and perform in traditional feminine ways. Nope. Not me! The first issue of *Ms.* magazine hit the stands right around the time I started clashing with my mother about women's rights. Wonder Woman was on the cover of that magazine. I realized that I wasn't alone in my hopes for a future of equality and opportunity for all.

Wonder Woman gave me permission to be an athlete. She showed me that muscles are amazing and that strength creates joy and safety. While I'm still bummed that there weren't many other female superheroes while I was growing up, I'm grateful for the one who changed my life and helped me dream of the large and in-charge life I've created for myself.

The chance to work on this book, as well as writing my own Wonder Woman graphic novel, has been a dream come true. No…that's not quite right.

This has been *better* than a dream come true! I've got a pretty good imagination, but I could never have imagined being able to work on projects like this.

For one thing, #TeamWonderWoman is filled with badasses. Look at the women and nonbinary people who fill these pages! Look at the incredible odds they faced, their moments of failure, how they dug deep, rose to meet the opposition, and overcame it! Read the book the first time for these inspiring stories. But read it again to bask in the talent of the writers and artists who bring these stories to life on the page. My role as editor was mainly to watch in awe as the creators of these stories did the labor of condensing lifetimes of hard work and activism down to a few magical pages. Make note of the names of the writers and artists who really connected with your heart, then look up their other books and comics. (Hint: most of them are on social media as well as their own websites.)

I hope these stories will inspire and strengthen you. I hope they help you understand the challenges faced by earlier generations, and how the battles for equality and justice are still going on right now. This book was created on the magical island of Themyscira that lives within all of us. I hope that when you read it, you'll see that there is a place waiting for you on that island, too. Welcome to the family!

Laurie

Laurie Halse Anderson is a *New York Times* bestselling author known for tackling tough subjects with humor and sensitivity. Two of her books, *Speak* and *Chains*, were National Book Award finalists. Laurie has been honored for her battles for intellectual freedom by the National Coalition Against Censorship and the National Council of Teachers of English. She is a member of RAINN's National Leadership Council and frequently speaks about sexual violence. Working on this book with these talented authors, artists, and the editorial team was one of two great things that happened to her in the sucky year of 2020. The other was when Lynda Carter, TV's Wonder Woman, followed her on Twitter.

WONDERFUL WOMEN of HISTORY

This book is an updated version of a feature that ran in Wonder Woman comic books from 1942 to 1954. The concept was to pair short biographies of women who had defied stereotypes and discrimination with comics-style illustrations. The woman who created and ran the project was named Alice Marble.

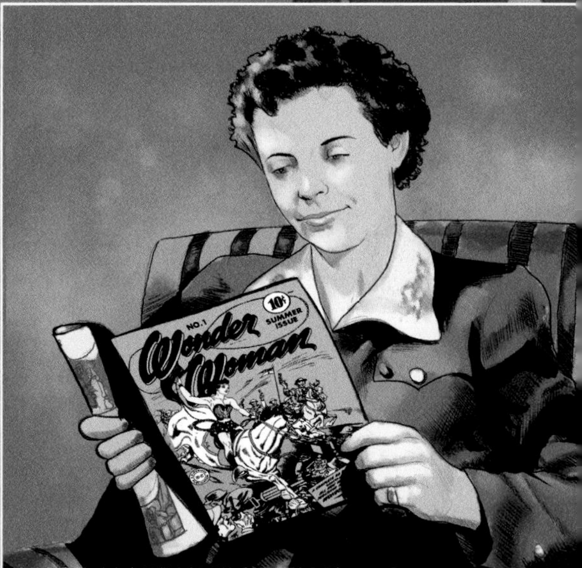
No. 1
10¢
Summer Issue
Wonder Woman
ALICE MARBLE BY CAT STAGGS

Alice was a Wonder Woman in her own right. She was a powerful, world-class tennis player before World War II broke out. She was a spy in Nazi-occupied Europe near the end of the war and continued to break barriers for the rest of her life. After her tennis career, Alice became an editor at DC Comics. Her first job was researching and writing the biographies for the original Wonder Women of History stories.

Alice shared many qualities with the heroes of this book. She broke through the challenges of poverty, she trusted her judgment, and she believed in her dreams. Later in life, Alice used her position to combat injustice. She publicly called out the American tennis community's exclusion of Black players. Her words helped open the door for Althea Gibson, the first Black player to win Wimbledon and the U.S. National Championships. Alice also mentored younger women, like tennis legend Billie Jean King and Sally Ride, the first female American astronaut.

Every generation has had people like Alice, like all of the people highlighted in this book, and like the writers and illustrators who combined their talents to make it. People of marginalized genders have all faced institutional discrimination, political and social injustice, and hatred. Those who live within intersectional identities face these issues in compounded and complex ways. But they didn't quit. They pushed on, pushed up, stood up, and claimed their rightful space. Because of the heroes in this book and countless others like them, our world is a better place.

But we have far to go.

We need *you* to join us.

There are three things you can do to help.

LEARN

Your best weapon is your education. It is the one thing that the bad guys can never steal from you. If you aren't happy with the quality of your education, speak up about it. Work with your teachers and librarians. Figure out your learning style and identify what you are curious about and what problems you want to solve. You need to sharpen your wits and create opportunities so that you can take your rightful place in the world. And know this — education comes in many forms. It's not always a straight line of high school > college > grad school > success. The most interesting and happy people I know (including me) took a winding road that included time off, jobs (I worked on a dairy farm, among other things), adventure, soul-searching, and then back to school. You have to walk your own path. Just make sure you're always feeding your brain and soul.

BUILD

Superheroes never do it all on their own. They understand the magical, magnifying power of community. There are the communities that you are born into and the communities that you create around yourself once you go out into the world. If you are feeling unseen or lonely, then you need more people in your life who will honor and respect you for who you are. This can be a challenge, especially if you are introverted (like me!). But Wonder Women do not shy away from doing the hard things. You'll find your people as you explore your passions: space exploration, nanotechnology, Nubian history, glass sculpture, surfing, political activism, cooking videos, voting rights, dancing, or petitioning for a full-time librarian at your school. That's where you will find your kindred spirits. Build your community with them.

DREAM

The greatest gift of all is the ability to imagine a better world. You have the opportunity and responsibility to be a part of that. It starts by dreaming of the world that you want to live in. What would that look like? What changes do you want to see in how food is produced? How we deal with air and water pollution? How can we make sure all schools are safe, welcoming spaces for all students? How many languages do you want to learn? What countries do you want to live in? What kind of art do you want to create, what inventions or programs? Dream big and dream bold, my friends. You are the next generation of Wonder Women, Wonder People, Wonder Men. You will make it better for everyone.

part one STRENGTH

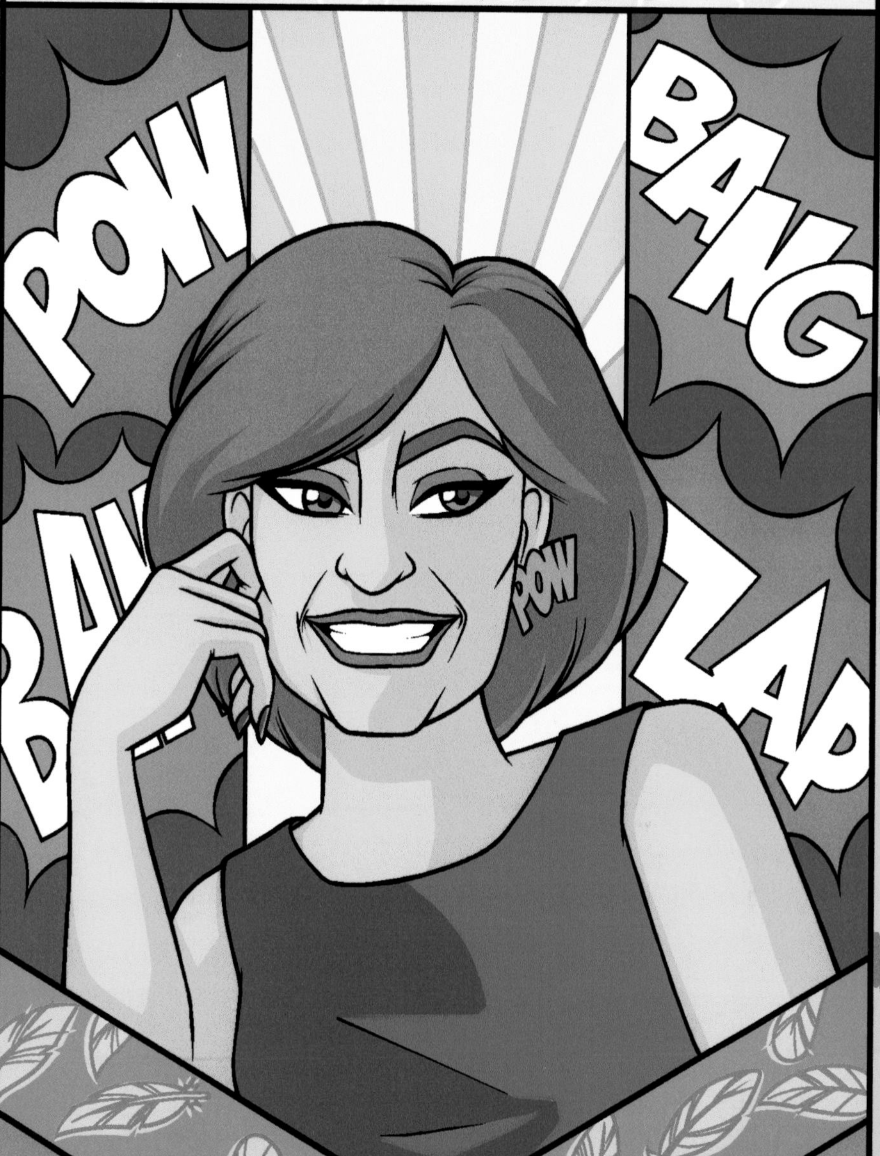
POW
BANG
BAM
ZAP
POW
AGNES '2020

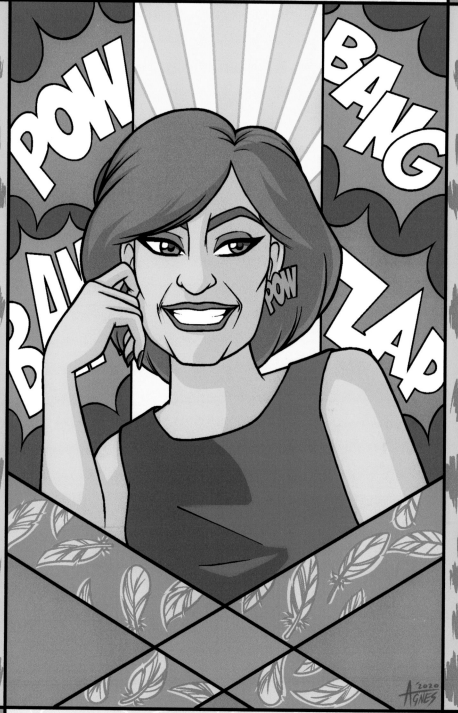

Jenette Kahn exemplifies the strength of character required to break new ground. A larger-than-life representative of women in business, the onetime president and publisher of DC Comics led with her values: championing creator rights, pursuing diversity among the people in the company and on the comics pages, and pushing boundaries to expose important issues to our audience were key elements that made her successful. DC Books for Young Readers is proud to continue those traditions!

SERENA WILLIAMS: SUPER SERENA–G.O.A.T.

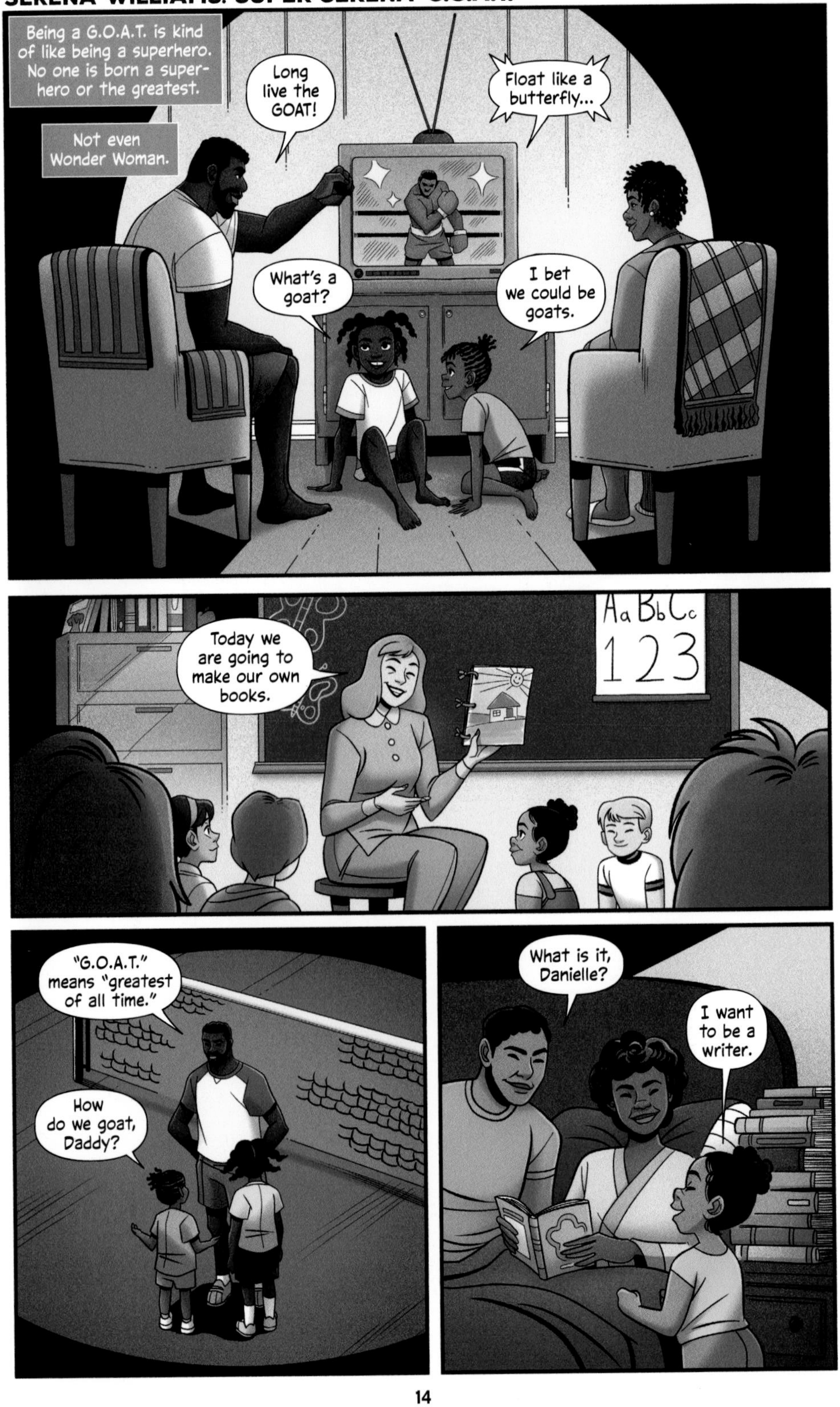

Being a G.O.A.T. is kind of like being a superhero. No one is born a superhero or the greatest.
Not even Wonder Woman.
Long live the GOAT!
Float like a butterfly...
What's a goat?
I bet we could be goats.
Today we are going to make our own books.
Aa Bb Cc
123
"G.O.A.T." means "greatest of all time."
How do we goat, Daddy?
What is it, Danielle?
I want to be a writer.

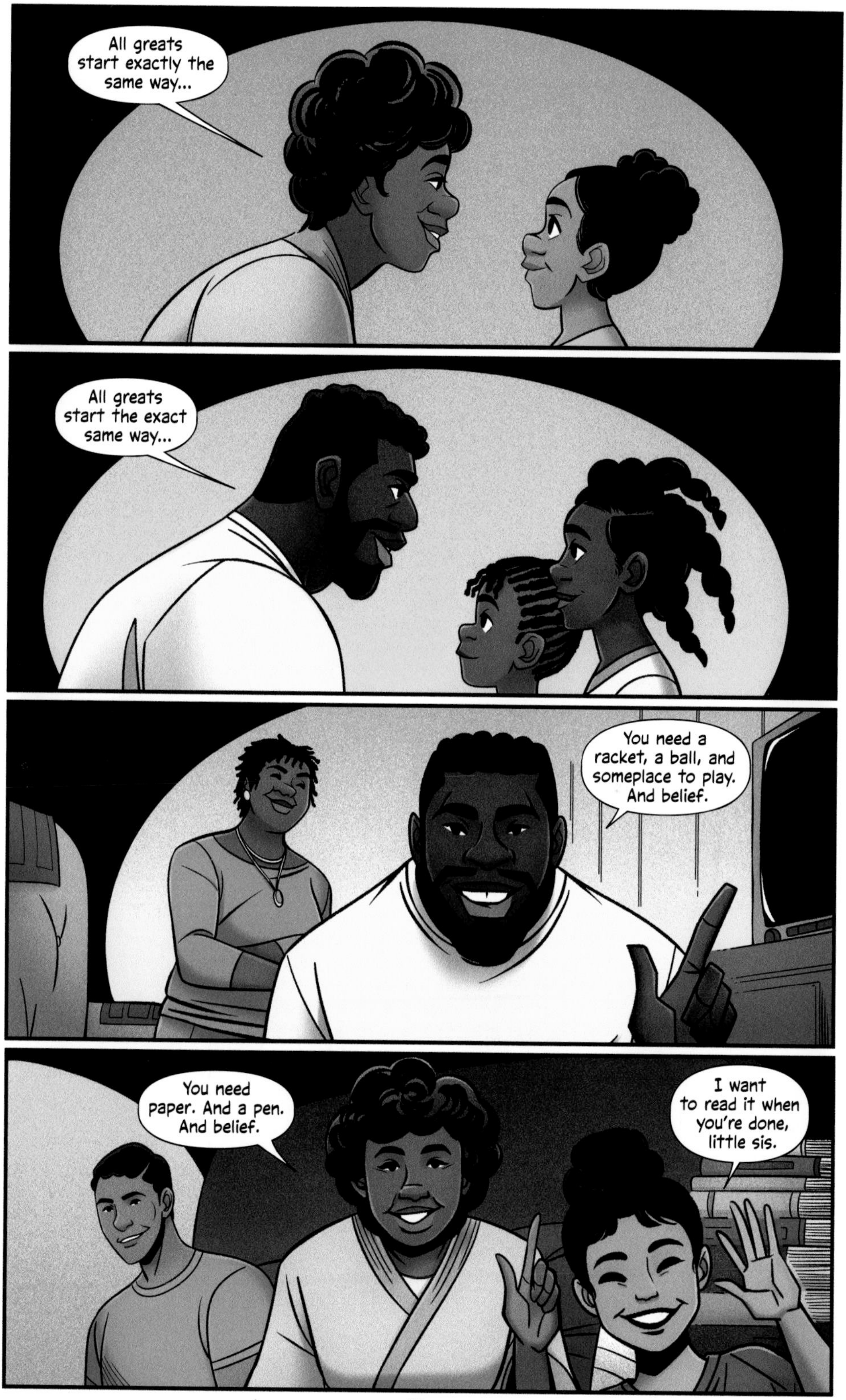
All greats start exactly the same way...
All greats start the exact same way...
You need a racket, a ball, and someplace to play. And belief.
You need paper. And a pen. And belief.
I want to read it when you're done, little sis.

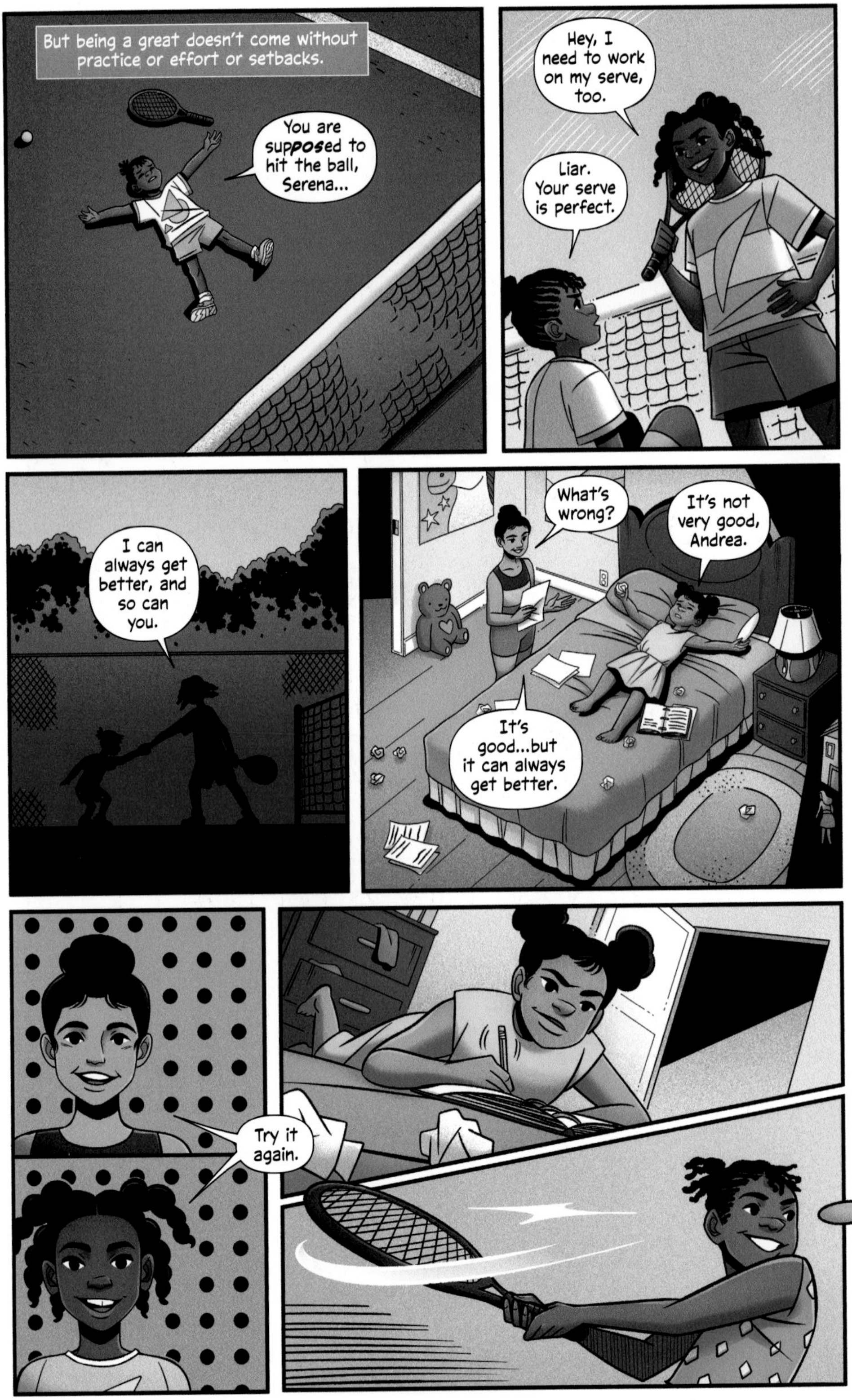
But being a great doesn't come without practice or effort or setbacks.
You are sup*pos*ed to hit the ball, Serena...
Hey, I need to work on my serve, too.
Liar. Your serve is perfect.
I can always get better, and so can you.
What's wrong?
It's not very good, Andrea.
It's good...but it can always get better.
Try it again.

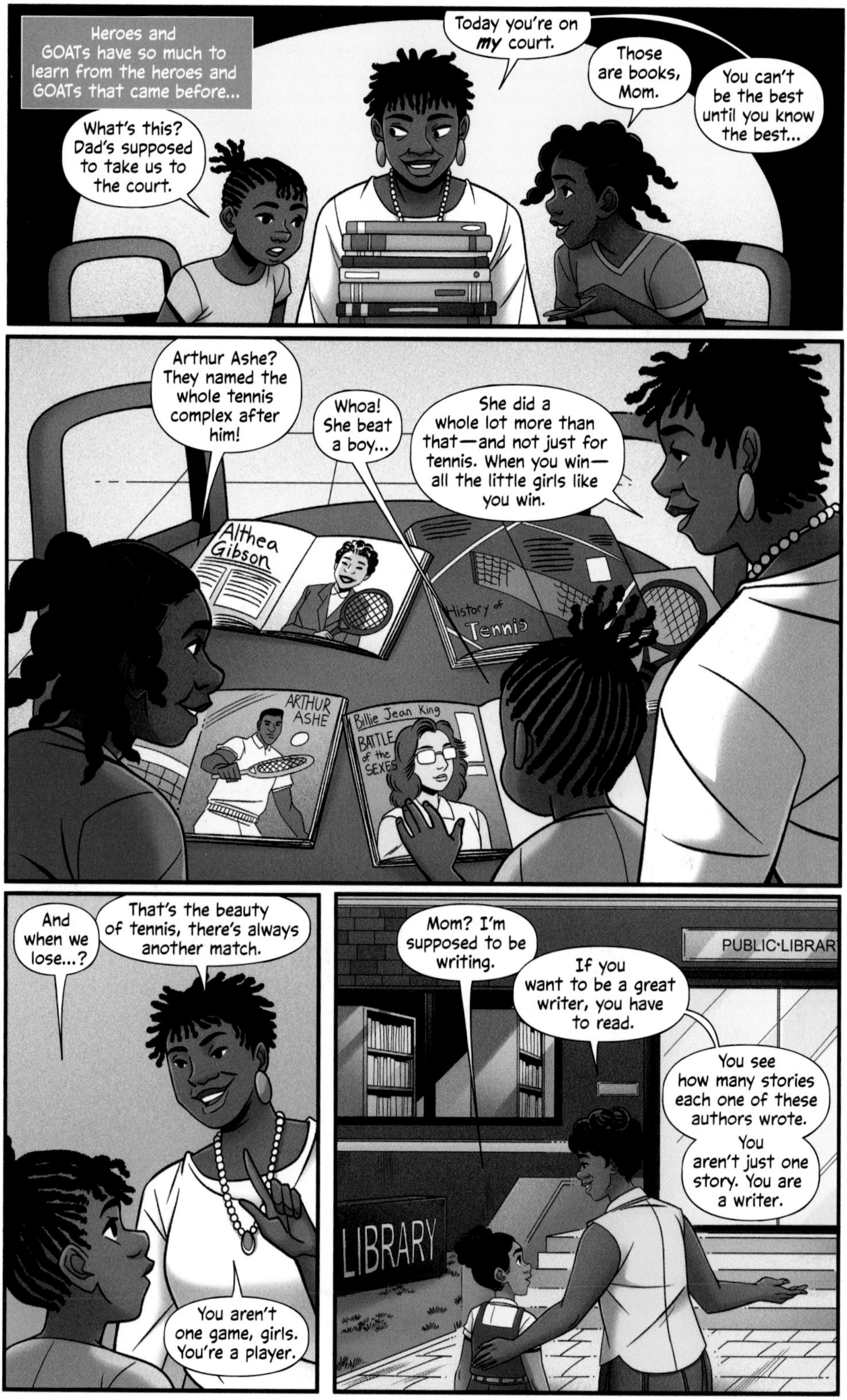
Heroes and GOATs have so much to learn from the heroes and GOATs that came before...
What's this? Dad's supposed to take us to the court.
Today you're on *my* court.
Those are books, Mom.
You can't be the best until you know the best...
Arthur Ashe? They named the whole tennis complex after him!
Whoa! She beat a boy...
She did a whole lot more than that—and not just for tennis. When you win—all the little girls like you win.
Althea Gibson
History of Tennis
ARTHUR ASHE
Billie Jean King
BATTLE of the SEXES
And when we lose...?
That's the beauty of tennis, there's always another match.
You aren't one game, girls. You're a player.
Mom? I'm supposed to be writing.
If you want to be a great writer, you have to read.
PUBLIC·LIBRARY
You see how many stories each one of these authors wrote.
You aren't just one story. You are a writer.
LIBRARY

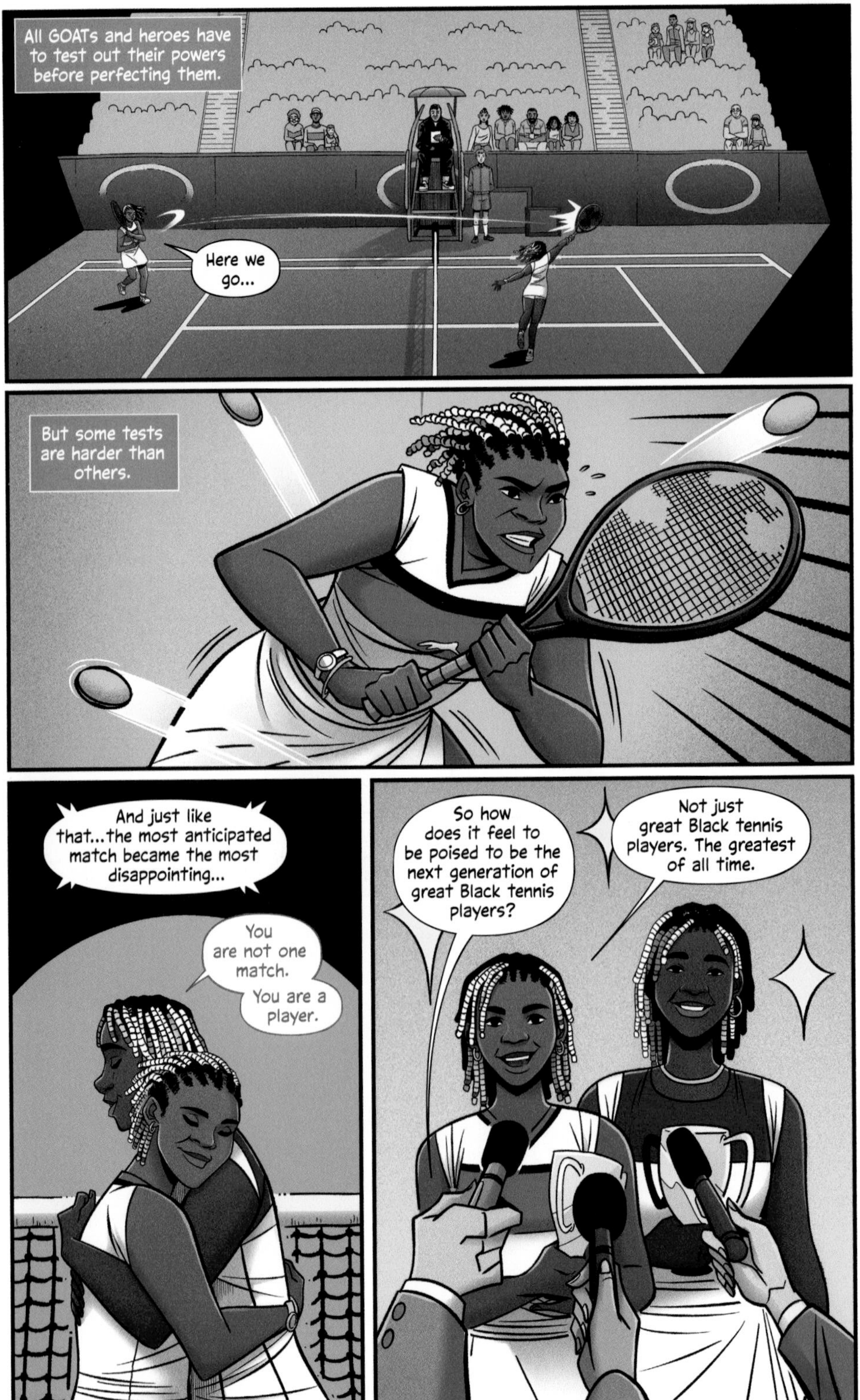
All GOATs and heroes have to test out their powers before perfecting them.
Here we go...
But some tests are harder than others.
And just like that...the most anticipated match became the most disappointing...
You are not one match.
You are a player.
So how does it feel to be poised to be the next generation of great Black tennis players?
Not just great Black tennis players. The greatest of all time.

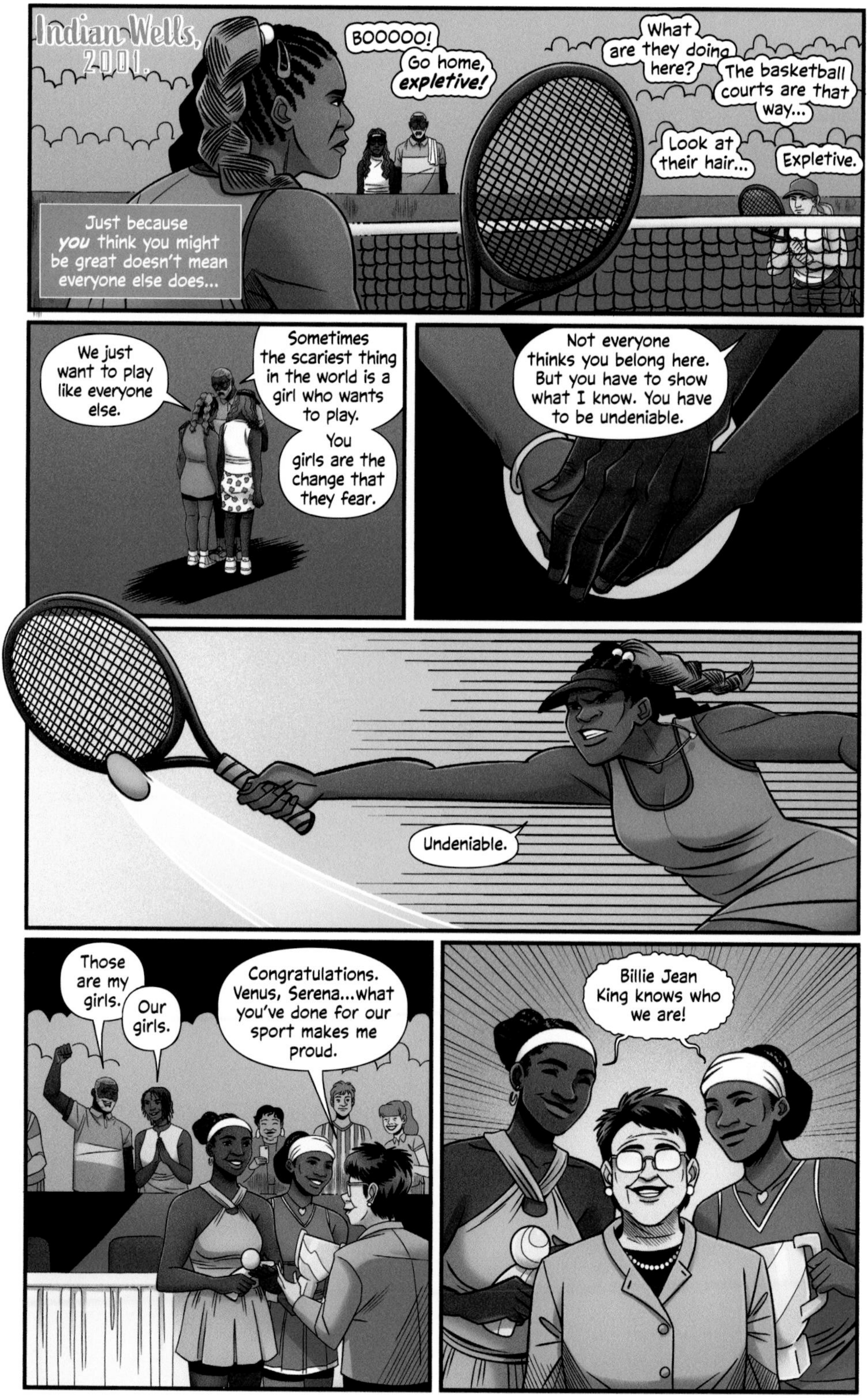
Indian Wells, 2001.
BOOOOO!
Go home, *expletive!*
What are they doing here?
The basketball courts are that way...
Look at their hair...
Expletive.
Just because *you* think you might be great doesn't mean everyone else does...
We just want to play like everyone else.
Sometimes the scariest thing in the world is a girl who wants to play.
You girls are the change that they fear.
Not everyone thinks you belong here. But you have to show what I know. You have to be undeniable.
Undeniable.
Those are my girls.
Our girls.
Congratulations. Venus, Serena...what you've done for our sport makes me proud.
Billie Jean King knows who we are!

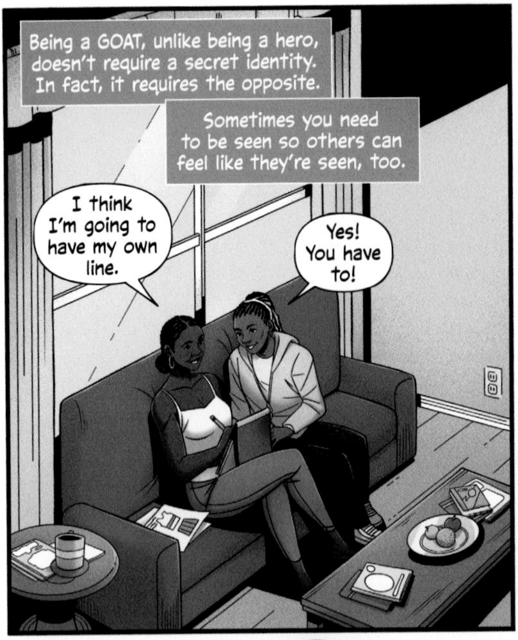
Being a GOAT, unlike being a hero, doesn't require a secret identity. In fact, it requires the opposite.
Sometimes you need to be seen so others can feel like they're seen, too.
I think I'm going to have my own line.
Yes! You have to!

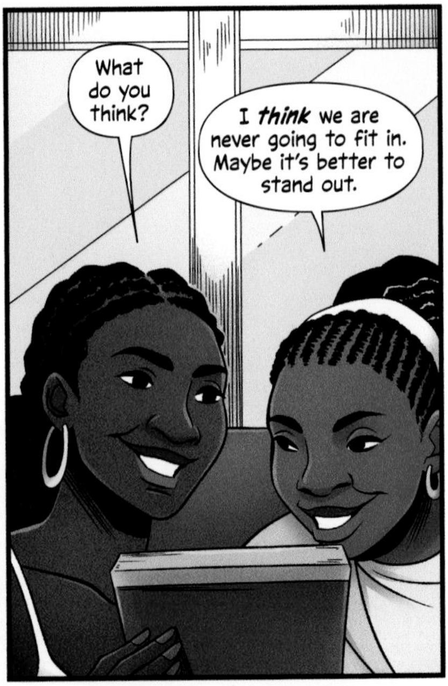
What do you think?
I *think* we are never going to fit in. Maybe it's better to stand out.

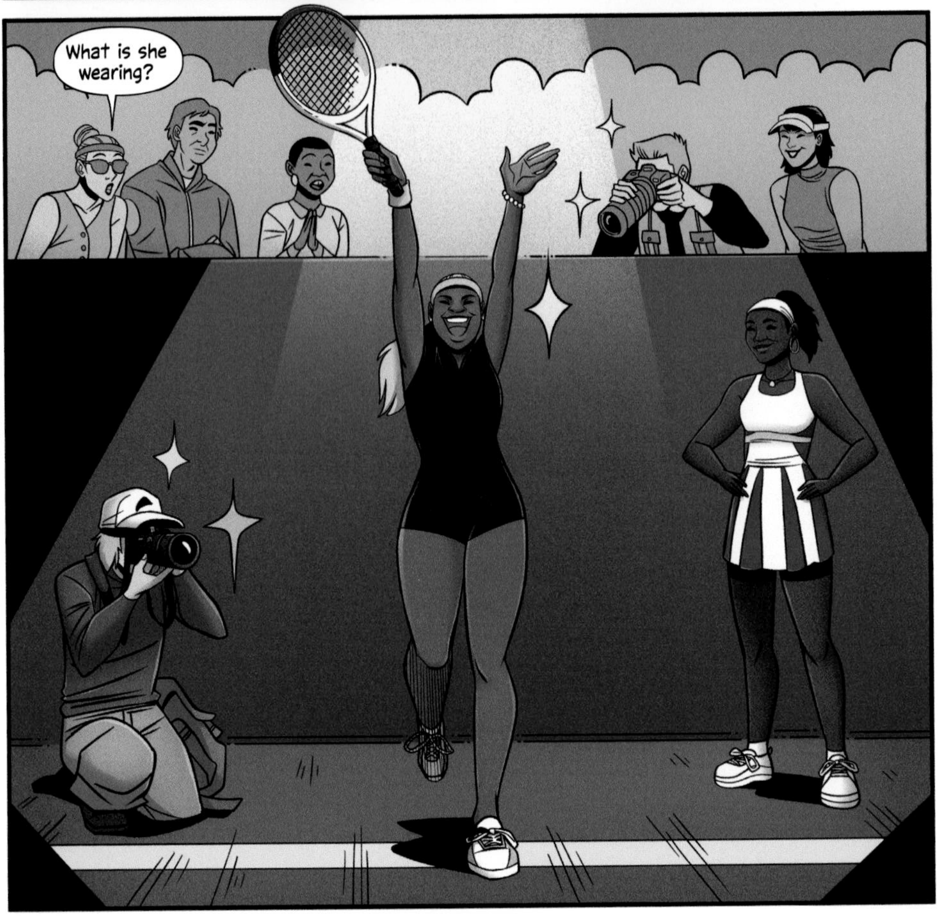
What is she wearing?

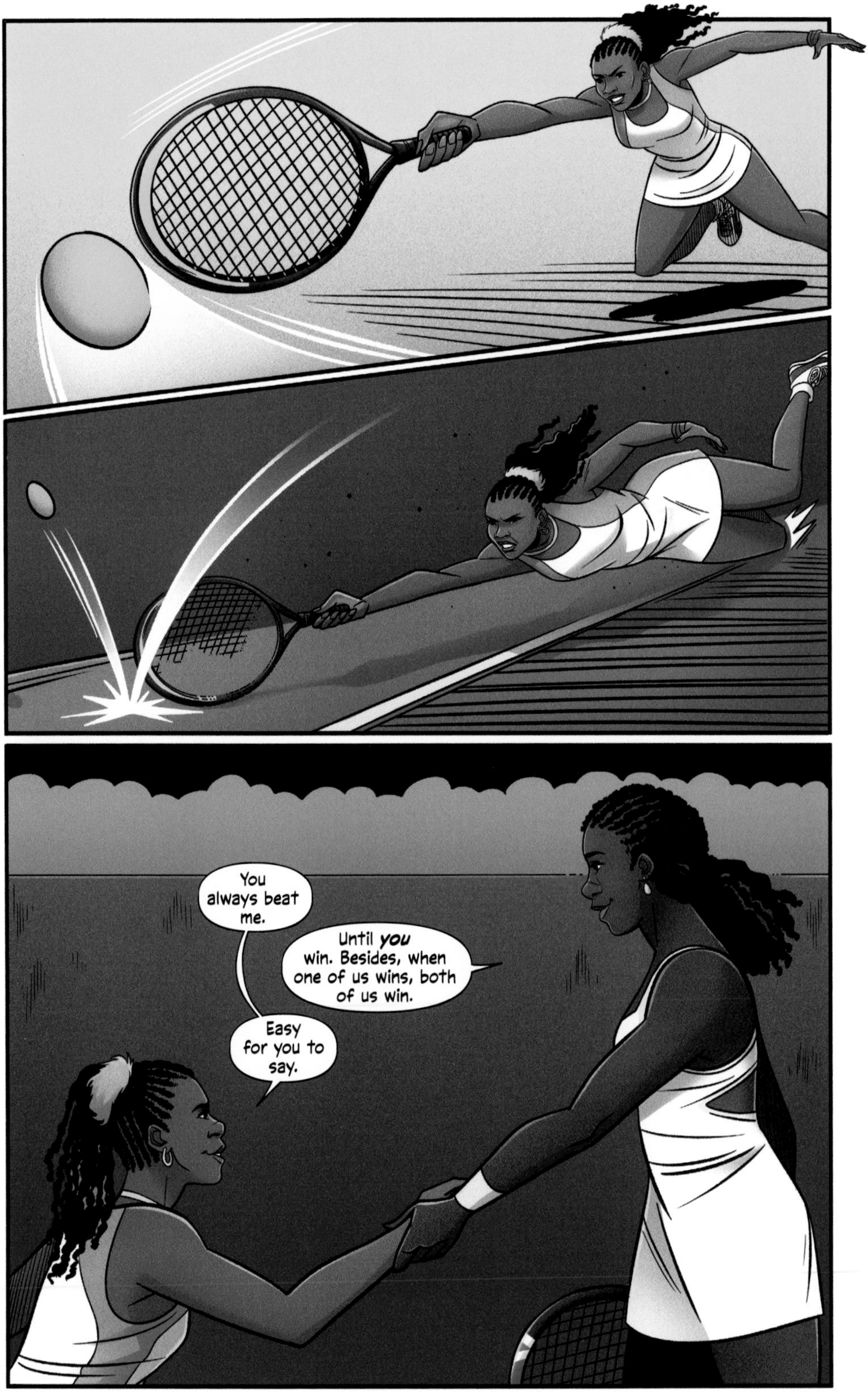
You always beat me.
Until *you* win. Besides, when one of us wins, both of us win.
Easy for you to say.

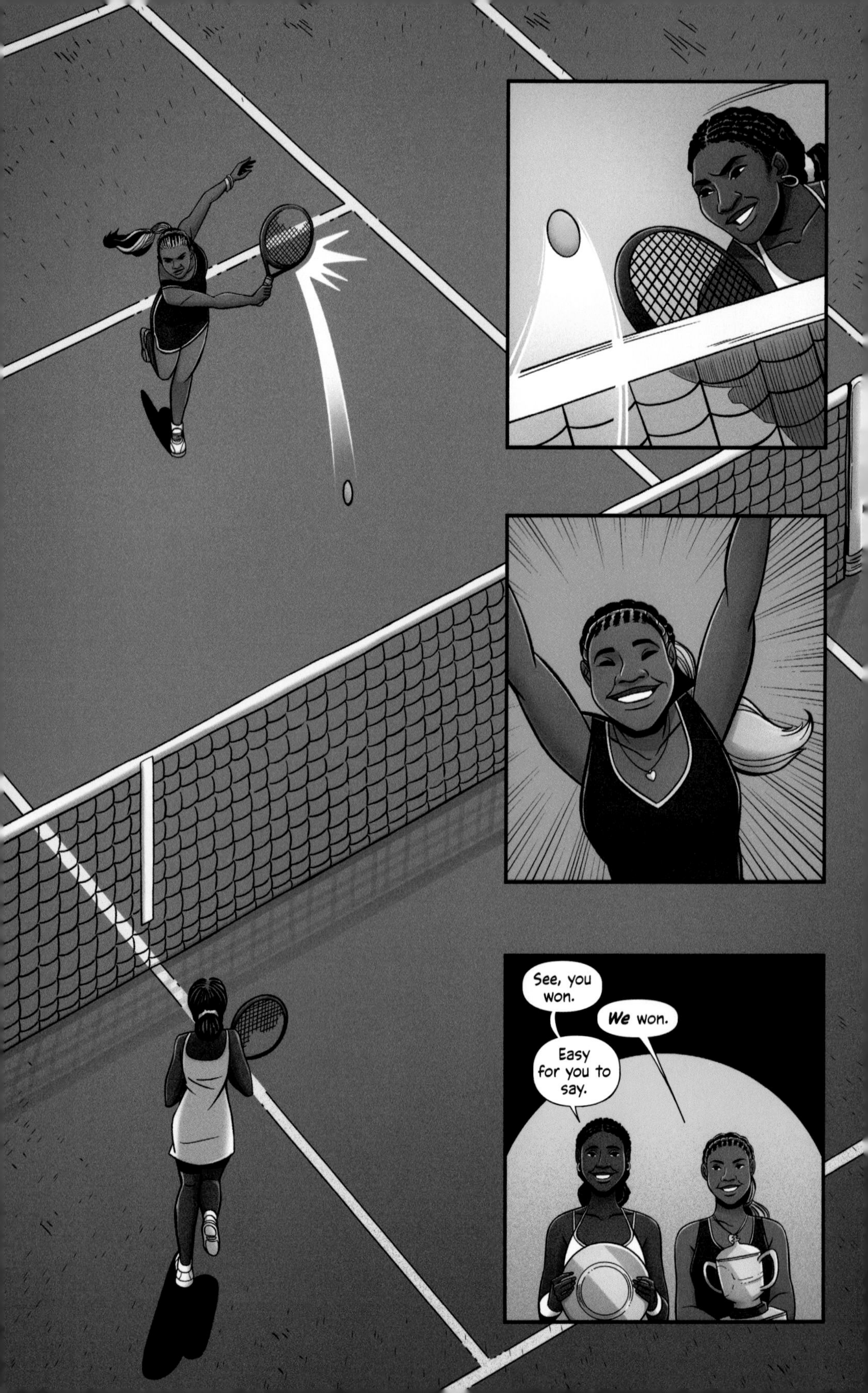
See, you won.
We won.
Easy for you to say.

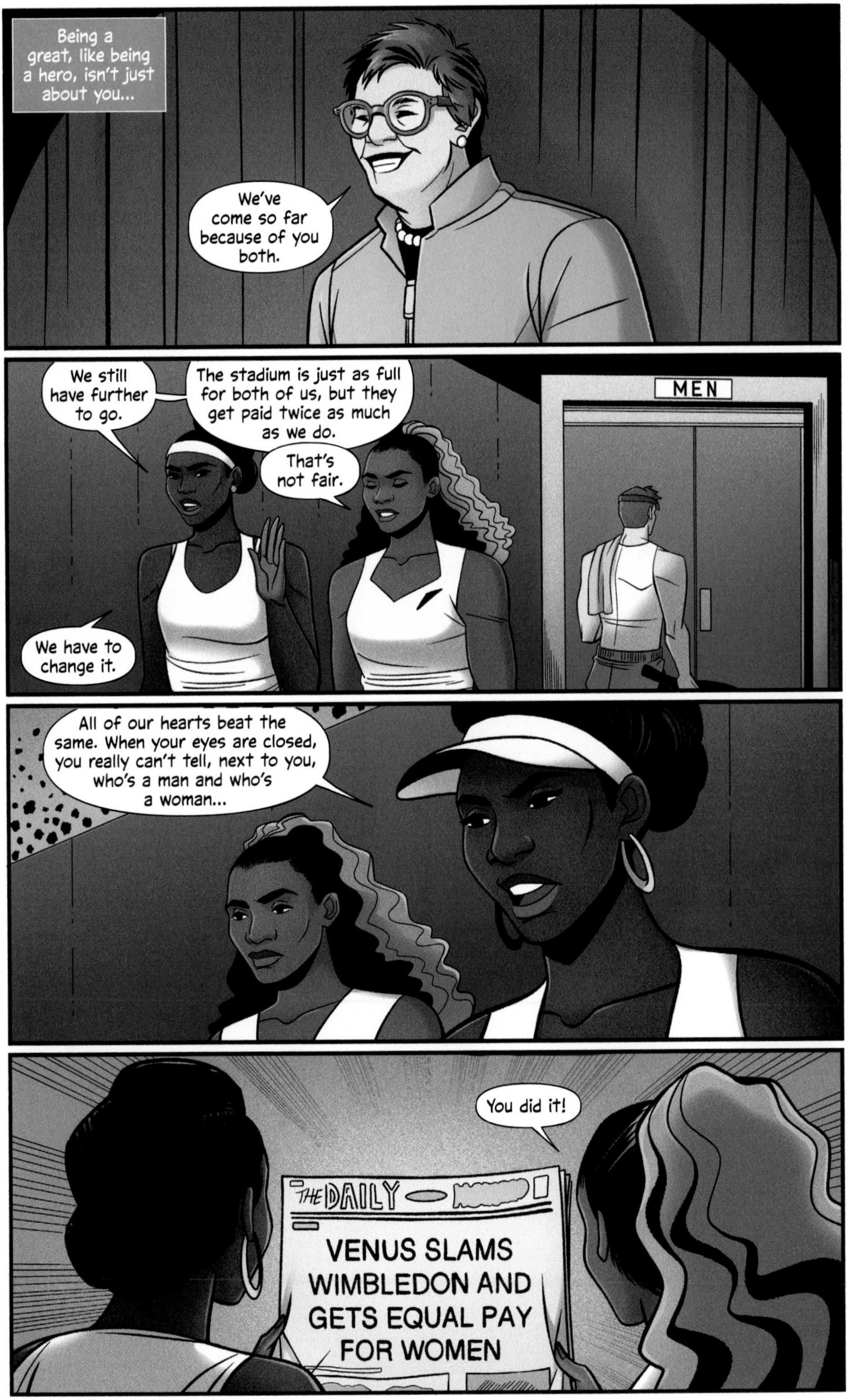
Being a great, like being a hero, isn't just about you...
We've come so far because of you both.
We still have further to go.
The stadium is just as full for both of us, but they get paid twice as much as we do.
That's not fair.
We have to change it.
MEN
All of our hearts beat the same. When your eyes are closed, you really can't tell, next to you, who's a man and who's a woman...
You did it!
THE DAILY
VENUS SLAMS WIMBLEDON AND GETS EQUAL PAY FOR WOMEN

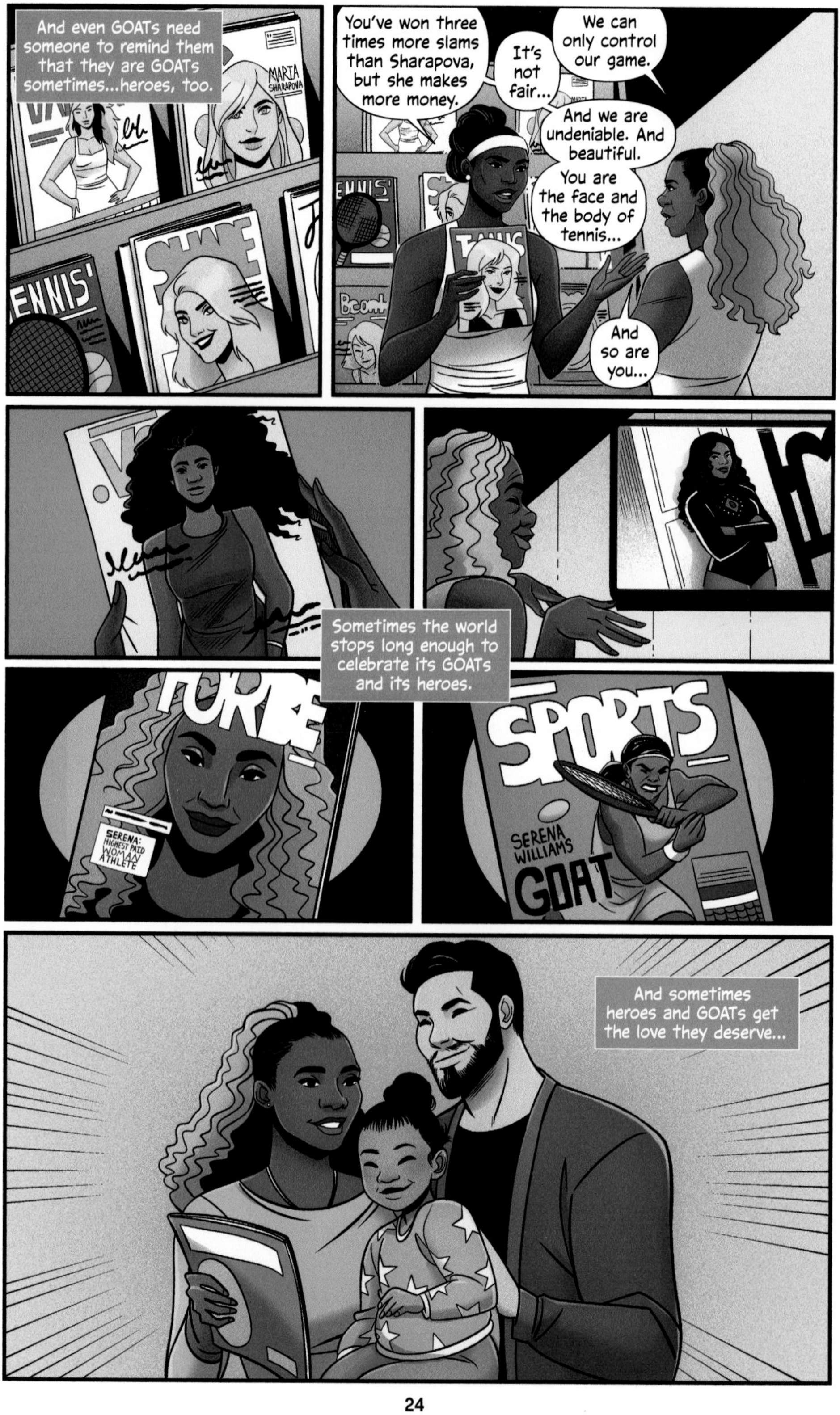
And even GOATs need someone to remind them that they are GOATs sometimes...heroes, too.
MARIA SHARAPOVA
TENNIS'
You've won three times more slams than Sharapova, but she makes more money.
It's not fair...
We can only control our game.
And we are undeniable. And beautiful.
You are the face and the body of tennis...
And so are you...
Sometimes the world stops long enough to celebrate its GOATs and its heroes.
SERENA: HIGHEST PAID WOMAN ATHLETE
SPORTS
SERENA WILLIAMS
GOAT
And sometimes heroes and GOATs get the love they deserve...

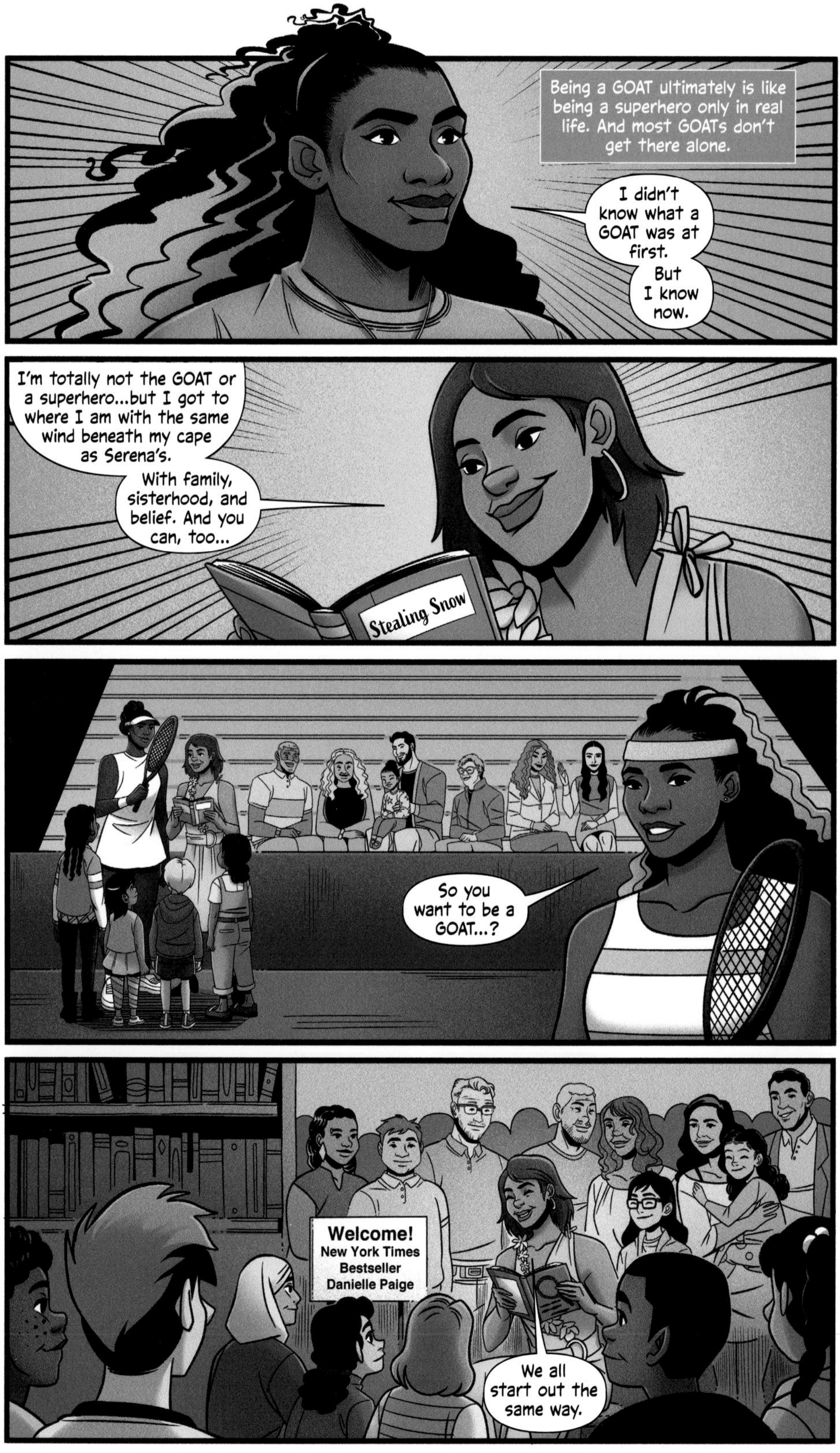
Being a GOAT ultimately is like being a superhero only in real life. And most GOATs don't get there alone.
I didn't know what a GOAT was at first.
But I know now.
I'm totally not the GOAT or a superhero...but I got to where I am with the same wind beneath my cape as Serena's.
With family, sisterhood, and belief. And you can, too...
Stealing Snow
So you want to be a GOAT...?
Welcome! New York Times Bestseller Danielle Paige
We all start out the same way.

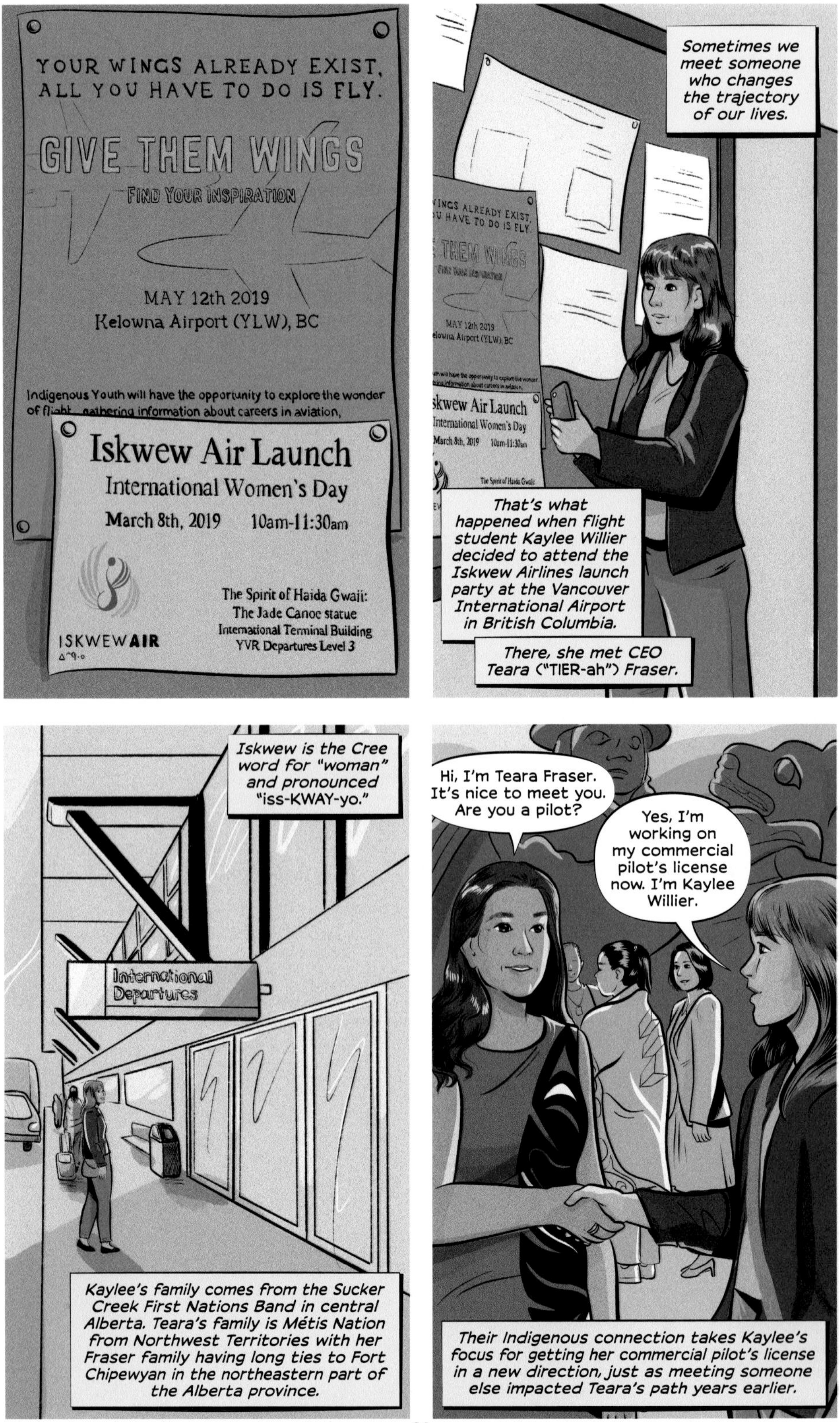
YOUR WINGS ALREADY EXIST, ALL YOU HAVE TO DO IS FLY.
GIVE THEM WINGS
FIND YOUR INSPIRATION
MAY 12th 2019
Kelowna Airport (YLW), BC
Indigenous Youth will have the opportunity to explore the wonder of flight, gathering information about careers in aviation,
Iskwew Air Launch
International Women's Day
March 8th, 2019 10am-11:30am
The Spirit of Haida Gwaii: The Jade Canoe statue International Terminal Building YVR Departures Level 3
ISKWEWAIR
Sometimes we meet someone who changes the trajectory of our lives.
That's what happened when flight student Kaylee Willier decided to attend the Iskwew Airlines launch party at the Vancouver International Airport in British Columbia.
There, she met CEO Teara ("TIER-ah") Fraser.
Iskwew is the Cree word for "woman" and pronounced "iss-KWAY-yo."
International Departures
Kaylee's family comes from the Sucker Creek First Nations Band in central Alberta. Teara's family is Métis Nation from Northwest Territories with her Fraser family having long ties to Fort Chipewyan in the northeastern part of the Alberta province.
Hi, I'm Teara Fraser. It's nice to meet you. Are you a pilot?
Yes, I'm working on my commercial pilot's license now. I'm Kaylee Willier.
Their Indigenous connection takes Kaylee's focus for getting her commercial pilot's license in a new direction, just as meeting someone else impacted Teara's path years earlier.

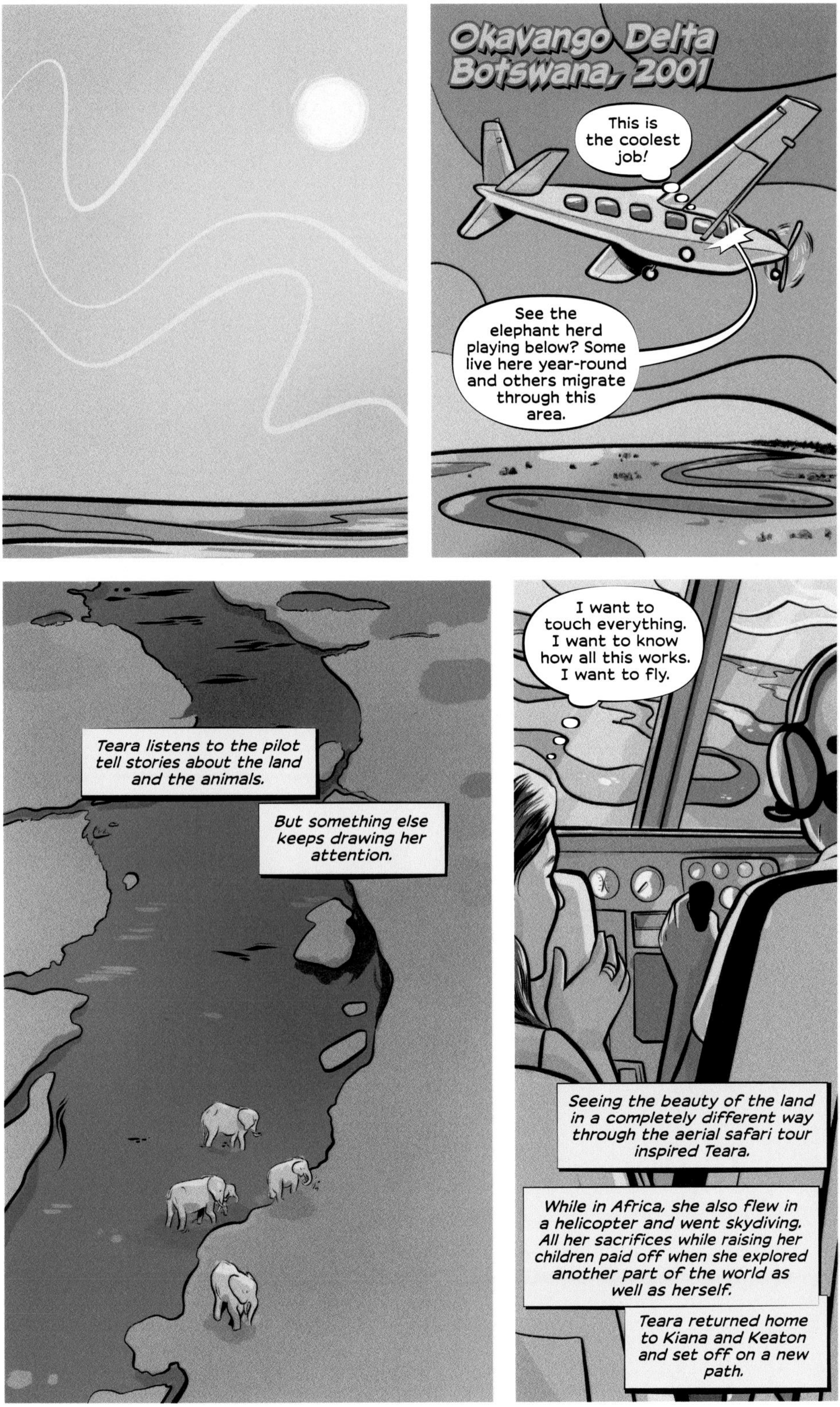

Okavango Delta
Botswana, 2001
This is the coolest job!
See the elephant herd playing below? Some live here year-round and others migrate through this area.
Teara listens to the pilot tell stories about the land and the animals.
But something else keeps drawing her attention.
I want to touch everything. I want to know how all this works. I want to fly.
Seeing the beauty of the land in a completely different way through the aerial safari tour inspired Teara.
While in Africa, she also flew in a helicopter and went skydiving. All her sacrifices while raising her children paid off when she explored another part of the world as well as herself.
Teara returned home to Kiana and Keaton and set off on a new path.

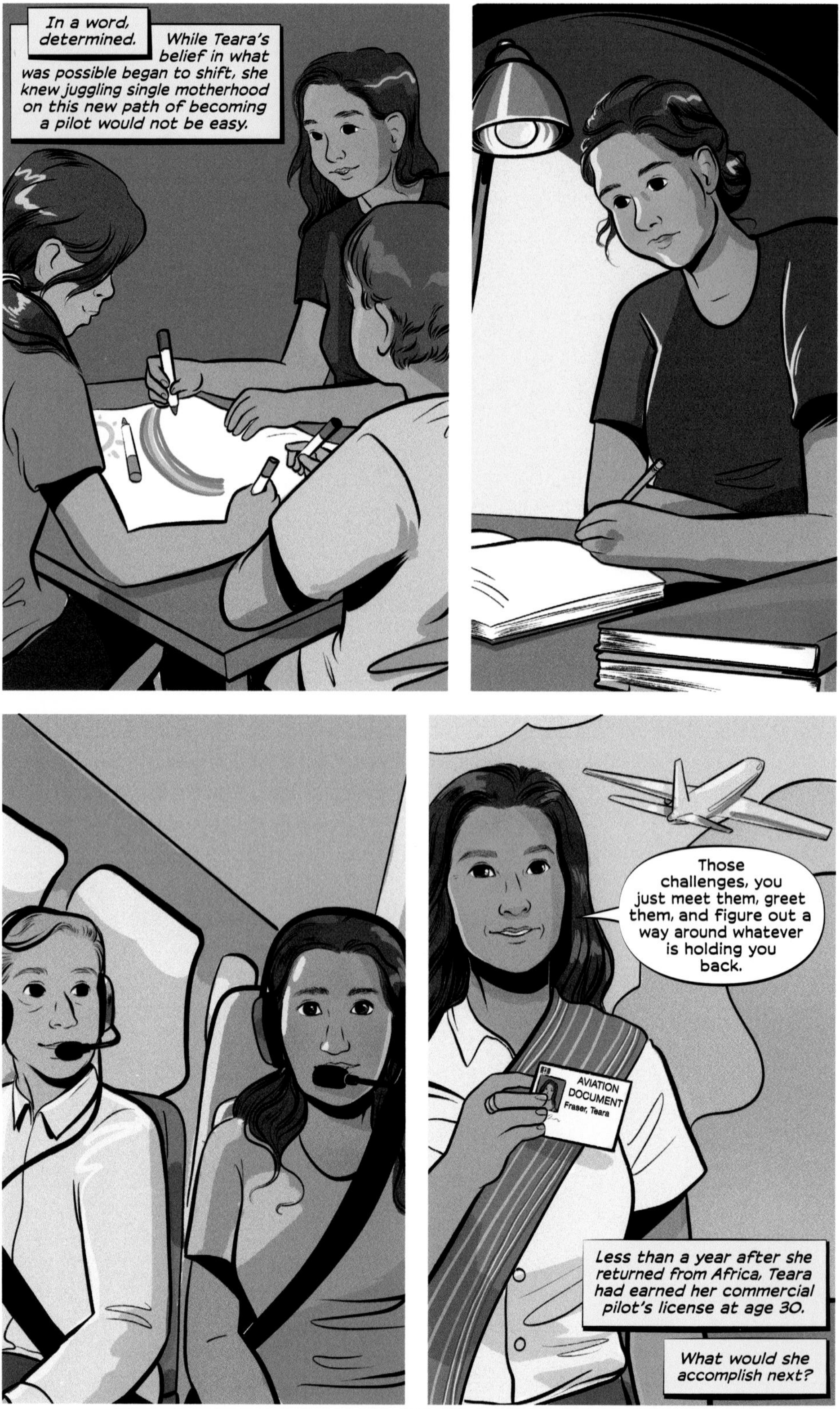
In a word, determined.
While Teara's belief in what was possible began to shift, she knew juggling single motherhood on this new path of becoming a pilot would not be easy.
Those challenges, you just meet them, greet them, and figure out a way around whatever is holding you back.
AVIATION DOCUMENT
Fraser, Teara
Less than a year after she returned from Africa, Teara had earned her commercial pilot's license at age 30.
What would she accomplish next?

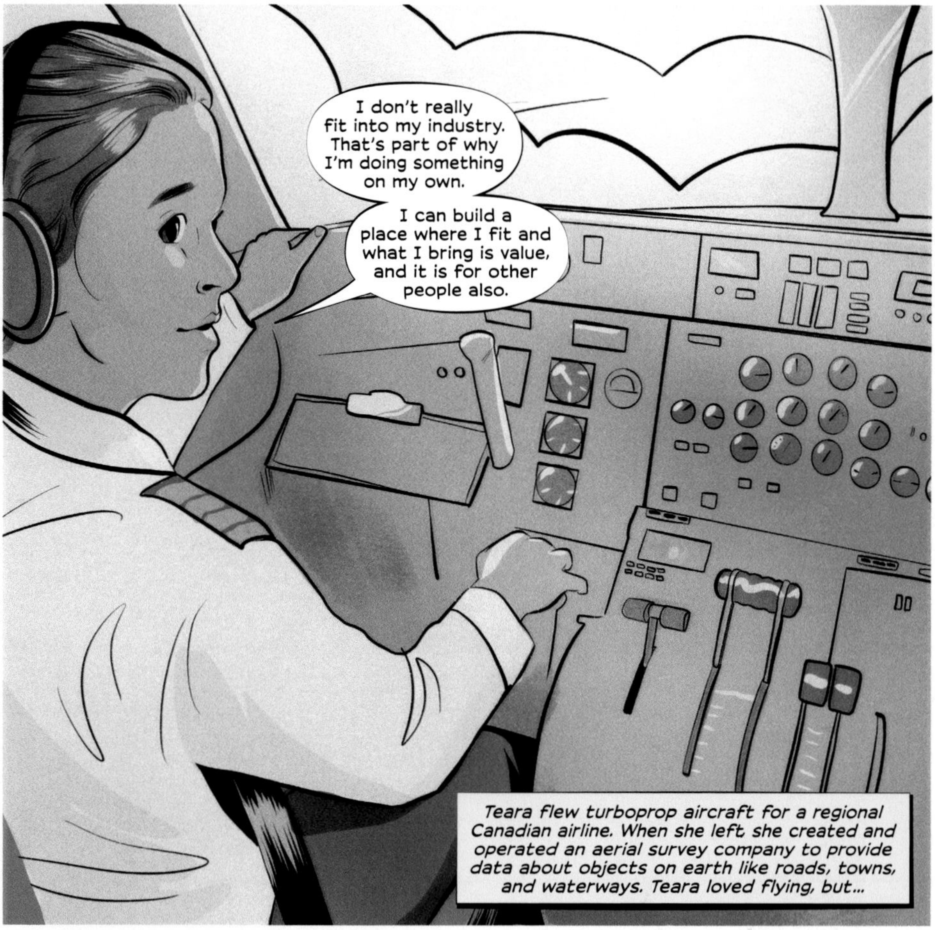
I don't really fit into my industry. That's part of why I'm doing something on my own.
I can build a place where I fit and what I bring is value, and it is for other people also.
Teara flew turboprop aircraft for a regional Canadian airline. When she left she created and operated an aerial survey company to provide data about objects on earth like roads, towns, and waterways. Teara loved flying, but...

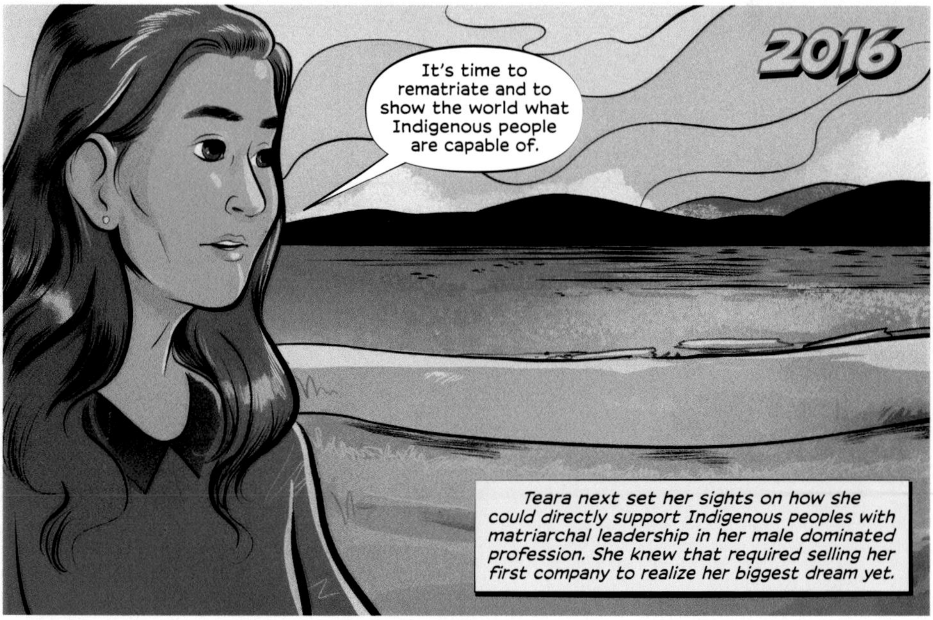
2016
It's time to rematriate and to show the world what Indigenous people are capable of.
Teara next set her sights on how she could directly support Indigenous peoples with matriarchal leadership in her male dominated profession. She knew that required selling her first company to realize her biggest dream yet.

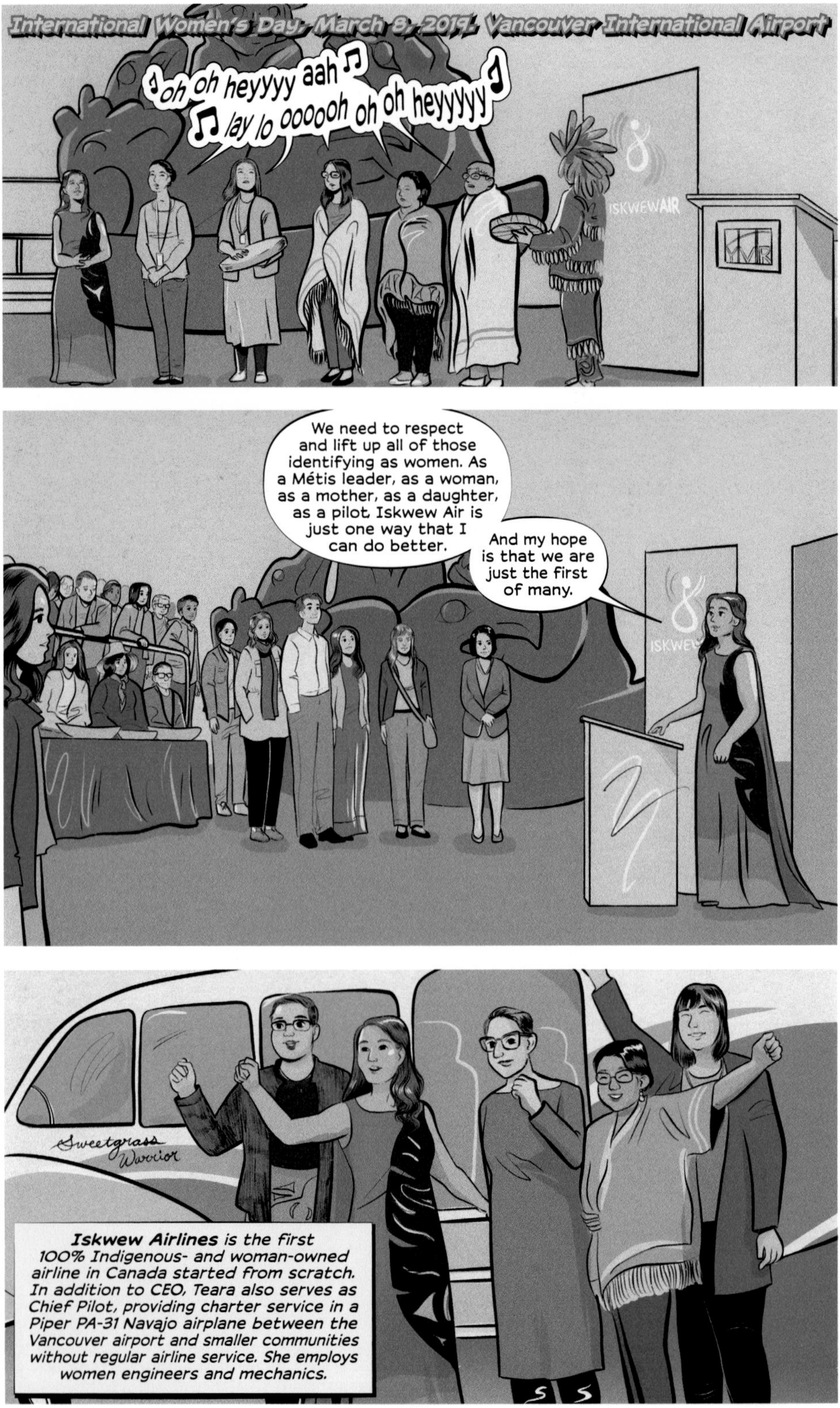
International Women's Day, March 8, 2019. Vancouver International Airport
oh oh heyyyy aah
lay lo oooooh oh oh heyyyyy
ISKWEWAIR
YVR
We need to respect and lift up all of those identifying as women. As a Métis leader, as a woman, as a mother, as a daughter, as a pilot Iskwew Air is just one way that I can do better.
And my hope is that we are just the first of many.
Sweetgrass Warrior
***Iskwew Airlines** is the first 100% Indigenous- and woman-owned airline in Canada started from scratch. In addition to CEO, Teara also serves as Chief Pilot, providing charter service in a Piper PA-31 Navajo airplane between the Vancouver airport and smaller communities without regular airline service. She employs women engineers and mechanics.*

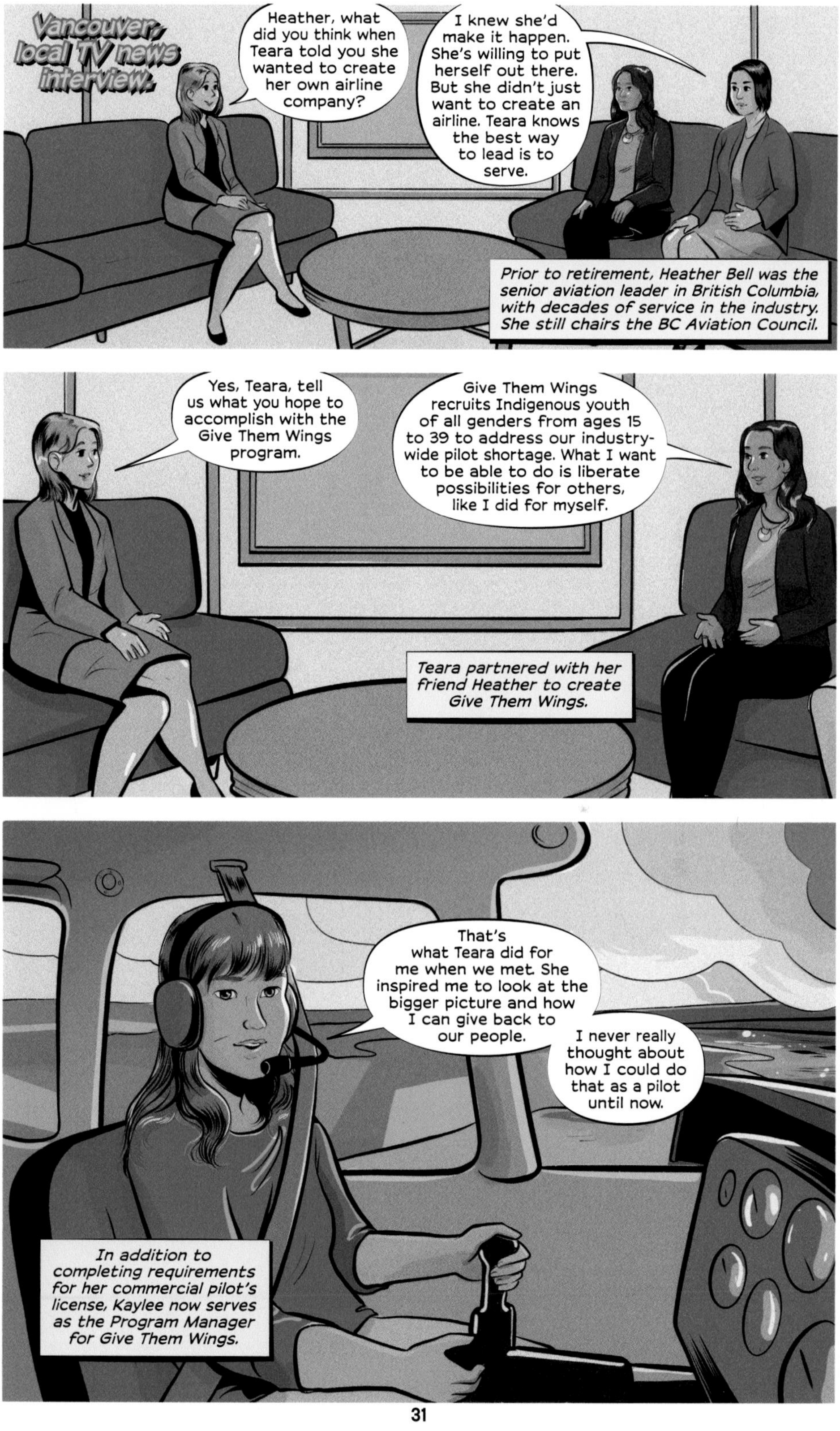
Vancouver, local TV news interview.
Heather, what did you think when Teara told you she wanted to create her own airline company?
I knew she'd make it happen. She's willing to put herself out there. But she didn't just want to create an airline. Teara knows the best way to lead is to serve.
Prior to retirement, Heather Bell was the senior aviation leader in British Columbia, with decades of service in the industry. She still chairs the BC Aviation Council.
Yes, Teara, tell us what you hope to accomplish with the Give Them Wings program.
Give Them Wings recruits Indigenous youth of all genders from ages 15 to 39 to address our industry-wide pilot shortage. What I want to be able to do is liberate possibilities for others, like I did for myself.
Teara partnered with her friend Heather to create Give Them Wings.
That's what Teara did for me when we met. She inspired me to look at the bigger picture and how I can give back to our people.
I never really thought about how I could do that as a pilot until now.
In addition to completing requirements for her commercial pilot's license, Kaylee now serves as the Program Manager for Give Them Wings.

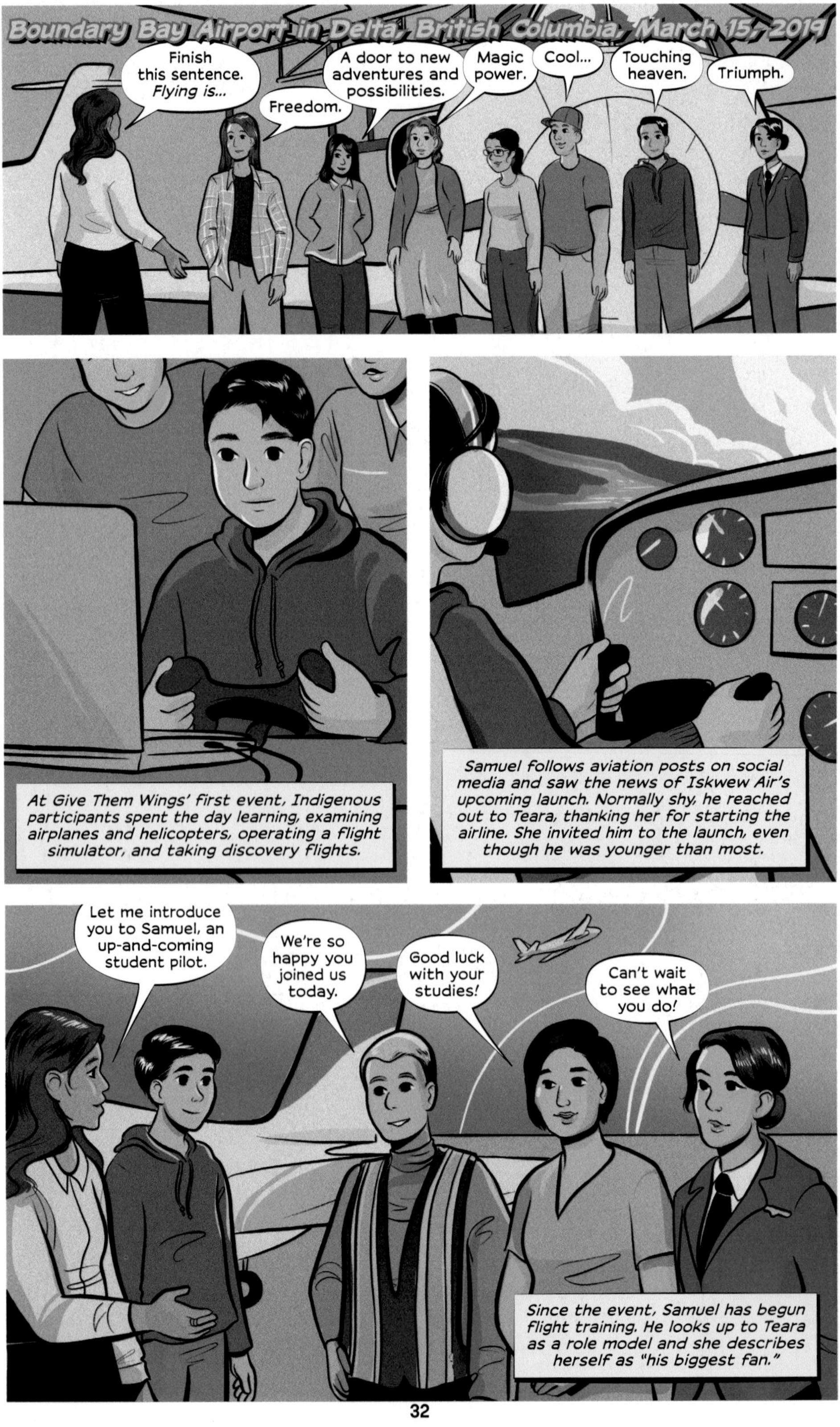
Boundary Bay Airport in Delta, British Columbia, March 15, 2019
Finish this sentence. *Flying is...*
Freedom.
A door to new adventures and possibilities.
Magic power.
Cool...
Touching heaven.
Triumph.
At Give Them Wings' first event, Indigenous participants spent the day learning, examining airplanes and helicopters, operating a flight simulator, and taking discovery flights.
Samuel follows aviation posts on social media and saw the news of Iskwew Air's upcoming launch. Normally shy, he reached out to Teara, thanking her for starting the airline. She invited him to the launch, even though he was younger than most.
Let me introduce you to Samuel, an up-and-coming student pilot.
We're so happy you joined us today.
Good luck with your studies!
Can't wait to see what you do!
Since the event, Samuel has begun flight training. He looks up to Teara as a role model and she describes herself as "his biggest fan."

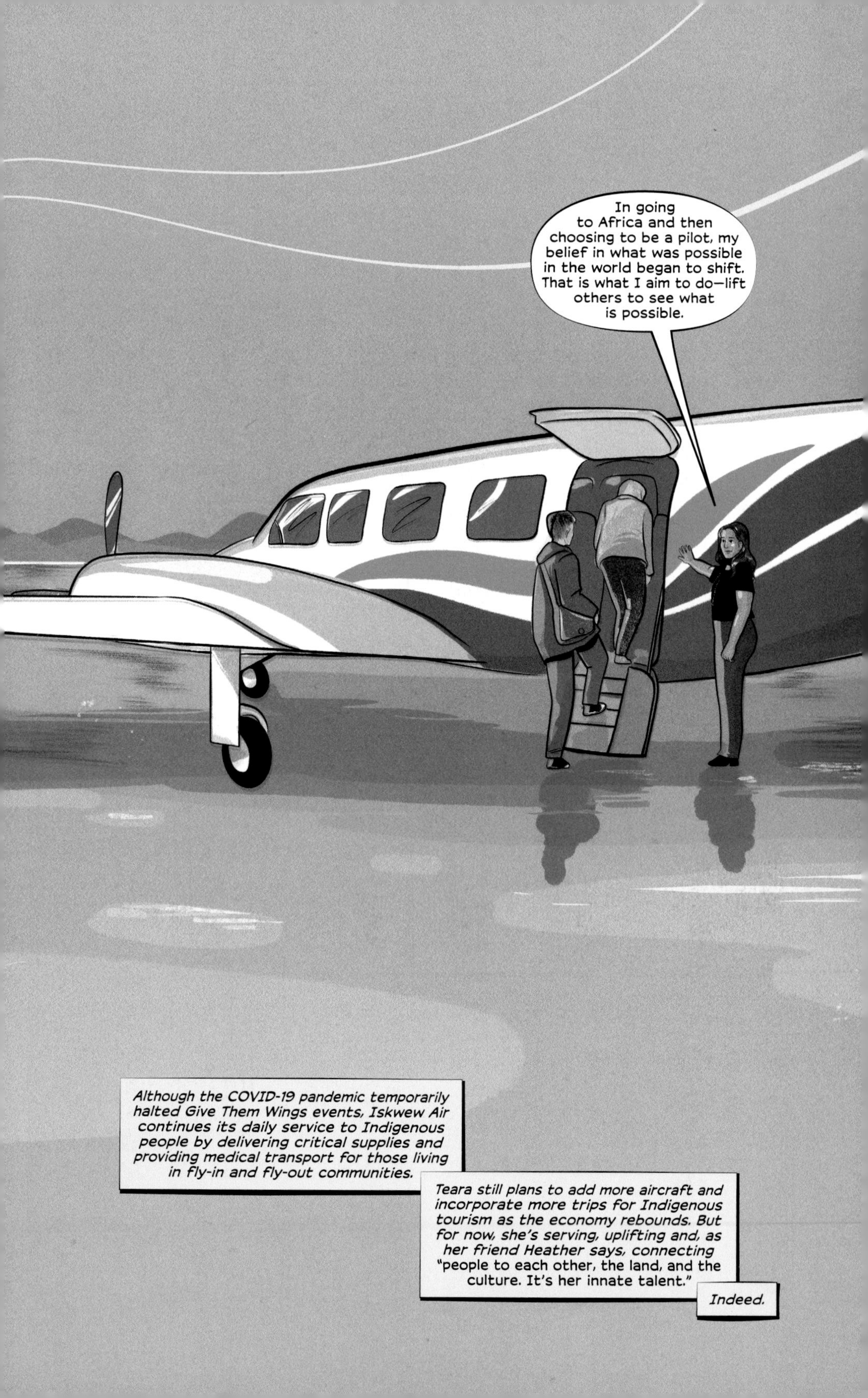
In going to Africa and then choosing to be a pilot, my belief in what was possible in the world began to shift. That is what I aim to do—lift others to see what is possible.
Although the COVID-19 pandemic temporarily halted Give Them Wings events, Iskwew Air continues its daily service to Indigenous people by delivering critical supplies and providing medical transport for those living in fly-in and fly-out communities.
Teara still plans to add more aircraft and incorporate more trips for Indigenous tourism as the economy rebounds. But for now, she's serving, uplifting and, as her friend Heather says, connecting "people to each other, the land, and the culture. It's her innate talent."
Indeed.

MALALA YOUSAFZAI: ONE FOR ALL

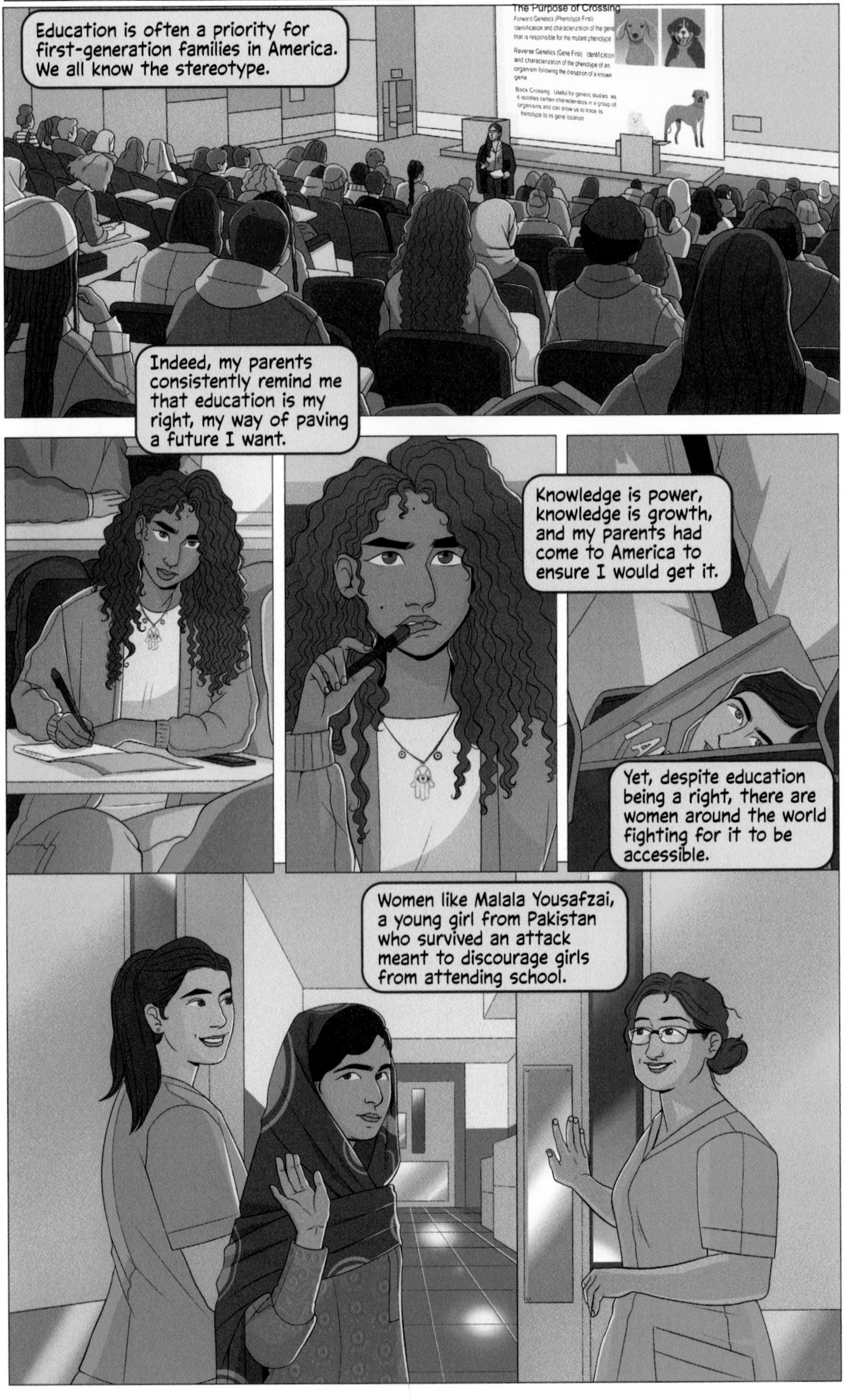

Education is often a priority for first-generation families in America. We all know the stereotype.
The Purpose of Crossing
Forward Genetics (Phenotype First) Identification and characterization of the gene that is responsible for the mutant phenotype
Reverse Genetics (Gene First) Identification and characterization of the phenotype of an organism following the disruption of a known gene
Back Crossing Useful for genetic studies as it isolates certain characteristics in a group of organisms and can allow us to trace its henotype to its gene location
Indeed, my parents consistently remind me that education is my right, my way of paving a future I want.
Knowledge is power, knowledge is growth, and my parents had come to America to ensure I would get it.
Yet, despite education being a right, there are women around the world fighting for it to be accessible.
Women like Malala Yousafzai, a young girl from Pakistan who survived an attack meant to discourage girls from attending school.

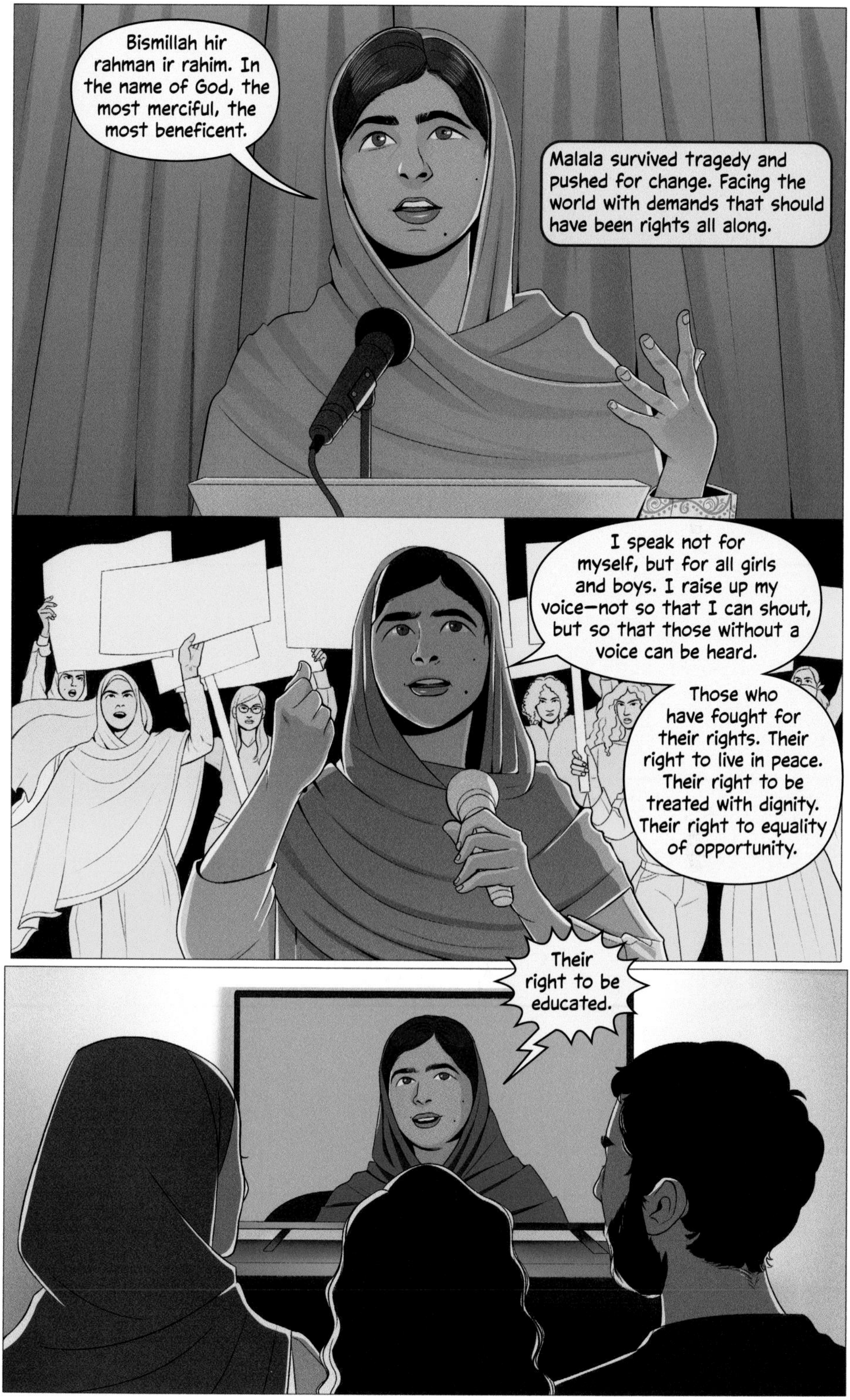
Bismillah hir rahman ir rahim. In the name of God, the most merciful, the most beneficent.
Malala survived tragedy and pushed for change. Facing the world with demands that should have been rights all along.
I speak not for myself, but for all girls and boys. I raise up my voice—not so that I can shout, but so that those without a voice can be heard.
Those who have fought for their rights. Their right to live in peace. Their right to be treated with dignity. Their right to equality of opportunity.
Their right to be educated.

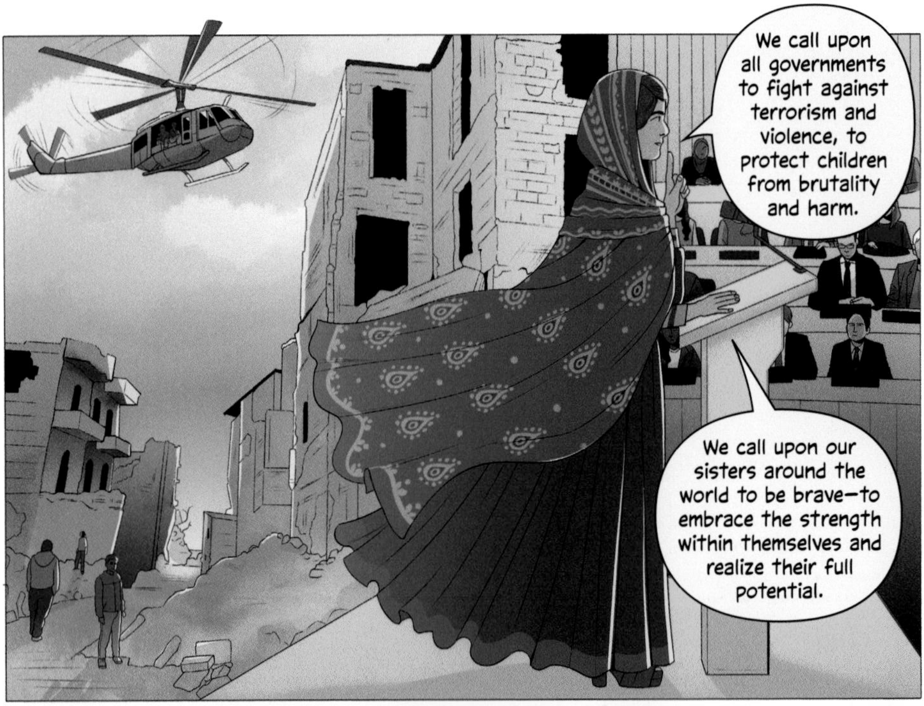
We call upon all governments to fight against terrorism and violence, to protect children from brutality and harm.
We call upon our sisters around the world to be brave—to embrace the strength within themselves and realize their full potential.

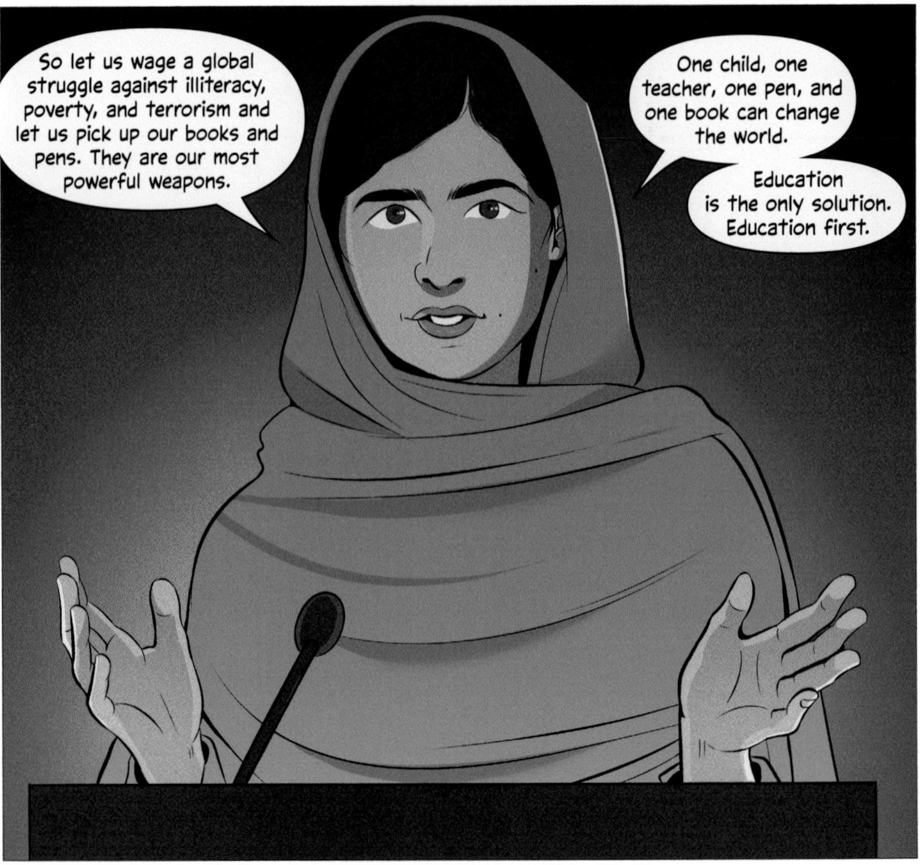
So let us wage a global struggle against illiteracy, poverty, and terrorism and let us pick up our books and pens. They are our most powerful weapons.
One child, one teacher, one pen, and one book can change the world.
Education is the only solution. Education first.

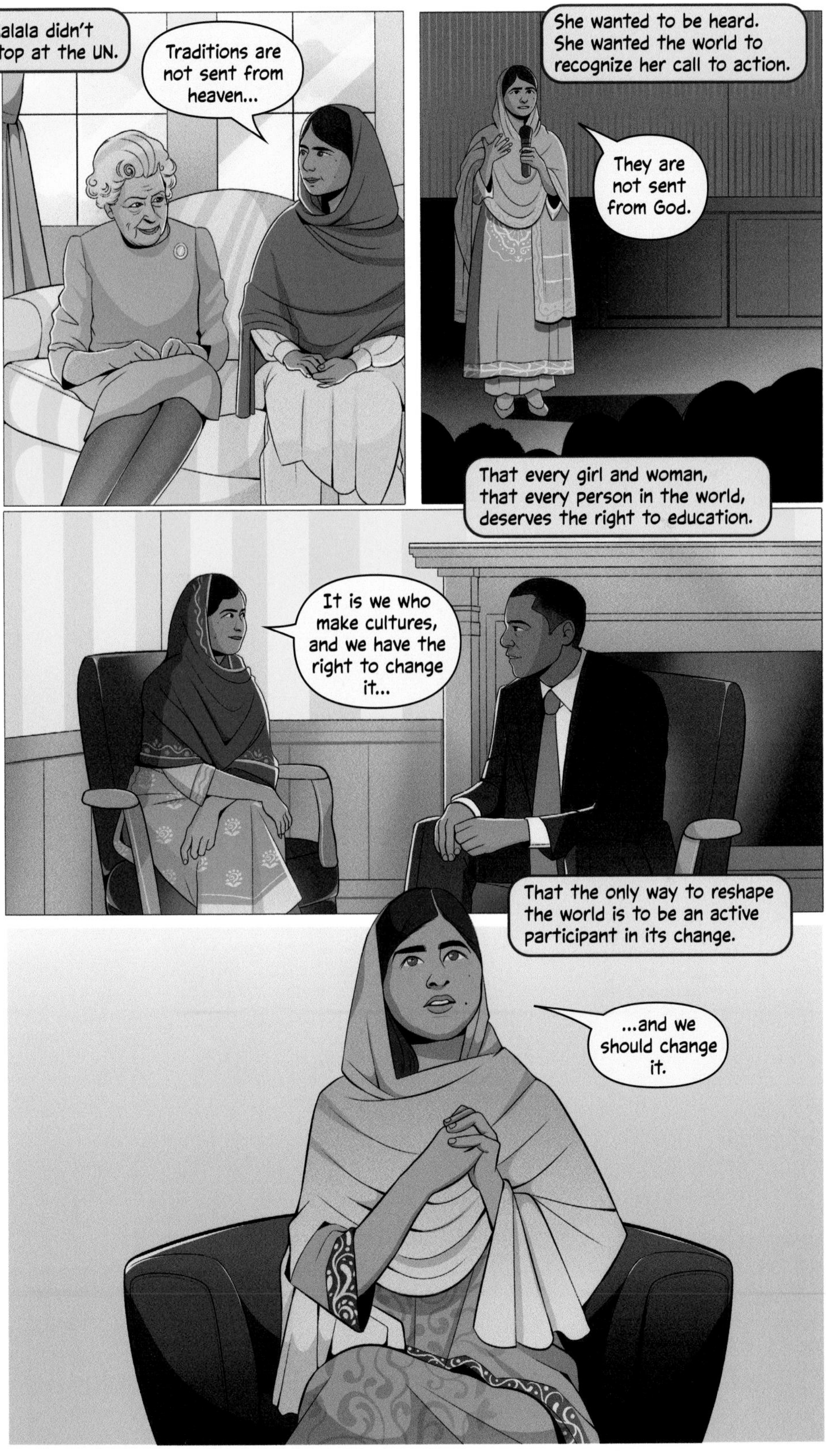
Malala didn't stop at the UN.
Traditions are not sent from heaven...
She wanted to be heard. She wanted the world to recognize her call to action.
They are not sent from God.
That every girl and woman, that every person in the world, deserves the right to education.
It is we who make cultures, and we have the right to change it...
That the only way to reshape the world is to be an active participant in its change.
...and we should change it.

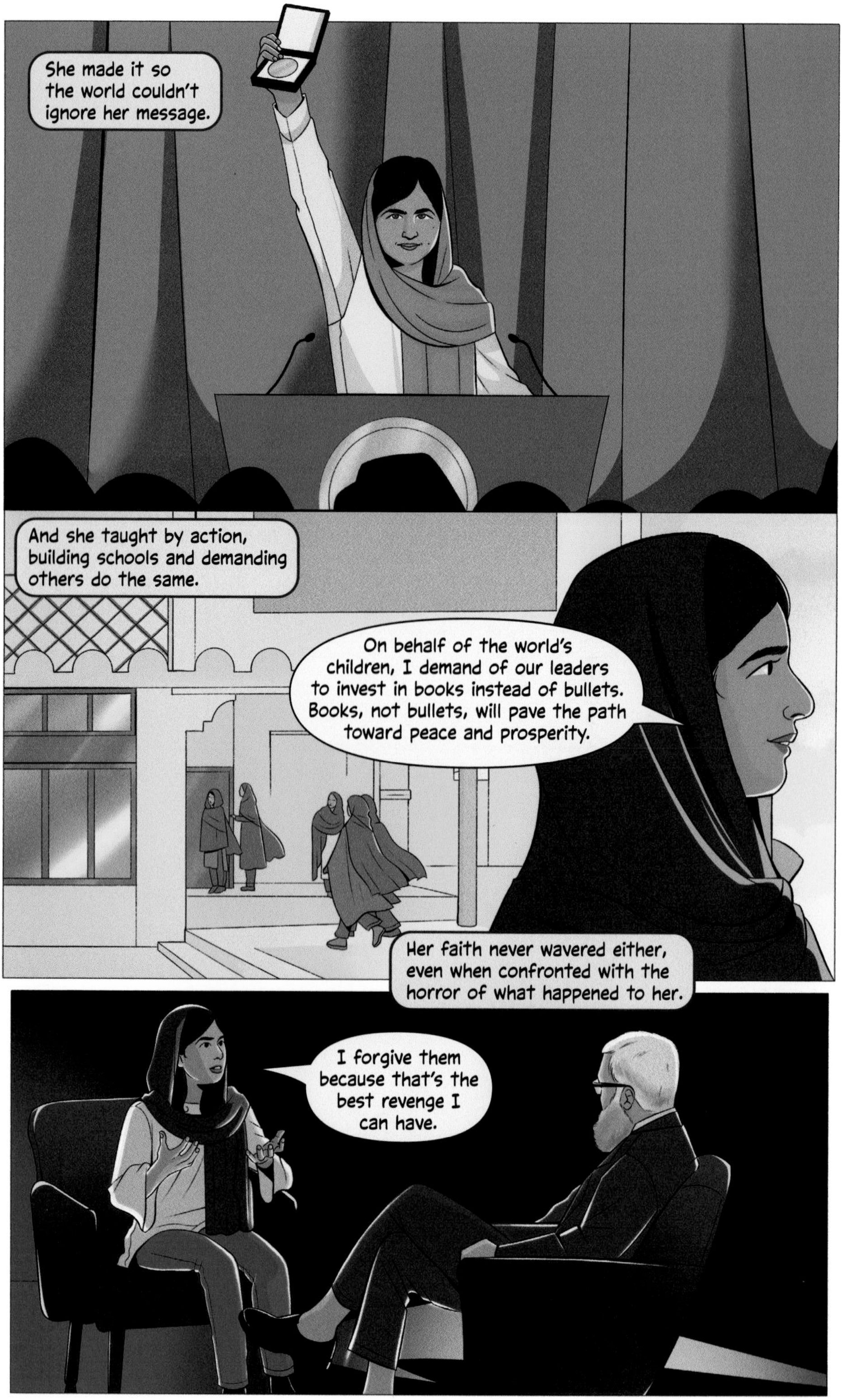
She made it so the world couldn't ignore her message.
And she taught by action, building schools and demanding others do the same.
On behalf of the world's children, I demand of our leaders to invest in books instead of bullets. Books, not bullets, will pave the path toward peace and prosperity.
Her faith never wavered either, even when confronted with the horror of what happened to her.
I forgive them because that's the best revenge I can have.

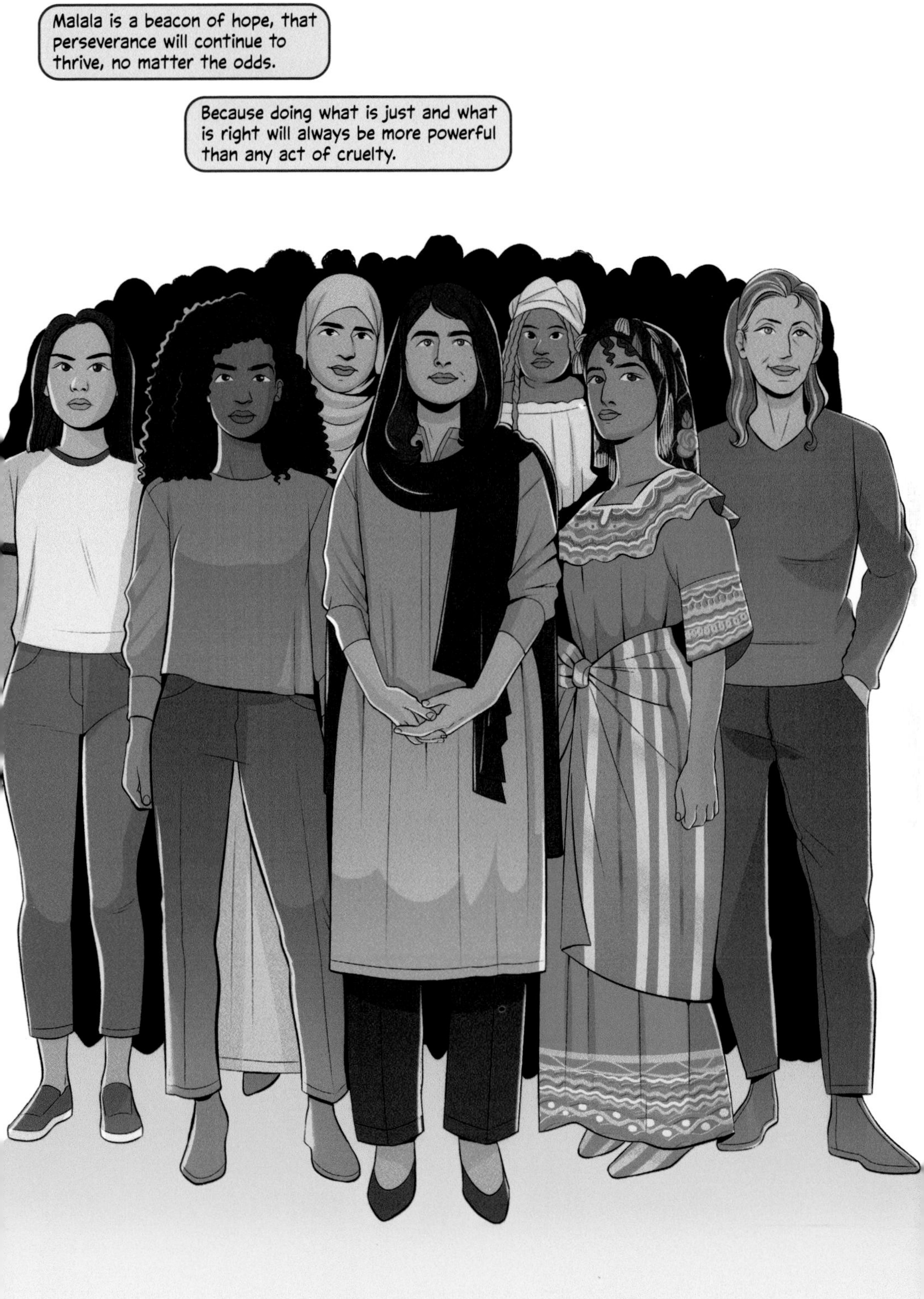
Malala is a beacon of hope, that perseverance will continue to thrive, no matter the odds.
Because doing what is just and what is right will always be more powerful than any act of cruelty.

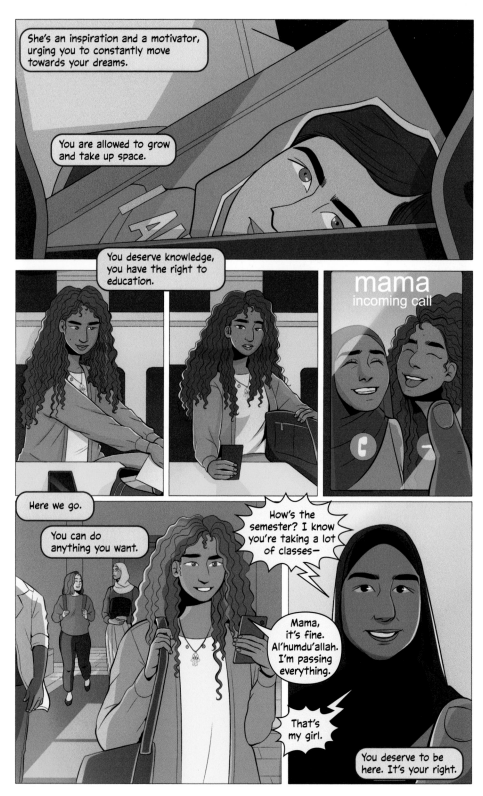

She's an inspiration and a motivator, urging you to constantly move towards your dreams.

You are allowed to grow and take up space.

You deserve knowledge, you have the right to education.

mama
incoming call

Here we go.

You can do anything you want.

How's the semester? I know you're taking a lot of classes—

Mama, it's fine. Al'humdu'allah. I'm passing everything.

That's my girl.

You deserve to be here. It's your right.

LEIOMY MALDONADO: GENERATIONAL

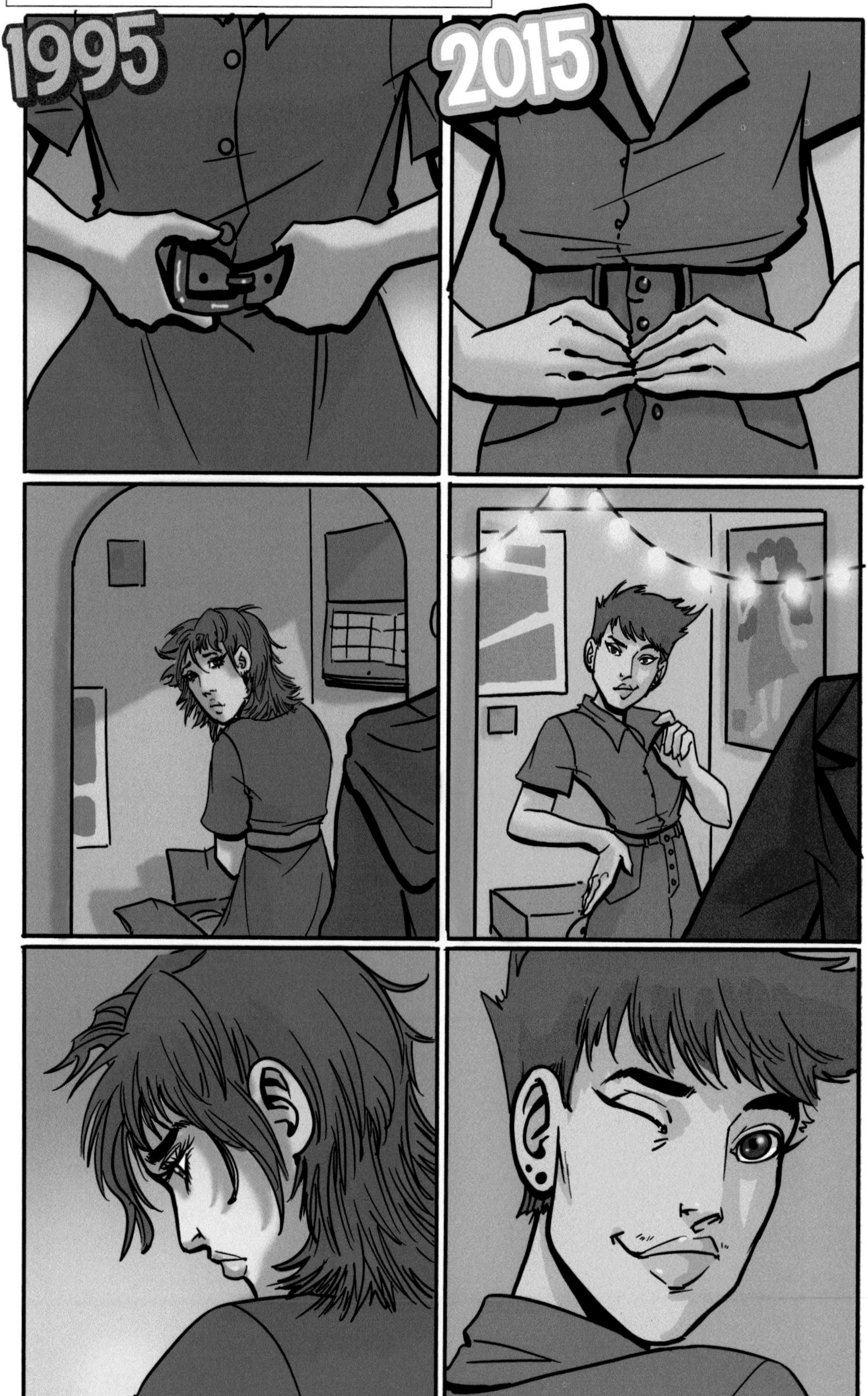
1995
2015

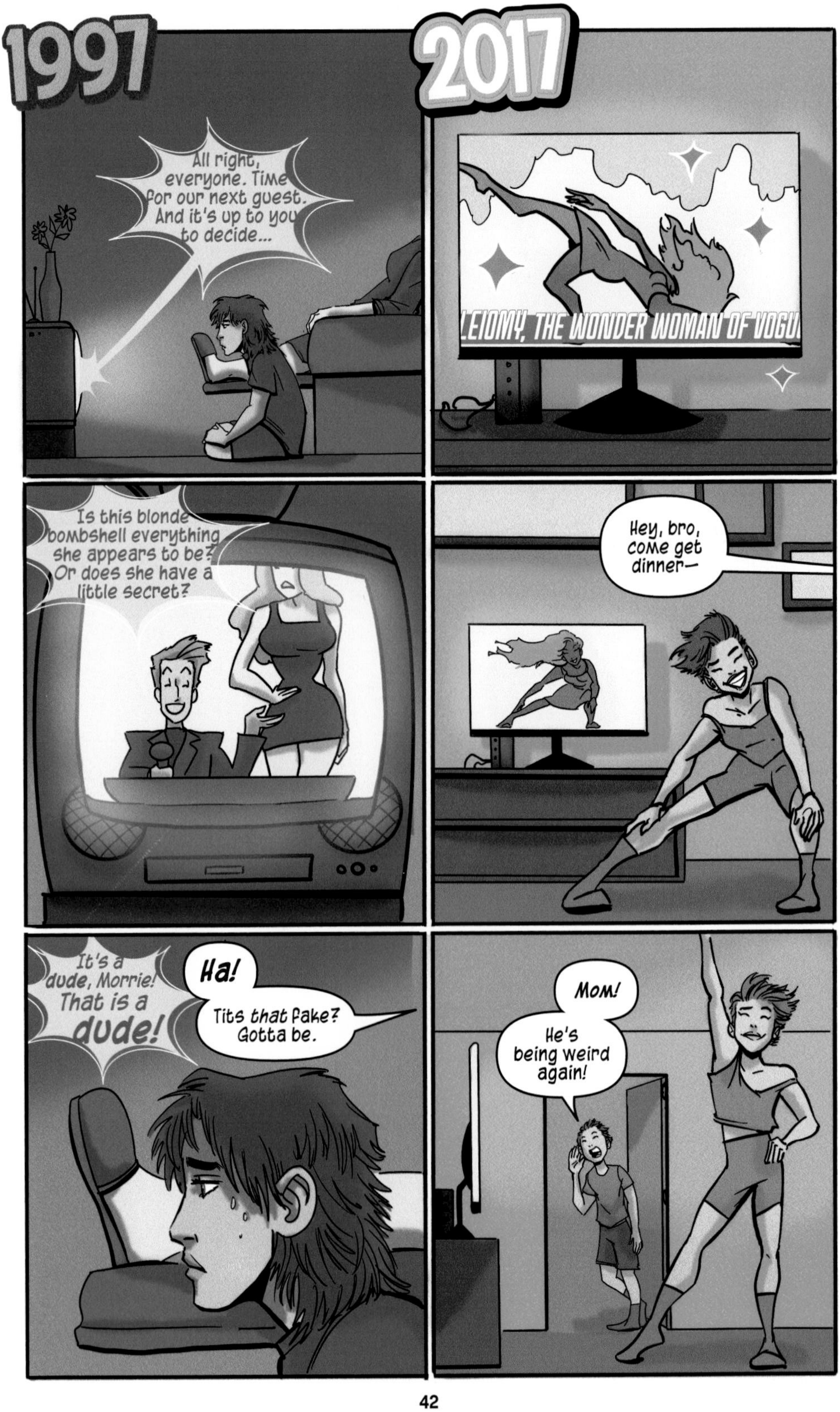
1997
2017
All right, everyone. Time for our next guest. And it's up to you to decide...
LEIOMY, THE WONDER WOMAN OF VOGU
Is this blonde bombshell everything she appears to be? Or does she have a little secret?
Hey, bro, come get dinner—
It's a dude, Morrie! That is a dude!
Ha!
Tits that fake? Gotta be.
Mom!
He's being weird again!

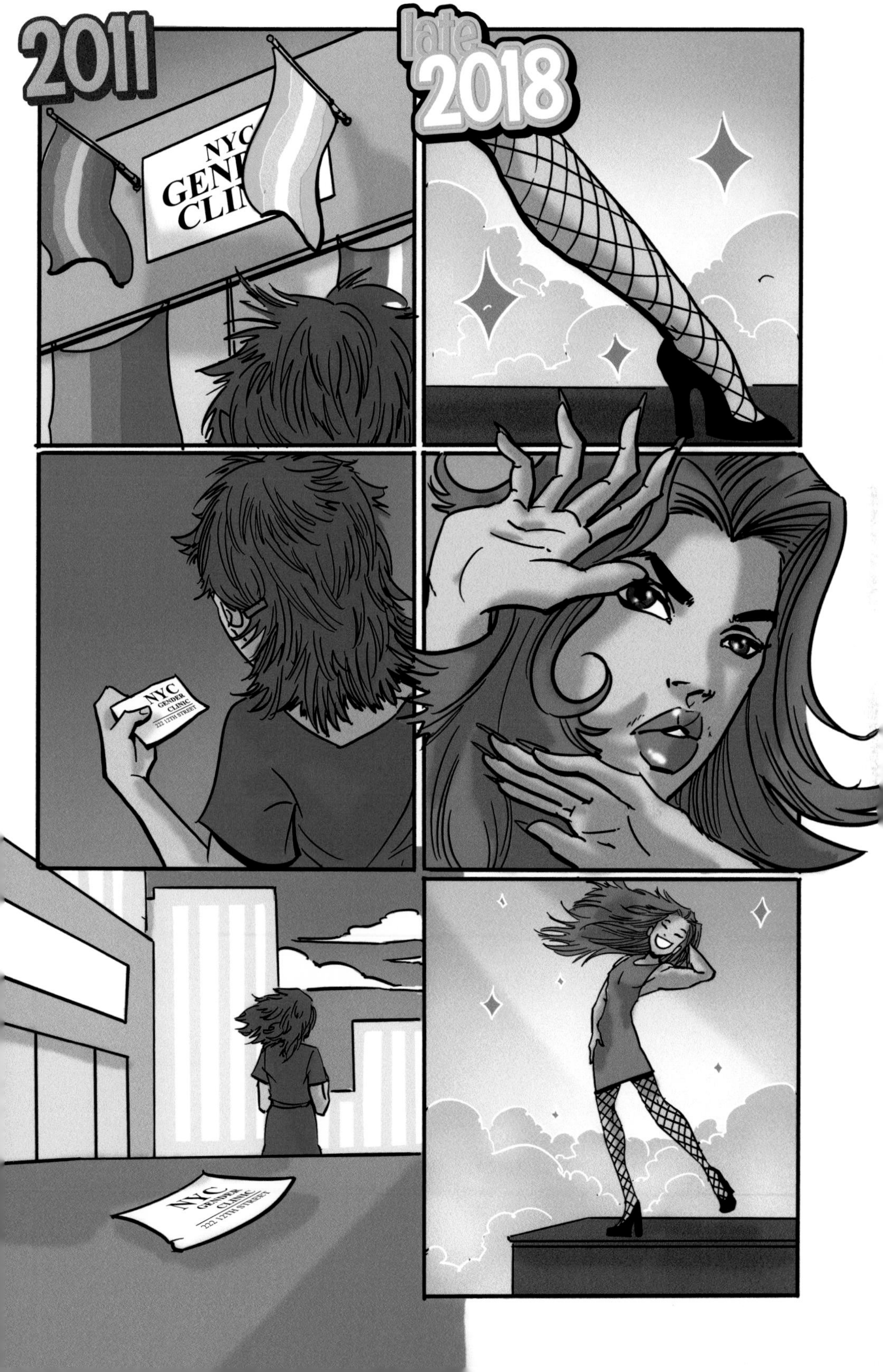
2011
late 2018
NYC GENDER CLINIC
NYC GENDER CLINIC 222 12TH STREET
NYC GENDER CLINIC 222 12TH STREET

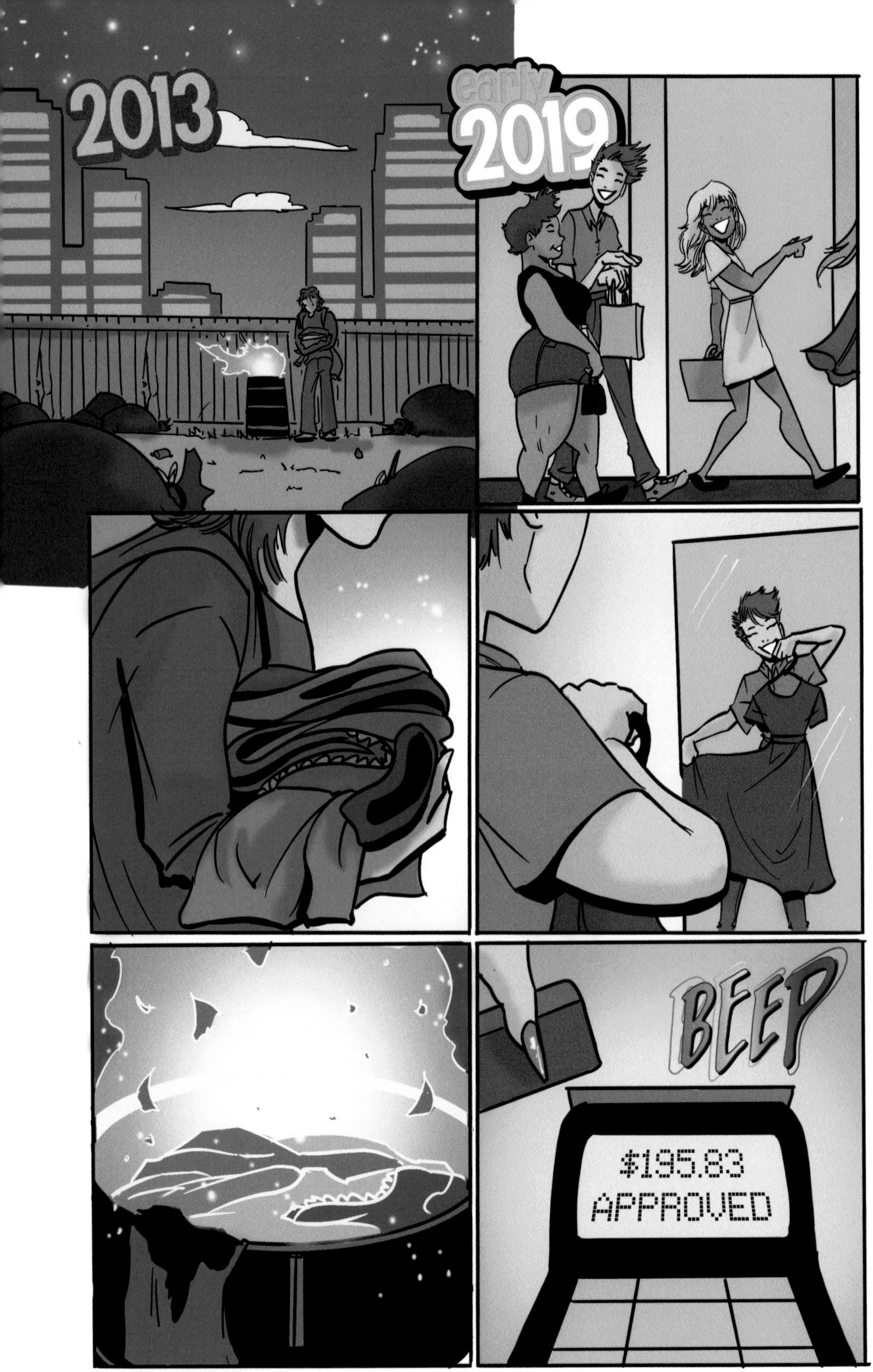
2013
early 2019
BEEP
$195.83
APPROVED

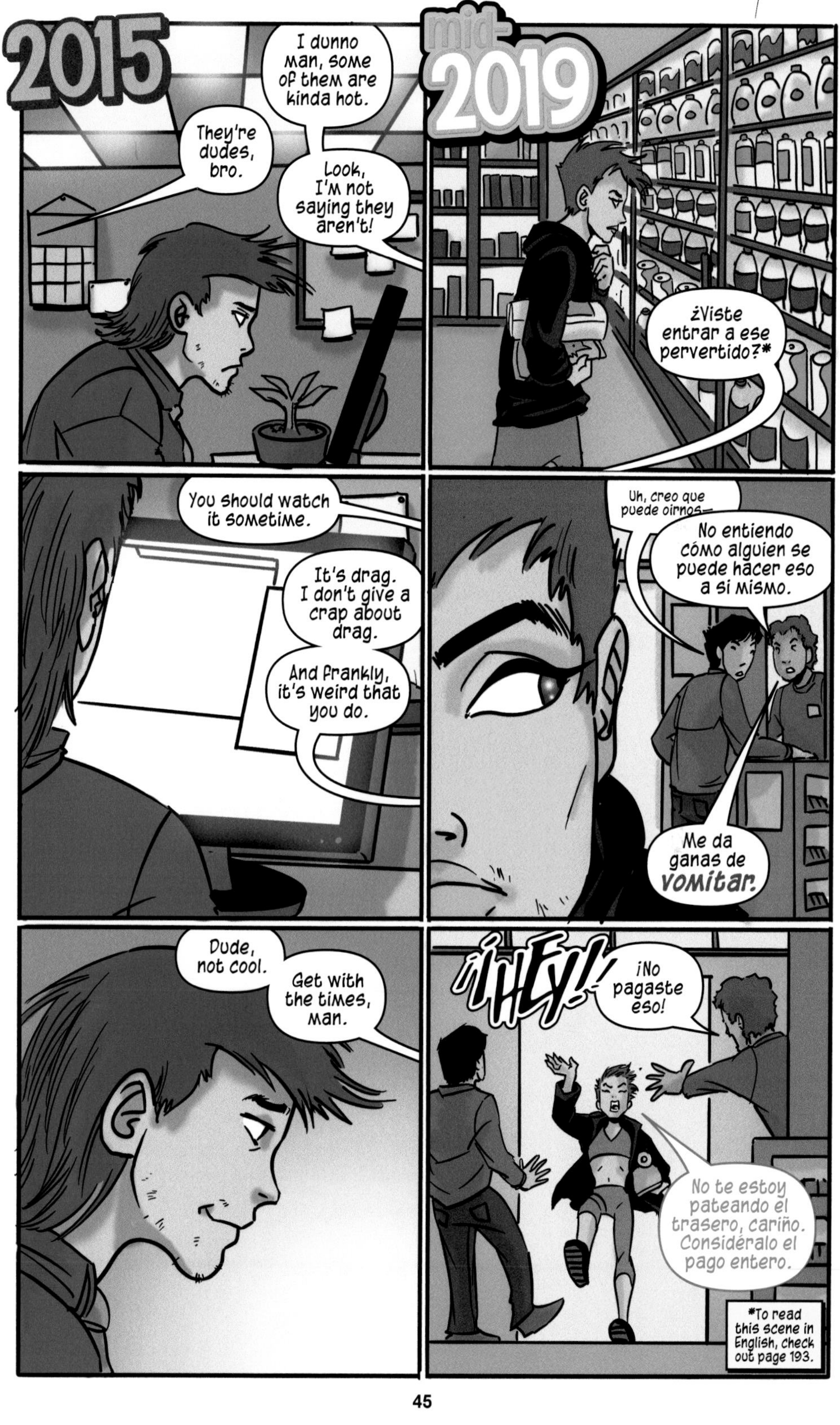
2015
They're dudes, bro.
I dunno man, some of them are kinda hot.
Look, I'm not saying they aren't!
mid-2019
¿Viste entrar a ese pervertido?*
You should watch it sometime.
It's drag. I don't give a crap about drag.
And frankly, it's weird that you do.
Uh, creo que puede oírnos—
No entiendo cómo alguien se puede hacer eso a sí mismo.
Me da ganas de vomitar.
Dude, not cool.
Get with the times, man.
¡¡Ey!!
¡No pagaste eso!
No te estoy pateando el trasero, cariño. Considéralo el pago entero.
*To read this scene in English, check out page 193.

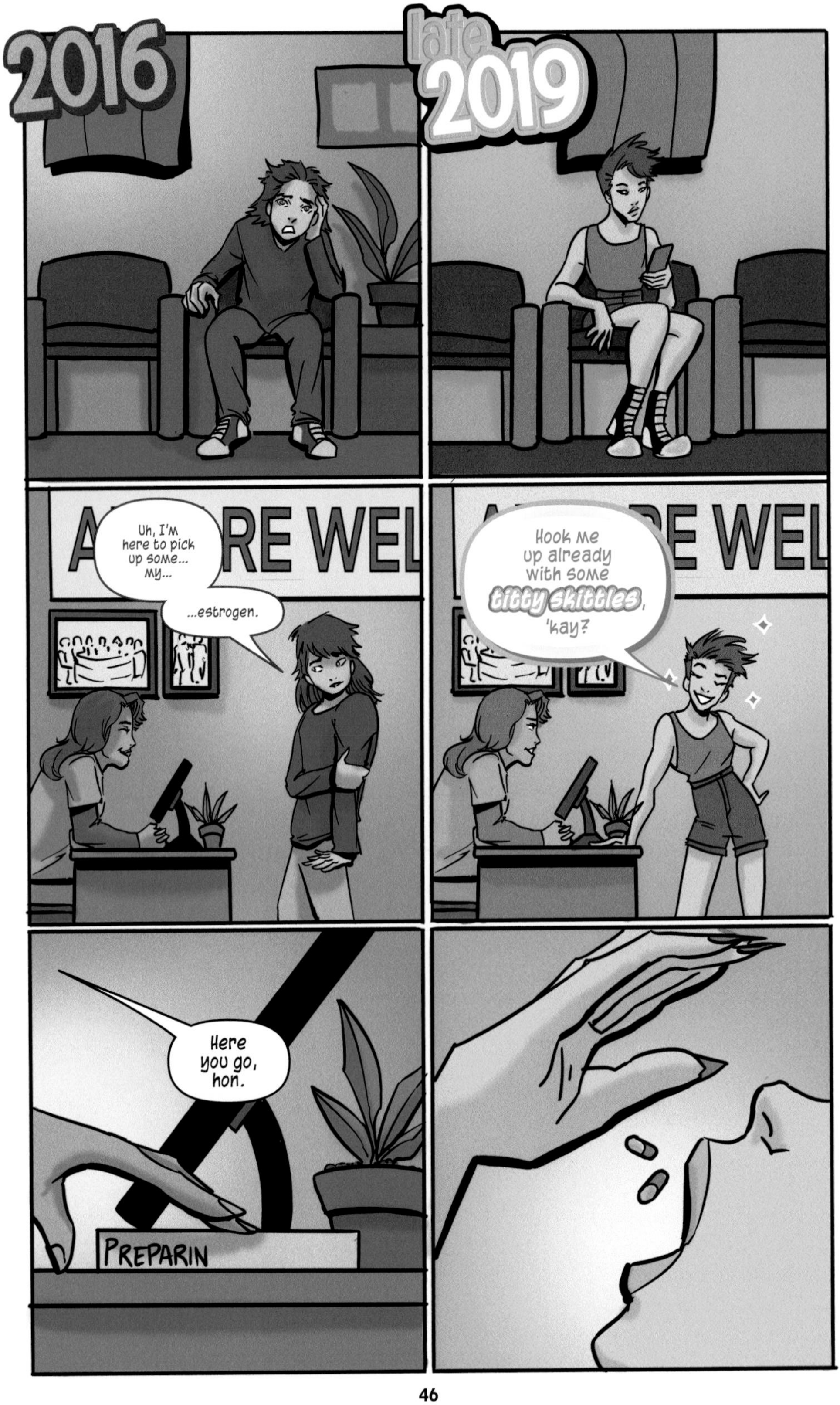
2016
late 2019
A RE WEL
Uh, I'm here to pick up some... my...
...estrogen.
A RE WEL
Hook me up already with some titty skittles, 'kay?
Here you go, hon.
PREPARIN

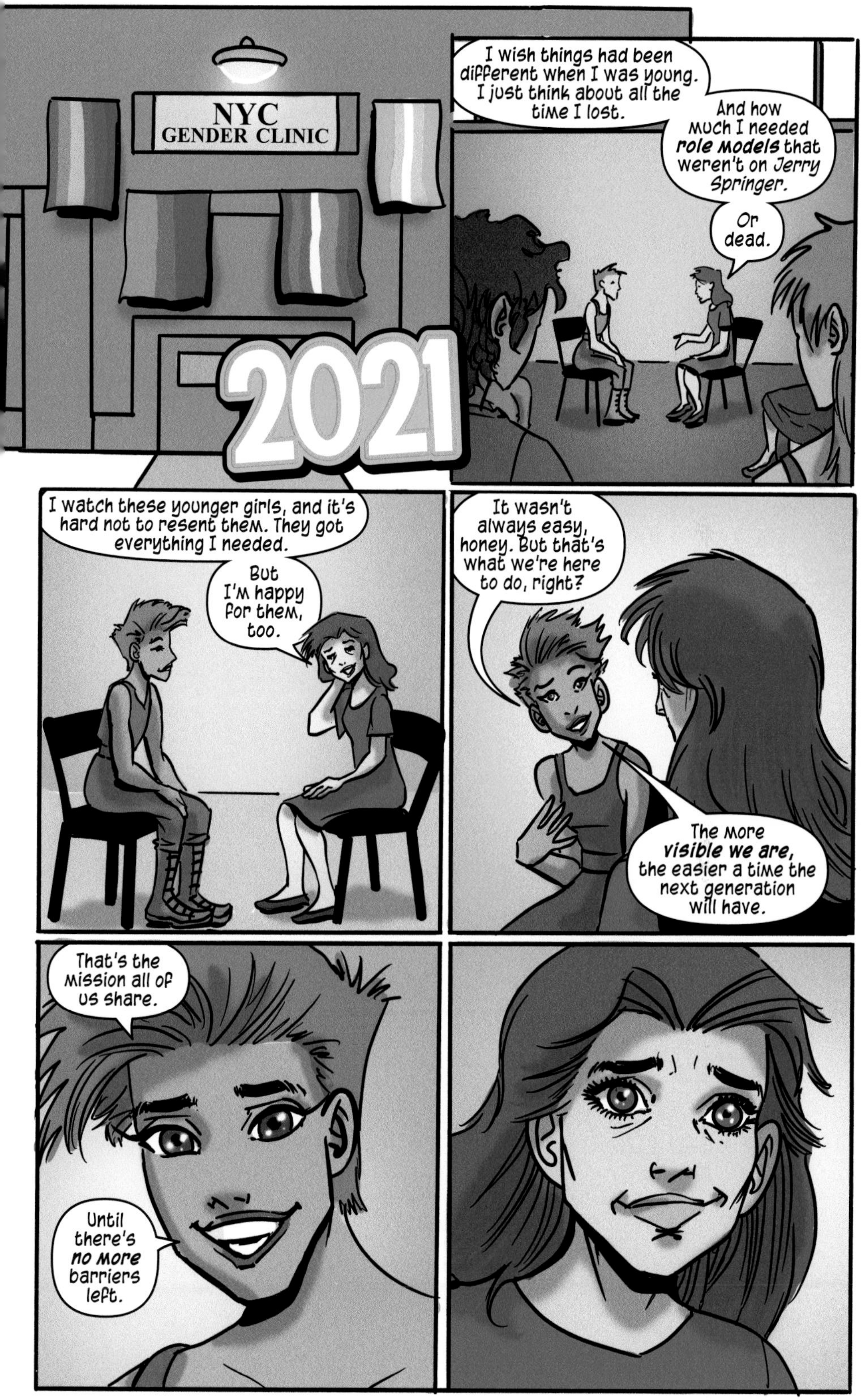
NYC GENDER CLINIC
2021
I wish things had been different when I was young. I just think about all the time I lost.
And how much I needed role models that weren't on Jerry Springer.
Or dead.
I watch these younger girls, and it's hard not to resent them. They got everything I needed.
But I'm happy for them, too.
It wasn't always easy, honey. But that's what we're here to do, right?
The more visible we are, the easier a time the next generation will have.
That's the mission all of us share.
Until there's no more barriers left.

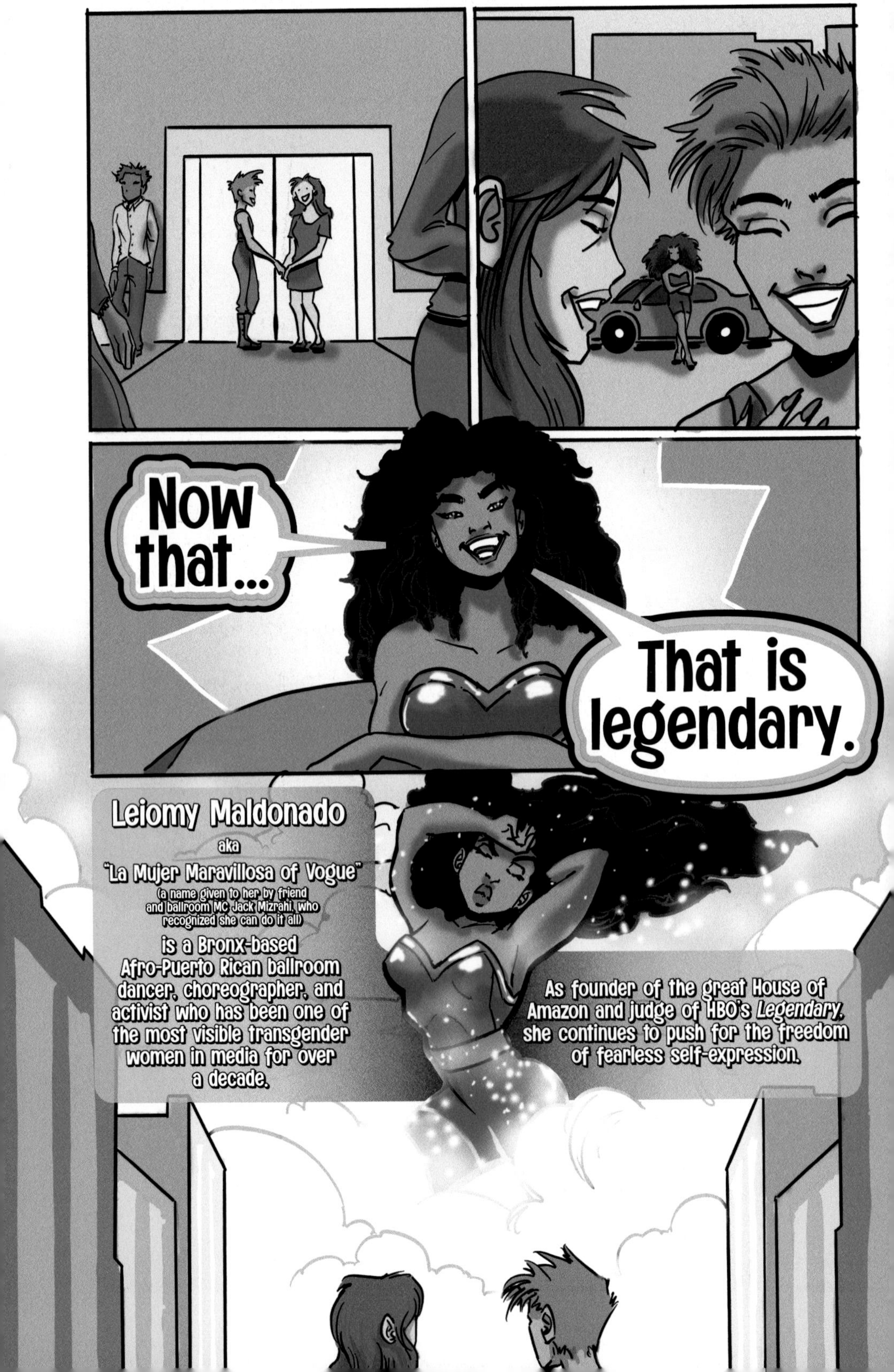
Now that...
That is legendary.
Leiomy Maldonado
aka
"La Mujer Maravillosa of Vogue"
(a name given to her by friend and ballroom MC Jack Mizrahi, who recognized she can do it all)
is a Bronx-based Afro-Puerto Rican ballroom dancer, choreographer, and activist who has been one of the most visible transgender women in media for over a decade.
As founder of the great House of Amazon and judge of HBO's *Legendary*, she continues to push for the freedom of fearless self-expression.

part two COMPASSION

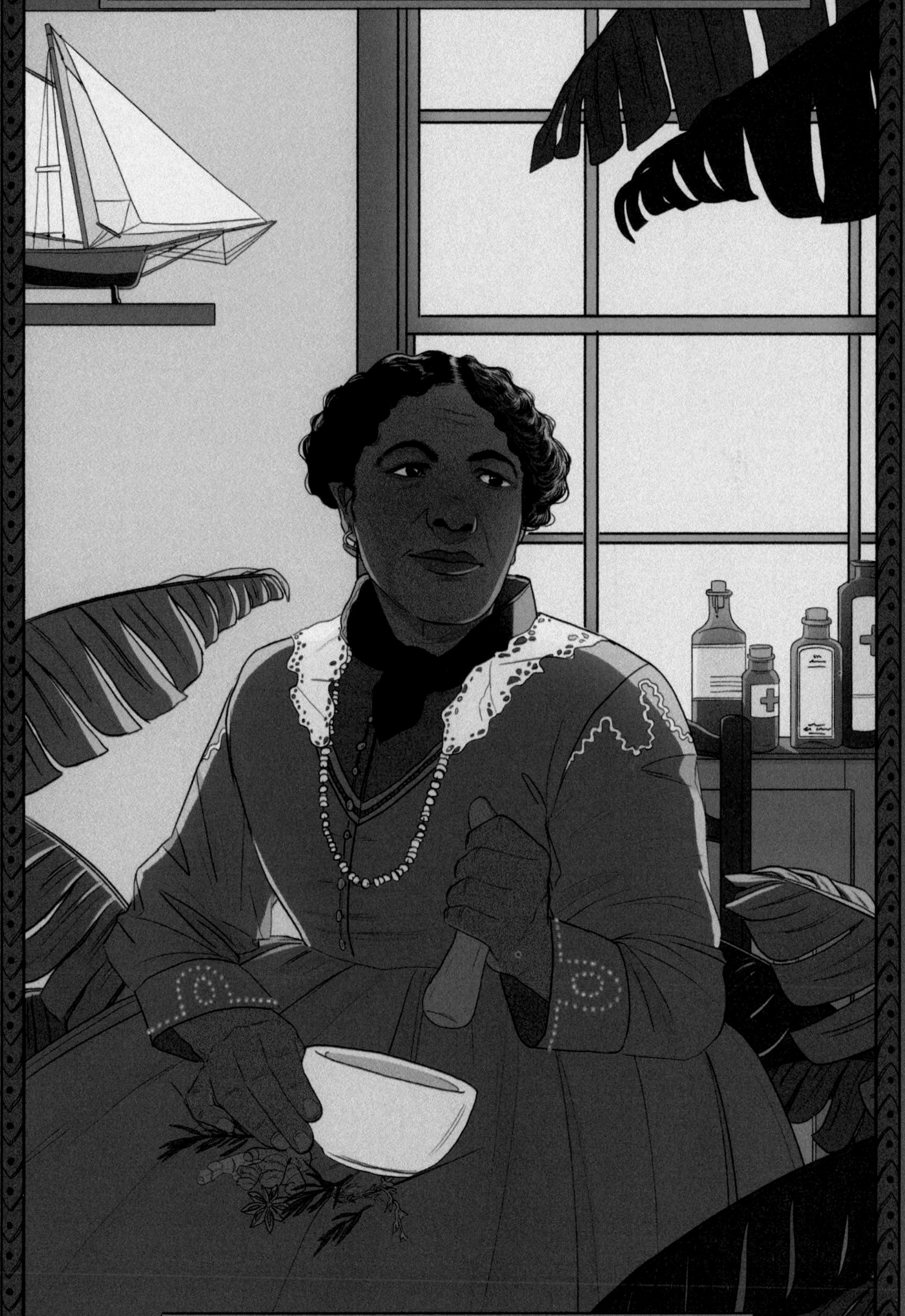

Mary Seacole (1805-1881) could have been a nurse, but her training in traditional Jamaican medicine wasn't recognized by the British establishment. Instead, she served the wounded soldiers of the Crimean War in the 1850s by setting up a hotel where they could recuperate and be restored to health. When official recognition is denied, showing compassion in direct ways can change the world.

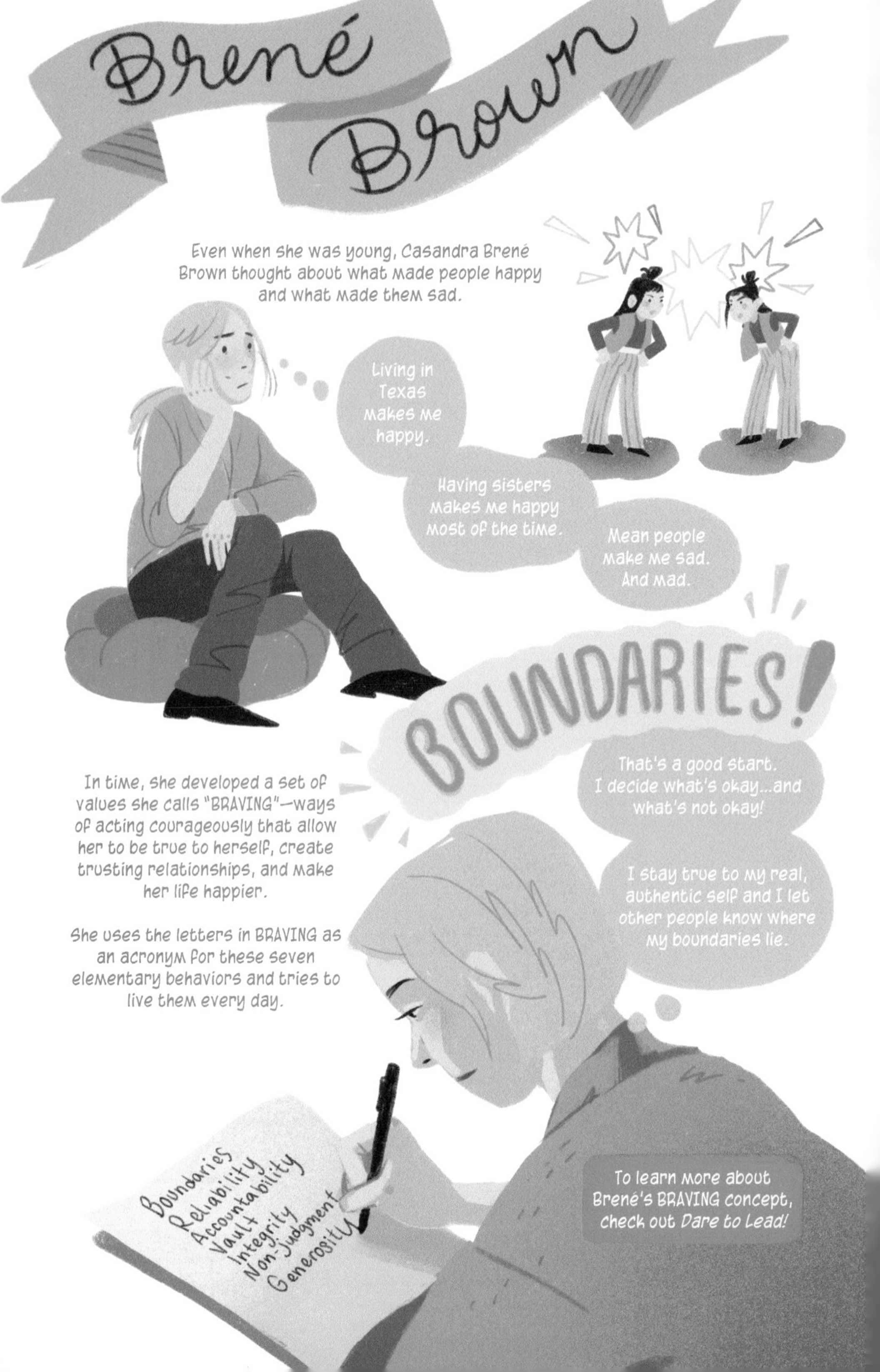
Brené Brown
Even when she was young, Casandra Brené Brown thought about what made people happy and what made them sad.
Living in Texas makes me happy.
Having sisters makes me happy most of the time.
Mean people make me sad. And mad.
BOUNDARIES!
That's a good start. I decide what's okay...and what's not okay!
I stay true to my real, authentic self and I let other people know where my boundaries lie.
In time, she developed a set of values she calls "BRAVING"—ways of acting courageously that allow her to be true to herself, create trusting relationships, and make her life happier.
She uses the letters in BRAVING as an acronym for these seven elementary behaviors and tries to live them every day.
Boundaries
Reliability
Accountability
Vault
Integrity
Non-Judgment
Generosity
To learn more about Brené's BRAVING concept, check out *Dare to Lead!*

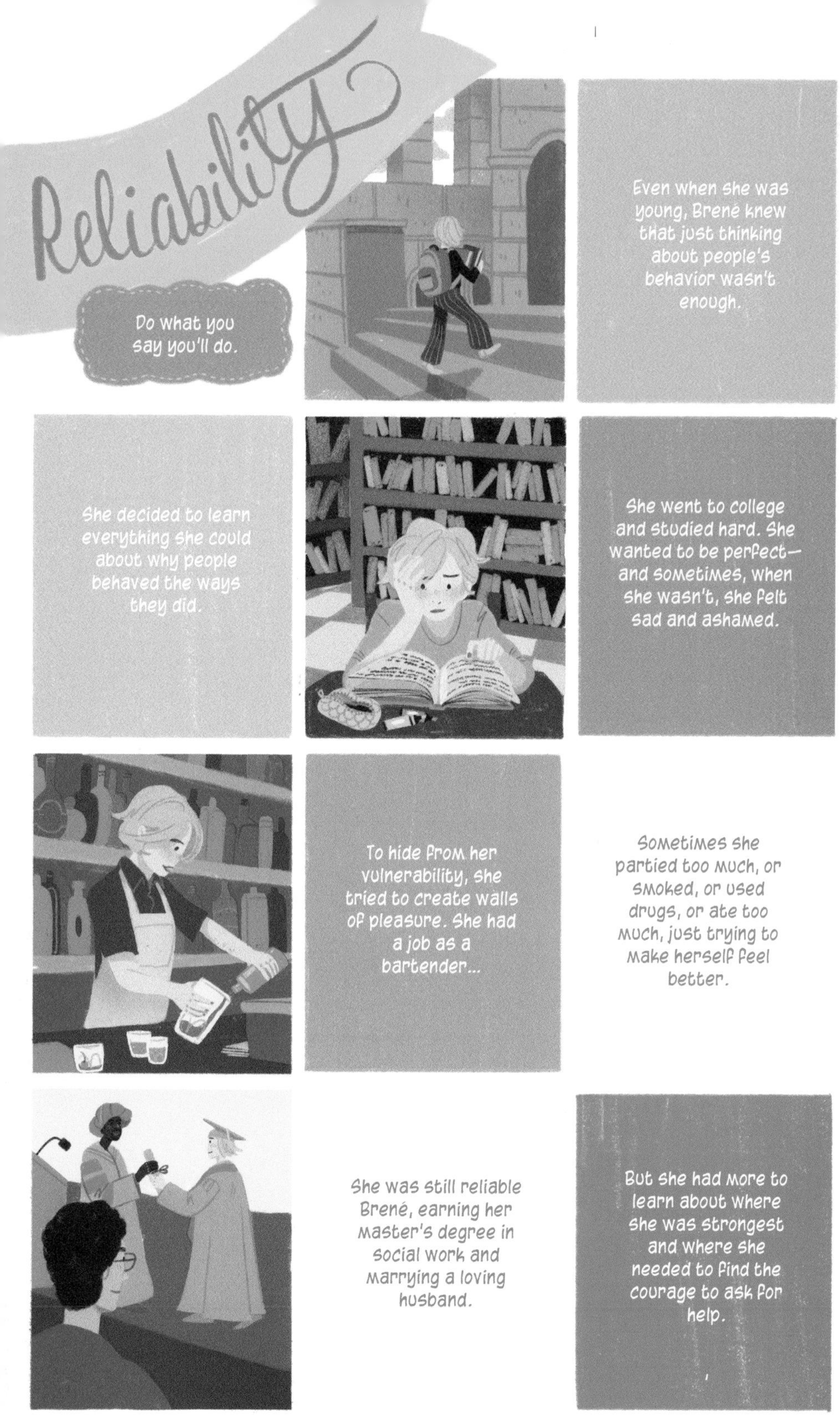
Reliability
Do what you say you'll do.
Even when she was young, Brené knew that just thinking about people's behavior wasn't enough.
She decided to learn everything she could about why people behaved the ways they did.
She went to college and studied hard. She wanted to be perfect—and sometimes, when she wasn't, she felt sad and ashamed.
To hide from her vulnerability, she tried to create walls of pleasure. She had a job as a bartender...
Sometimes she partied too much, or smoked, or used drugs, or ate too much, just trying to make herself feel better.
She was still reliable Brené, earning her master's degree in social work and marrying a loving husband.
But she had more to learn about where she was strongest and where she needed to find the courage to ask for help.

ACCOUNTABILITY

Own your mistakes, apologize, and make amends.

In grad school, Brené was asked to create a genogram—a visual diagram of family behavior patterns over several generations.

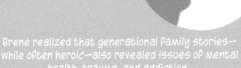

So, of course, she asked her mom about her family history.

Brené realized that generational family stories—while often heroic—also revealed issues of mental health, trauma, and addiction.

The day after she received her master's degree, Brené went to her first meeting of Alcoholics Anonymous.

She worried, at first, that she didn't really belong there—that compared to many, her addictions weren't severe.

But she also realized she had a family history of addiction and that she had been using substances like armor, trying to deflect feelings of vulnerability.

That was the day she quit drinking, smoking, and drugs. She's been sober ever since, and is grateful to AA for keeping her on the right path.

Living without those protective barriers has sometimes made her feel "like a turtle without a shell."

People who wade into discomfort and vulnerability and tell the truth about their stories are the real badasses.*

*Rising Strong is where she explores these ideas.

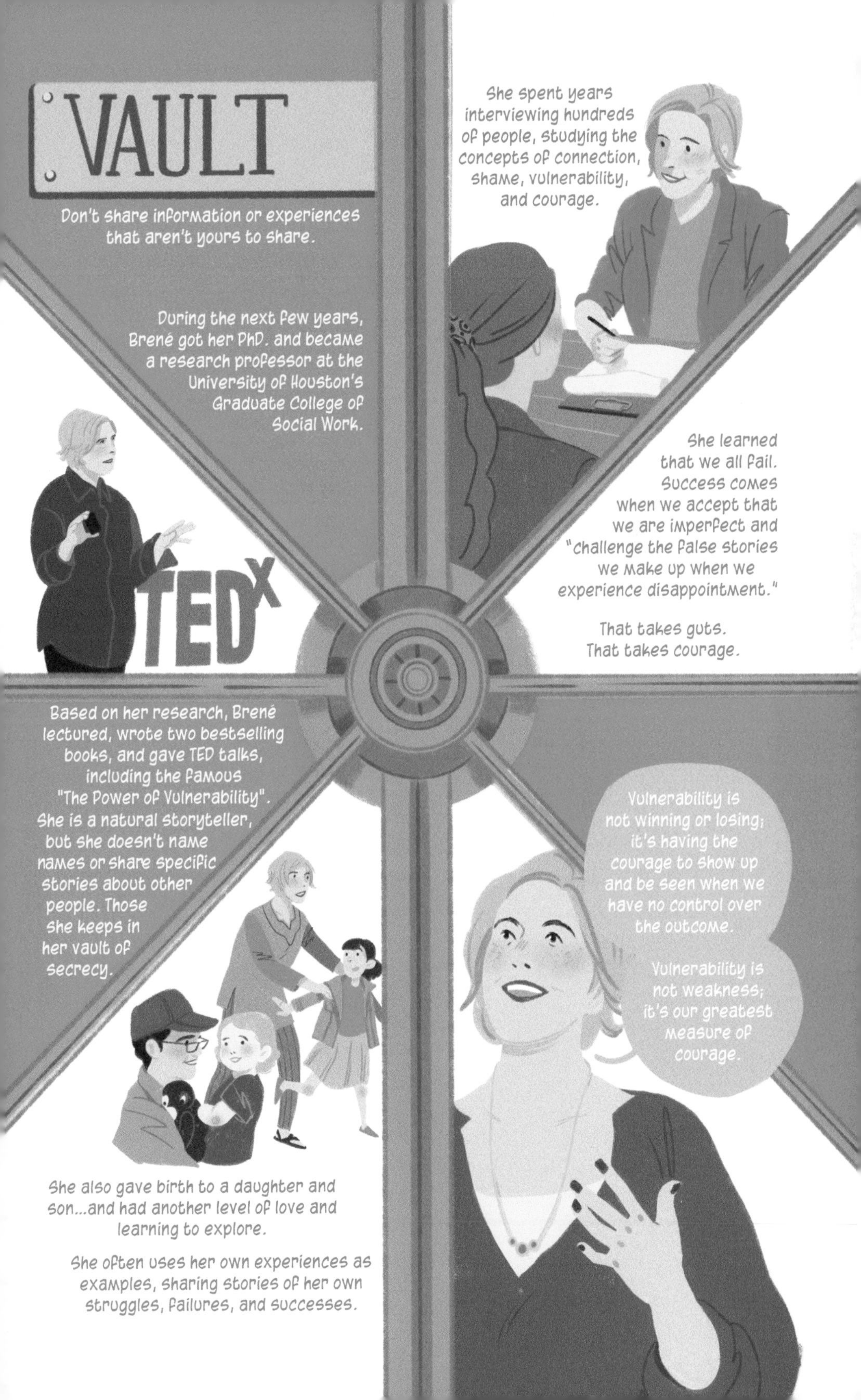
VAULT
Don't share information or experiences that aren't yours to share.
During the next few years, Brené got her PhD. and became a research professor at the University of Houston's Graduate College of Social Work.
TEDx
She spent years interviewing hundreds of people, studying the concepts of connection, shame, vulnerability, and courage.
She learned that we all fail. Success comes when we accept that we are imperfect and "challenge the false stories we make up when we experience disappointment."
That takes guts. That takes courage.
Based on her research, Brené lectured, wrote two bestselling books, and gave TED talks, including the famous "The Power of Vulnerability". She is a natural storyteller, but she doesn't name names or share specific stories about other people. Those she keeps in her vault of secrecy.
She also gave birth to a daughter and son...and had another level of love and learning to explore.
She often uses her own experiences as examples, sharing stories of her own struggles, failures, and successes.
Vulnerability is not winning or losing; it's having the courage to show up and be seen when we have no control over the outcome.
Vulnerability is not weakness; it's our greatest measure of courage.

Integrity

Choose courage over comfort. Practice your values rather than simply professing them.

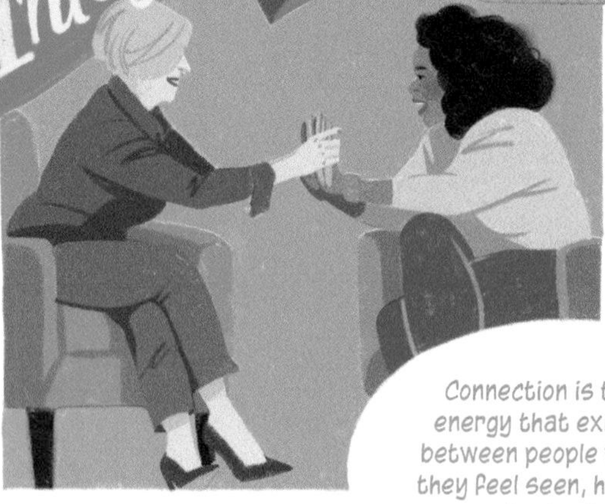

Brené's integrity, her willingness to be her honest and authentic self, to make hard choices, and to take chances (even in situations she couldn't control) were about to pay off, big time!

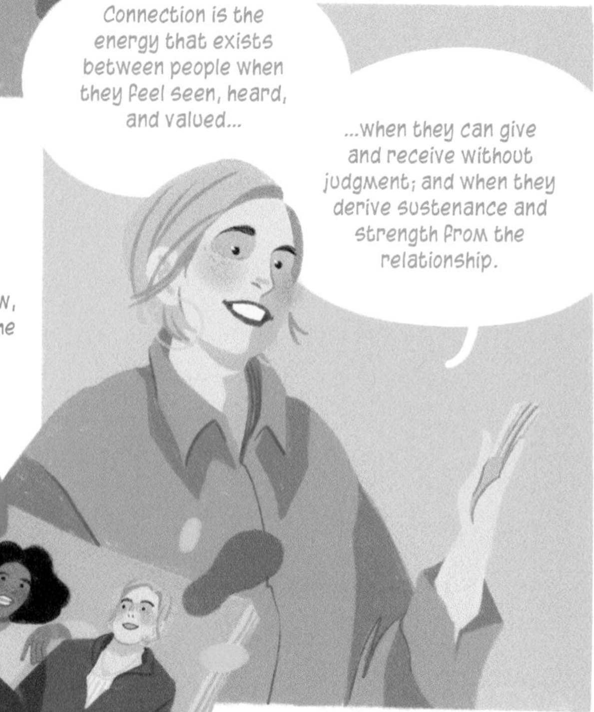
Connection is the energy that exists between people when they feel seen, heard, and valued...
...when they can give and receive without judgment; and when they derive sustenance and strength from the relationship.

Oprah Winfrey loved her TED talk "The Power of Vulnerability"!

When Oprah invited Brené to appear on her *Super Soul Sunday* TV show, Brené was thrilled, and she and Oprah instantly connected.

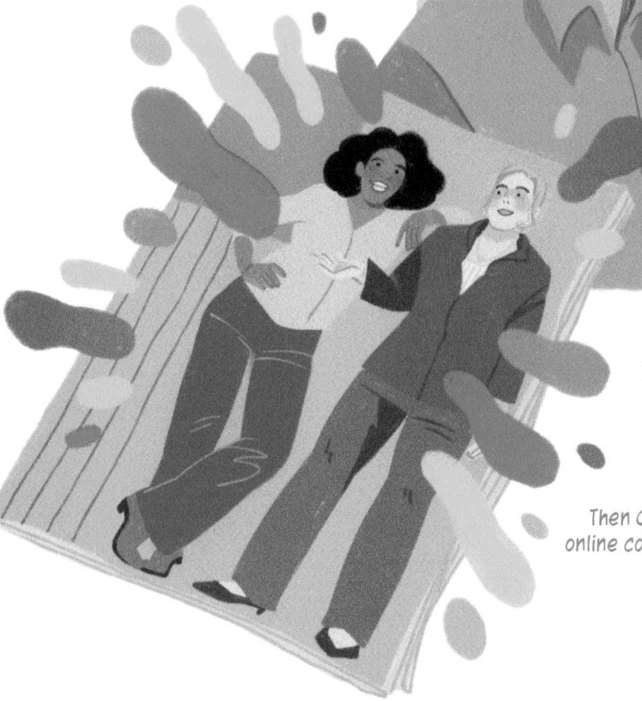

Her appearance was a huge success. Oprah was so engaged by Brené, that the interview was featured in *O* magazine.

Then Oprah asked Brené to give an online course for Oprah's OWN network.

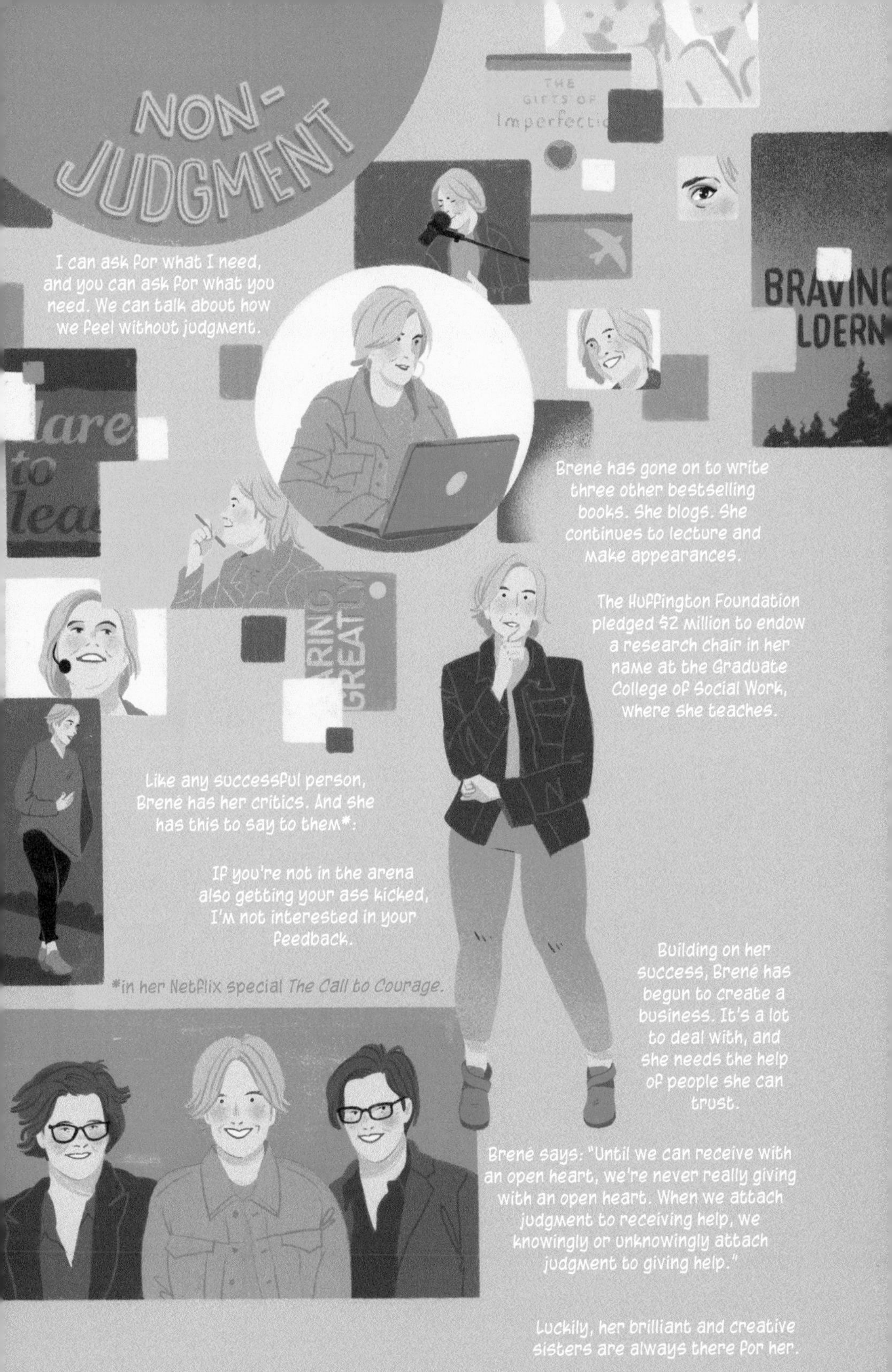
NON-JUDGMENT
THE GIFTS OF
I can ask for what I need, and you can ask for what you need. We can talk about how we feel without judgment.
Brené has gone on to write three other bestselling books. She blogs. She continues to lecture and make appearances.
The Huffington Foundation pledged $2 million to endow a research chair in her name at the Graduate College of Social Work, where she teaches.
Like any successful person, Brené has her critics. And she has this to say to them*:
If you're not in the arena also getting your ass kicked, I'm not interested in your feedback.
*in her Netflix special The Call to Courage.
Building on her success, Brené has begun to create a business. It's a lot to deal with, and she needs the help of people she can trust.
Brené says: "Until we can receive with an open heart, we're never really giving with an open heart. When we attach judgment to receiving help, we knowingly or unknowingly attach judgment to giving help."
Luckily, her brilliant and creative sisters are always there for her.

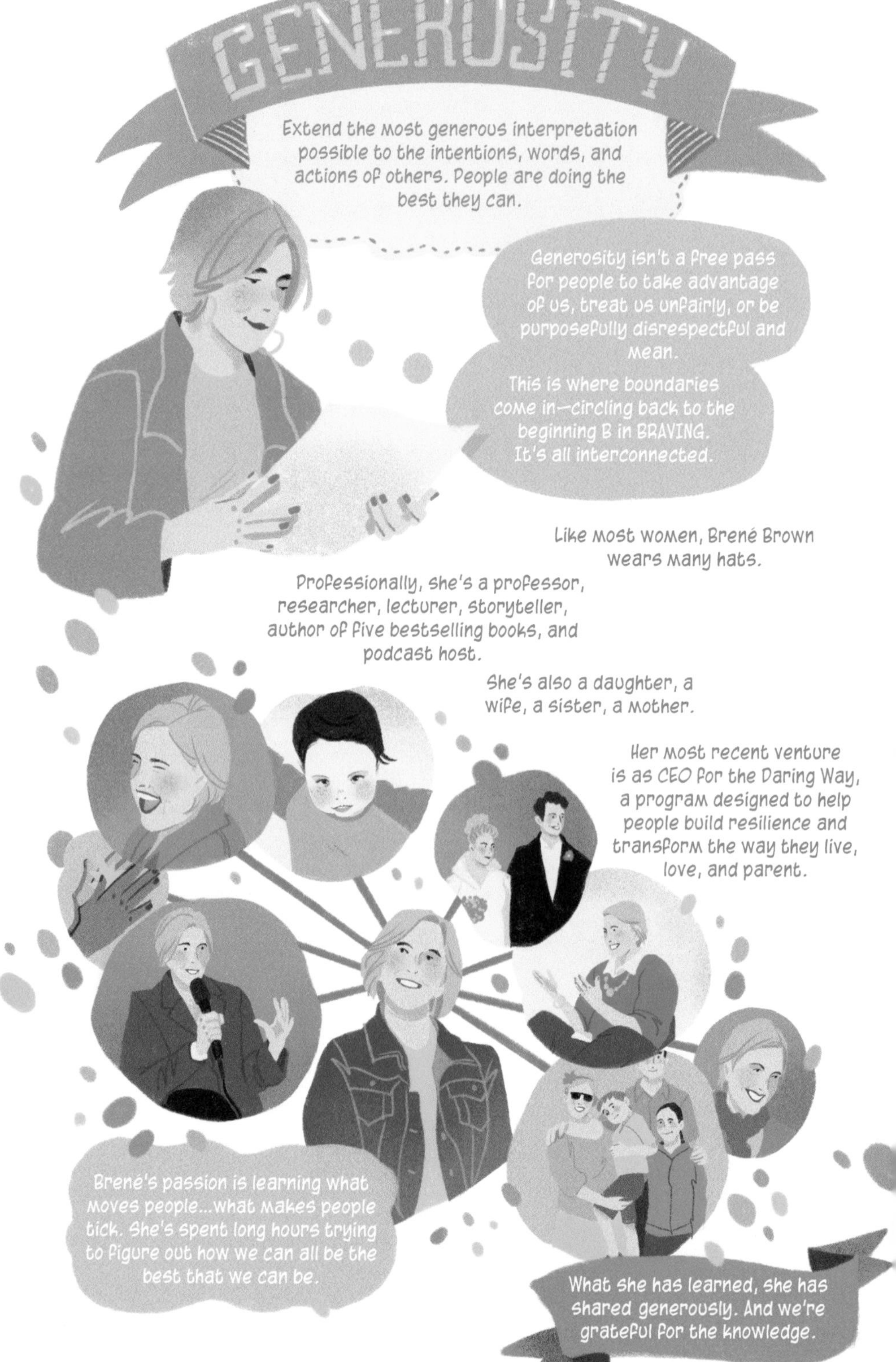
GENEROSITY
Extend the most generous interpretation possible to the intentions, words, and actions of others. People are doing the best they can.
Generosity isn't a free pass for people to take advantage of us, treat us unfairly, or be purposefully disrespectful and mean.
This is where boundaries come in—circling back to the beginning B in BRAVING. It's all interconnected.
Like most women, Brené Brown wears many hats.
Professionally, she's a professor, researcher, lecturer, storyteller, author of five bestselling books, and podcast host.
She's also a daughter, a wife, a sister, a mother.
Her most recent venture is as CEO for the Daring Way, a program designed to help people build resilience and transform the way they live, love, and parent.
Brené's passion is learning what moves people...what makes people tick. She's spent long hours trying to figure out how we can all be the best that we can be.
What she has learned, she has shared generously. And we're grateful for the knowledge.

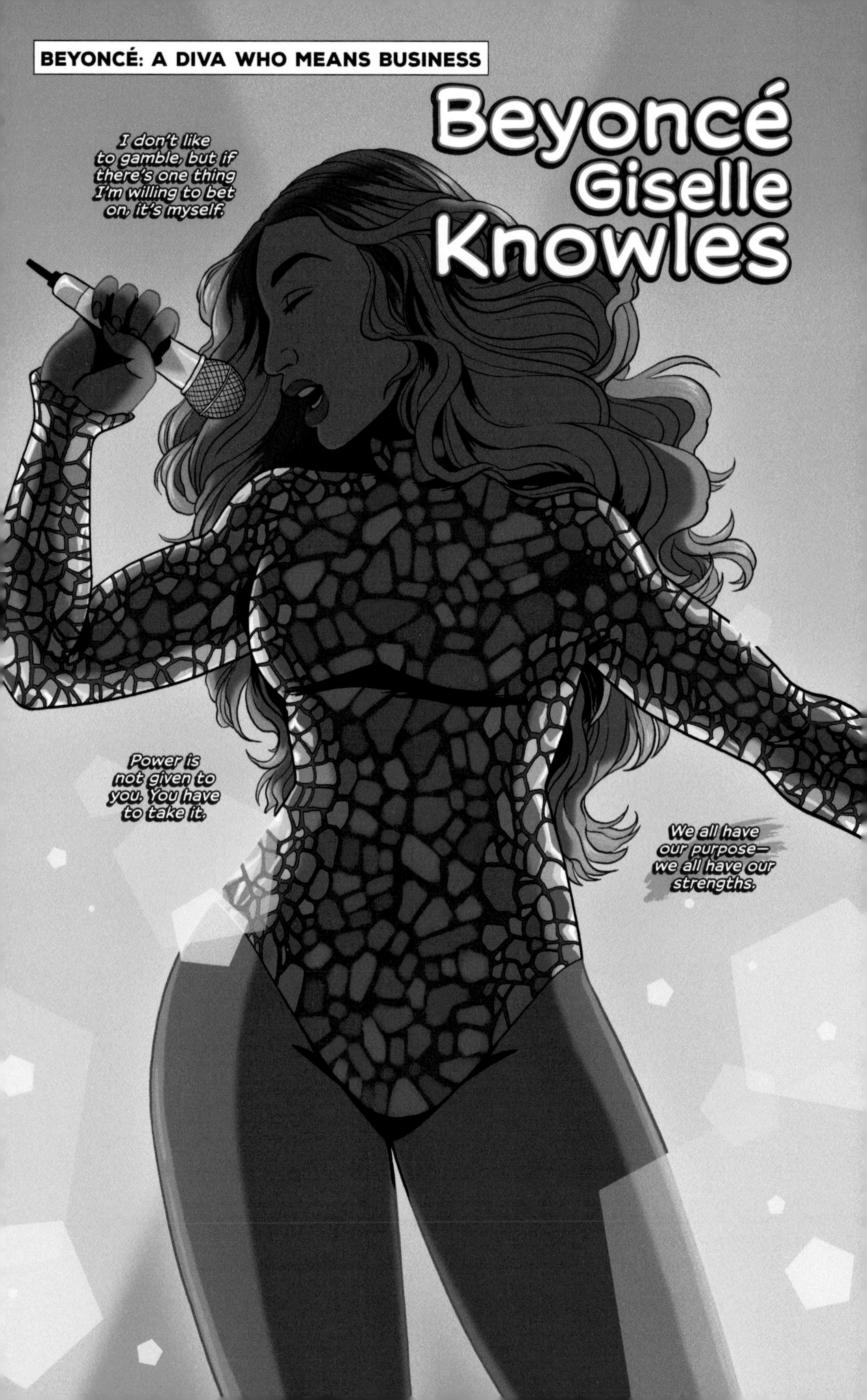

BEYONCÉ: A DIVA WHO MEANS BUSINESS
Beyoncé Giselle Knowles
I don't like to gamble, but if there's one thing I'm willing to bet on, it's myself.
Power is not given to you. You have to take it.
We all have our purpose—we all have our strengths.

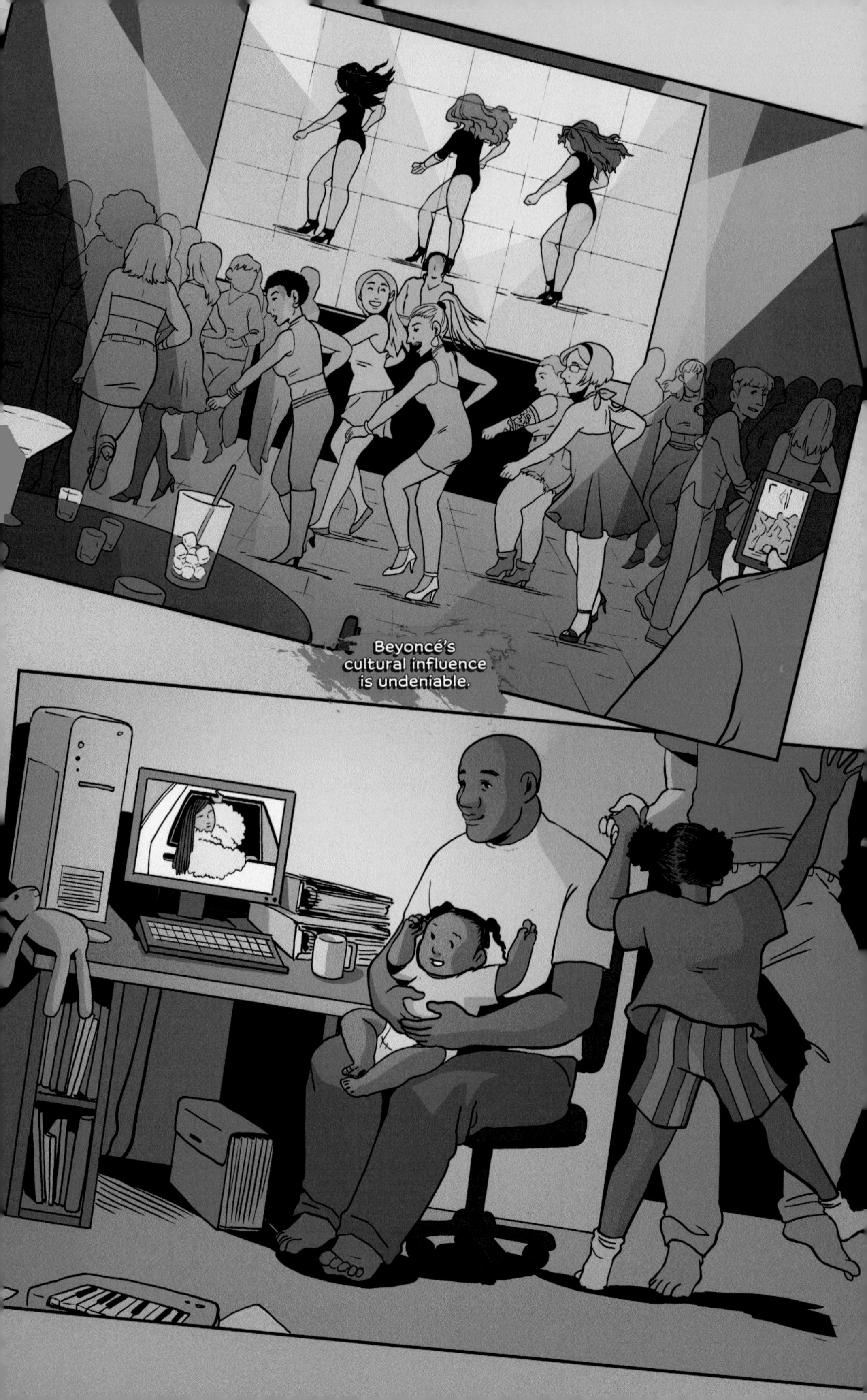
Beyoncé's cultural influence is undeniable.

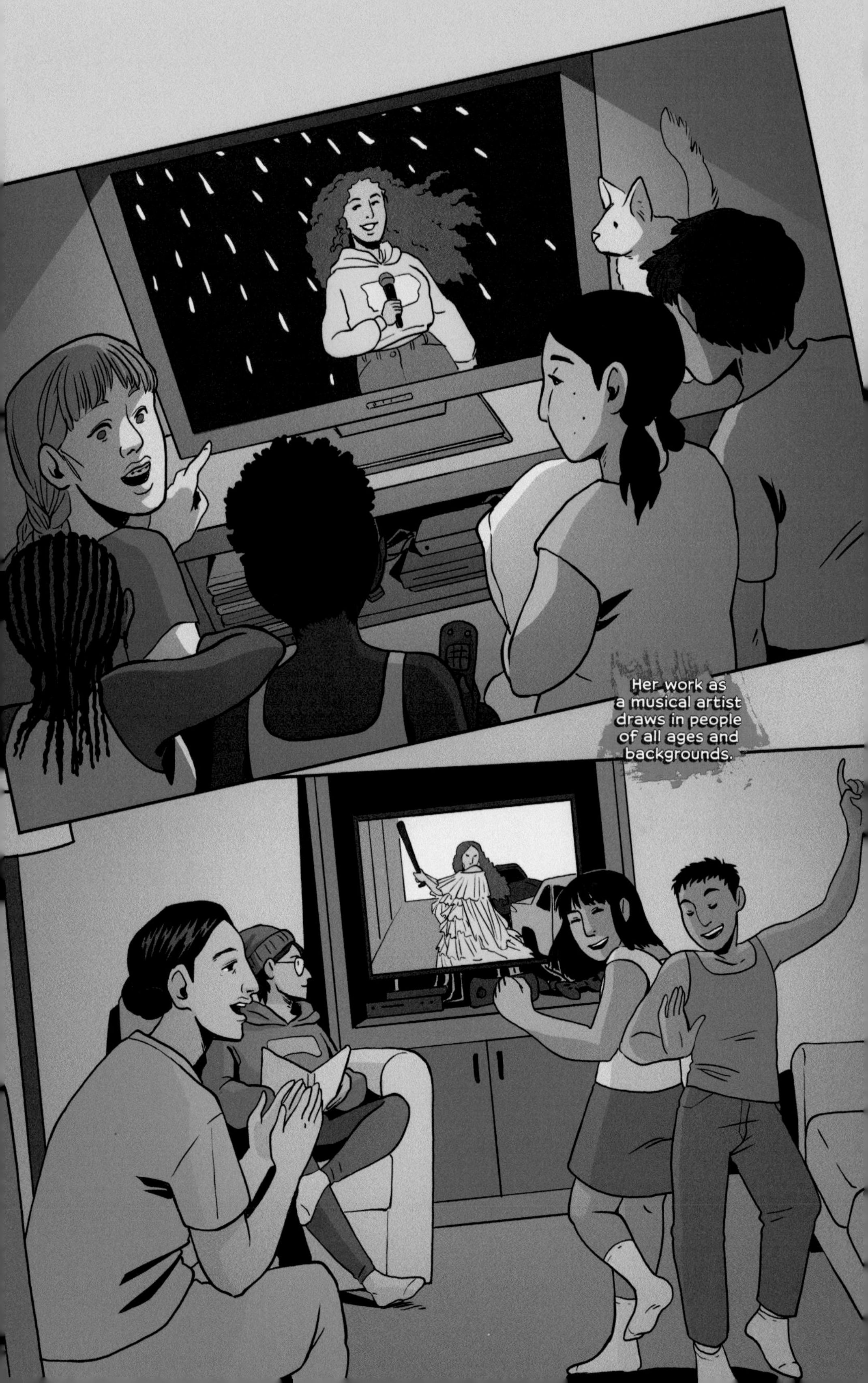
Her work as a musical artist draws in people of all ages and backgrounds.

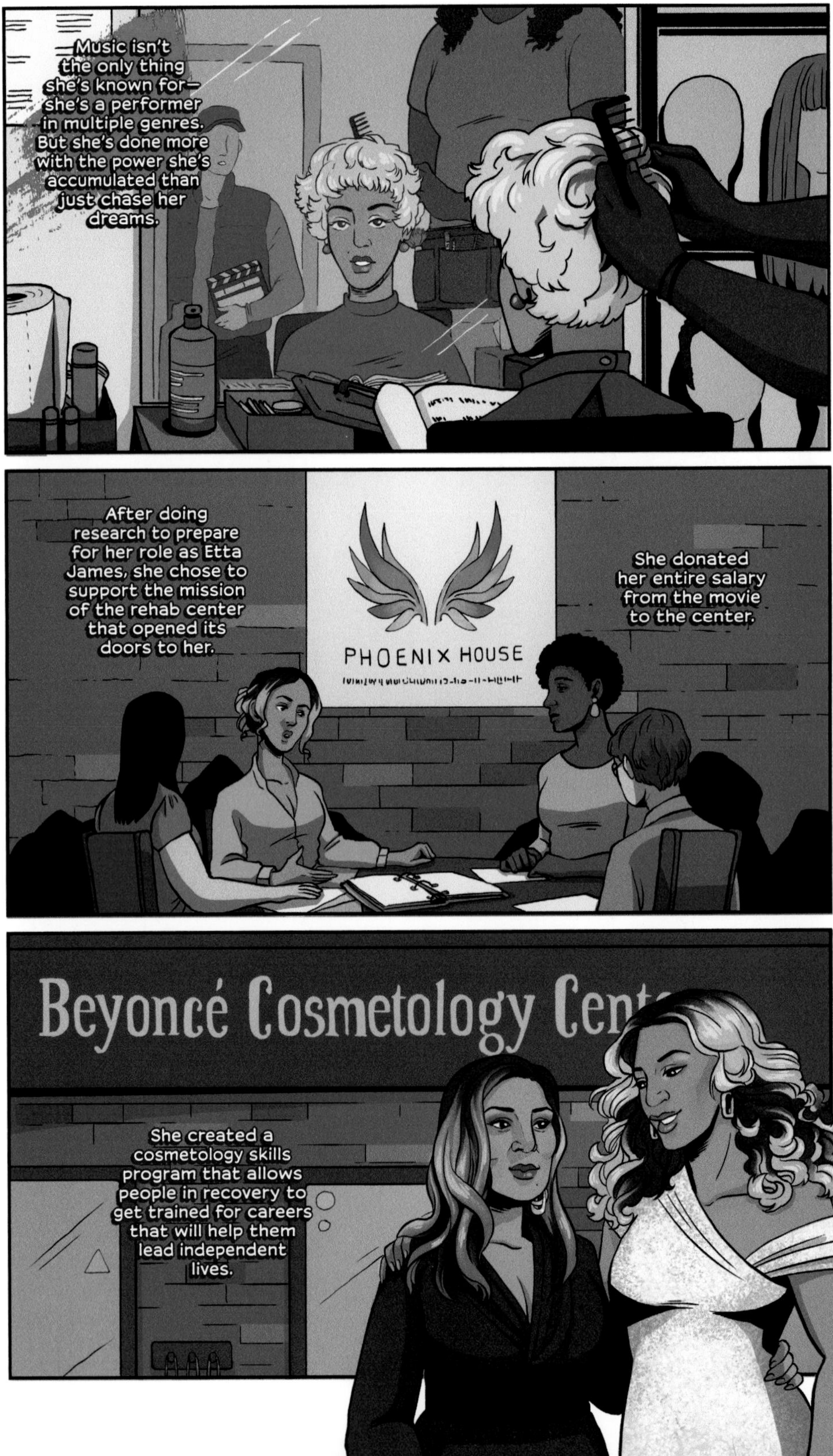
Music isn't the only thing she's known for—she's a performer in multiple genres. But she's done more with the power she's accumulated than just chase her dreams.
After doing research to prepare for her role as Etta James, she chose to support the mission of the rehab center that opened its doors to her.
PHOENIX HOUSE
She donated her entire salary from the movie to the center.
Beyoncé Cosmetology Cent
She created a cosmetology skills program that allows people in recovery to get trained for careers that will help them lead independent lives.

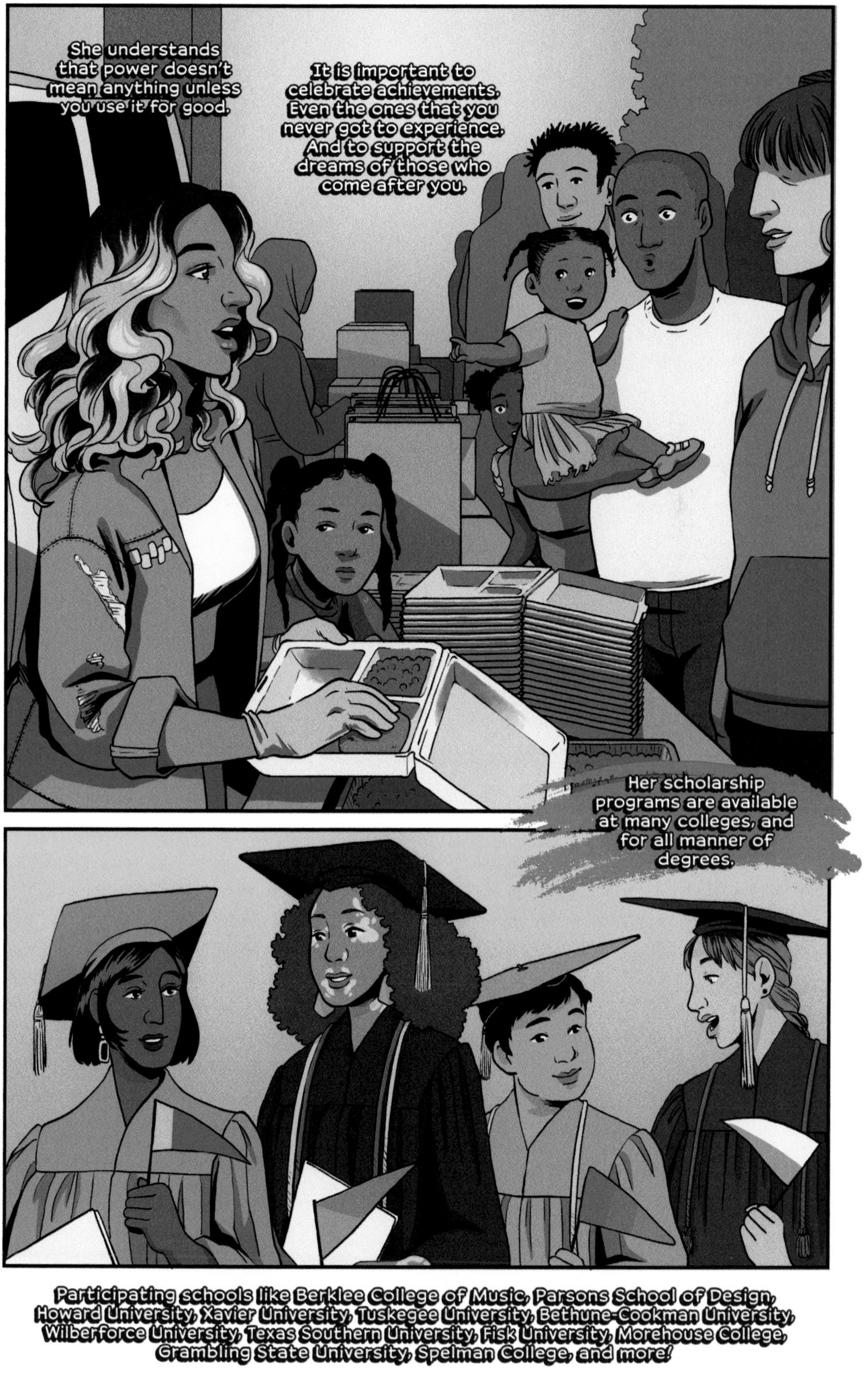
She understands that power doesn't mean anything unless you use it for good.
It is important to celebrate achievements. Even the ones that you never got to experience. And to support the dreams of those who come after you.
Her scholarship programs are available at many colleges, and for all manner of degrees.

Participating schools like Berklee College of Music, Parsons School of Design, Howard University, Xavier University, Tuskegee University, Bethune-Cookman University, Wilberforce University, Texas Southern University, Fisk University, Morehouse College, Grambling State University, Spelman College, and more!

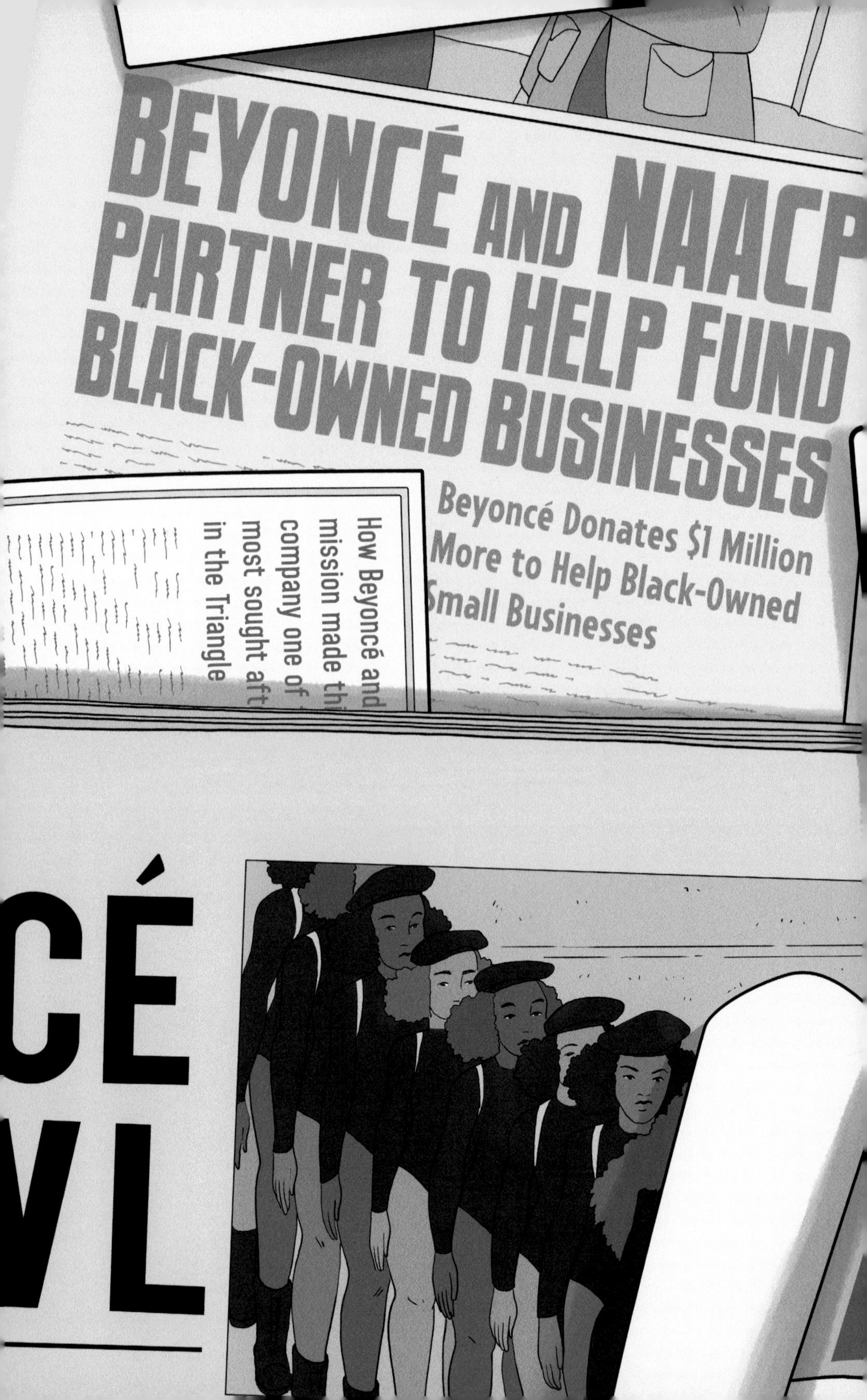
BEYONCÉ AND NAACP PARTNER TO HELP FUND BLACK-OWNED BUSINESSES
Beyoncé Donates $1 Million More to Help Black-Owned Small Businesses
How Beyoncé and
mission made thi
company one of
most sought aft
in the Triangle
CÉ
VL

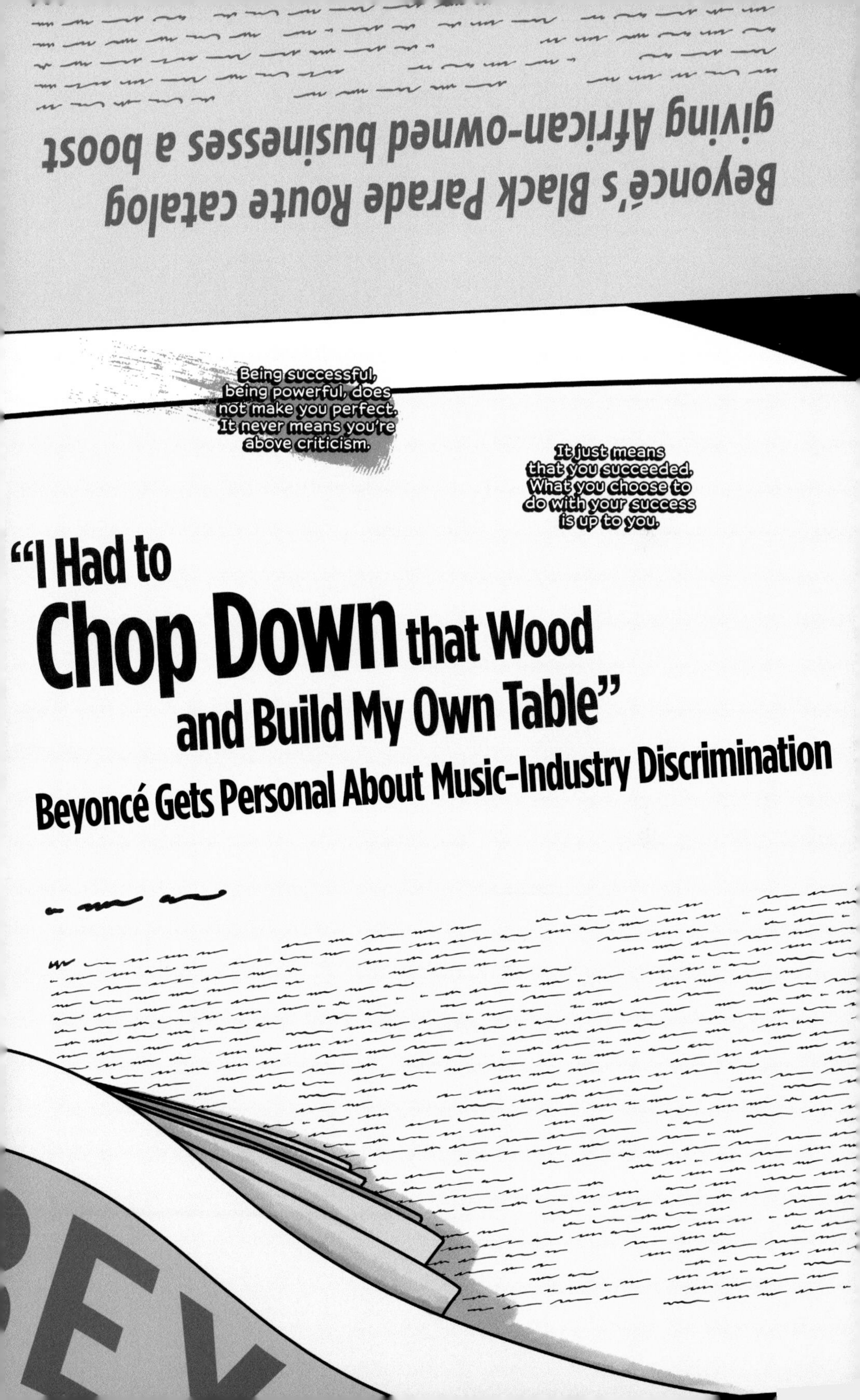

Beyoncé's Black Parade Route catalog giving African-owned businesses a boost
Being successful, being powerful, does not make you perfect. It never means you're above criticism.
It just means that you succeeded. What you choose to do with your success is up to you.
"I Had to Chop Down that Wood and Build My Own Table"
Beyoncé Gets Personal About Music-Industry Discrimination

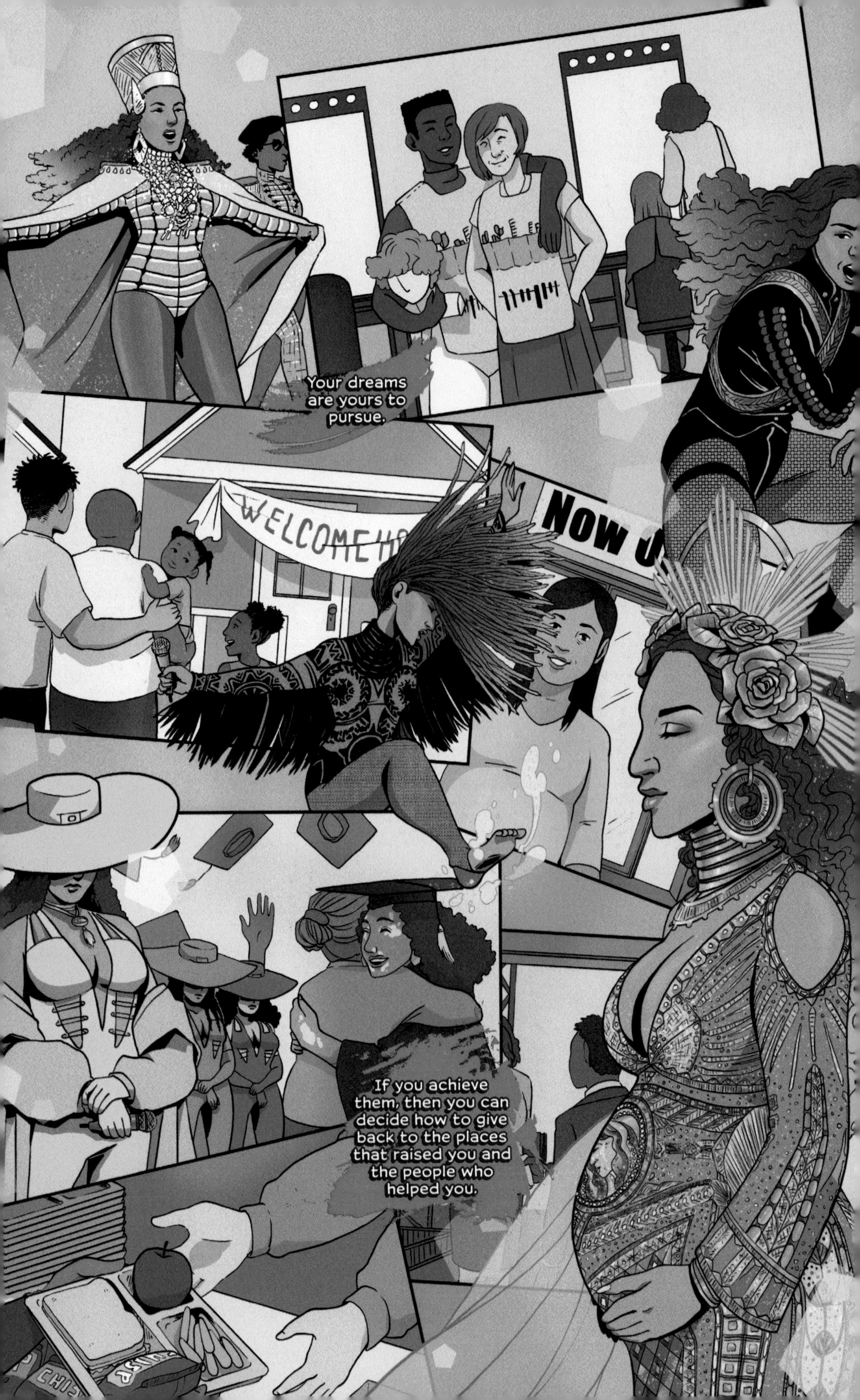
Your dreams are yours to pursue.
If you achieve them, then you can decide how to give back to the places that raised you and the people who helped you.

MARI COPENY: FIGHTING FOR FLINT

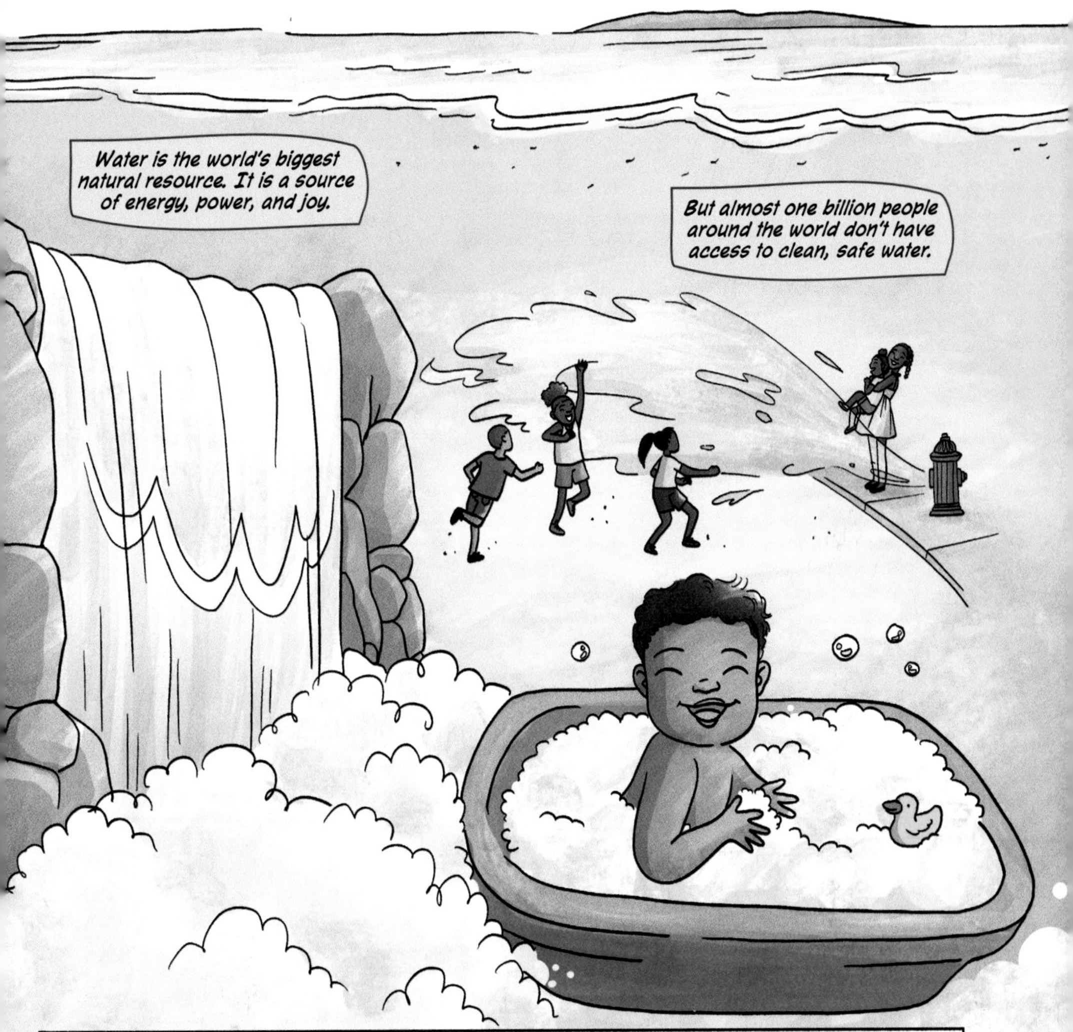
Water is the world's biggest natural resource. It is a source of energy, power, and joy.
But almost one billion people around the world don't have access to clean, safe water.

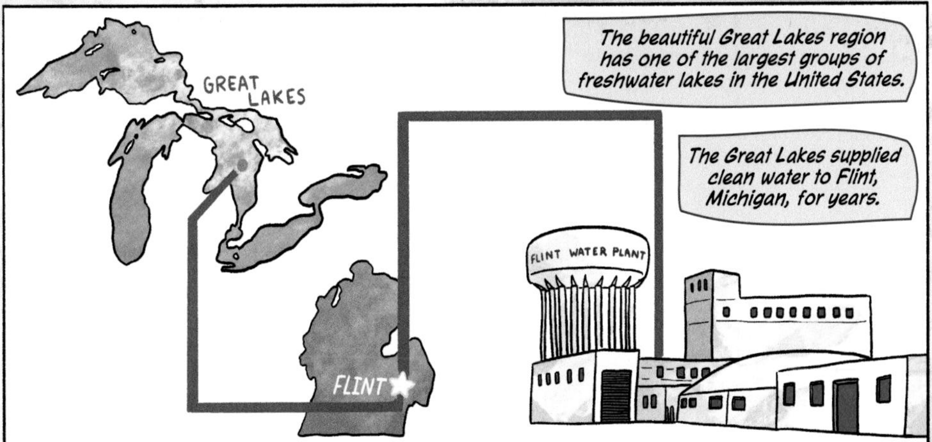
The beautiful Great Lakes region has one of the largest groups of freshwater lakes in the United States.
GREAT LAKES
The Great Lakes supplied clean water to Flint, Michigan, for years.
FLINT WATER PLANT
FLINT

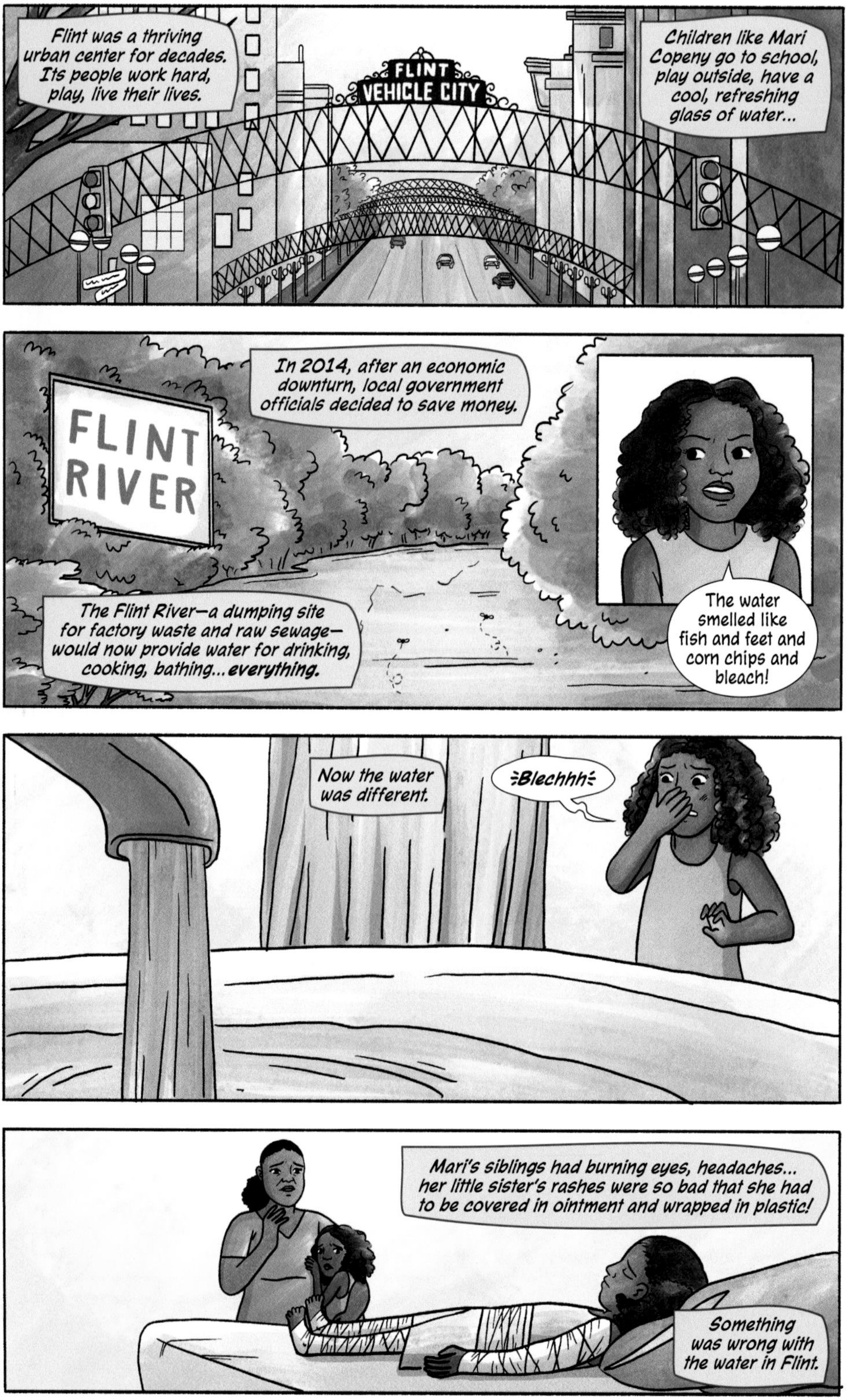
Flint was a thriving urban center for decades. Its people work hard, play, live their lives.
FLINT
VEHICLE CITY
Children like Mari Copeny go to school, play outside, have a cool, refreshing glass of water...
In 2014, after an economic downturn, local government officials decided to save money.
FLINT RIVER
The water smelled like fish and feet and corn chips and bleach!
The Flint River—a dumping site for factory waste and raw sewage—would now provide water for drinking, cooking, bathing... **everything.**
Now the water was different.
Blechhh
Mari's siblings had burning eyes, headaches... her little sister's rashes were so bad that she had to be covered in ointment and wrapped in plastic!
Something was wrong with the water in Flint.

Dr. Mona Hanna-Attisha is a local physician who served her patients by bringing their troubles to the media.

Hello, I have some important information about the water in Flint. My patients are showing signs of—

Click

The Flint River water wasn't properly treated for human use, and traveling through old, corroded pipes left the water contaminated with high levels of lead.

WATER IS LIFE

JUSTICE FOR FLINT

People made calls and wrote letters about the dirty, smelly water making them sick.

Residents contacted the federal Environmental Protection Agency (EPA), and protested...but their government wasn't listening.

Mari Copeny was only eight, but she knew a lot about helping her community.

When she was even younger, she would go with her grandmother to bring food to hungry people.

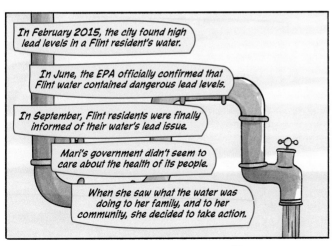

In February 2015, the city found high lead levels in a Flint resident's water.

In June, the EPA officially confirmed that Flint water contained dangerous lead levels.

In September, Flint residents were finally informed of their water's lead issue.

Mari's government didn't seem to care about the health of its people.

When she saw what the water was doing to her family, and to her community, she decided to take action.

Mari's mom, LuLu Brezzell.

You either deal with it or you try to take a stand, and her choice was she wanted to stand up for the kids in Flint.

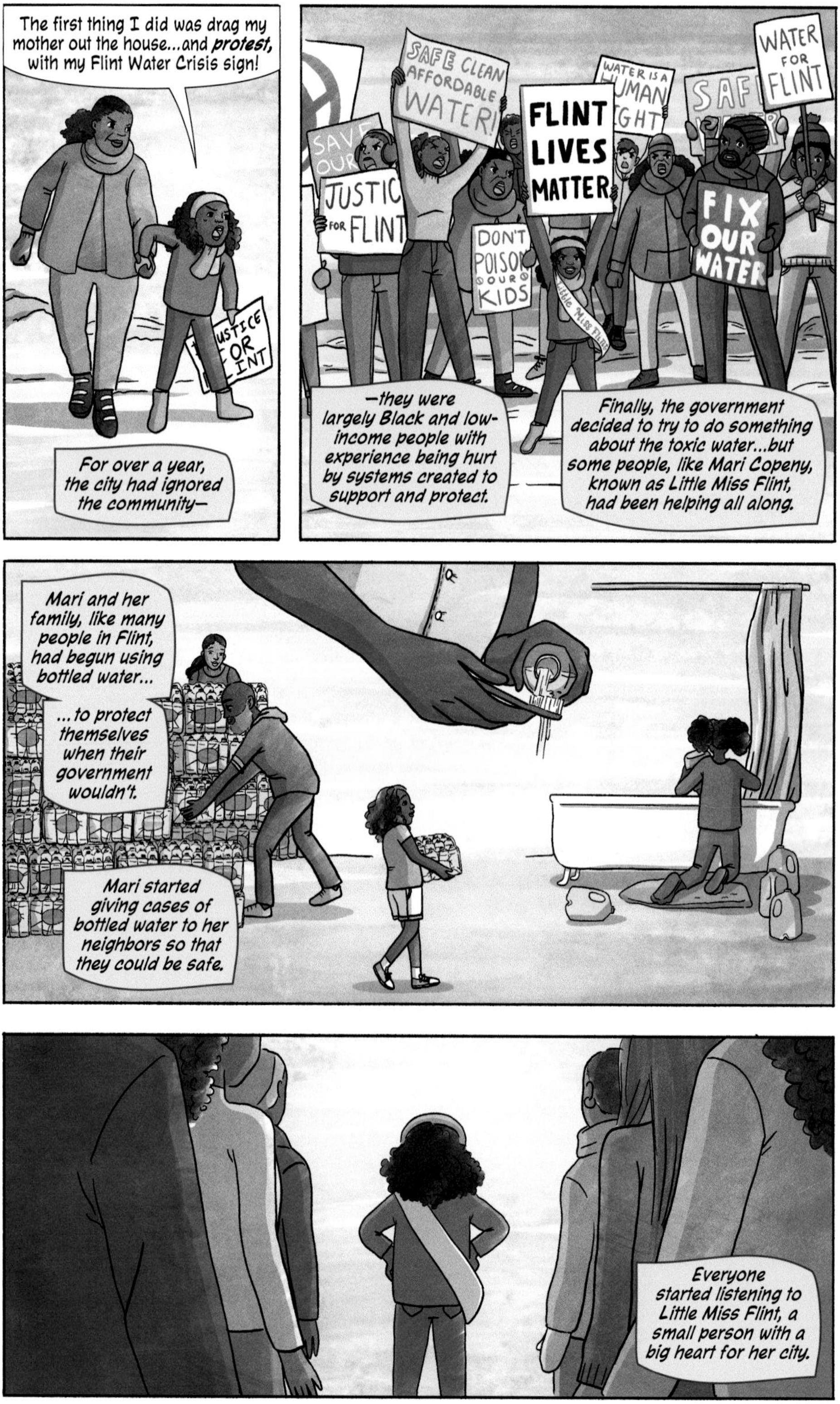
The first thing I did was drag my mother out the house...and ***protest,*** with my Flint Water Crisis sign!
For over a year, the city had ignored the community—
SAFE CLEAN AFFORDABLE WATER!
FLINT LIVES MATTER
WATER FOR FLINT
JUSTICE FOR FLINT
DON'T POISON OUR KIDS
FIX OUR WATER
Little Miss Flint
—they were largely Black and low-income people with experience being hurt by systems created to support and protect.
Finally, the government decided to try to do something about the toxic water...but some people, like Mari Copeny, known as Little Miss Flint, had been helping all along.
Mari and her family, like many people in Flint, had begun using bottled water...
...to protect themselves when their government wouldn't.
Mari started giving cases of bottled water to her neighbors so that they could be safe.
Everyone started listening to Little Miss Flint, a small person with a big heart for her city.

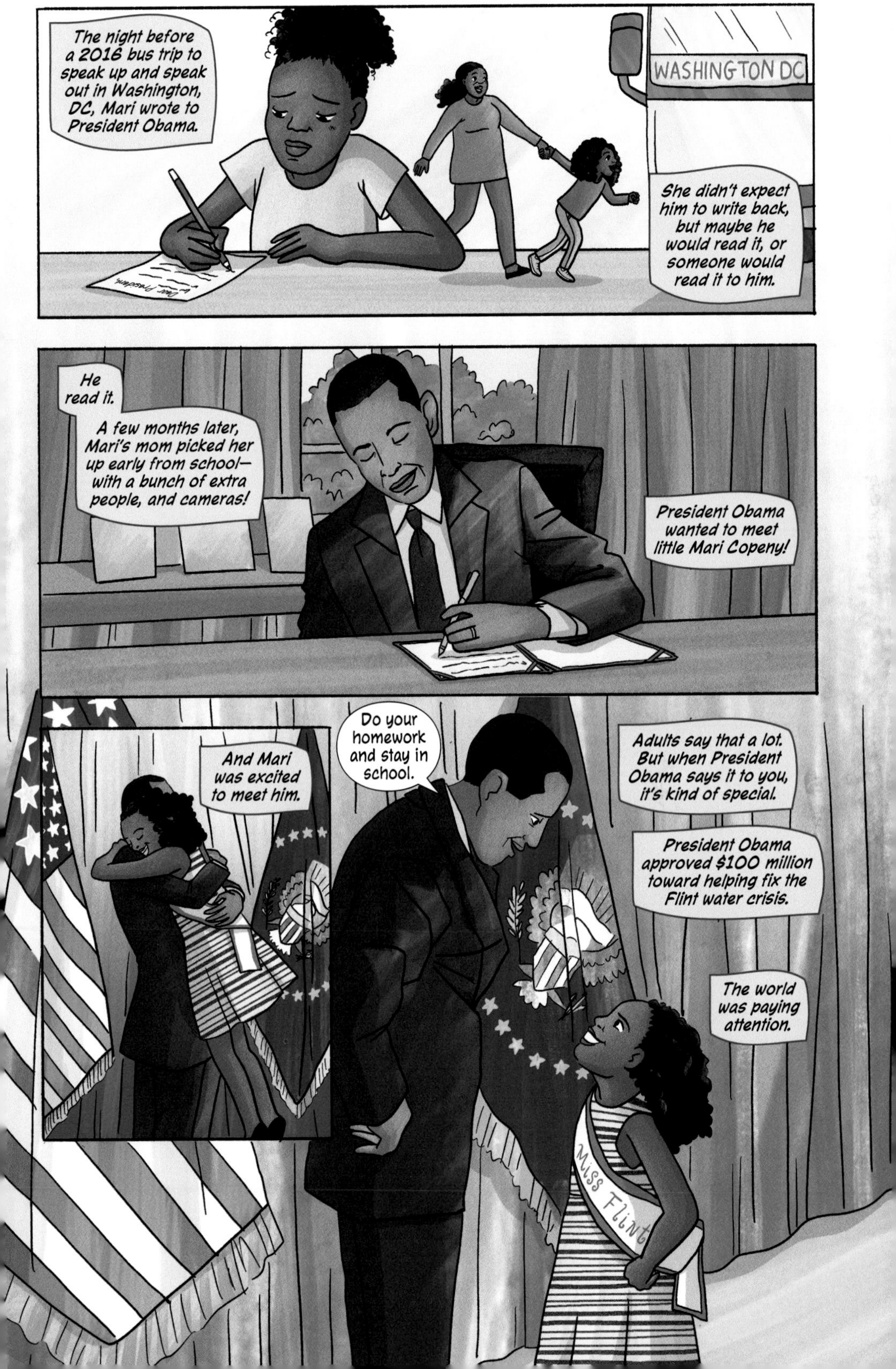
The night before a 2016 bus trip to speak up and speak out in Washington, DC, Mari wrote to President Obama.
WASHINGTON DC
She didn't expect him to write back, but maybe he would read it, or someone would read it to him.
He read it.
A few months later, Mari's mom picked her up early from school—with a bunch of extra people, and cameras!
President Obama wanted to meet little Mari Copeny!
And Mari was excited to meet him.
Do your homework and stay in school.
Adults say that a lot. But when President Obama says it to you, it's kind of special.
President Obama approved $100 million toward helping fix the Flint water crisis.
The world was paying attention.
Miss Flint

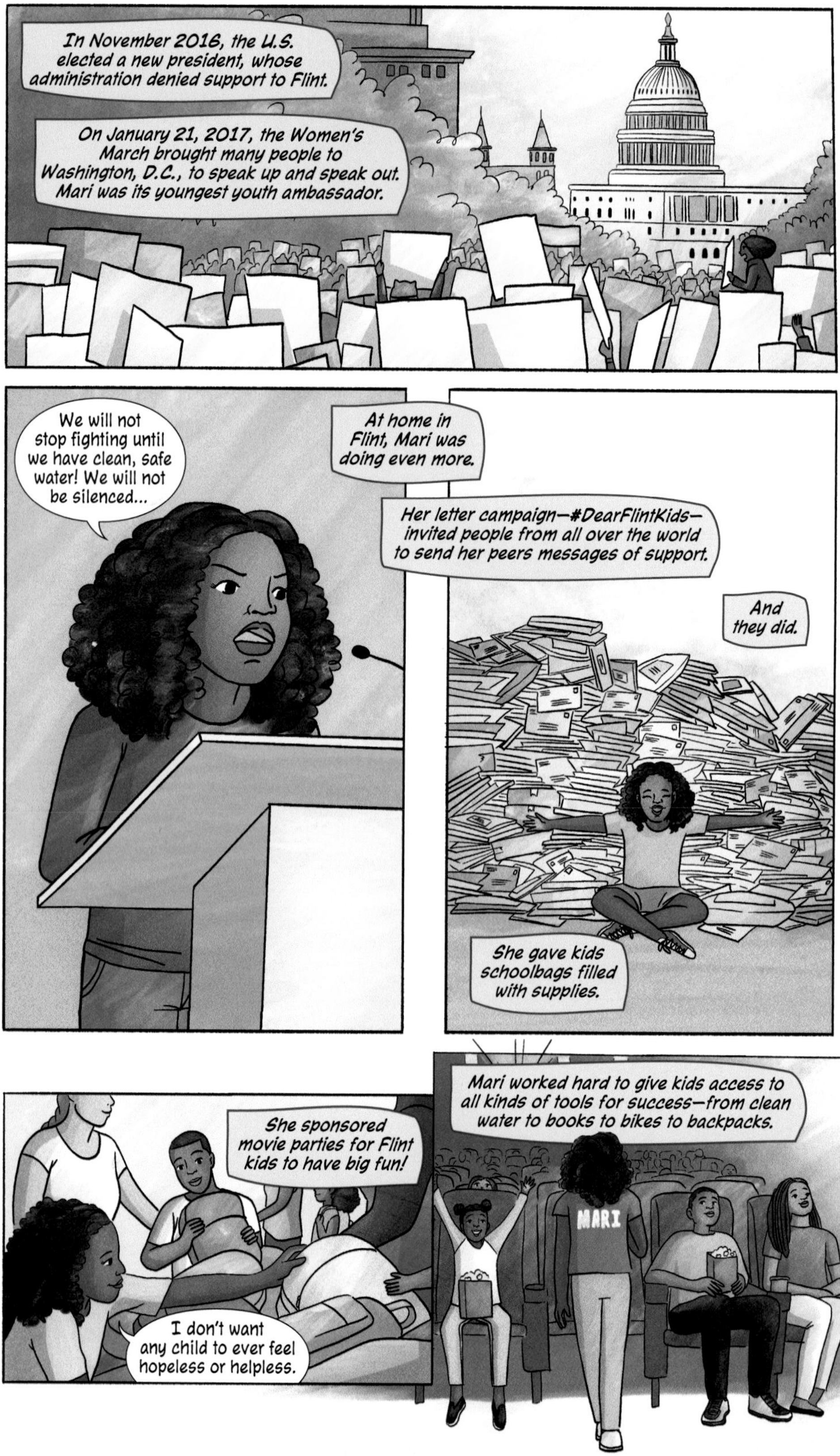

In November 2016, the U.S. elected a new president, whose administration denied support to Flint.
On January 21, 2017, the Women's March brought many people to Washington, D.C., to speak up and speak out. Mari was its youngest youth ambassador.
We will not stop fighting until we have clean, safe water! We will not be silenced...
At home in Flint, Mari was doing even more.
Her letter campaign—#DearFlintKids—invited people from all over the world to send her peers messages of support.
And they did.
She gave kids schoolbags filled with supplies.
She sponsored movie parties for Flint kids to have big fun!
I don't want any child to ever feel hopeless or helpless.
Mari worked hard to give kids access to all kinds of tools for success—from clean water to books to bikes to backpacks.
MARI

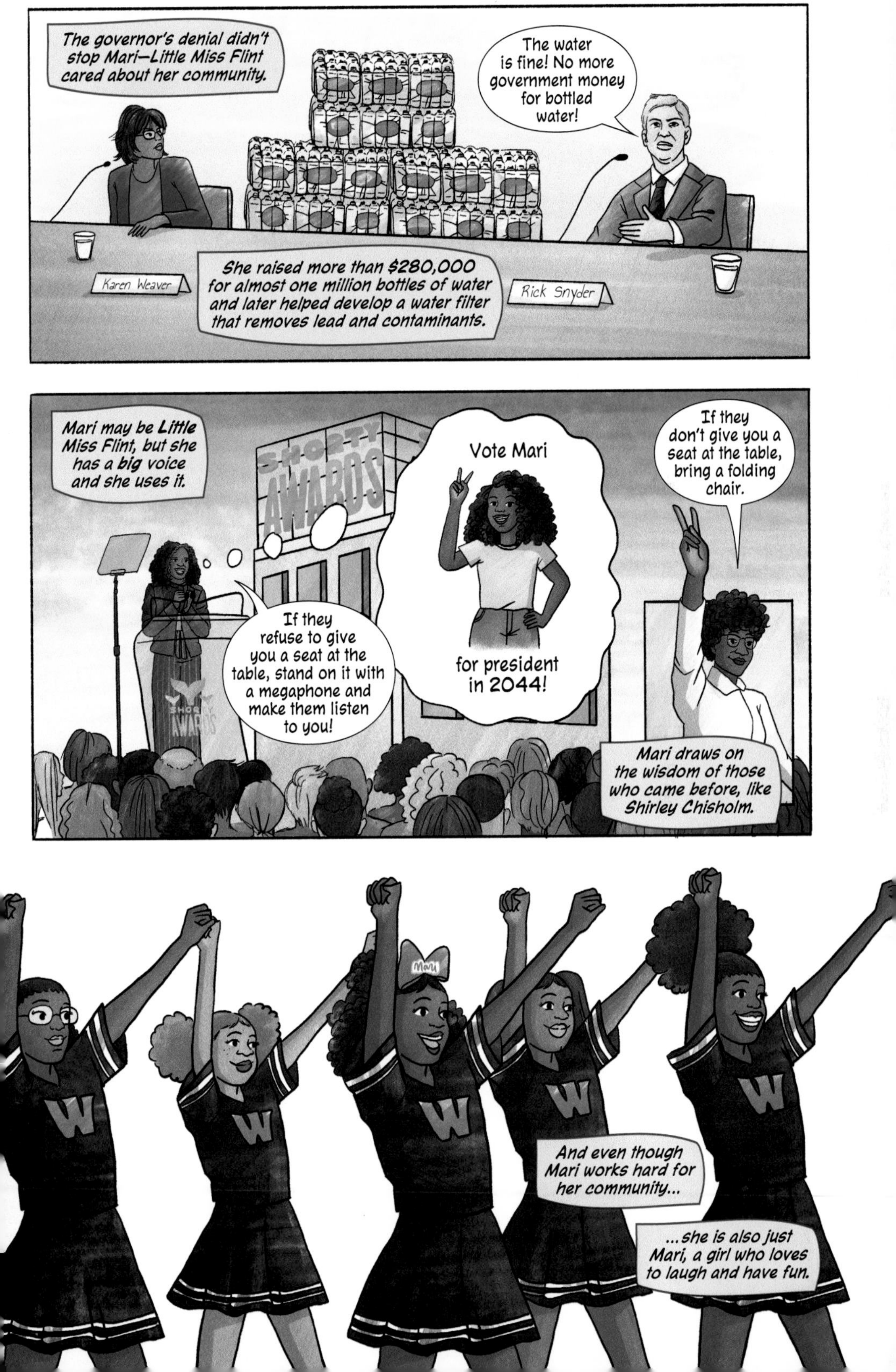
The governor's denial didn't stop Mari—Little Miss Flint cared about her community.
The water is fine! No more government money for bottled water!
Karen Weaver
Rick Snyder
She raised more than $280,000 for almost one million bottles of water and later helped develop a water filter that removes lead and contaminants.
Mari may be Little Miss Flint, but she has a big voice and she uses it.
SHORTY AWARDS
If they refuse to give you a seat at the table, stand on it with a megaphone and make them listen to you!
Vote Mari for president in 2044!
If they don't give you a seat at the table, bring a folding chair.
Mari draws on the wisdom of those who came before, like Shirley Chisholm.
Mari
And even though Mari works hard for her community...
...she is also just Mari, a girl who loves to laugh and have fun.

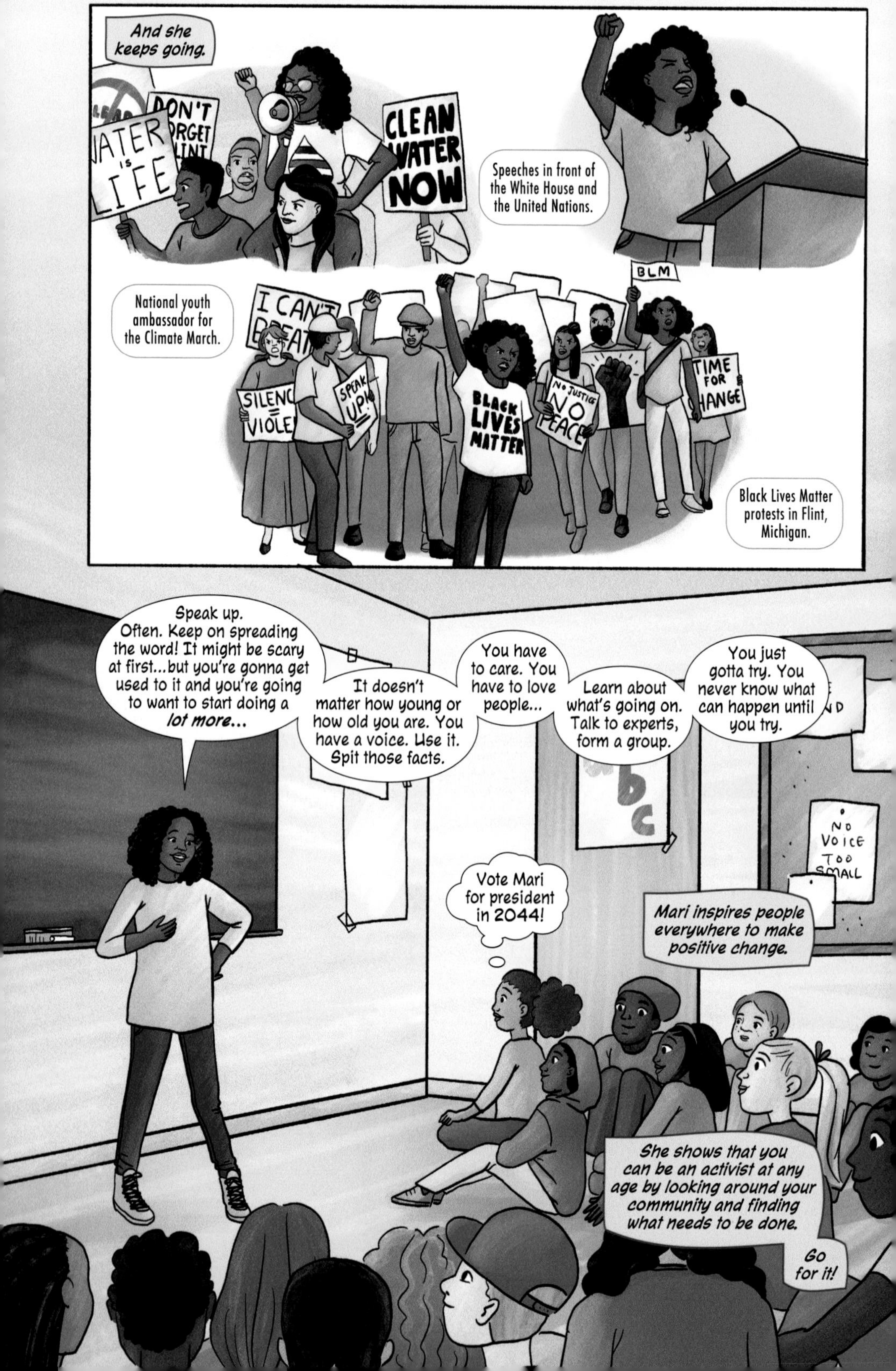
And she keeps going.
CLEAN WATER NOW
Speeches in front of the White House and the United Nations.
National youth ambassador for the Climate March.
BLM
SPEAK UP!
BLACK LIVES MATTER
NO JUSTICE NO PEACE
Black Lives Matter protests in Flint, Michigan.
Speak up. Often. Keep on spreading the word! It might be scary at first...but you're gonna get used to it and you're going to want to start doing a *lot more...*
It doesn't matter how young or how old you are. You have a voice. Use it. Spit those facts.
You have to care. You have to love people...
Learn about what's going on. Talk to experts, form a group.
You just gotta try. You never know what can happen until you try.
NO VOICE TOO SMALL
Vote Mari for president in 2044!
Mari inspires people everywhere to make positive change.
She shows that you can be an activist at any age by looking around your community and finding what needs to be done.
Go for it!

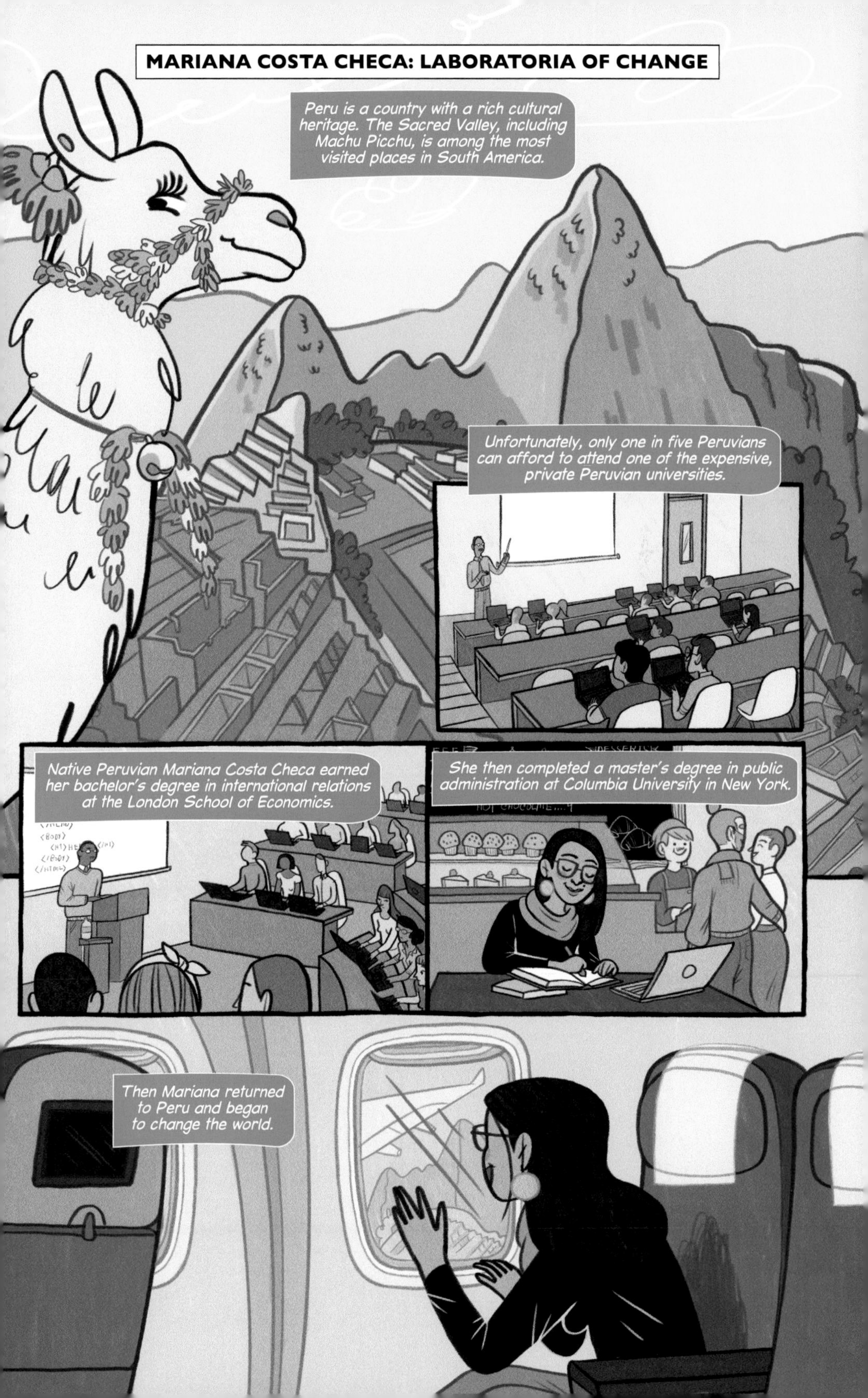
MARIANA COSTA CHECA: LABORATORIA OF CHANGE
Peru is a country with a rich cultural heritage. The Sacred Valley, including Machu Picchu, is among the most visited places in South America.
Unfortunately, only one in five Peruvians can afford to attend one of the expensive, private Peruvian universities.
Native Peruvian Mariana Costa Checa earned her bachelor's degree in international relations at the London School of Economics.
She then completed a master's degree in public administration at Columbia University in New York.
Then Mariana returned to Peru and began to change the world.

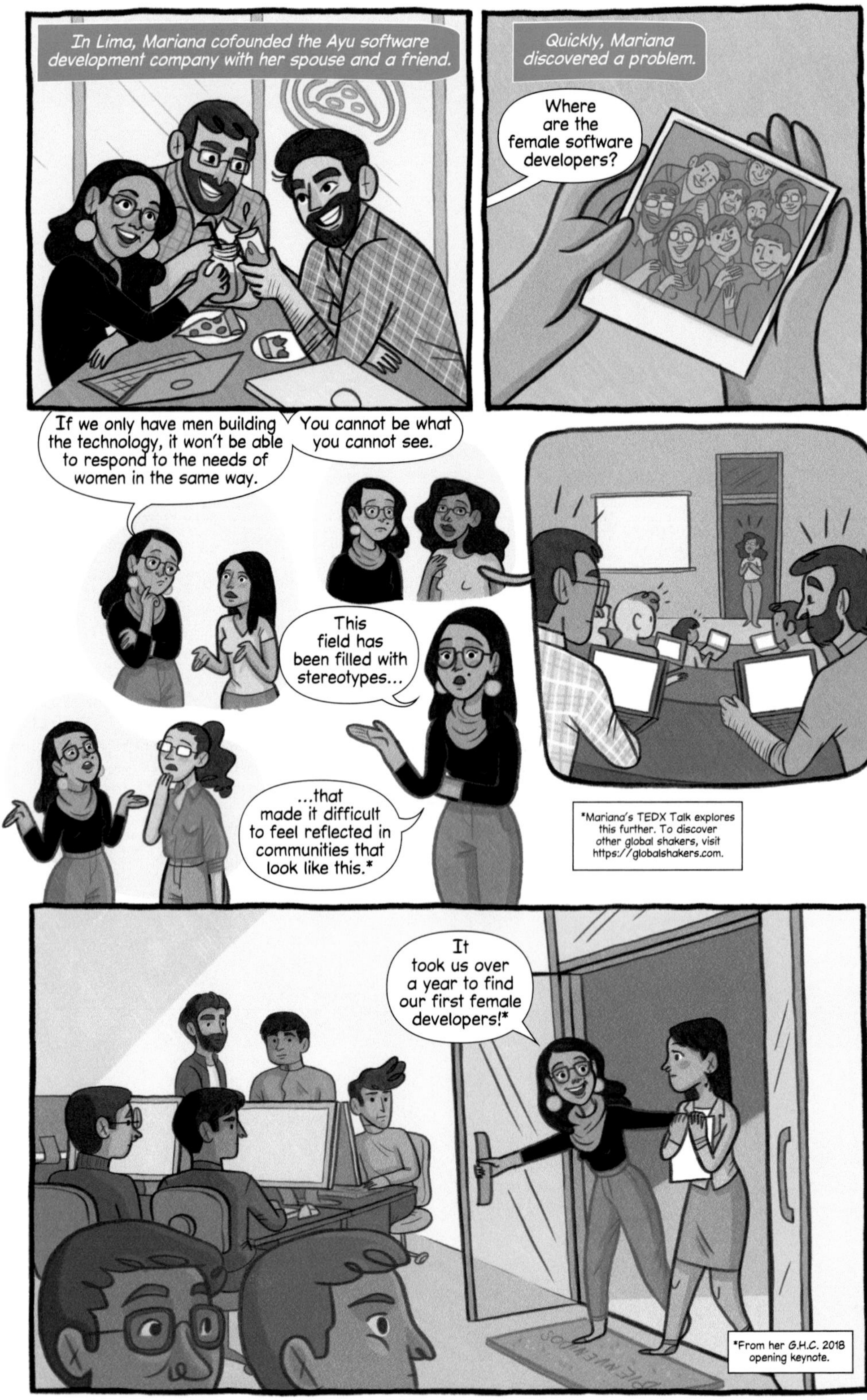
In Lima, Mariana cofounded the Ayu software development company with her spouse and a friend.
Quickly, Mariana discovered a problem.
Where are the female software developers?
If we only have men building the technology, it won't be able to respond to the needs of women in the same way.
You cannot be what you cannot see.
This field has been filled with stereotypes...
...that made it difficult to feel reflected in communities that look like this.*
*Mariana's TEDX Talk explores this further. To discover other global shakers, visit https://globalshakers.com.
It took us over a year to find our first female developers!*
*From her G.H.C. 2018 opening keynote.

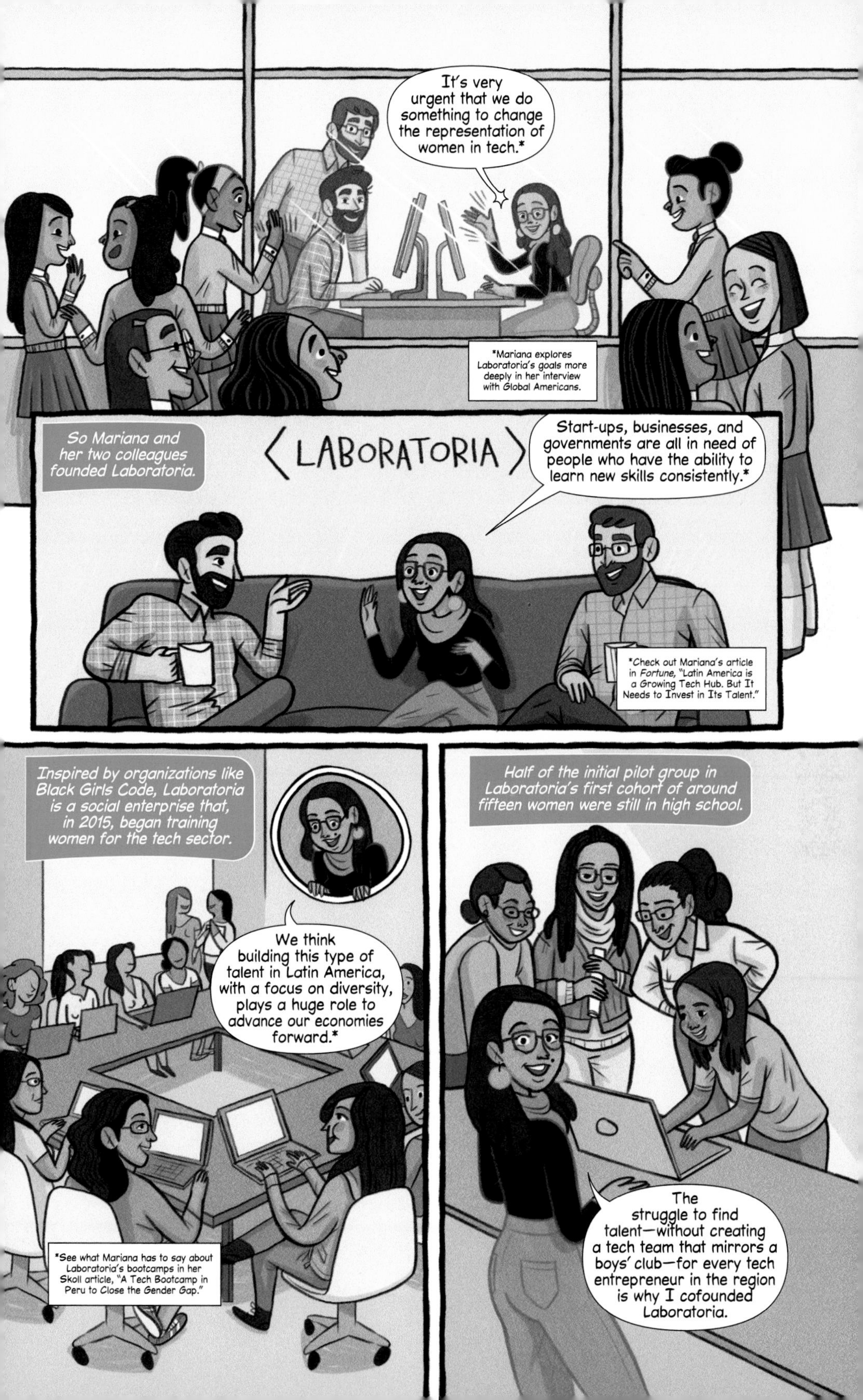
It's very urgent that we do something to change the representation of women in tech.*
*Mariana explores Laboratoria's goals more deeply in her interview with Global Americans.
So Mariana and her two colleagues founded Laboratoria.
LABORATORIA
Start-ups, businesses, and governments are all in need of people who have the ability to learn new skills consistently.*
*Check out Mariana's article in Fortune, "Latin America is a Growing Tech Hub. But It Needs to Invest in Its Talent."
Inspired by organizations like Black Girls Code, Laboratoria is a social enterprise that, in 2015, began training women for the tech sector.
We think building this type of talent in Latin America, with a focus on diversity, plays a huge role to advance our economies forward.*
*See what Mariana has to say about Laboratoria's bootcamps in her Skoll article, "A Tech Bootcamp in Peru to Close the Gender Gap."
Half of the initial pilot group in Laboratoria's first cohort of around fifteen women were still in high school.
The struggle to find talent—without creating a tech team that mirrors a boys' club—for every tech entrepreneur in the region is why I cofounded Laboratoria.

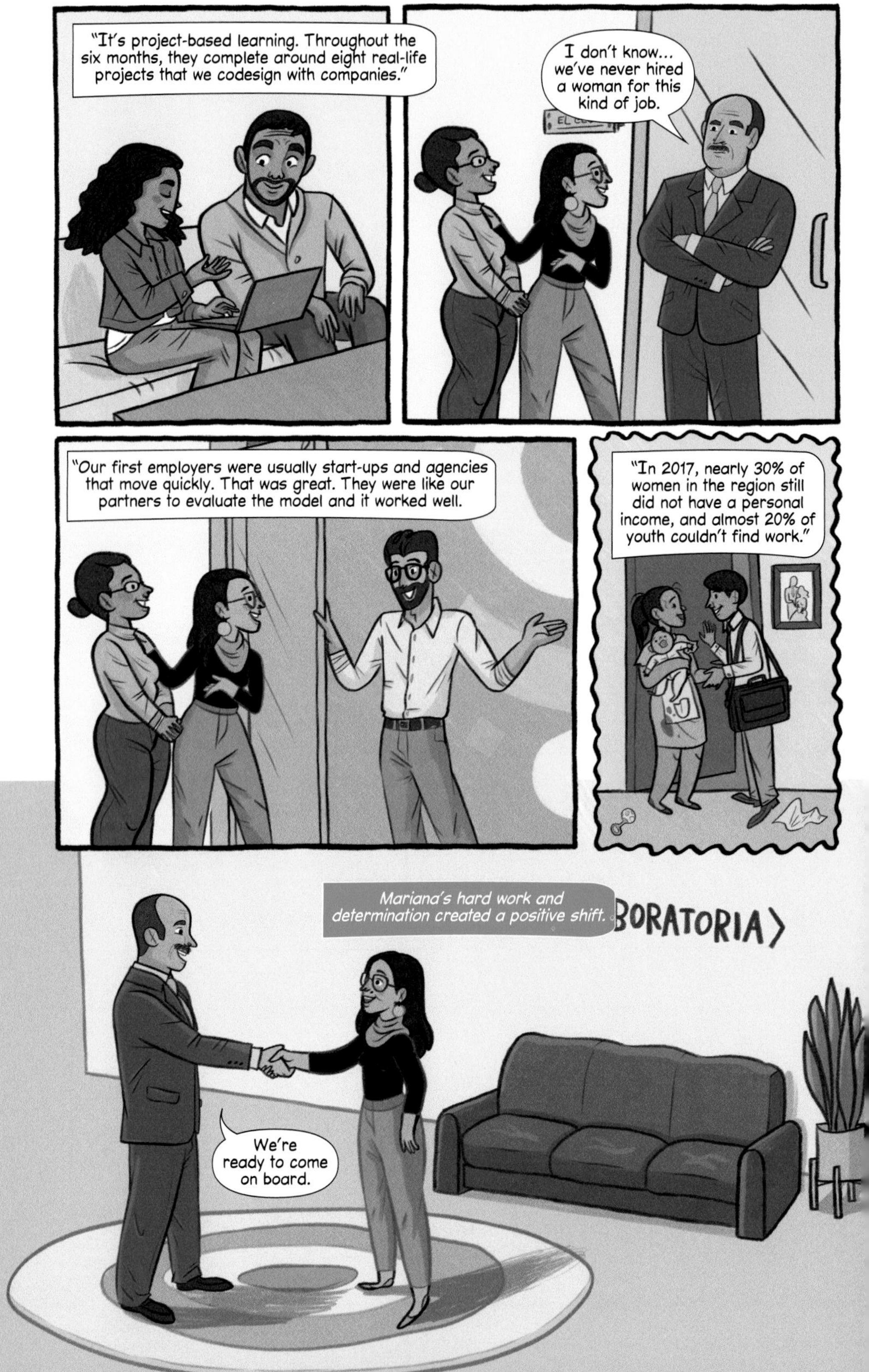
"It's project-based learning. Throughout the six months, they complete around eight real-life projects that we codesign with companies."
I don't know... we've never hired a woman for this kind of job.
"Our first employers were usually start-ups and agencies that move quickly. That was great. They were like our partners to evaluate the model and it worked well.
"In 2017, nearly 30% of women in the region still did not have a personal income, and almost 20% of youth couldn't find work."
Mariana's hard work and determination created a positive shift.
BORATORIA>
We're ready to come on board.

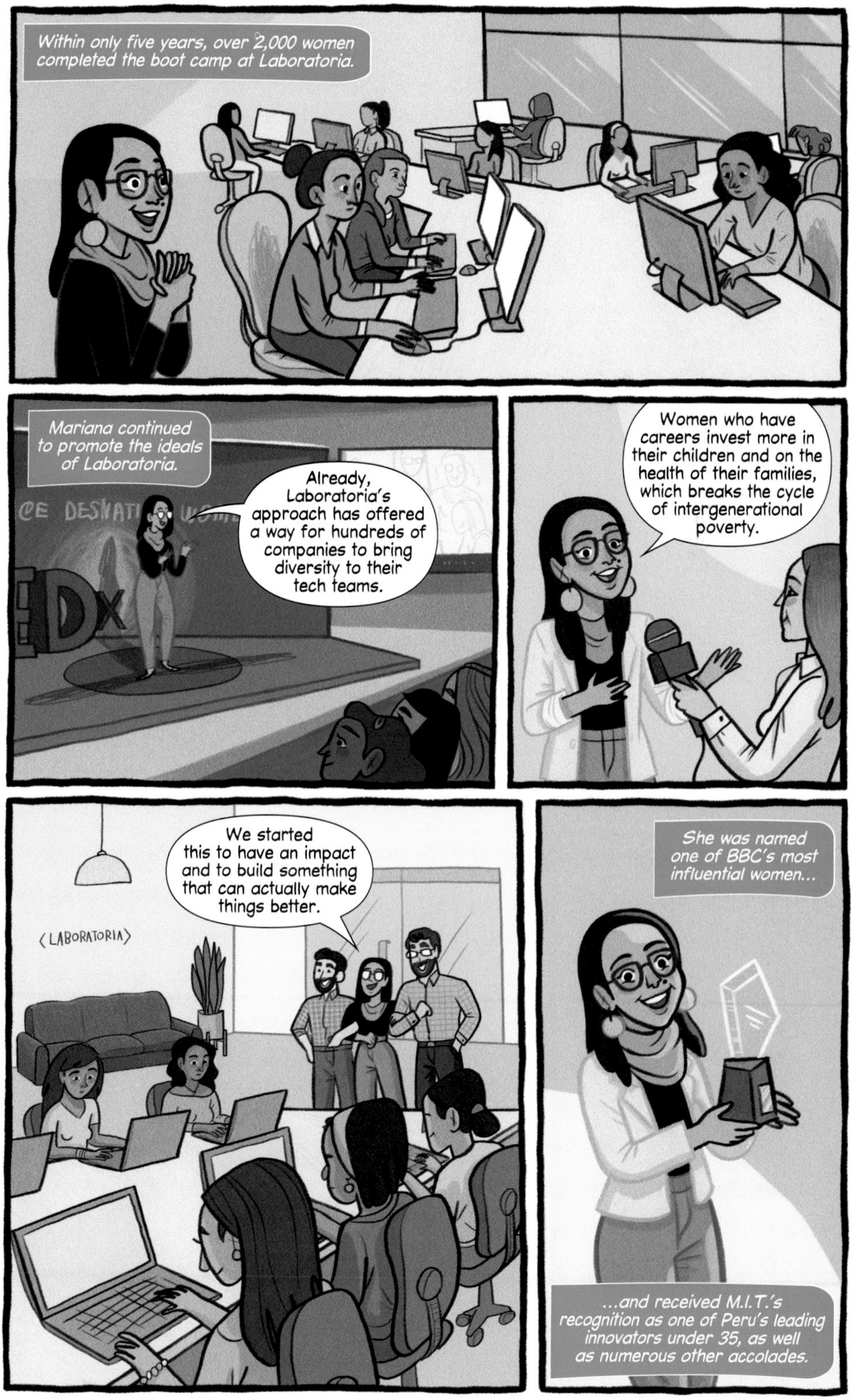
Within only five years, over 2,000 women completed the boot camp at Laboratoria.
Mariana continued to promote the ideals of Laboratoria.
Already, Laboratoria's approach has offered a way for hundreds of companies to bring diversity to their tech teams.
Women who have careers invest more in their children and on the health of their families, which breaks the cycle of intergenerational poverty.
We started this to have an impact and to build something that can actually make things better.
<LABORATORIA>
She was named one of BBC's most influential women...
...and received M.I.T.'s recognition as one of Peru's leading innovators under 35, as well as numerous other accolades.

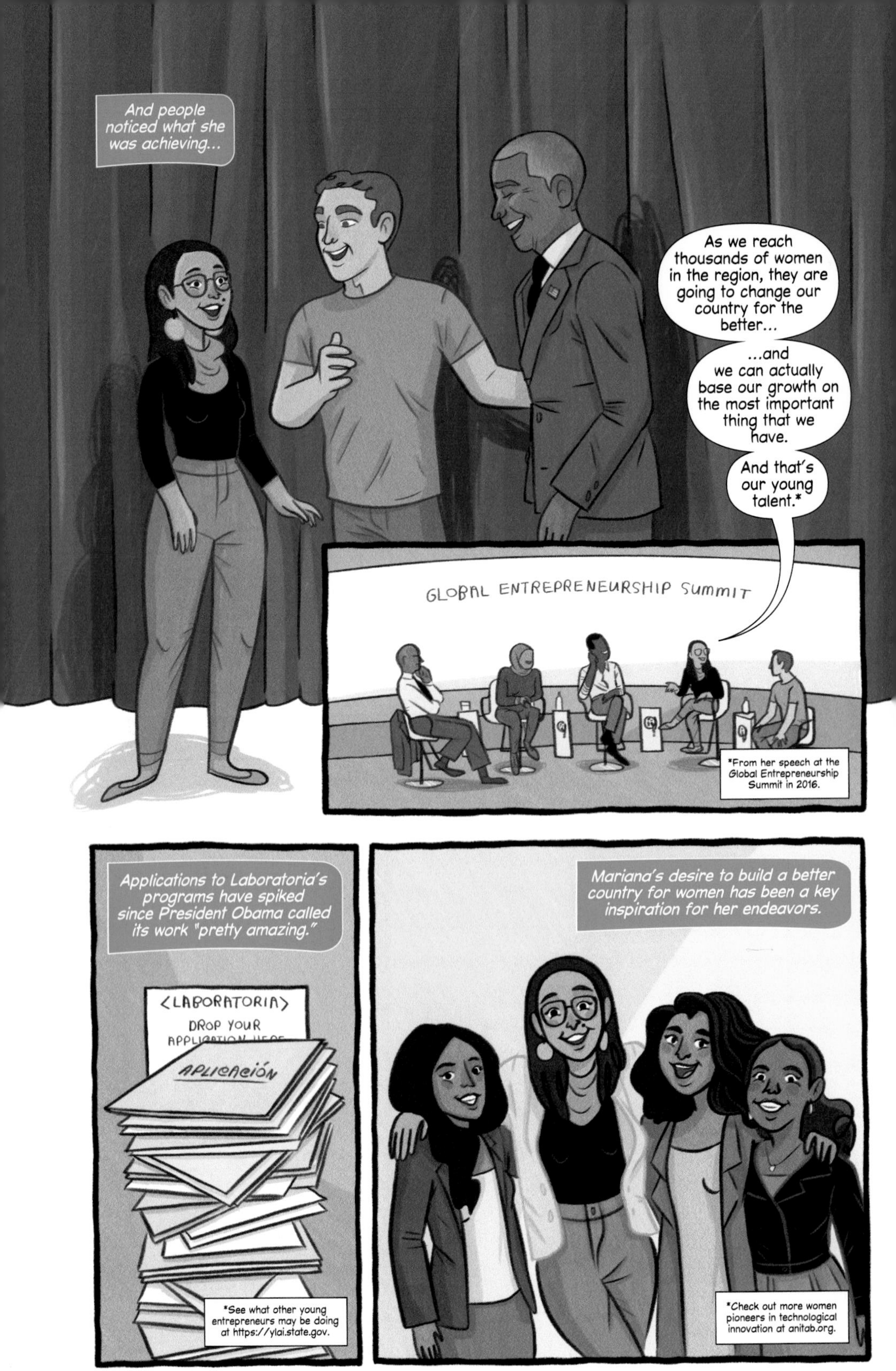

And people noticed what she was achieving...
As we reach thousands of women in the region, they are going to change our country for the better...
...and we can actually base our growth on the most important thing that we have.
And that's our young talent.*
GLOBAL ENTREPRENEURSHIP SUMMIT
*From her speech at the Global Entrepreneurship Summit in 2016.
Applications to Laboratoria's programs have spiked since President Obama called its work "pretty amazing."
<LABORATORIA>
DROP YOUR
APLICACIÓN
*See what other young entrepreneurs may be doing at https://ylai.state.gov.
Mariana's desire to build a better country for women has been a key inspiration for her endeavors.
*Check out more women pioneers in technological innovation at anitab.org.

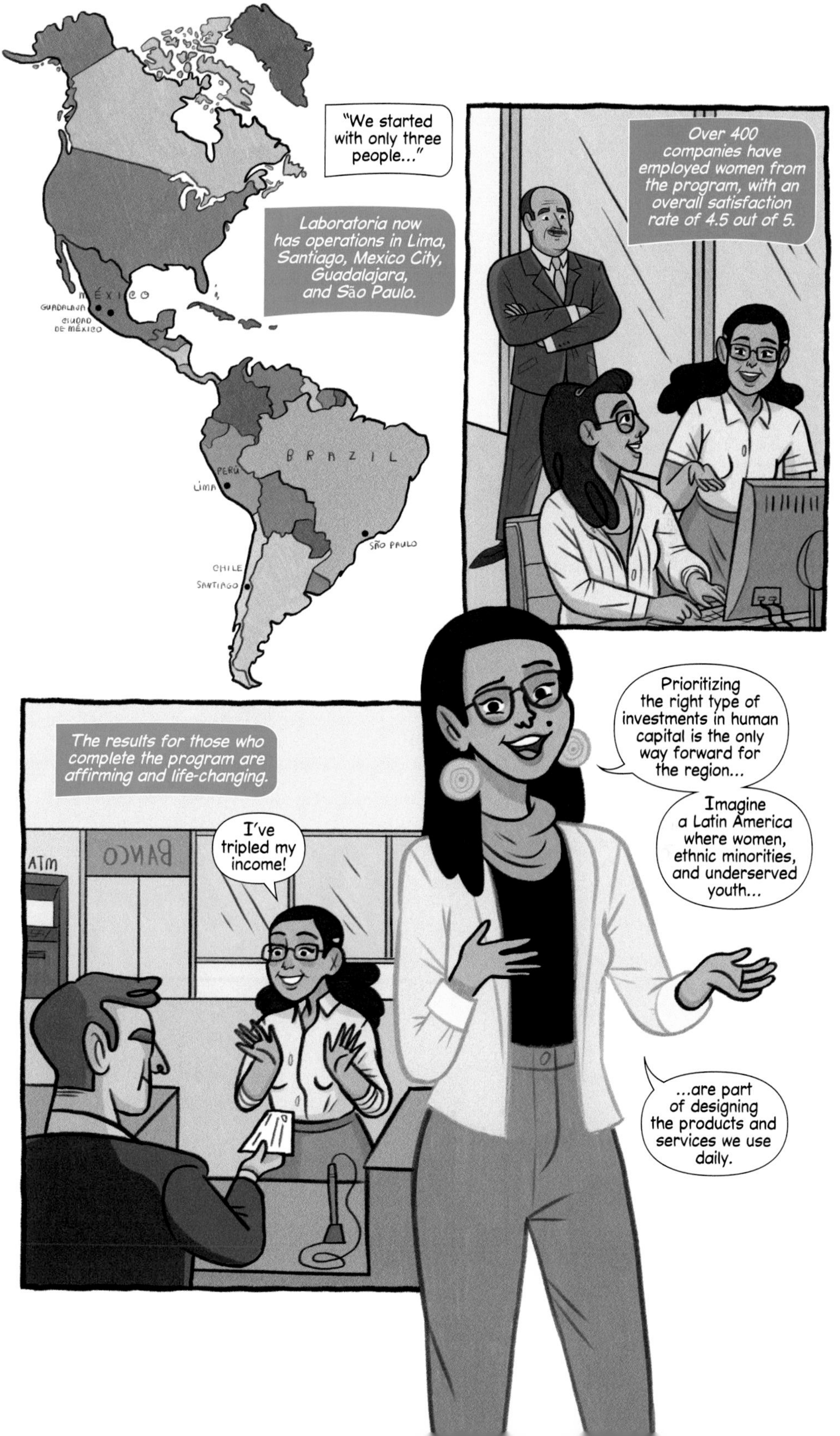

"We started with only three people..."
Laboratoria now has operations in Lima, Santiago, Mexico City, Guadalajara, and São Paulo.
MÉXICO
GUADALAJA
CIUDAD DE MÉXICO
BRAZIL
PERÚ
LIMA
CHILE
SANTIAGO
SÃO PAULO
Over 400 companies have employed women from the program, with an overall satisfaction rate of 4.5 out of 5.
The results for those who complete the program are affirming and life-changing.
ATM
I've tripled my income!
Prioritizing the right type of investments in human capital is the only way forward for the region...
Imagine a Latin America where women, ethnic minorities, and underserved youth...
...are part of designing the products and services we use daily.

part three
JUSTICE

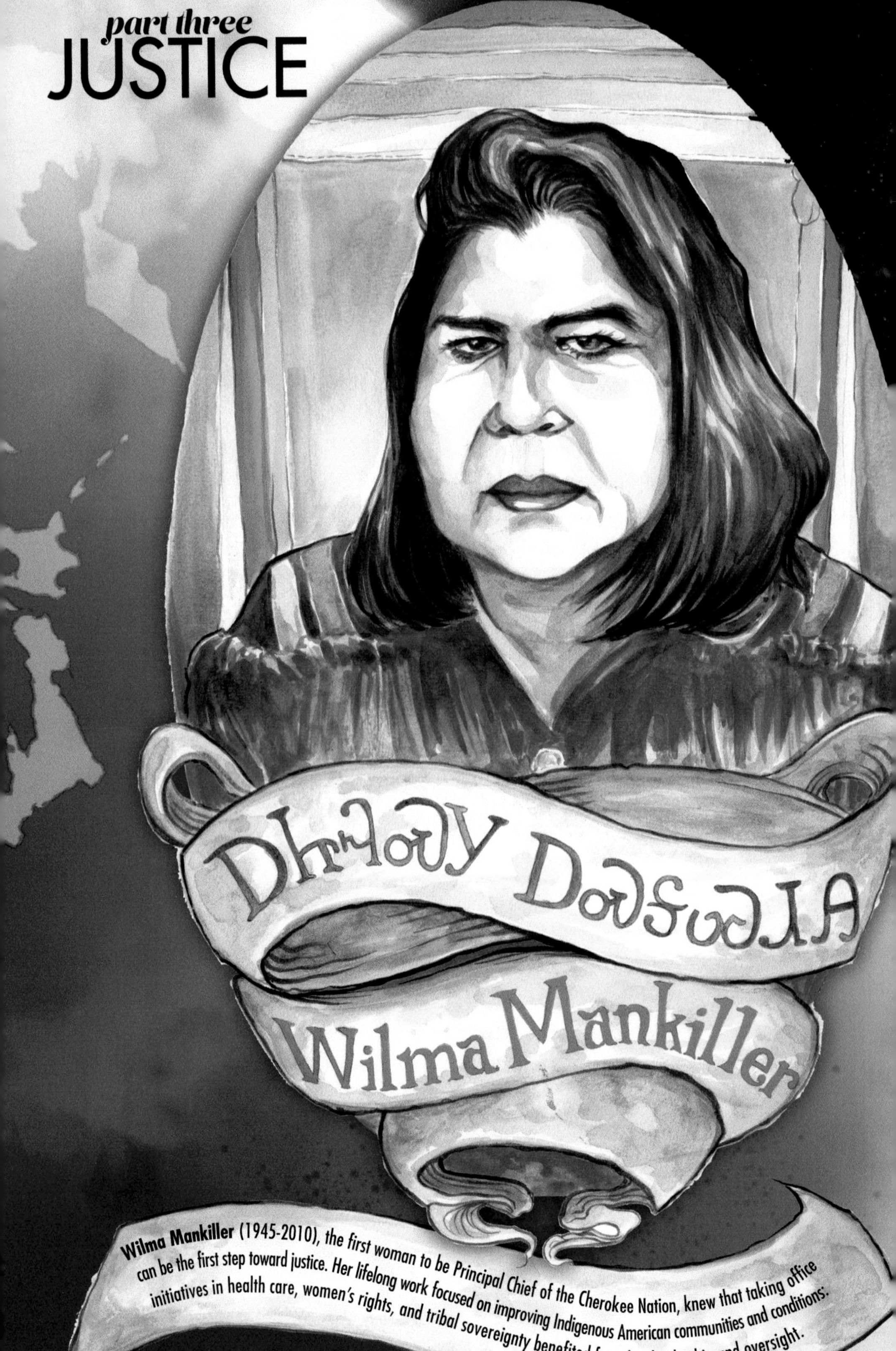
Wilma Mankiller

Wilma Mankiller (1945-2010), the first woman to be Principal Chief of the Cherokee Nation, knew that taking office can be the first step toward justice. Her lifelong work focused on improving Indigenous American communities and conditions: initiatives in health care, women's rights, and tribal sovereignty benefited from her leadership and oversight.

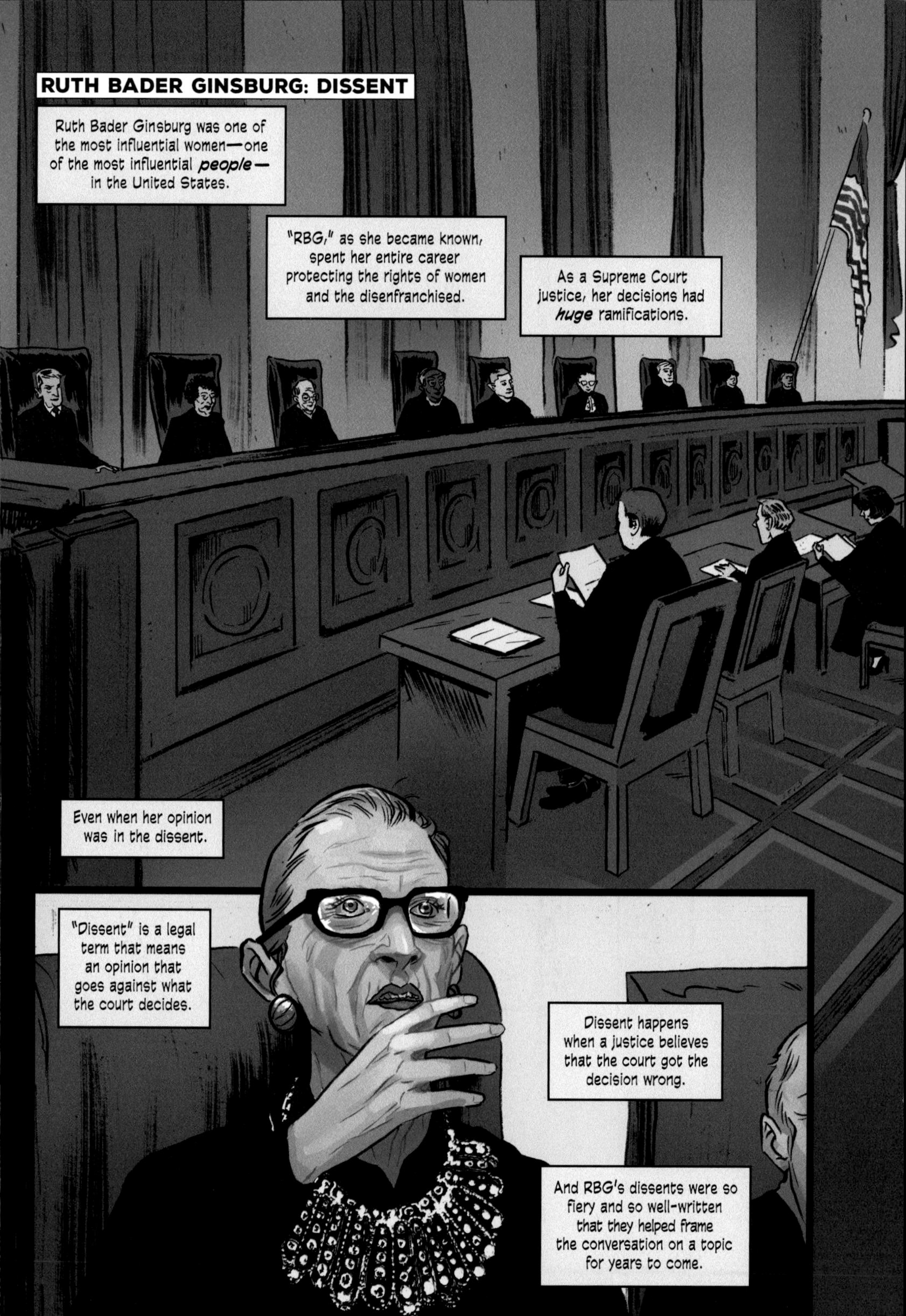
RUTH BADER GINSBURG: DISSENT
Ruth Bader Ginsburg was one of the most influential women—one of the most influential *people*—in the United States.
"RBG," as she became known, spent her entire career protecting the rights of women and the disenfranchised.
As a Supreme Court justice, her decisions had *huge* ramifications.
Even when her opinion was in the dissent.
"Dissent" is a legal term that means an opinion that goes against what the court decides.
Dissent happens when a justice believes that the court got the decision wrong.
And RBG's dissents were so fiery and so well-written that they helped frame the conversation on a topic for years to come.

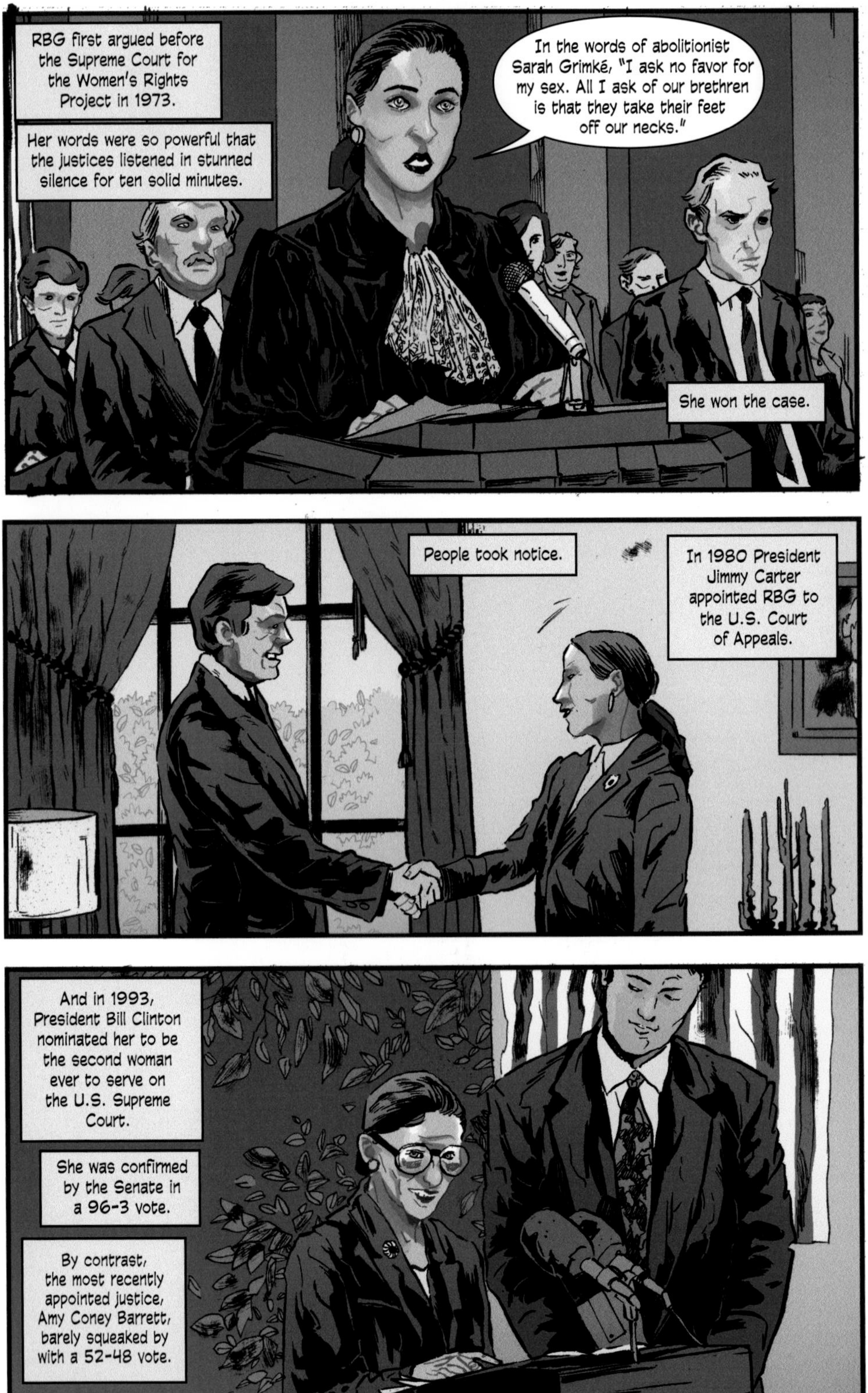
RBG first argued before the Supreme Court for the Women's Rights Project in 1973.
Her words were so powerful that the justices listened in stunned silence for ten solid minutes.
In the words of abolitionist Sarah Grimké, "I ask no favor for my sex. All I ask of our brethren is that they take their feet off our necks."
She won the case.
People took notice.
In 1980 President Jimmy Carter appointed RBG to the U.S. Court of Appeals.
And in 1993, President Bill Clinton nominated her to be the second woman ever to serve on the U.S. Supreme Court.
She was confirmed by the Senate in a 96-3 vote.
By contrast, the most recently appointed justice, Amy Coney Barrett, barely squeaked by with a 52-48 vote.

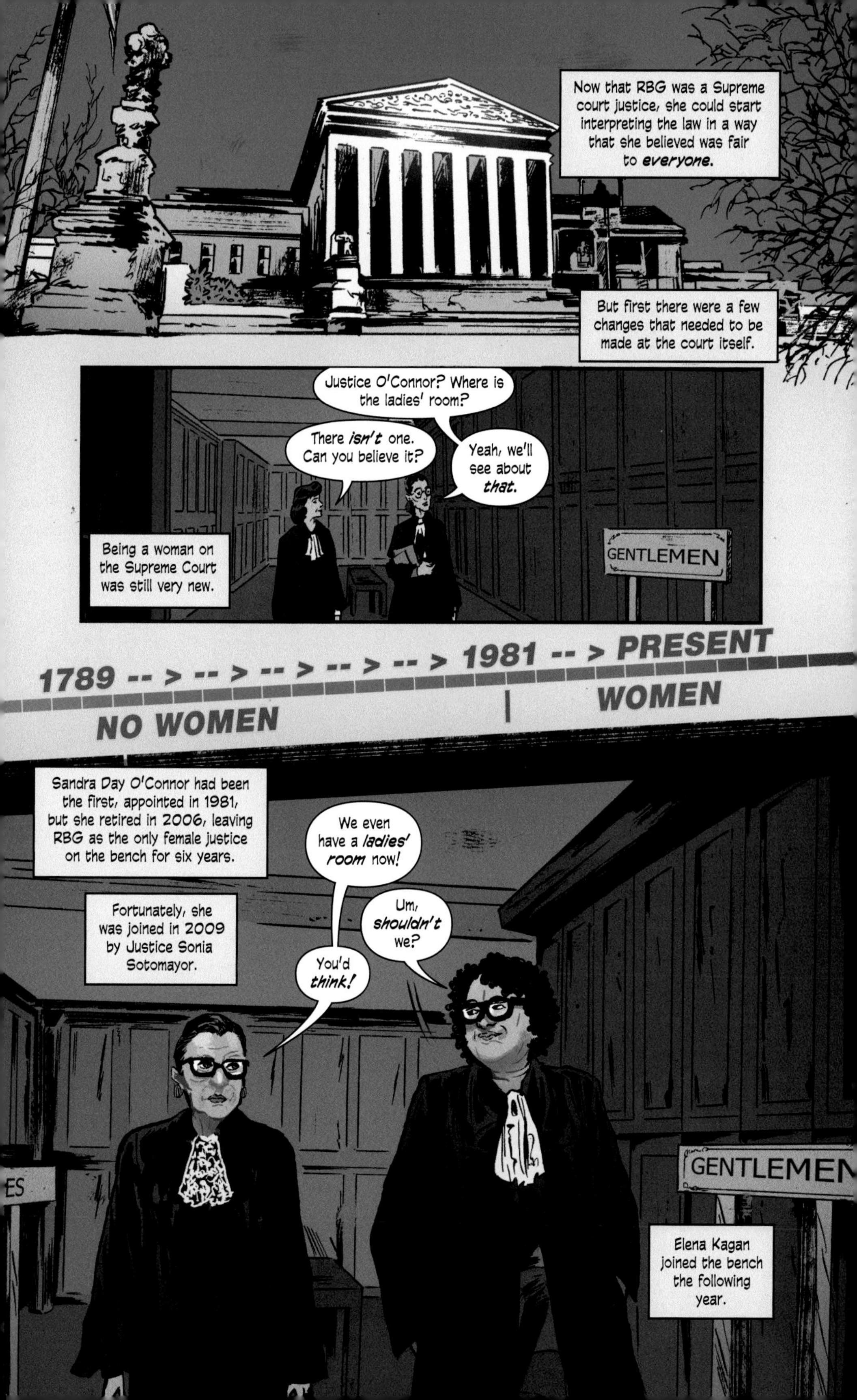
Now that RBG was a Supreme court justice, she could start interpreting the law in a way that she believed was fair to *everyone*.
But first there were a few changes that needed to be made at the court itself.
Justice O'Connor? Where is the ladies' room?
There *isn't* one. Can you believe it?
Yeah, we'll see about *that*.
Being a woman on the Supreme Court was still very new.
GENTLEMEN
1789 -- > -- > -- > -- > -- > 1981 -- > PRESENT
NO WOMEN
WOMEN
Sandra Day O'Connor had been the first, appointed in 1981, but she retired in 2006, leaving RBG as the only female justice on the bench for six years.
Fortunately, she was joined in 2009 by Justice Sonia Sotomayor.
We even have a *ladies' room* now!
Um, *shouldn't* we?
You'd *think!*
ES
GENTLEMEN
Elena Kagan joined the bench the following year.

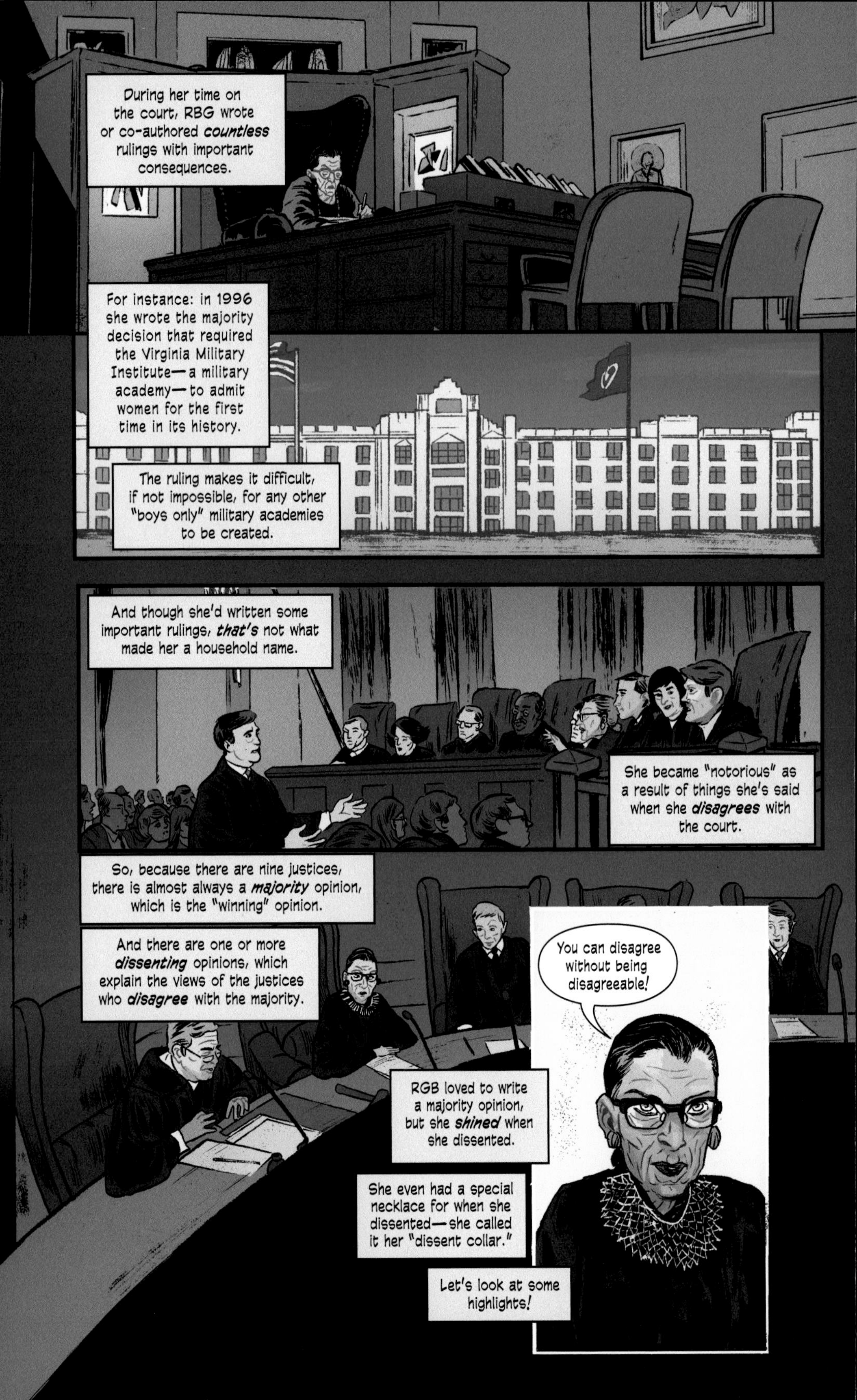
During her time on the court, RBG wrote or co-authored *countless* rulings with important consequences.
For instance: in 1996 she wrote the majority decision that required the Virginia Military Institute—a military academy—to admit women for the first time in its history.
The ruling makes it difficult, if not impossible, for any other "boys only" military academies to be created.
And though she'd written some important rulings, *that's* not what made her a household name.
She became "notorious" as a result of things she's said when she *disagrees* with the court.
So, because there are nine justices, there is almost always a *majority* opinion, which is the "winning" opinion.
And there are one or more *dissenting* opinions, which explain the views of the justices who *disagree* with the majority.
You can disagree without being disagreeable!
RGB loved to write a majority opinion, but she *shined* when she dissented.
She even had a special necklace for when she dissented—she called it her "dissent collar."
Let's look at some highlights!

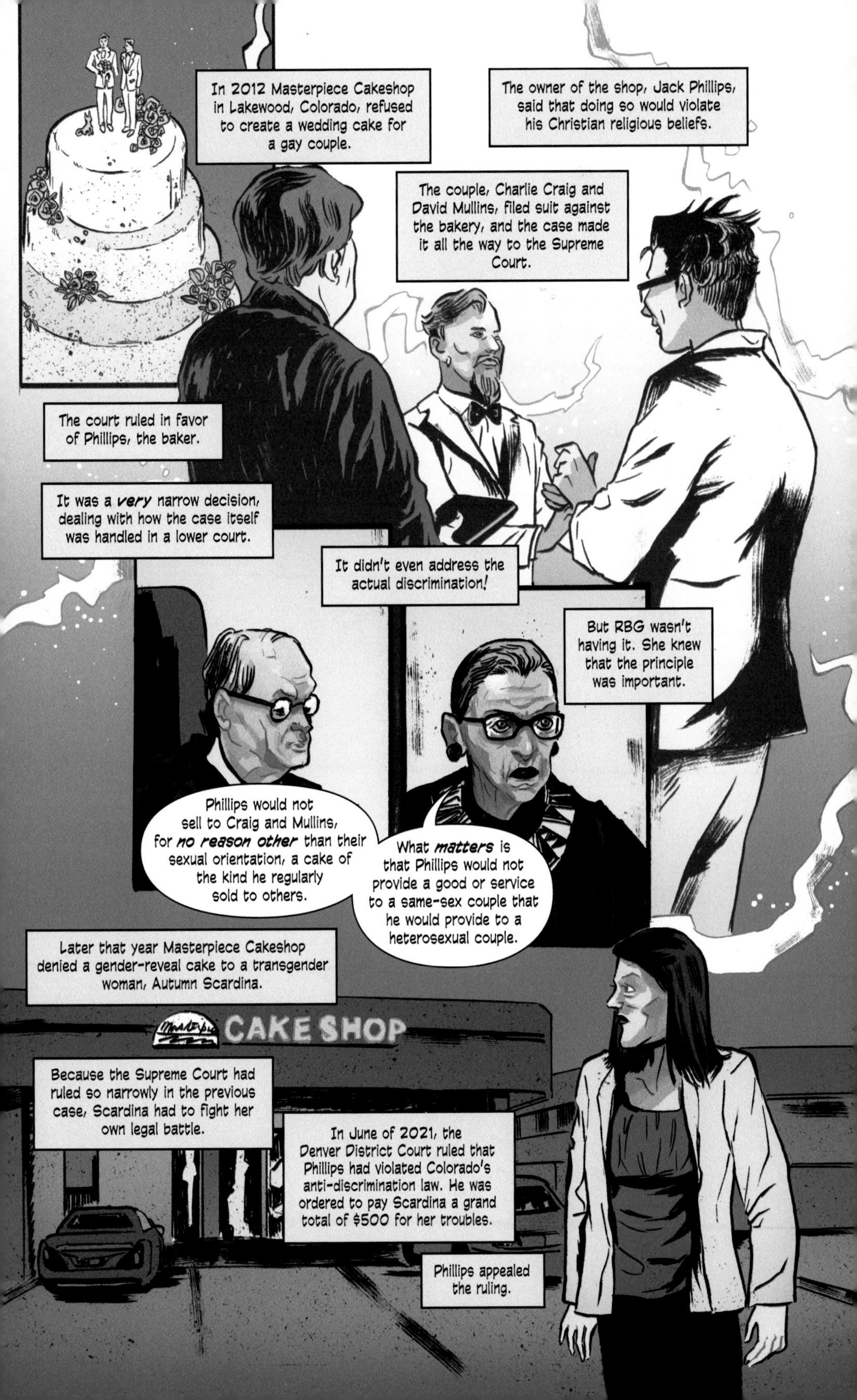
In 2012 Masterpiece Cakeshop in Lakewood, Colorado, refused to create a wedding cake for a gay couple.
The owner of the shop, Jack Phillips, said that doing so would violate his Christian religious beliefs.
The couple, Charlie Craig and David Mullins, filed suit against the bakery, and the case made it all the way to the Supreme Court.
The court ruled in favor of Phillips, the baker.
It was a *very* narrow decision, dealing with how the case itself was handled in a lower court.
It didn't even address the actual discrimination!
But RBG wasn't having it. She knew that the principle was important.
Phillips would not sell to Craig and Mullins, for *no reason other* than their sexual orientation, a cake of the kind he regularly sold to others.
What *matters* is that Phillips would not provide a good or service to a same-sex couple that he would provide to a heterosexual couple.
Later that year Masterpiece Cakeshop denied a gender-reveal cake to a transgender woman, Autumn Scardina.
CAKE SHOP
Because the Supreme Court had ruled so narrowly in the previous case, Scardina had to fight her own legal battle.
In June of 2021, the Denver District Court ruled that Phillips had violated Colorado's anti-discrimination law. He was ordered to pay Scardina a grand total of $500 for her troubles.
Phillips appealed the ruling.

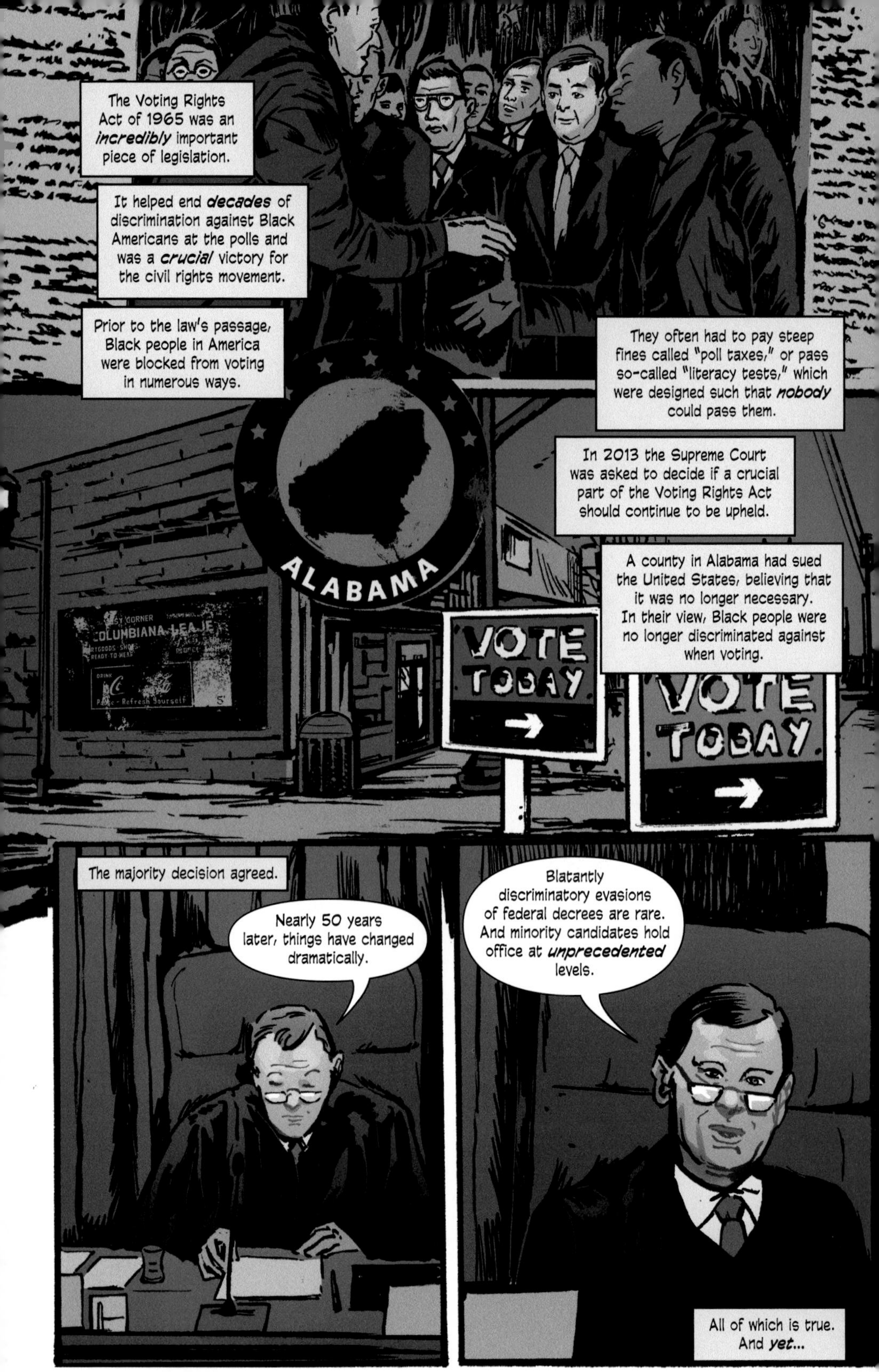

The Voting Rights Act of 1965 was an *incredibly* important piece of legislation.
It helped end *decades* of discrimination against Black Americans at the polls and was a *crucial* victory for the civil rights movement.
Prior to the law's passage, Black people in America were blocked from voting in numerous ways.
They often had to pay steep fines called "poll taxes," or pass so-called "literacy tests," which were designed such that *nobody* could pass them.
ALABAMA
In 2013 the Supreme Court was asked to decide if a crucial part of the Voting Rights Act should continue to be upheld.
A county in Alabama had sued the United States, believing that it was no longer necessary. In their view, Black people were no longer discriminated against when voting.
VOTE TODAY
VOTE TODAY
The majority decision agreed.
Nearly 50 years later, things have changed dramatically.
Blatantly discriminatory evasions of federal decrees are rare. And minority candidates hold office at *unprecedented* levels.
All of which is true. And *yet*...

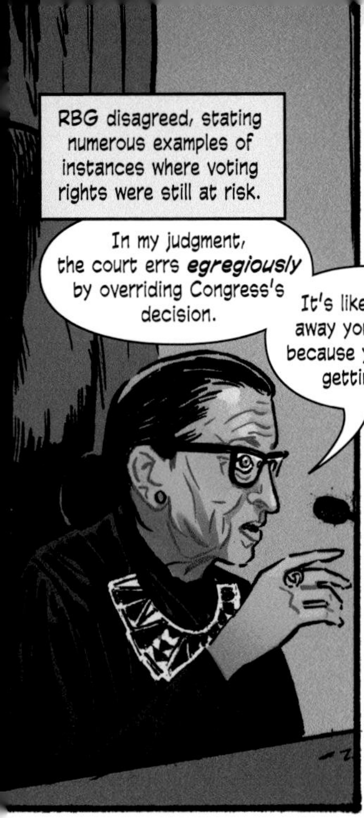
RBG disagreed, stating numerous examples of instances where voting rights were still at risk.
In my judgment, the court errs *egregiously* by overriding Congress's decision.
It's like throwing away your umbrella because you are not getting wet.

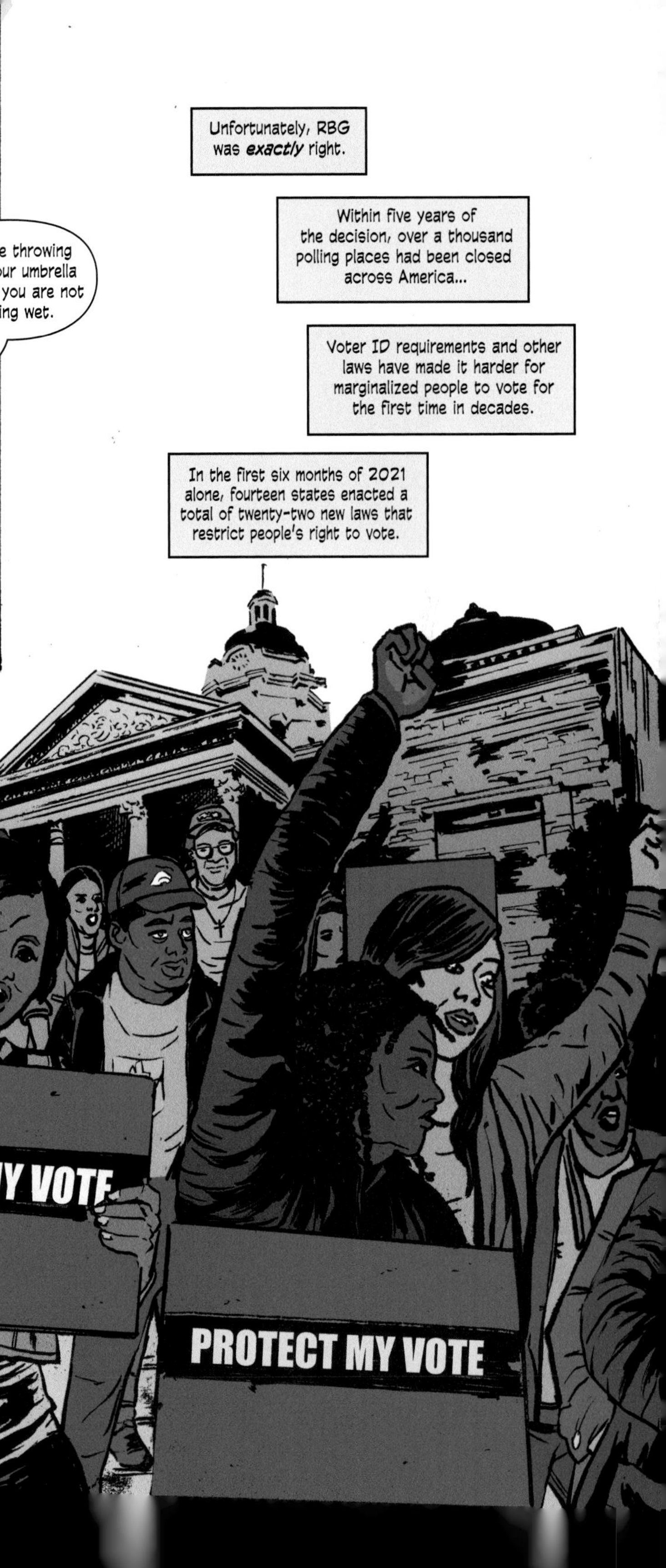
Unfortunately, RBG was *exactly* right.
Within five years of the decision, over a thousand polling places had been closed across America...
Voter ID requirements and other laws have made it harder for marginalized people to vote for the first time in decades.
In the first six months of 2021 alone, fourteen states enacted a total of twenty-two new laws that restrict people's right to vote.
PROTECT MY VOTE
PROTECT MY VOTE

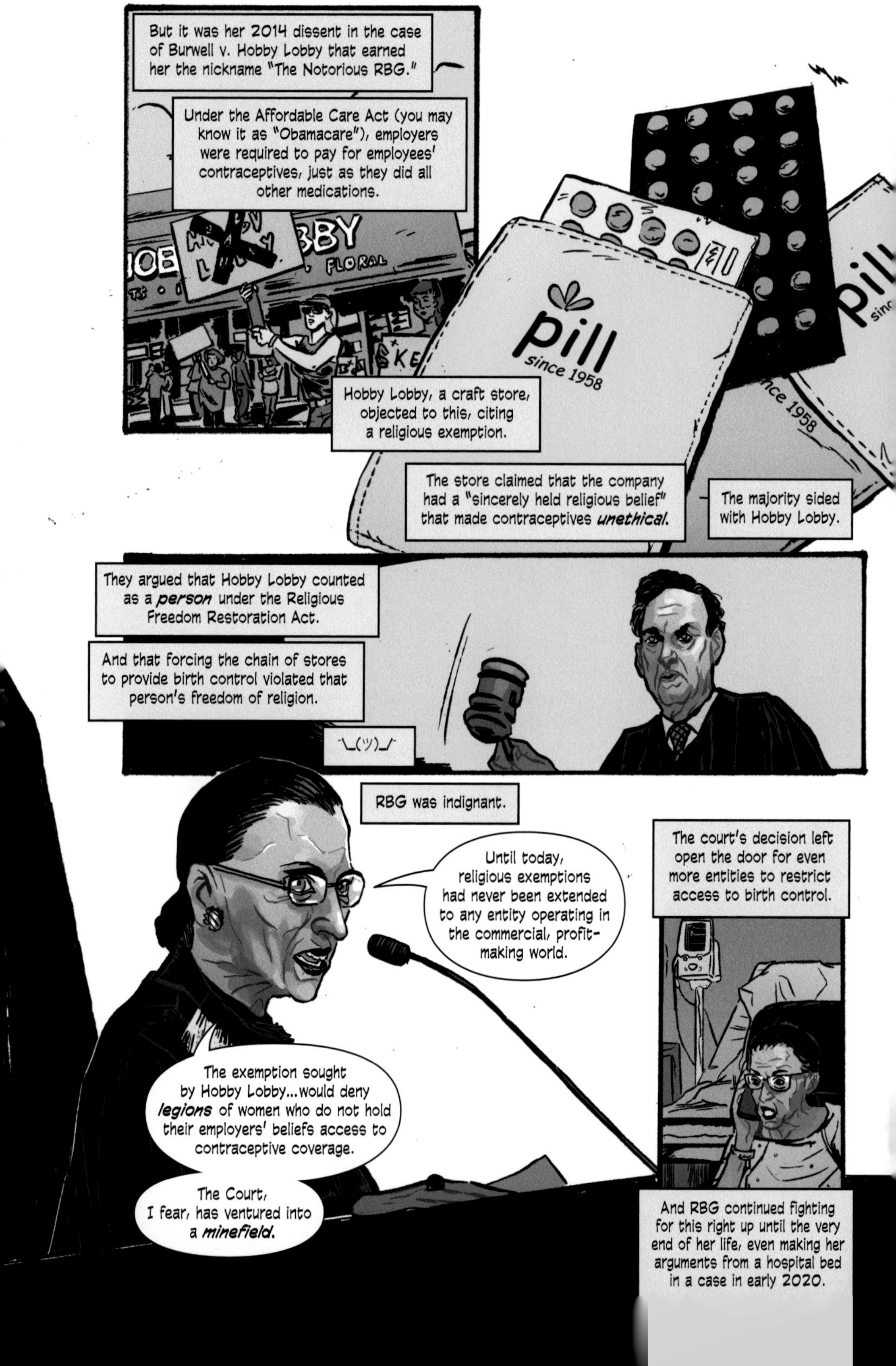
But it was her 2014 dissent in the case of Burwell v. Hobby Lobby that earned her the nickname "The Notorious RBG."
Under the Affordable Care Act (you may know it as "Obamacare"), employers were required to pay for employees' contraceptives, just as they did all other medications.
FLORAL
Hobby Lobby, a craft store, objected to this, citing a religious exemption.
pill since 1958
The store claimed that the company had a "sincerely held religious belief" that made contraceptives *unethical*.
The majority sided with Hobby Lobby.
They argued that Hobby Lobby counted as a *person* under the Religious Freedom Restoration Act.
And that forcing the chain of stores to provide birth control violated that person's freedom of religion.
¯_(ツ)_/¯
RBG was indignant.
Until today, religious exemptions had never been extended to any entity operating in the commercial, profit-making world.
The exemption sought by Hobby Lobby...would deny *legions* of women who do not hold their employers' beliefs access to contraceptive coverage.
The Court, I fear, has ventured into a *minefield*.
The court's decision left open the door for even more entities to restrict access to birth control.
And RBG continued fighting for this right up until the very end of her life, even making her arguments from a hospital bed in a case in early 2020.

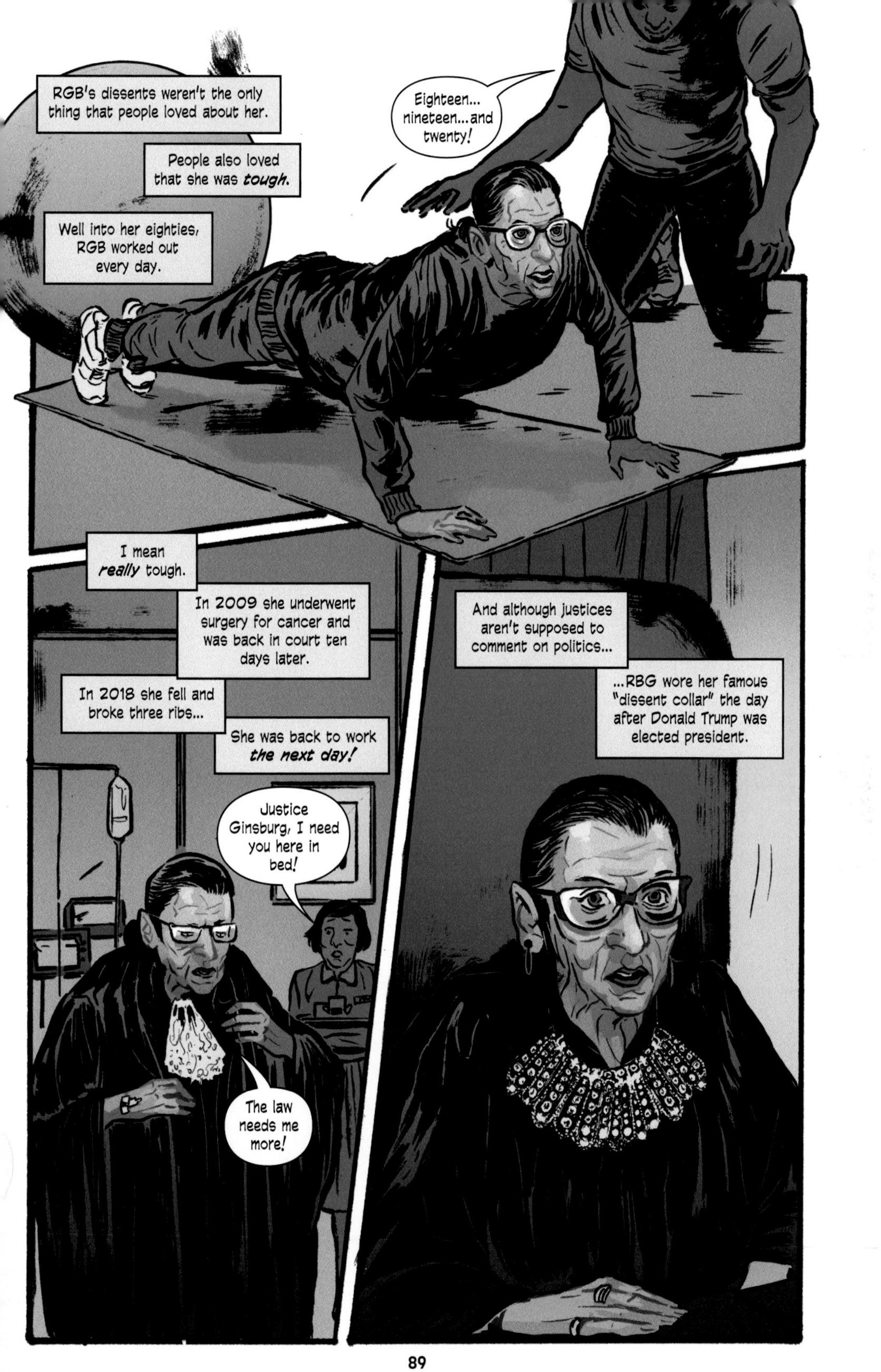
RGB's dissents weren't the only thing that people loved about her.
People also loved that she was *tough.*
Well into her eighties, RGB worked out every day.
Eighteen... nineteen...and twenty!
I mean *really* tough.
In 2009 she underwent surgery for cancer and was back in court ten days later.
In 2018 she fell and broke three ribs...
She was back to work *the next day!*
Justice Ginsburg, I need you here in bed!
The law needs me more!
And although justices aren't supposed to comment on politics...
...RBG wore her famous "dissent collar" the day after Donald Trump was elected president.

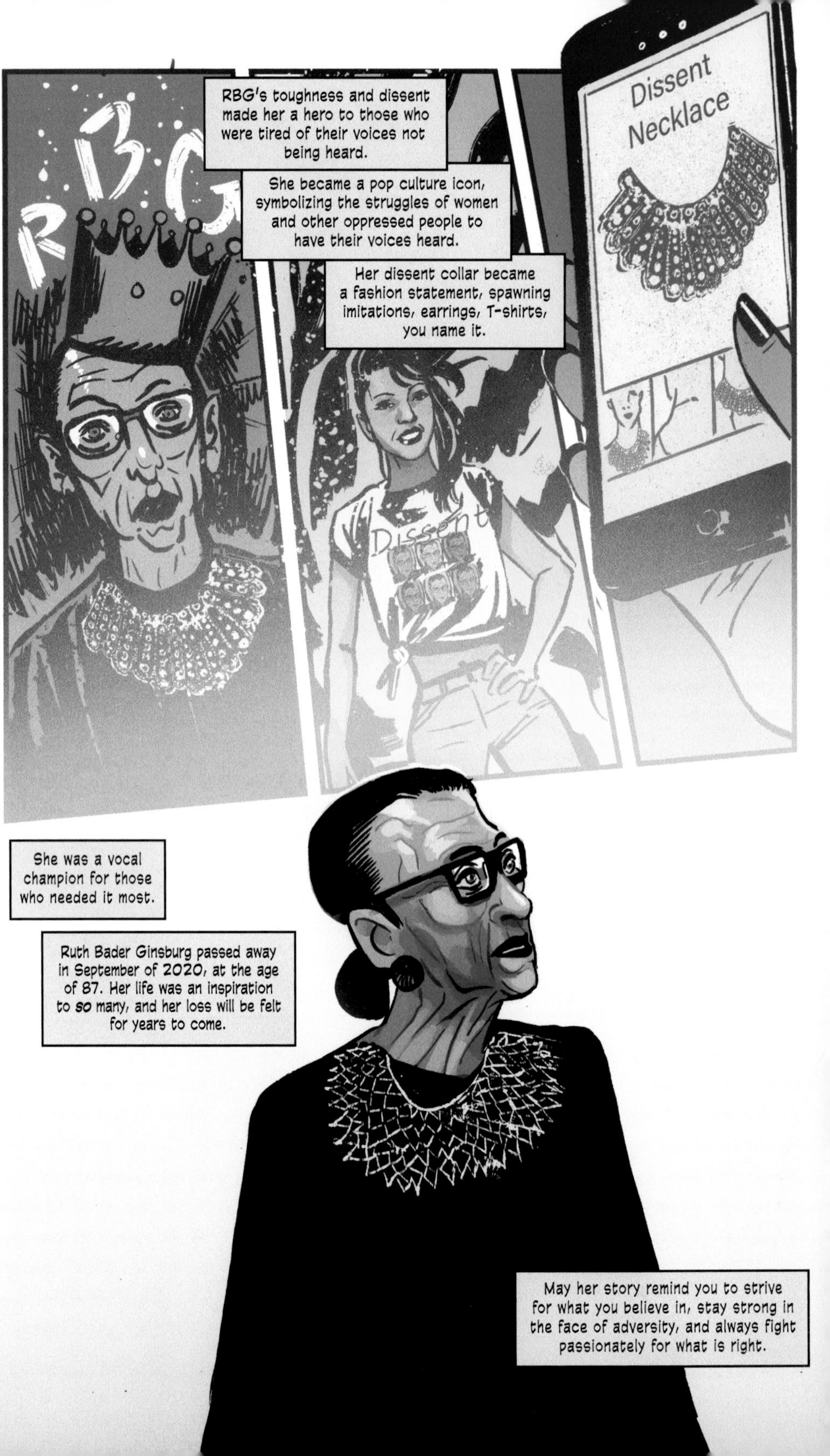
RBG
RBG's toughness and dissent made her a hero to those who were tired of their voices not being heard.
She became a pop culture icon, symbolizing the struggles of women and other oppressed people to have their voices heard.
Her dissent collar became a fashion statement, spawning imitations, earrings, T-shirts, you name it.
Dissent
Dissent Necklace
She was a vocal champion for those who needed it most.
Ruth Bader Ginsburg passed away in September of 2020, at the age of 87. Her life was an inspiration to *so* many, and her loss will be felt for years to come.
May her story remind you to strive for what you believe in, stay strong in the face of adversity, and always fight passionately for what is right.

GRETA THUNBERG: CLIMATE JUSTICE

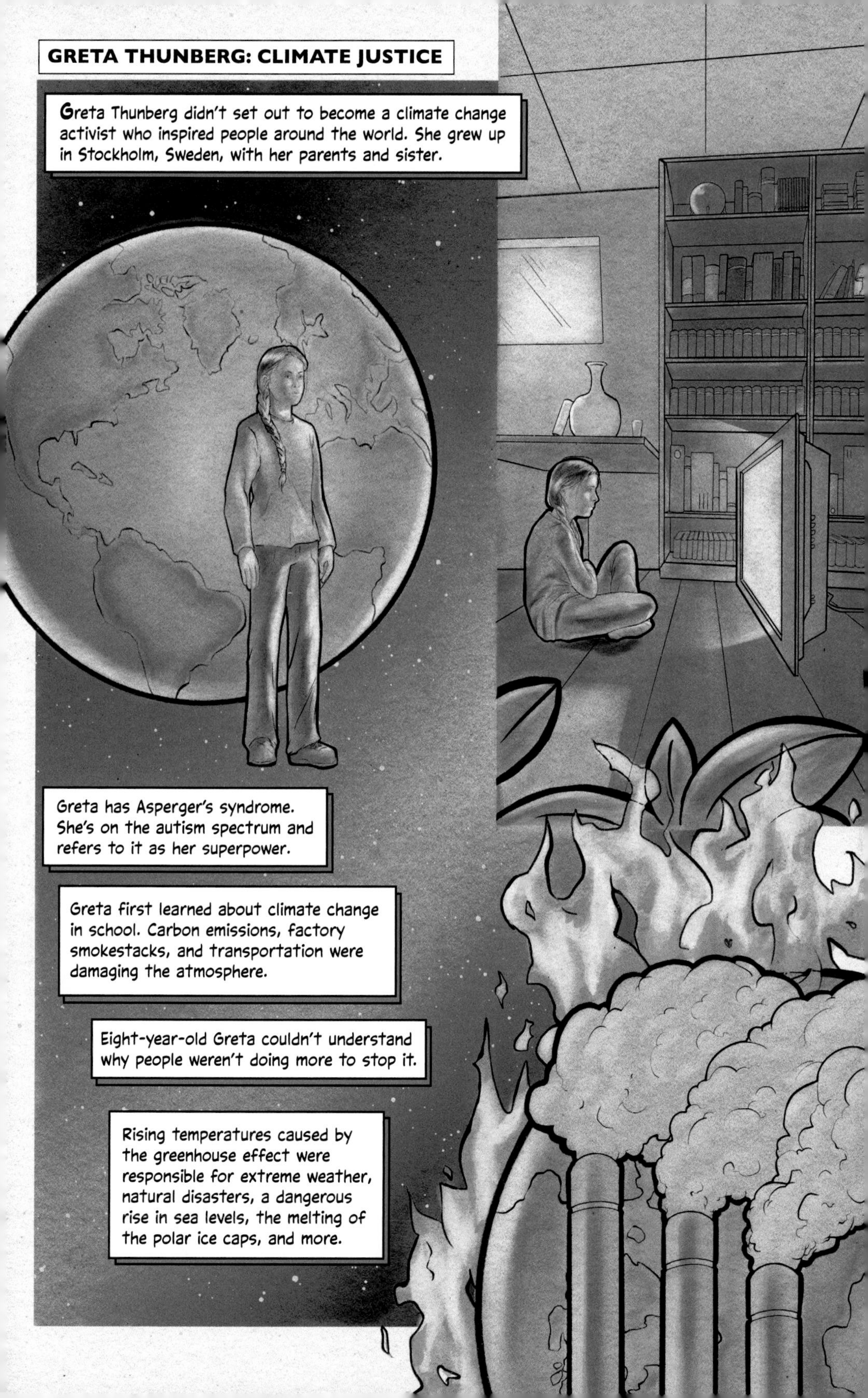
Greta Thunberg didn't set out to become a climate change activist who inspired people around the world. She grew up in Stockholm, Sweden, with her parents and sister.
Greta has Asperger's syndrome. She's on the autism spectrum and refers to it as her superpower.
Greta first learned about climate change in school. Carbon emissions, factory smokestacks, and transportation were damaging the atmosphere.
Eight-year-old Greta couldn't understand why people weren't doing more to stop it.
Rising temperatures caused by the greenhouse effect were responsible for extreme weather, natural disasters, a dangerous rise in sea levels, the melting of the polar ice caps, and more.

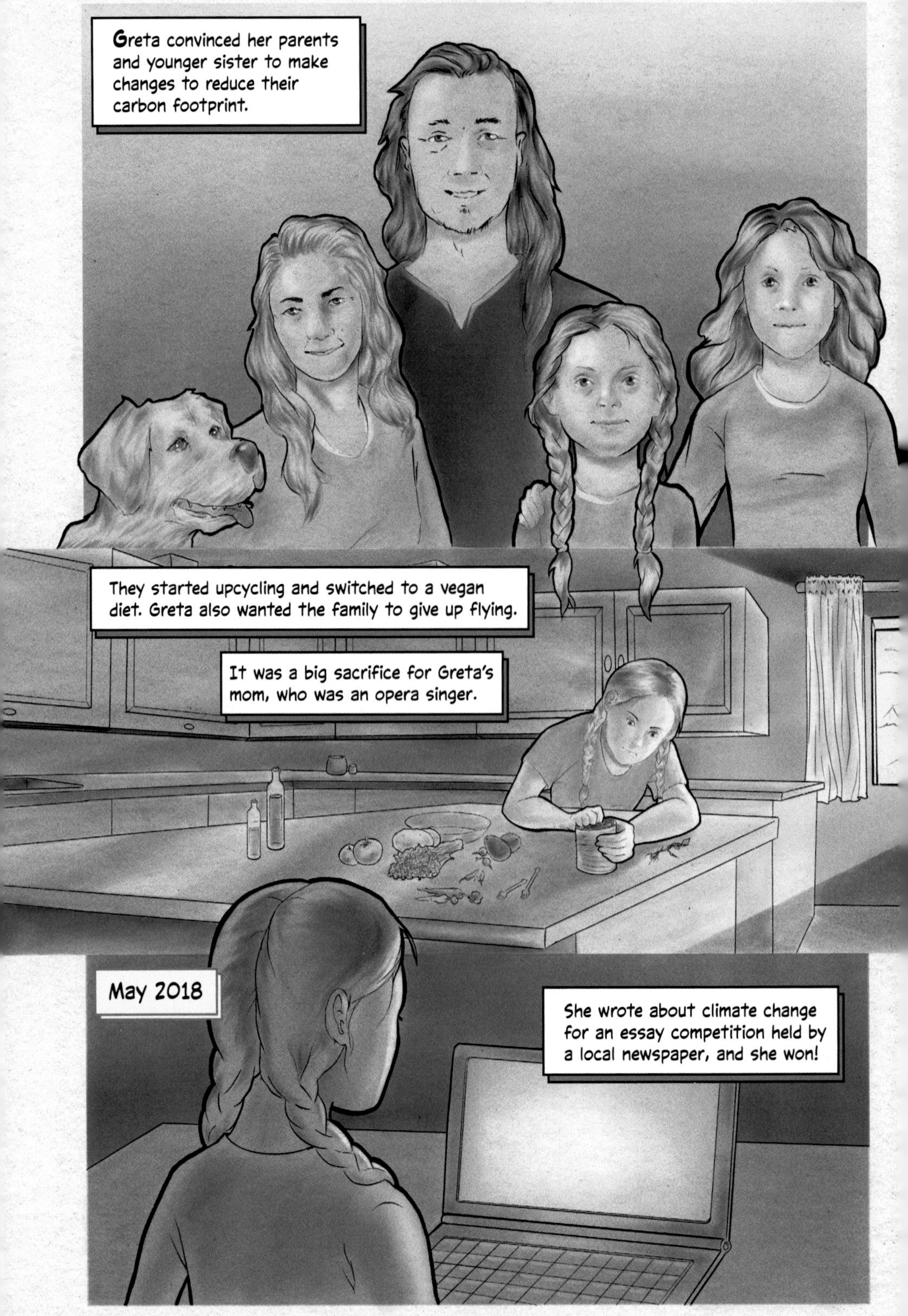
Greta convinced her parents and younger sister to make changes to reduce their carbon footprint.
They started upcycling and switched to a vegan diet. Greta also wanted the family to give up flying.
It was a big sacrifice for Greta's mom, who was an opera singer.
May 2018
She wrote about climate change for an essay competition held by a local newspaper, and she won!

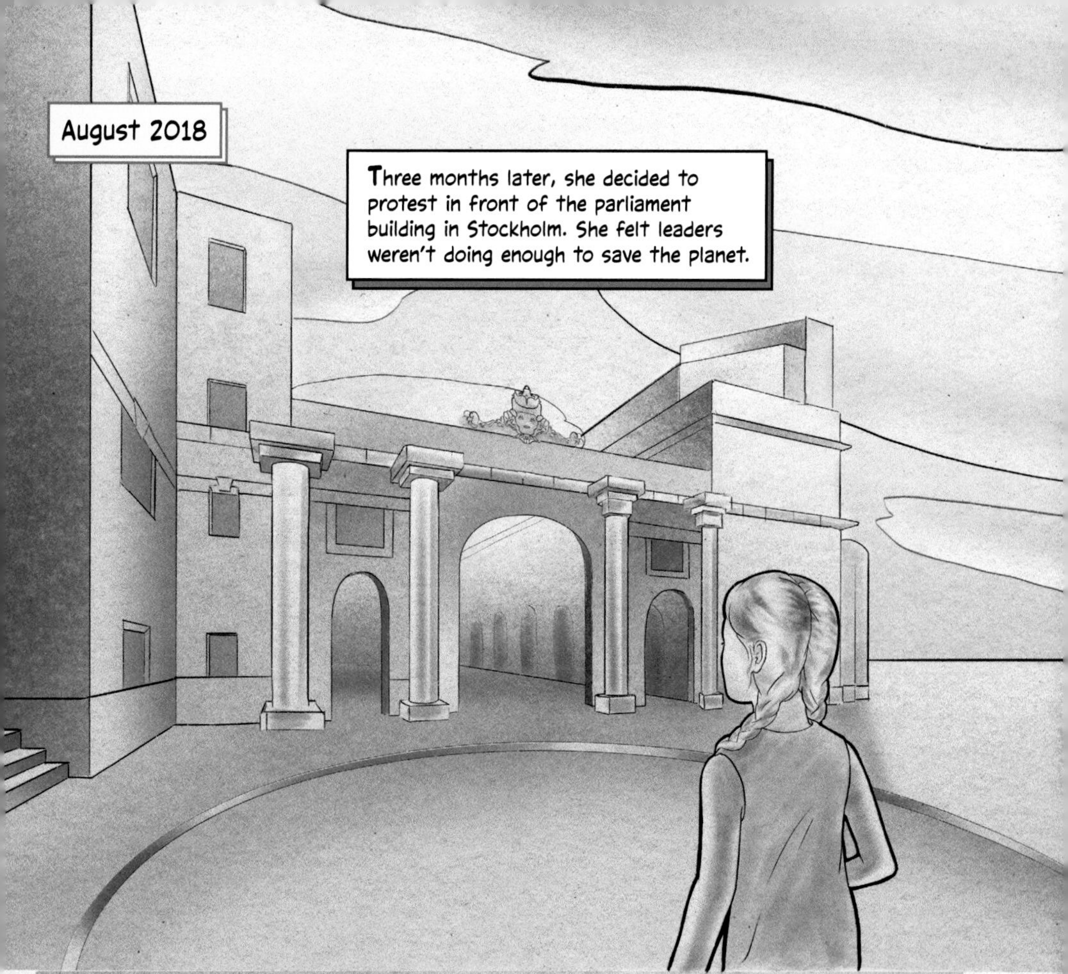
August 2018
Three months later, she decided to protest in front of the parliament building in Stockholm. She felt leaders weren't doing enough to save the planet.

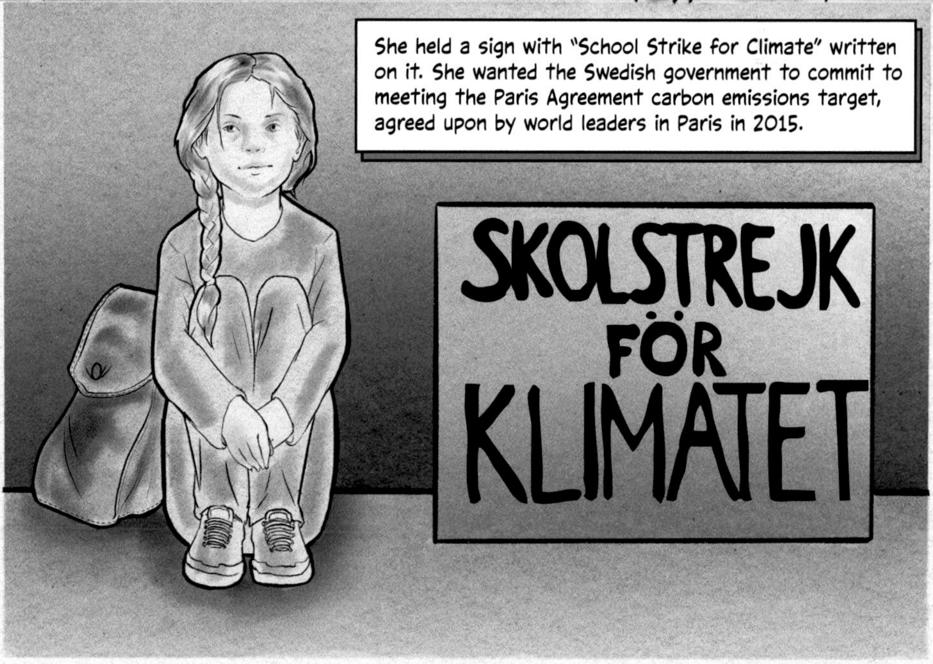
She held a sign with "School Strike for Climate" written on it. She wanted the Swedish government to commit to meeting the Paris Agreement carbon emissions target, agreed upon by world leaders in Paris in 2015.
SKOLSTREJK FÖR KLIMATET

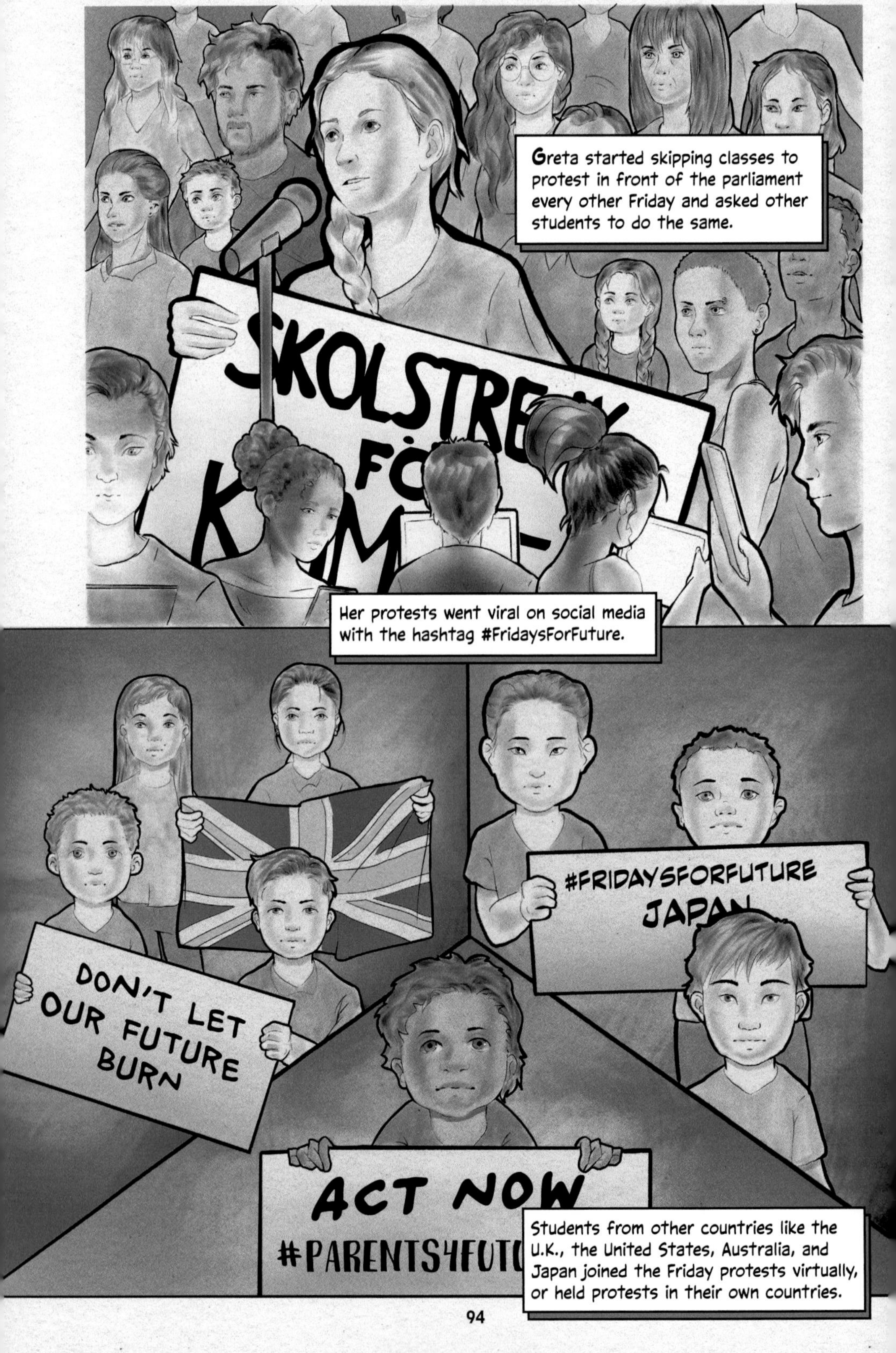
Greta started skipping classes to protest in front of the parliament every other Friday and asked other students to do the same.
Her protests went viral on social media with the hashtag #FridaysForFuture.
DON'T LET OUR FUTURE BURN
#FRIDAYSFORFUTURE JAPAN
ACT NOW
Students from other countries like the U.K., the United States, Australia, and Japan joined the Friday protests virtually, or held protests in their own countries.

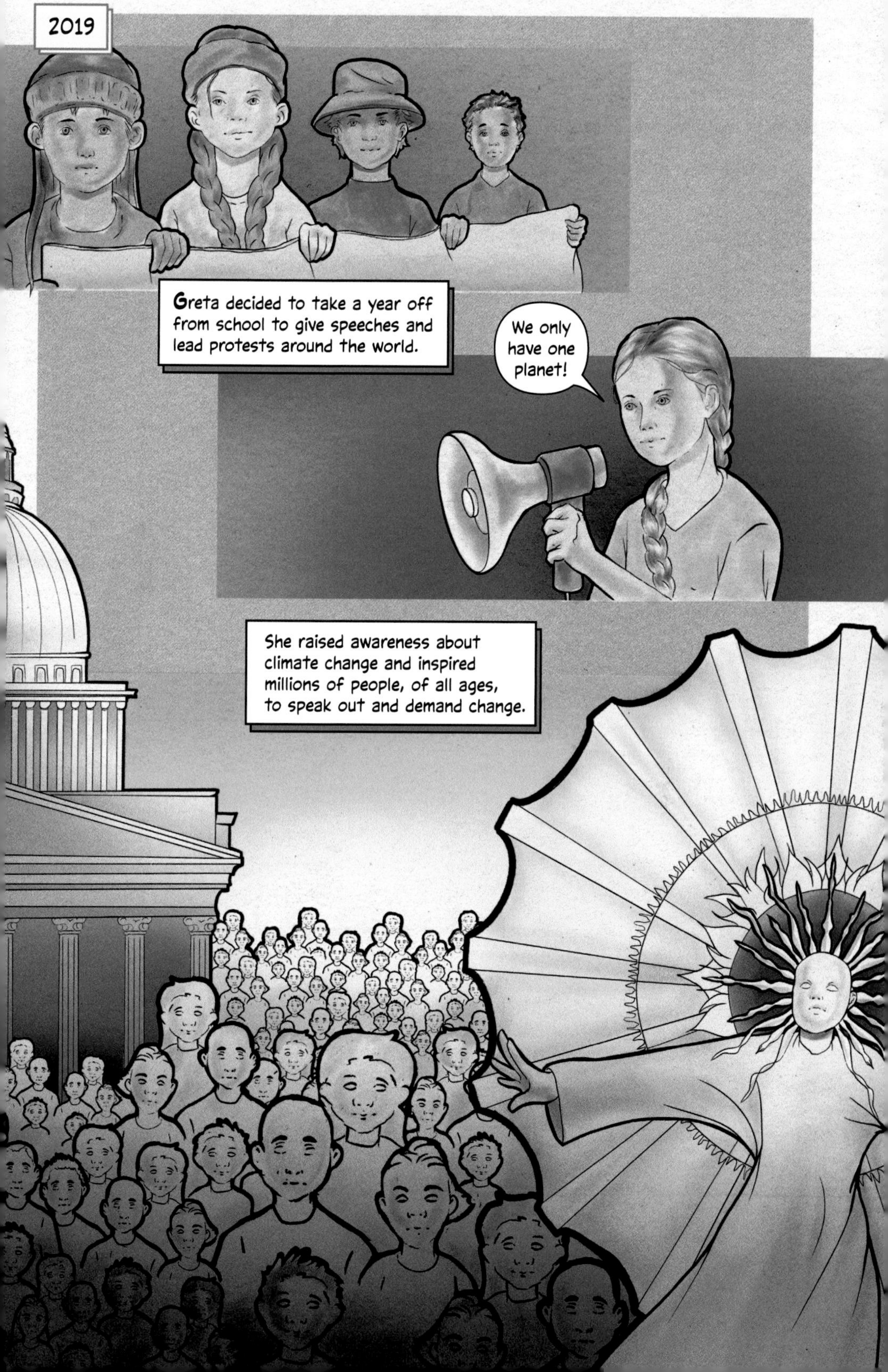
2019
Greta decided to take a year off from school to give speeches and lead protests around the world.
We only have one planet!
She raised awareness about climate change and inspired millions of people, of all ages, to speak out and demand change.

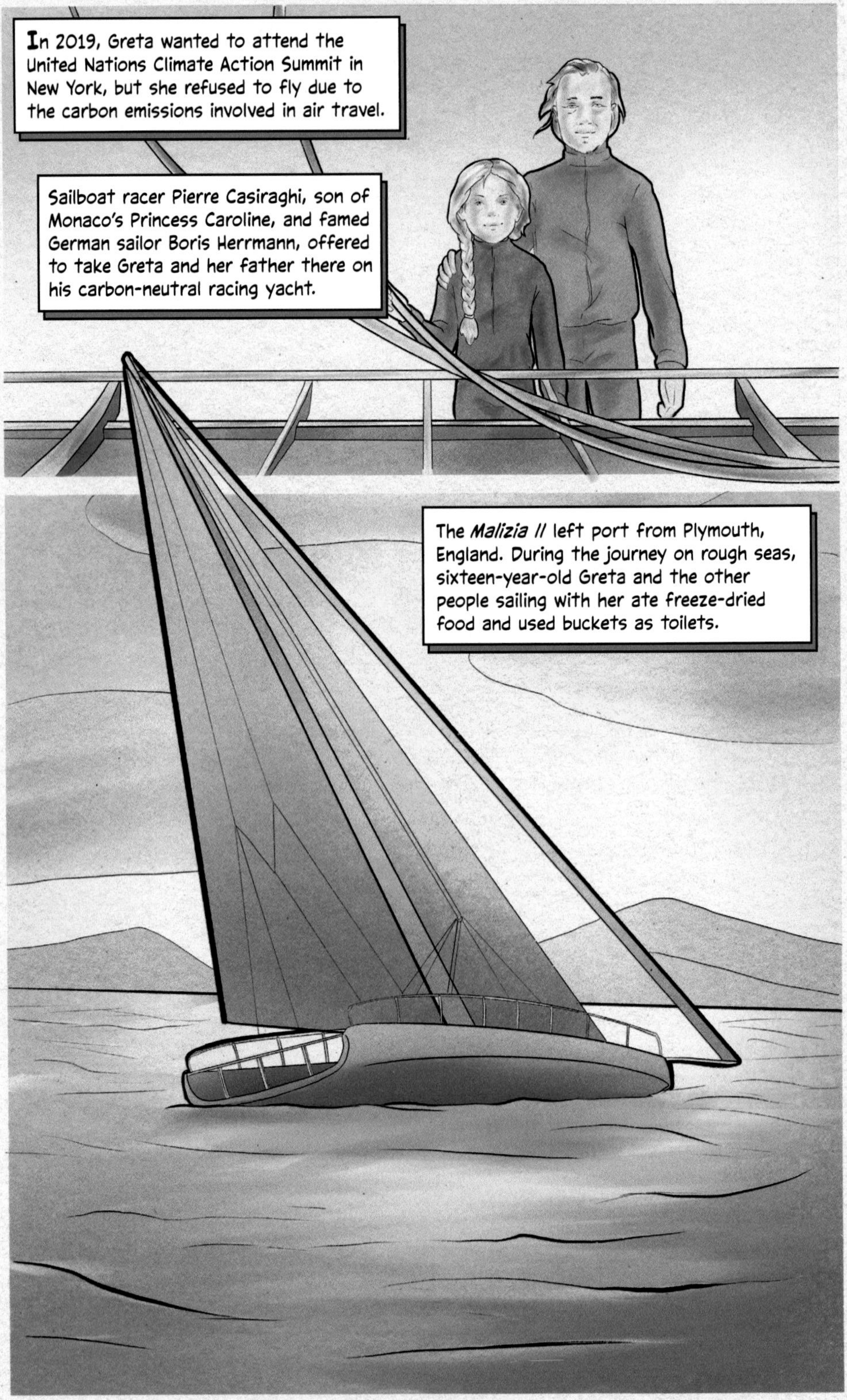
In 2019, Greta wanted to attend the United Nations Climate Action Summit in New York, but she refused to fly due to the carbon emissions involved in air travel.
Sailboat racer Pierre Casiraghi, son of Monaco's Princess Caroline, and famed German sailor Boris Herrmann, offered to take Greta and her father there on his carbon-neutral racing yacht.
The *Malizia II* left port from Plymouth, England. During the journey on rough seas, sixteen-year-old Greta and the other people sailing with her ate freeze-dried food and used buckets as toilets.

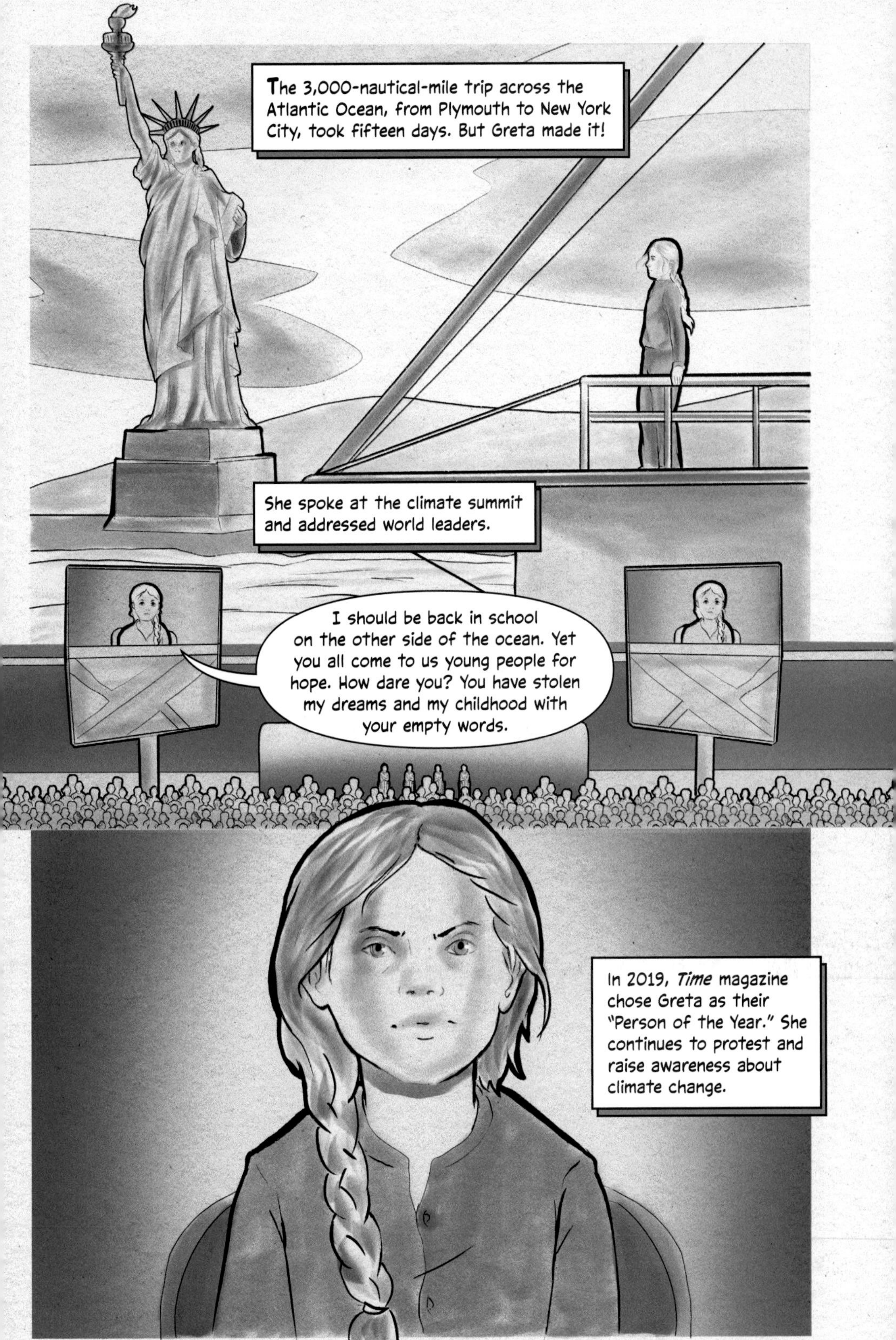
The 3,000-nautical-mile trip across the Atlantic Ocean, from Plymouth to New York City, took fifteen days. But Greta made it!
She spoke at the climate summit and addressed world leaders.
I should be back in school on the other side of the ocean. Yet you all come to us young people for hope. How dare you? You have stolen my dreams and my childhood with your empty words.
In 2019, *Time* magazine chose Greta as their "Person of the Year." She continues to protest and raise awareness about climate change.

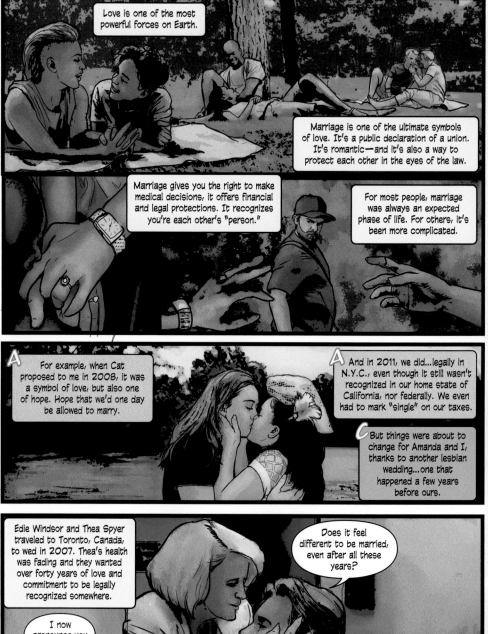

Love is one of the most powerful forces on Earth.

Marriage is one of the ultimate symbols of love. It's a public declaration of a union. It's romantic—and it's also a way to protect each other in the eyes of the law.

Marriage gives you the right to make medical decisions, it offers financial and legal protections. It recognizes you're each other's "person."

For most people, marriage was always an expected phase of life. For others, it's been more complicated.

For example, when Cat proposed to me in 2008, it was a symbol of love, but also one of hope. Hope that we'd one day be allowed to marry.

And in 2011, we did...legally in N.Y.C., even though it still wasn't recognized in our home state of California, nor federally. We even had to mark "single" on our taxes.

But things were about to change for Amanda and I, thanks to another lesbian wedding...one that happened a few years before ours.

Edie Windsor and Thea Spyer traveled to Toronto, Canada, to wed in 2007. Thea's health was fading and they wanted over forty years of love and commitment to be legally recognized somewhere.

I now pronounce you wife and wife.

Does it feel different to be married, even after all these years?

Yes.

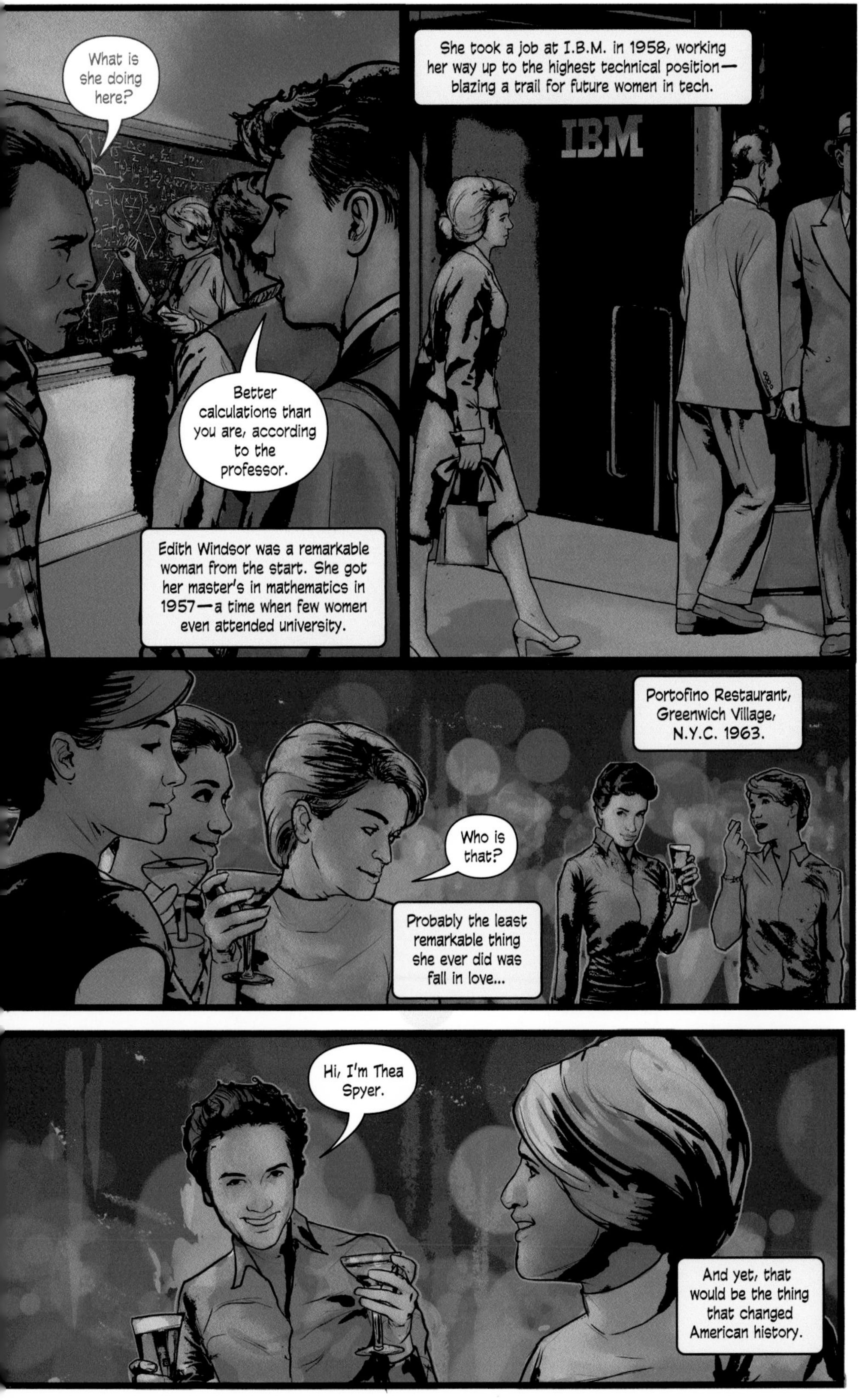
What is she doing here?
Better calculations than you are, according to the professor.
Edith Windsor was a remarkable woman from the start. She got her master's in mathematics in 1957—a time when few women even attended university.
She took a job at I.B.M. in 1958, working her way up to the highest technical position—blazing a trail for future women in tech.
IBM
Portofino Restaurant, Greenwich Village, N.Y.C. 1963.
Who is that?
Probably the least remarkable thing she ever did was fall in love...
Hi, I'm Thea Spyer.
And yet, that would be the thing that changed American history.

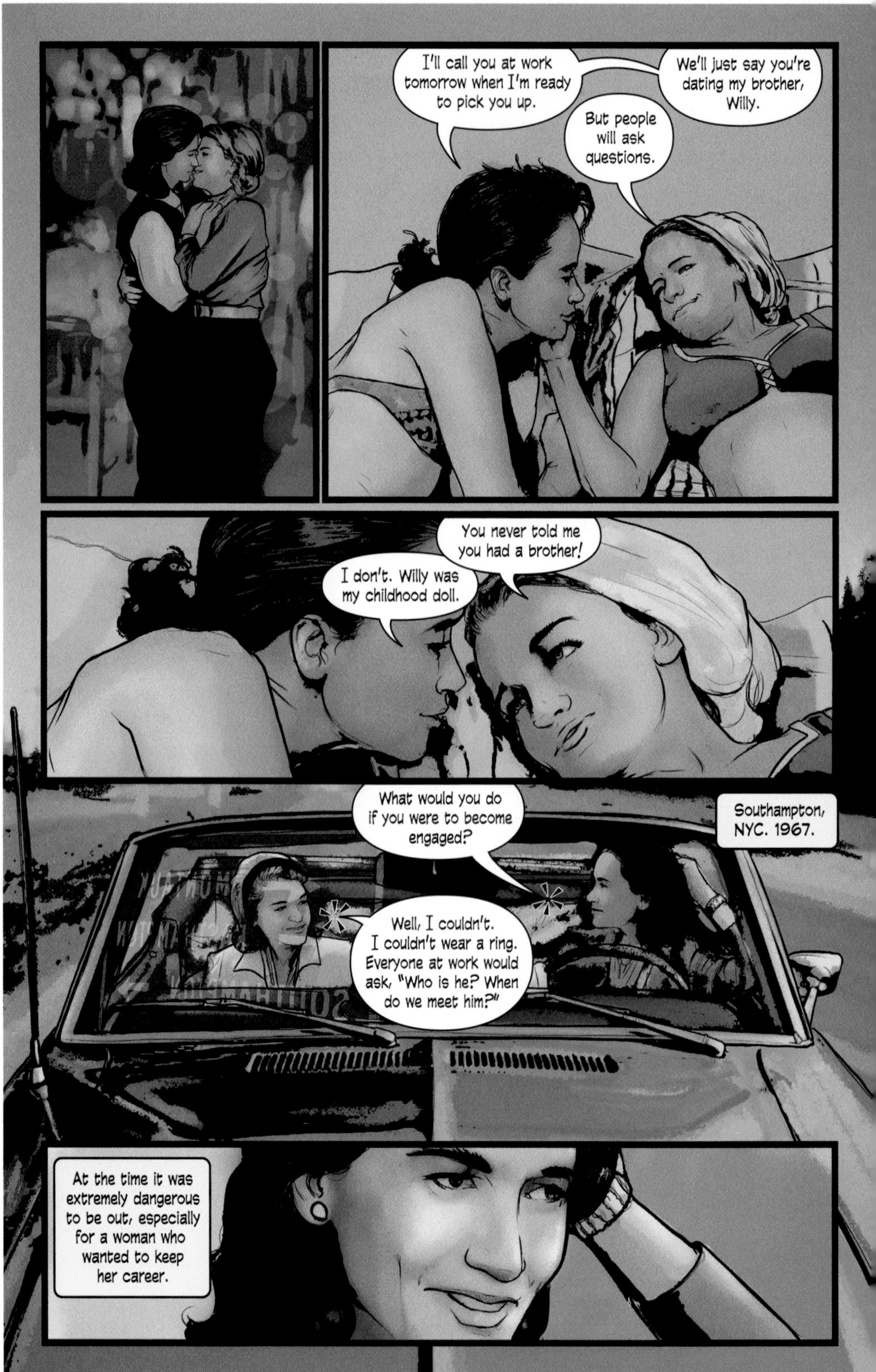
I'll call you at work tomorrow when I'm ready to pick you up.
But people will ask questions.
We'll just say you're dating my brother, Willy.
You never told me you had a brother!
I don't. Willy was my childhood doll.
Southampton, NYC. 1967.
What would you do if you were to become engaged?
Well, I couldn't. I couldn't wear a ring. Everyone at work would ask, "Who is he? When do we meet him?"
At the time it was extremely dangerous to be out, especially for a woman who wanted to keep her career.

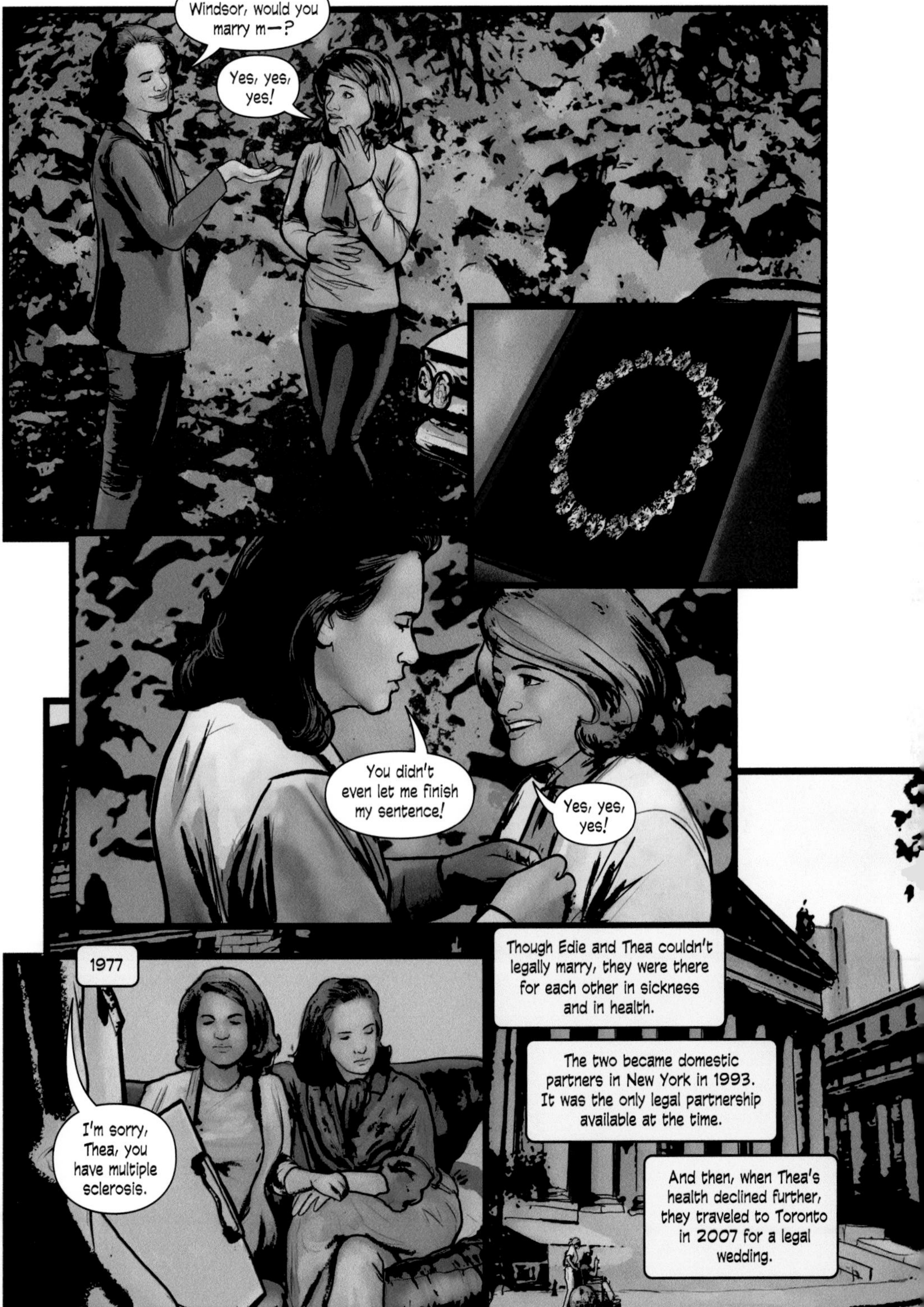
Edie Windsor, would you marry m—?
Yes, yes, yes!
You didn't even let me finish my sentence!
Yes, yes, yes!
1977
I'm sorry, Thea, you have multiple sclerosis.
Though Edie and Thea couldn't legally marry, they were there for each other in sickness and in health.
The two became domestic partners in New York in 1993. It was the only legal partnership available at the time.
And then, when Thea's health declined further, they traveled to Toronto in 2007 for a legal wedding.

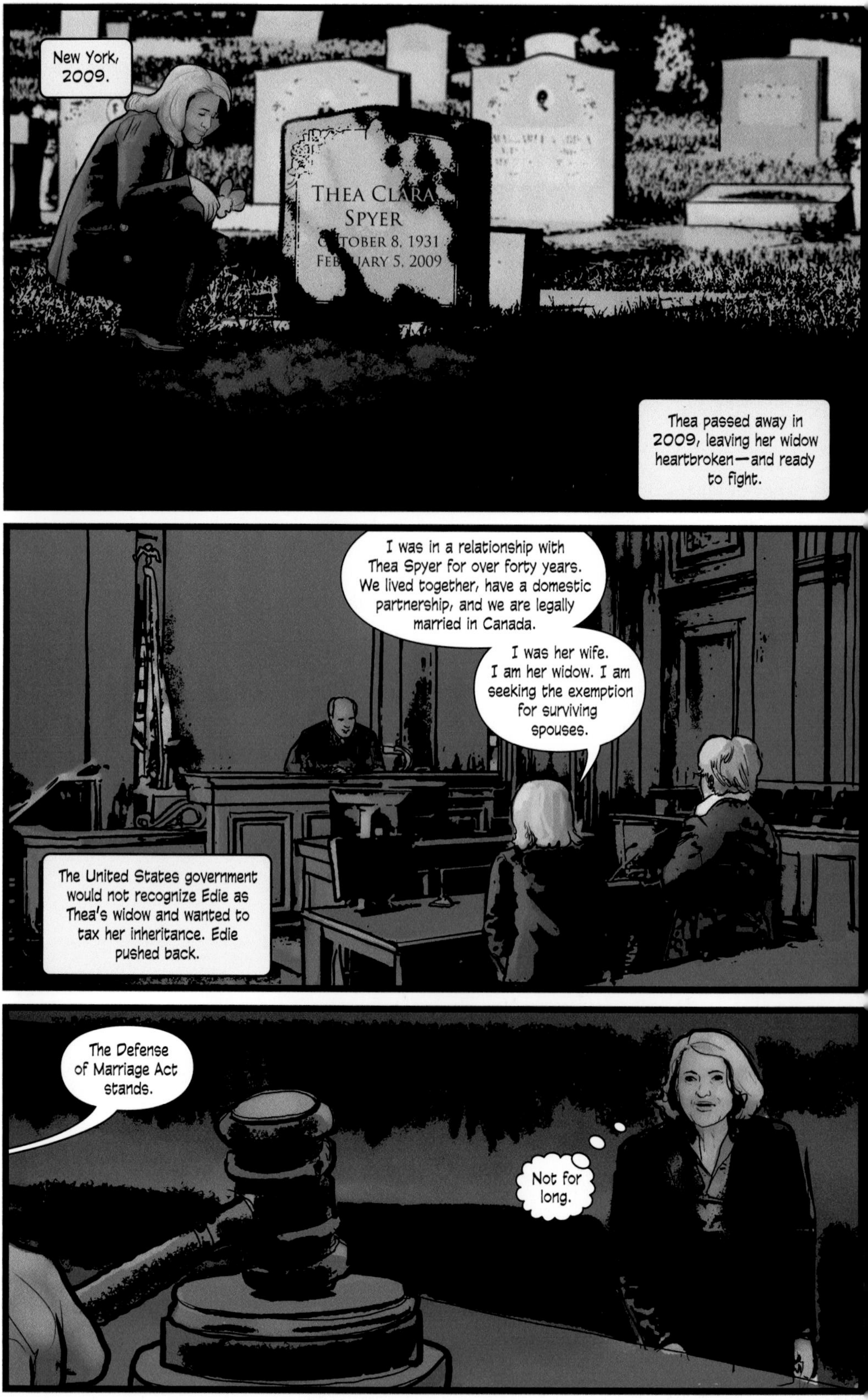
New York, 2009.
THEA CLARA SPYER
Thea passed away in 2009, leaving her widow heartbroken—and ready to fight.
I was in a relationship with Thea Spyer for over forty years. We lived together, have a domestic partnership, and we are legally married in Canada.
I was her wife. I am her widow. I am seeking the exemption for surviving spouses.
The United States government would not recognize Edie as Thea's widow and wanted to tax her inheritance. Edie pushed back.
The Defense of Marriage Act stands.
Not for long.

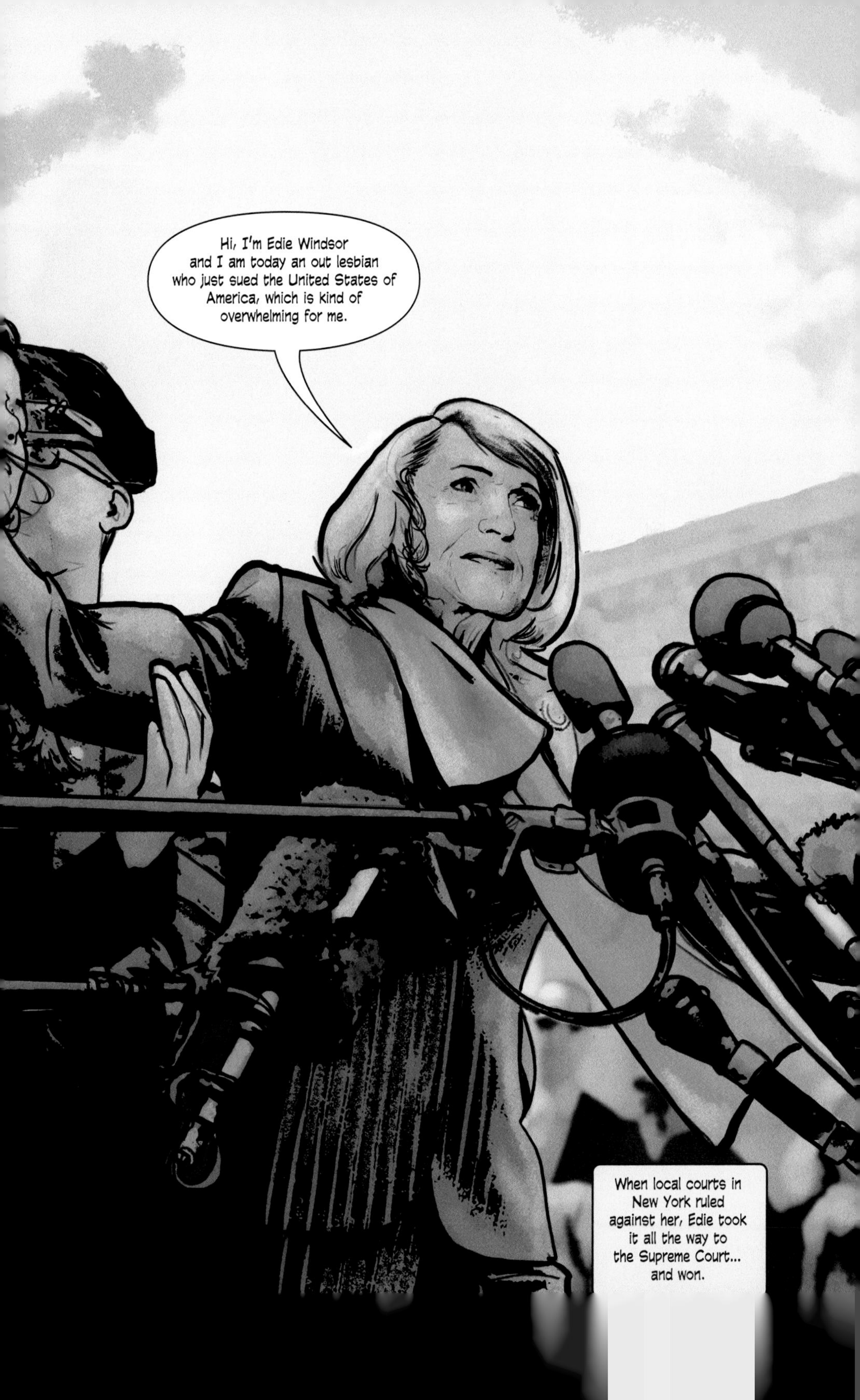
Hi, I'm Edie Windsor and I am today an out lesbian who just sued the United States of America, which is kind of overwhelming for me.
When local courts in New York ruled against her, Edie took it all the way to the Supreme Court... and won.

On June 26, 2013, the U.S. Supreme Court ruled section three of the so-called "Defense of Marriage Act" (D.O.M.A) unconstitutional.

LIFE FE
DIFFERENT W
YOU'RE MARRIE

Thank you, Edie!

This ruling prevents the federal government from discriminating against married lesbian and gay couples when it comes to federal benefits and protections.

Edie's overturning of this one part of D.O.M.A. set the stage, and a precedent, for the future...

No union is more profound than marriage, for it embodies the highest ideals of love, fidelity, devotion, sacrifice, and family...

They ask for equal dignity in the eyes of the law. The Constitution grants them that right...

On the *second anniversary* of Edie's win in *United States v. Windsor,* all of D.O.M.A. was finally overturned with the Supreme Court ruling in *Obergefell v. Hodges.*

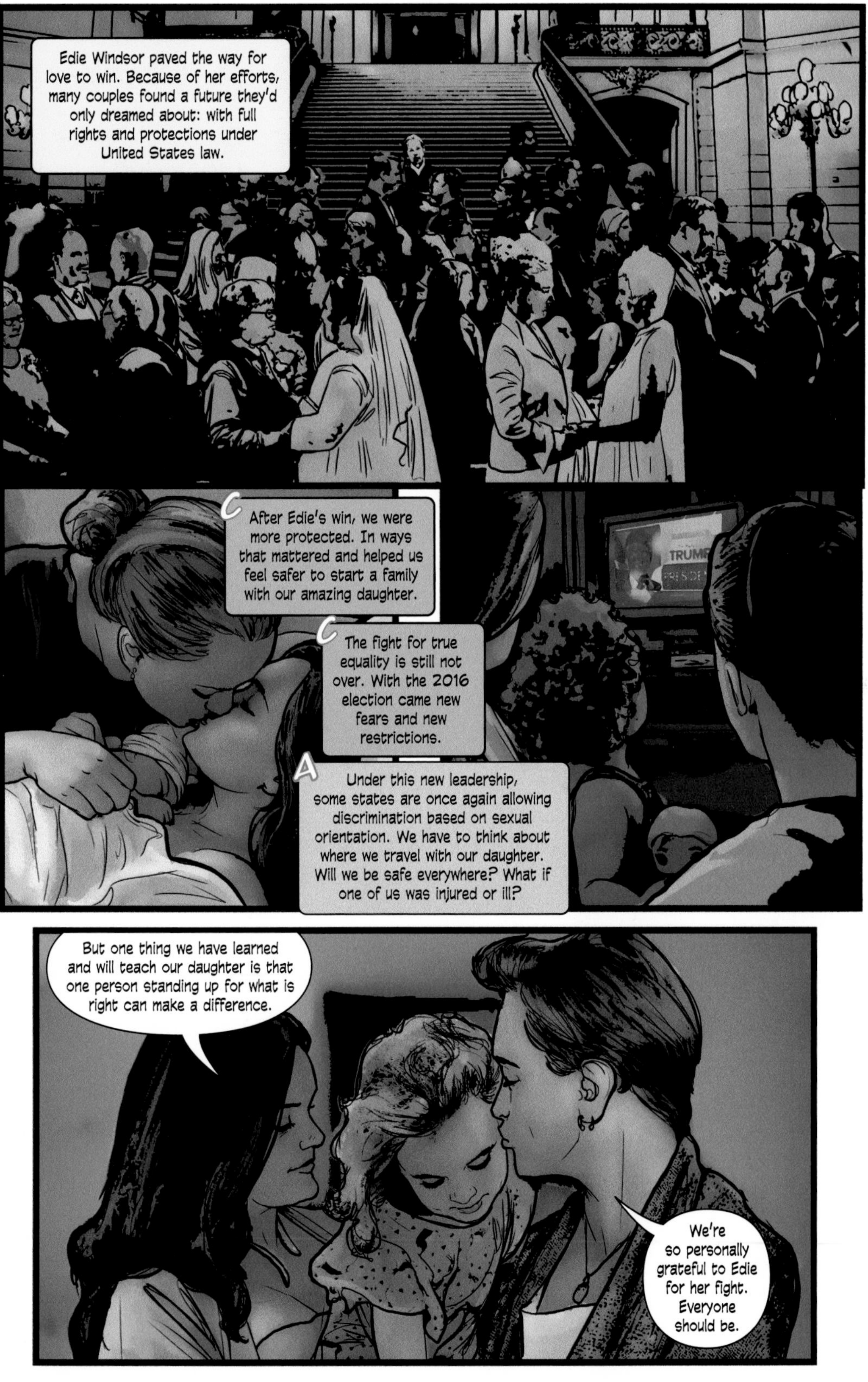
Edie Windsor paved the way for love to win. Because of her efforts, many couples found a future they'd only dreamed about: with full rights and protections under United States law.
C
After Edie's win, we were more protected. In ways that mattered and helped us feel safer to start a family with our amazing daughter.
C
The fight for true equality is still not over. With the 2016 election came new fears and new restrictions.
A
Under this new leadership, some states are once again allowing discrimination based on sexual orientation. We have to think about where we travel with our daughter. Will we be safe everywhere? What if one of us was injured or ill?
But one thing we have learned and will teach our daughter is that one person standing up for what is right can make a difference.
We're so personally grateful to Edie for her fight. Everyone should be.

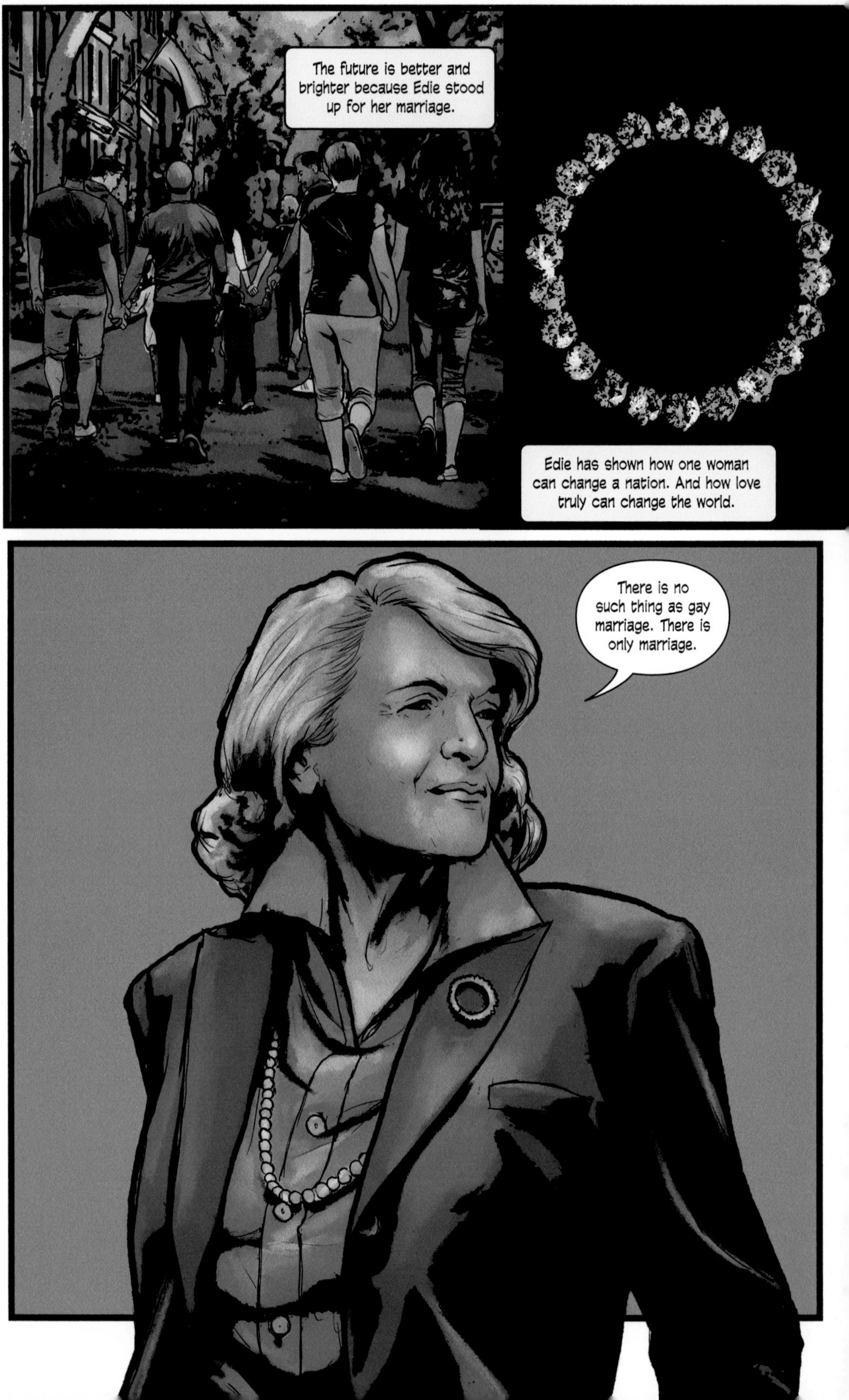
The future is better and brighter because Edie stood up for her marriage.
Edie has shown how one woman can change a nation. And how love truly can change the world.
There is no such thing as gay marriage. There is only marriage.

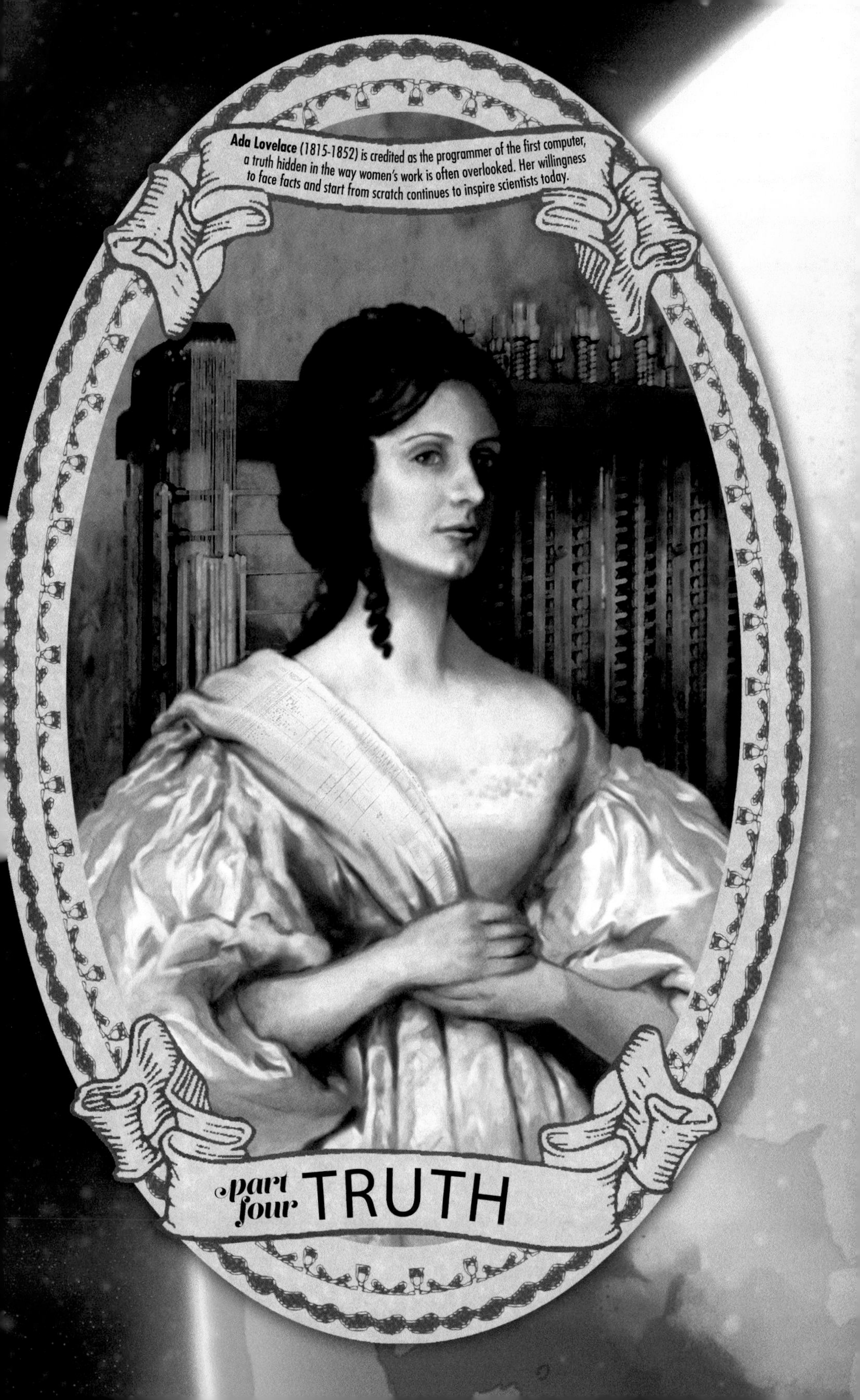

Ada Lovelace (1815-1852) is credited as the programmer of the first computer, a truth hidden in the way women's work is often overlooked. Her willingness to face facts and start from scratch continues to inspire scientists today.
part four TRUTH

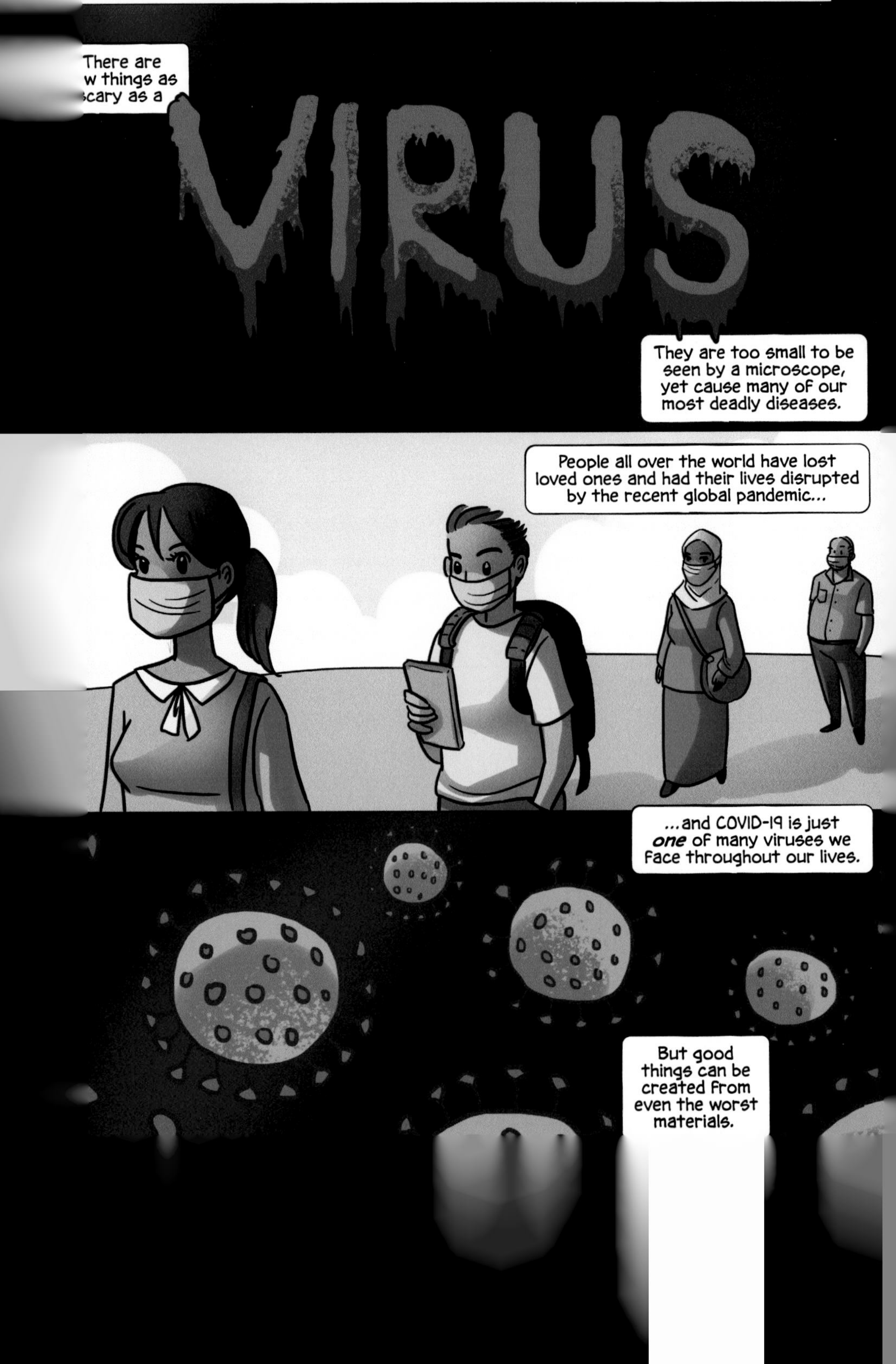
There are
w things as
scary as a
VIRUS
They are too small to be seen by a microscope, yet cause many of our most deadly diseases.
People all over the world have lost loved ones and had their lives disrupted by the recent global pandemic...
...and COVID-19 is just *one* of many viruses we face throughout our lives.
But good things can be created from even the worst materials.

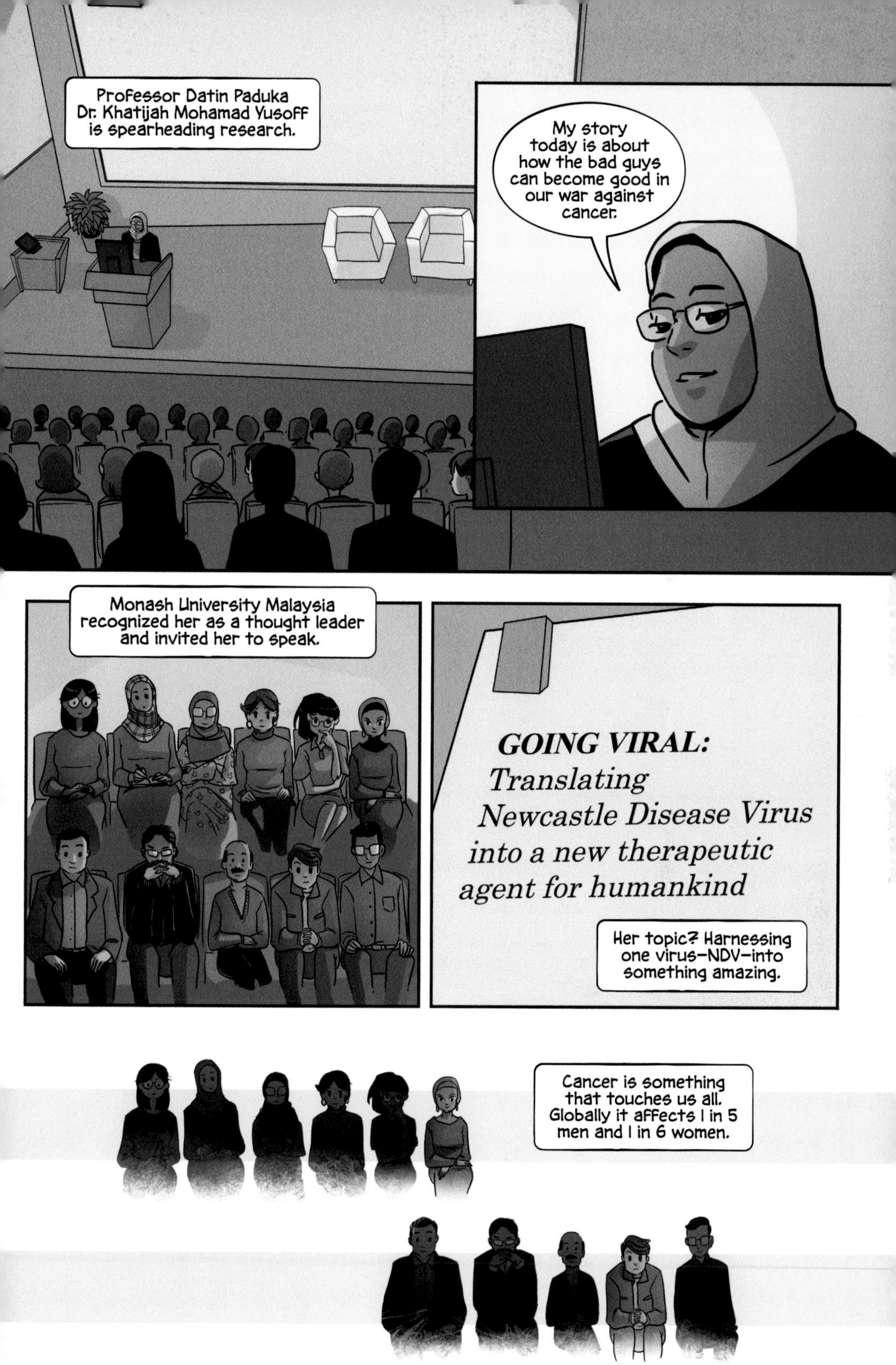

Professor Datin Paduka Dr. Khatijah Mohamad Yusoff is spearheading research.
My story today is about how the bad guys can become good in our war against cancer.
Monash University Malaysia recognized her as a thought leader and invited her to speak.
GOING VIRAL: Translating Newcastle Disease Virus into a new therapeutic agent for humankind
Her topic? Harnessing one virus—NDV—into something amazing.
Cancer is something that touches us all. Globally it affects 1 in 5 men and 1 in 6 women.

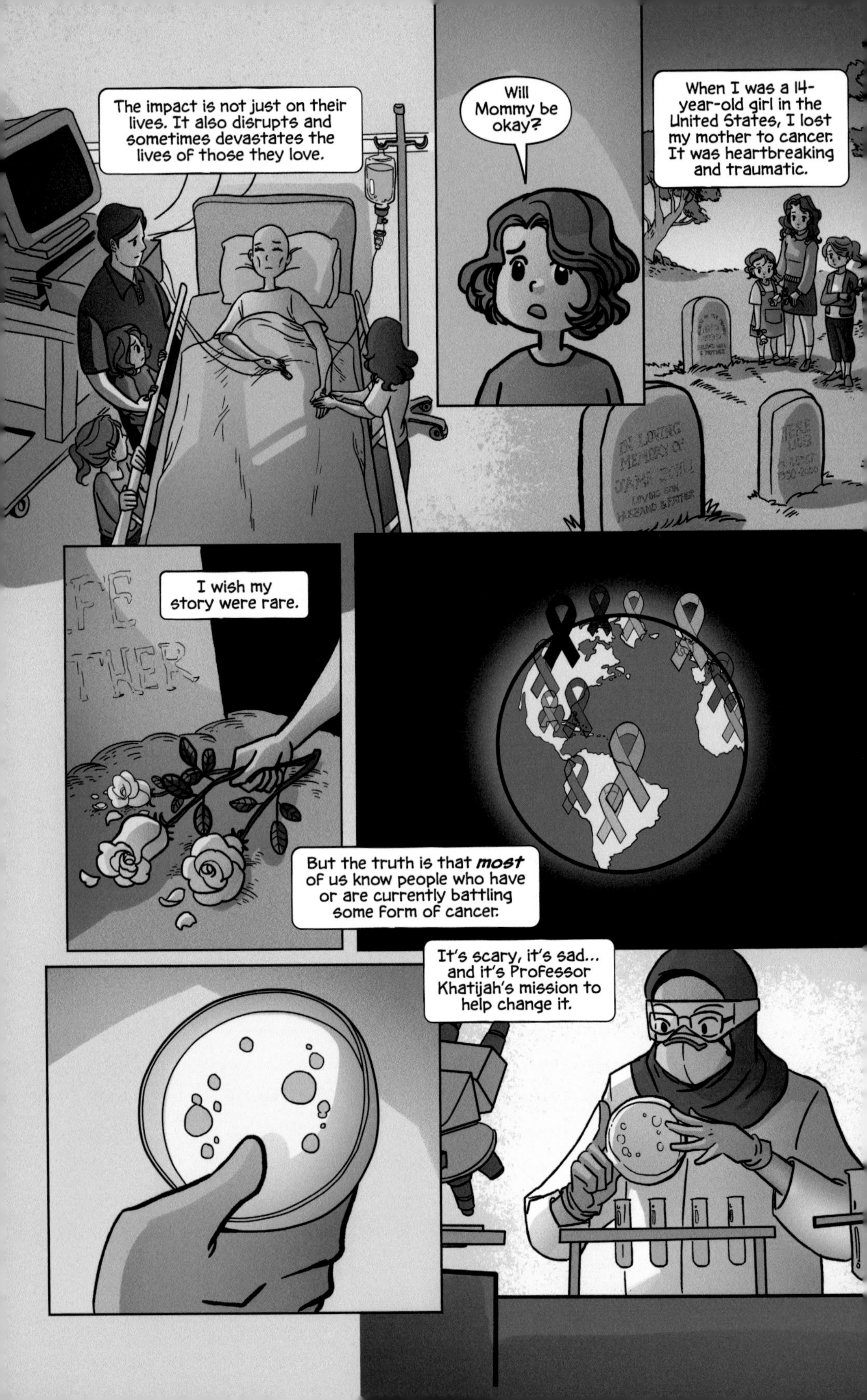
The impact is not just on their lives. It also disrupts and sometimes devastates the lives of those they love.
Will Mommy be okay?
When I was a 14-year-old girl in the United States, I lost my mother to cancer. It was heartbreaking and traumatic.
I wish my story were rare.
But the truth is that *most* of us know people who have or are currently battling some form of cancer.
It's scary, it's sad... and it's Professor Khatijah's mission to help change it.

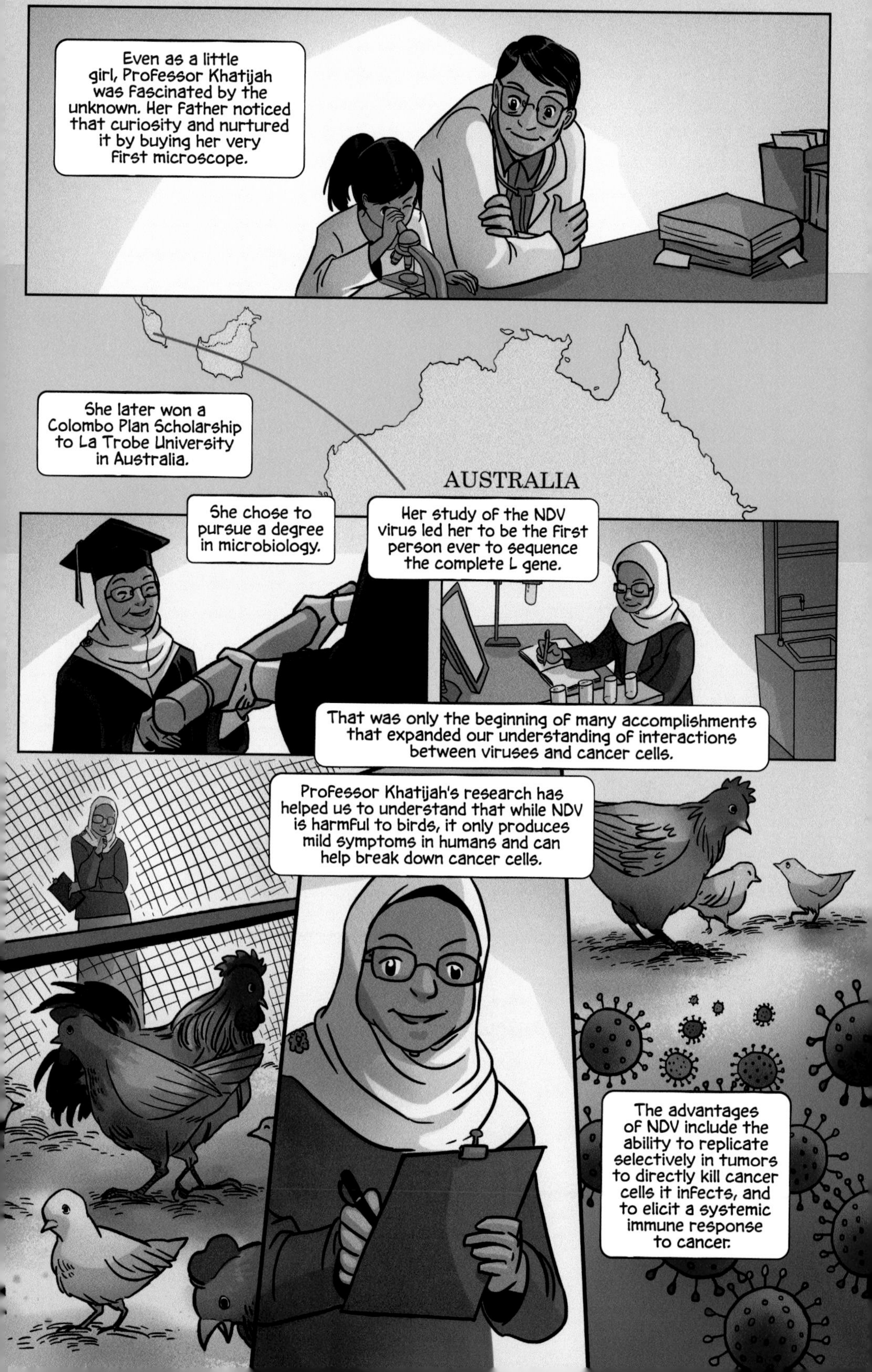
Even as a little girl, Professor Khatijah was fascinated by the unknown. Her father noticed that curiosity and nurtured it by buying her very first microscope.
She later won a Colombo Plan Scholarship to La Trobe University in Australia.
AUSTRALIA
She chose to pursue a degree in microbiology.
Her study of the NDV virus led her to be the first person ever to sequence the complete L gene.
That was only the beginning of many accomplishments that expanded our understanding of interactions between viruses and cancer cells.
Professor Khatijah's research has helped us to understand that while NDV is harmful to birds, it only produces mild symptoms in humans and can help break down cancer cells.
The advantages of NDV include the ability to replicate selectively in tumors to directly kill cancer cells it infects, and to elicit a systemic immune response to cancer.

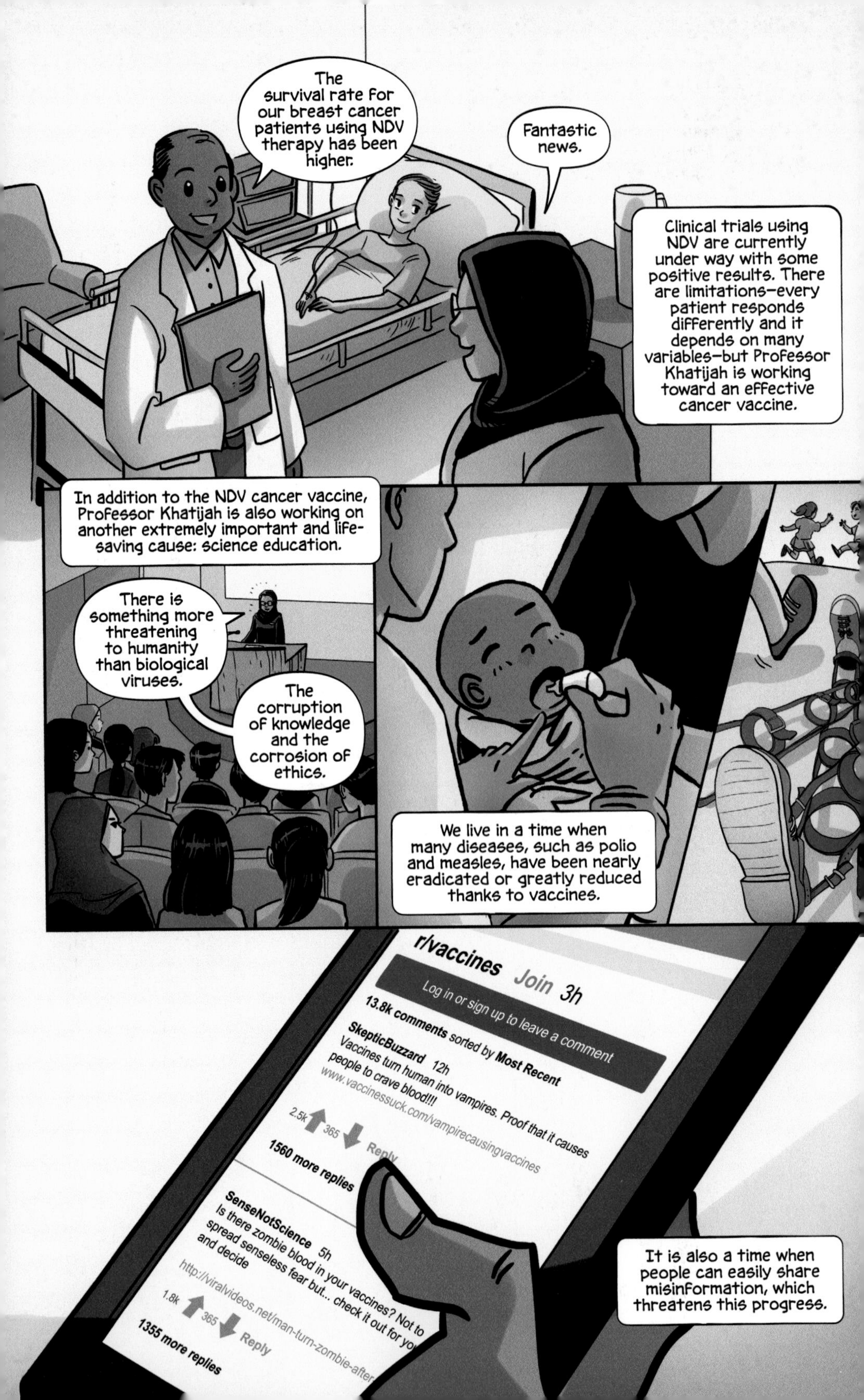

The survival rate for our breast cancer patients using NDV therapy has been higher.
Fantastic news.
Clinical trials using NDV are currently under way with some positive results. There are limitations—every patient responds differently and it depends on many variables—but Professor Khatijah is working toward an effective cancer vaccine.
In addition to the NDV cancer vaccine, Professor Khatijah is also working on another extremely important and life-saving cause: science education.
There is something more threatening to humanity than biological viruses.
The corruption of knowledge and the corrosion of ethics.
We live in a time when many diseases, such as polio and measles, have been nearly eradicated or greatly reduced thanks to vaccines.
r/vaccines Join 3h
Log in or sign up to leave a comment
13.8k comments sorted by Most Recent
SkepticBuzzard 12h
Vaccines turn human into vampires. Proof that it causes people to crave blood!!!
www.vaccinessuck.com/vampirecausingvaccines
2.5k 365 Reply
1560 more replies
SenseNotScience 5h
Is there zombie blood in your vaccines? Not to spread senseless fear but... check it out for yo and decide
http://viralvideos.net/man-turn-zombie-after
1.8k 365 Reply
1355 more replies
It is also a time when people can easily share misinformation, which threatens this progress.

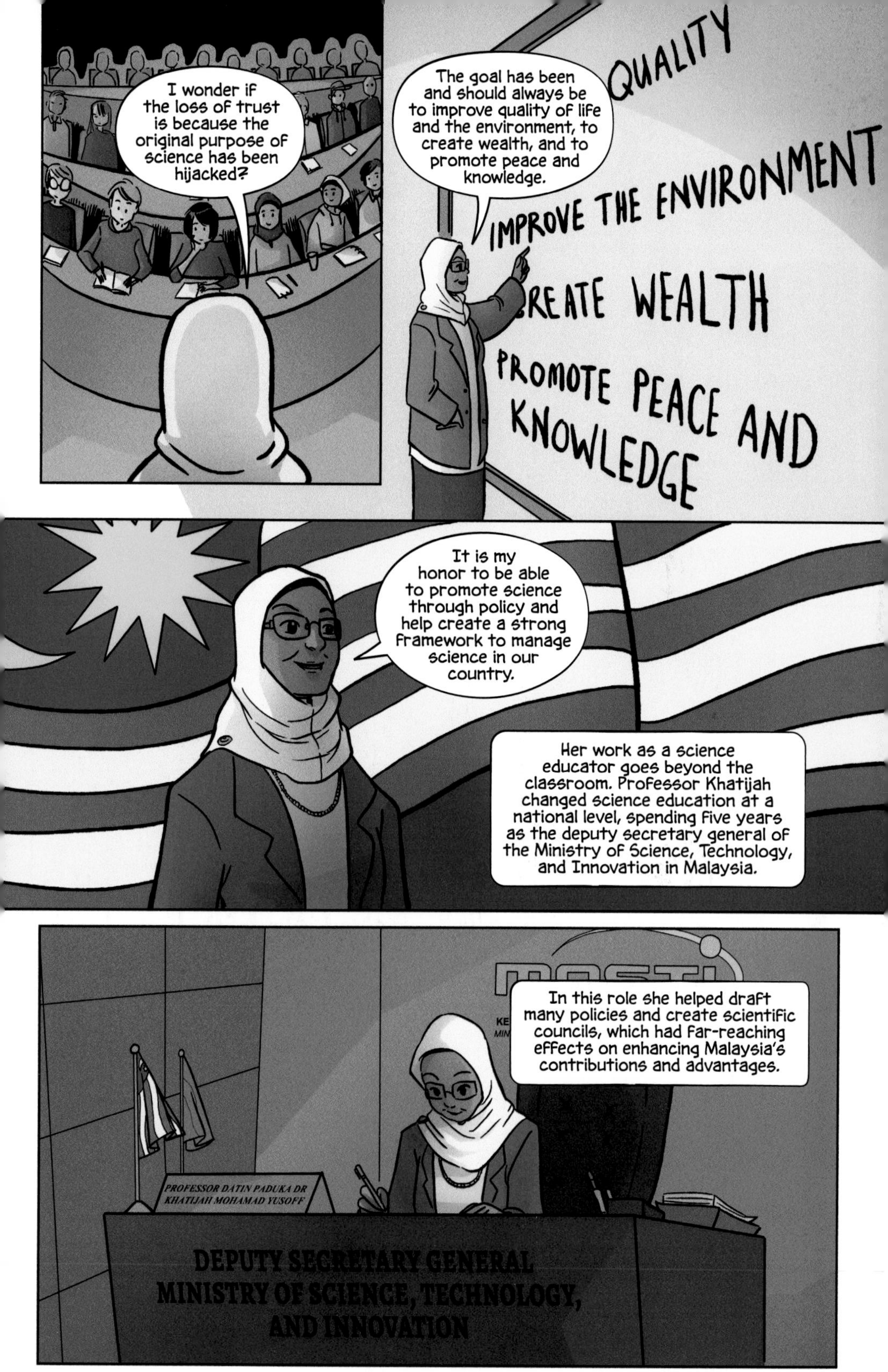

I wonder if the loss of trust is because the original purpose of science has been hijacked?
The goal has been and should always be to improve quality of life and the environment, to create wealth, and to promote peace and knowledge.
QUALITY
IMPROVE THE ENVIRONMENT
CREATE WEALTH
PROMOTE PEACE AND KNOWLEDGE
It is my honor to be able to promote science through policy and help create a strong framework to manage science in our country.
Her work as a science educator goes beyond the classroom. Professor Khatijah changed science education at a national level, spending five years as the deputy secretary general of the Ministry of Science, Technology, and Innovation in Malaysia.
In this role she helped draft many policies and create scientific councils, which had far-reaching effects on enhancing Malaysia's contributions and advantages.
PROFESSOR DATIN PADUKA DR KHATIJAH MOHAMAD YUSOFF
DEPUTY SECRETARY GENERAL MINISTRY OF SCIENCE, TECHNOLOGY, AND INNOVATION

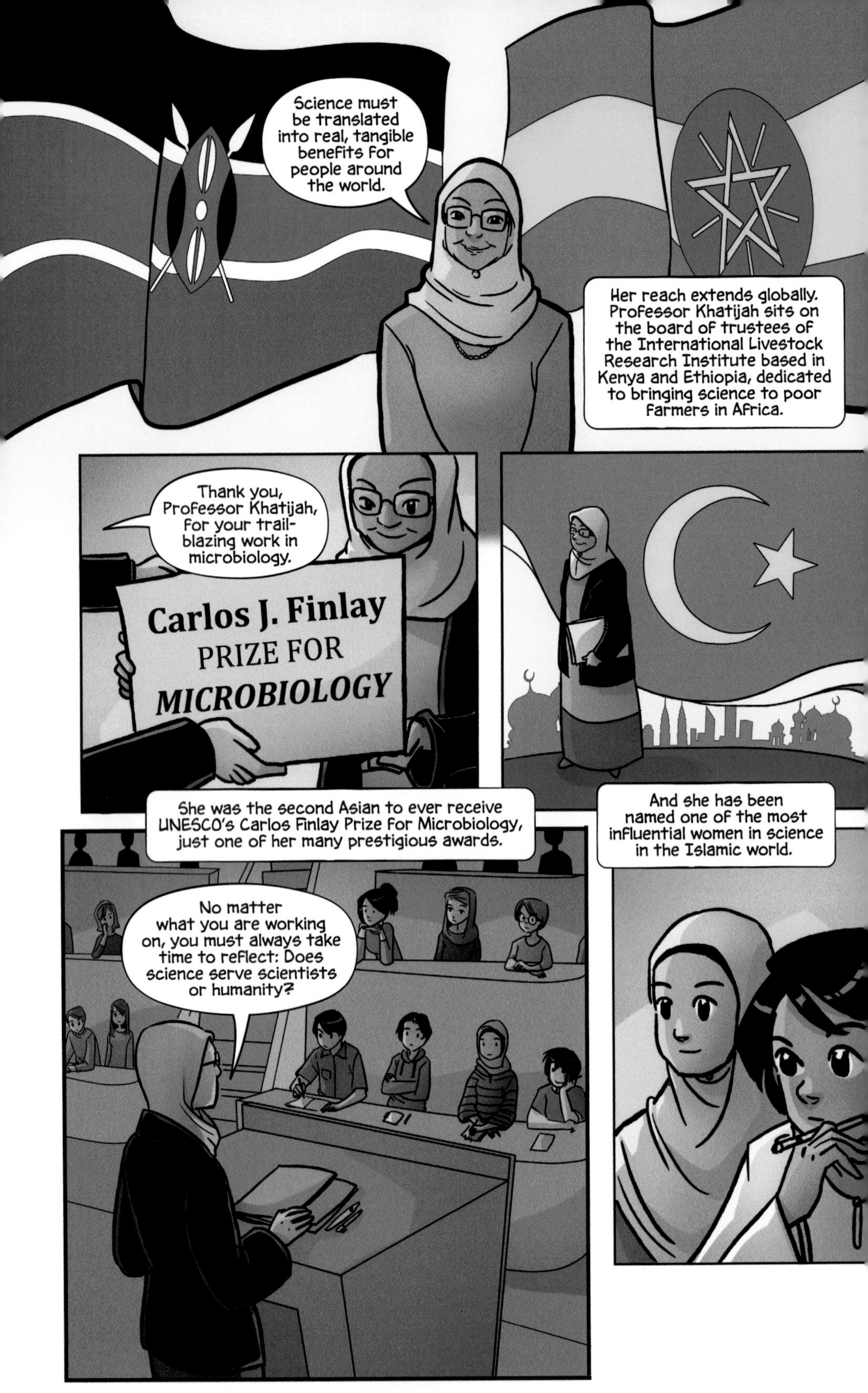
Science must be translated into real, tangible benefits for people around the world.
Her reach extends globally. Professor Khatijah sits on the board of trustees of the International Livestock Research Institute based in Kenya and Ethiopia, dedicated to bringing science to poor farmers in Africa.
Thank you, Professor Khatijah, for your trail-blazing work in microbiology.
Carlos J. Finlay PRIZE FOR MICROBIOLOGY
She was the second Asian to ever receive UNESCO's Carlos Finlay Prize for Microbiology, just one of her many prestigious awards.
And she has been named one of the most influential women in science in the Islamic world.
No matter what you are working on, you must always take time to reflect: Does science serve scientists or humanity?

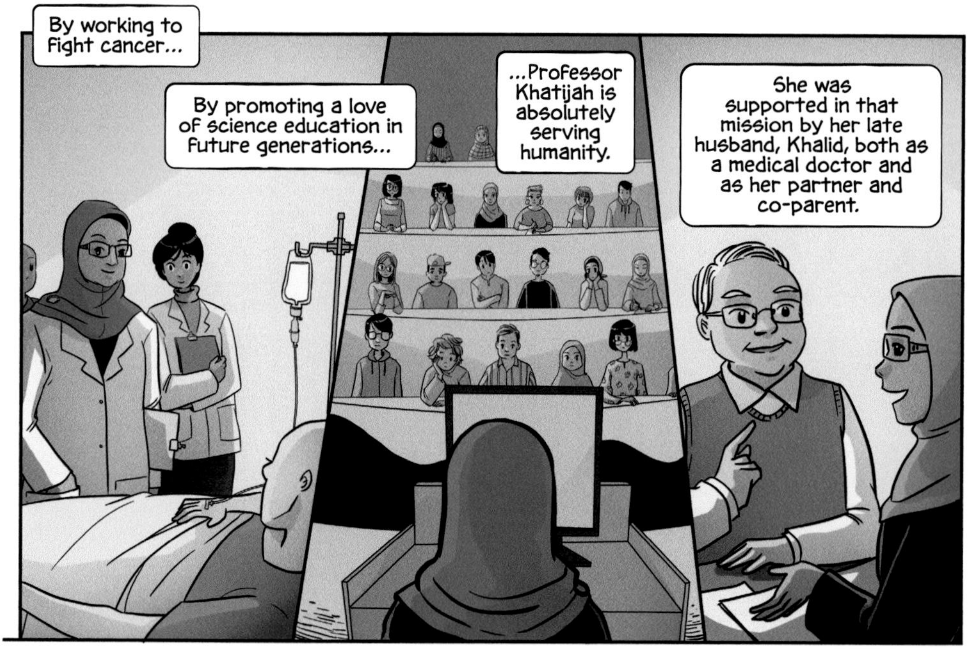
By working to fight cancer...
By promoting a love of science education in future generations...
...Professor Khatijah is absolutely serving humanity.
She was supported in that mission by her late husband, Khalid, both as a medical doctor and as her partner and co-parent.

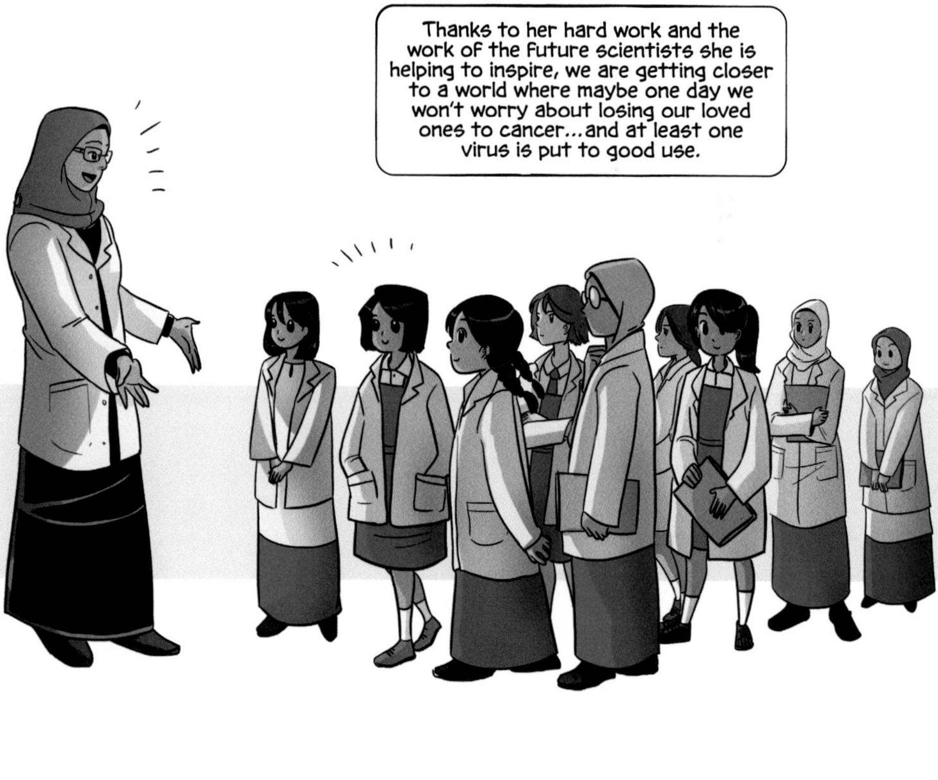
Thanks to her hard work and the work of the future scientists she is helping to inspire, we are getting closer to a world where maybe one day we won't worry about losing our loved ones to cancer...and at least one virus is put to good use.

FRANCISCA NNEKA OKEKE: CLIMATE CHANGE ACTIVIST AND SHERO

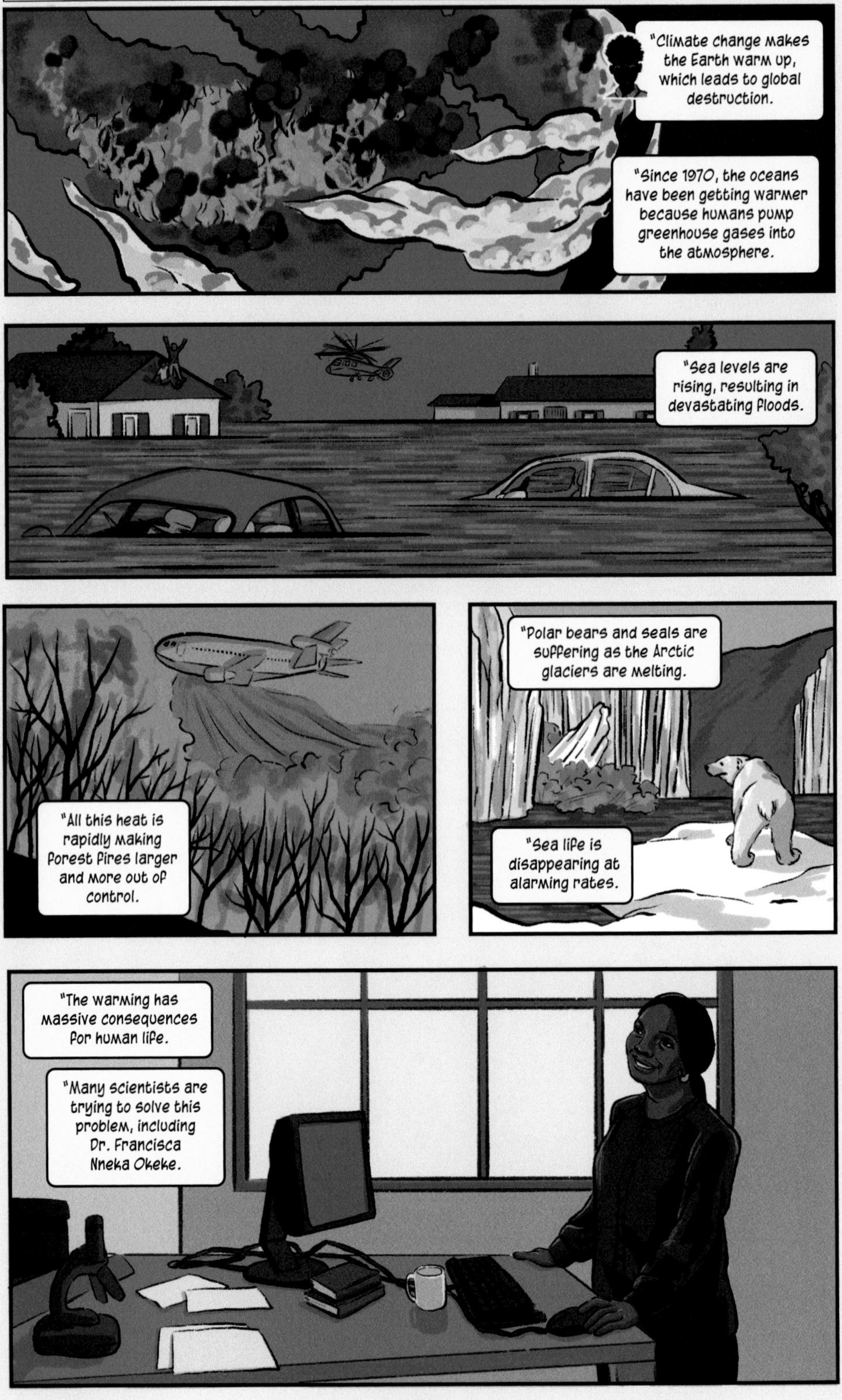
"Climate change makes the Earth warm up, which leads to global destruction.
"Since 1970, the oceans have been getting warmer because humans pump greenhouse gases into the atmosphere.
"Sea levels are rising, resulting in devastating floods.
"All this heat is rapidly making forest fires larger and more out of control.
"Polar bears and seals are suffering as the Arctic glaciers are melting.
"Sea life is disappearing at alarming rates.
"The warming has massive consequences for human life.
"Many scientists are trying to solve this problem, including Dr. Francisca Nneka Okeke.

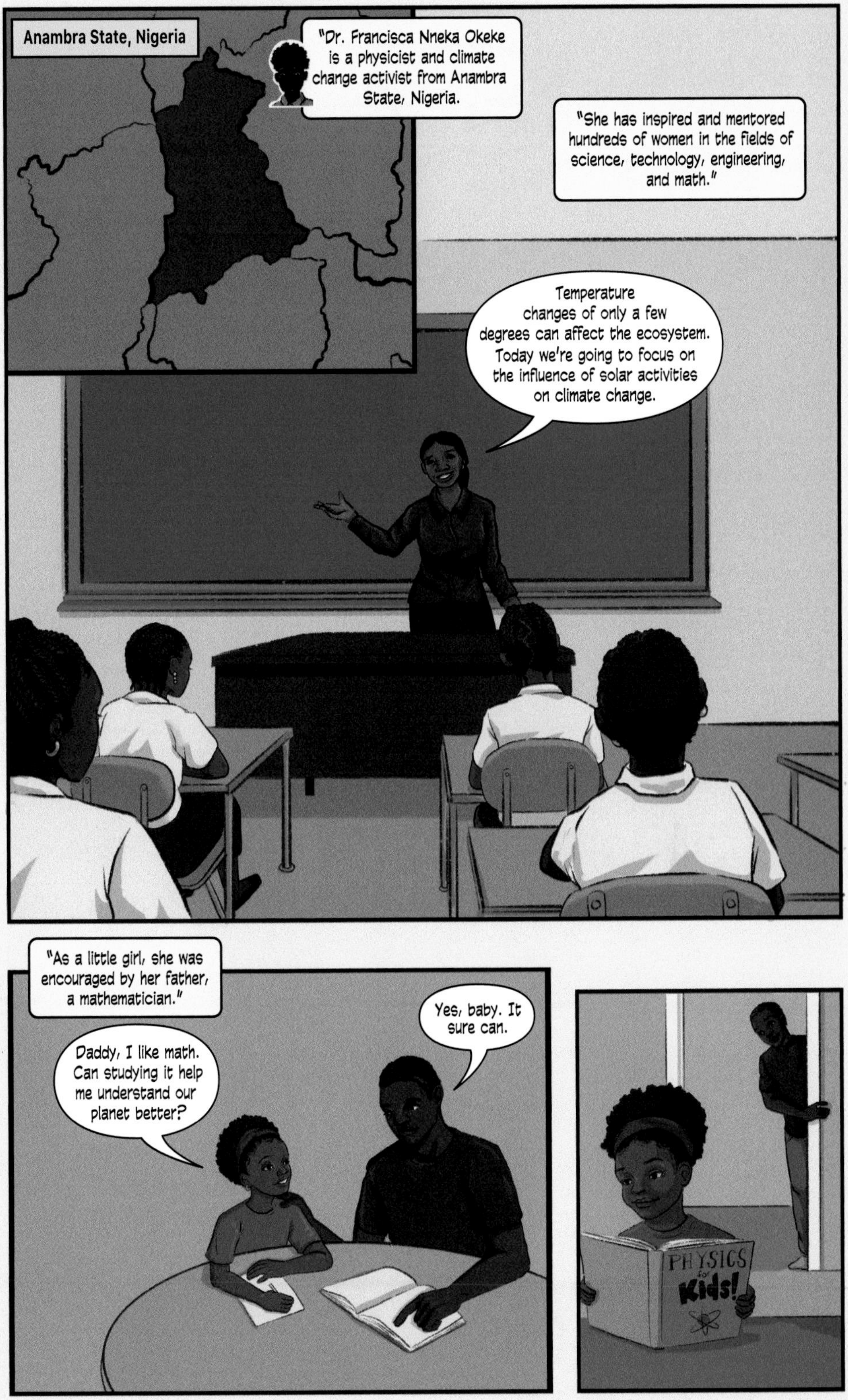
Anambra State, Nigeria
"Dr. Francisca Nneka Okeke is a physicist and climate change activist from Anambra State, Nigeria.
"She has inspired and mentored hundreds of women in the fields of science, technology, engineering, and math."
Temperature changes of only a few degrees can affect the ecosystem. Today we're going to focus on the influence of solar activities on climate change.
"As a little girl, she was encouraged by her father, a mathematician."
Daddy, I like math. Can studying it help me understand our planet better?
Yes, baby. It sure can.
PHYSICS for Kids!

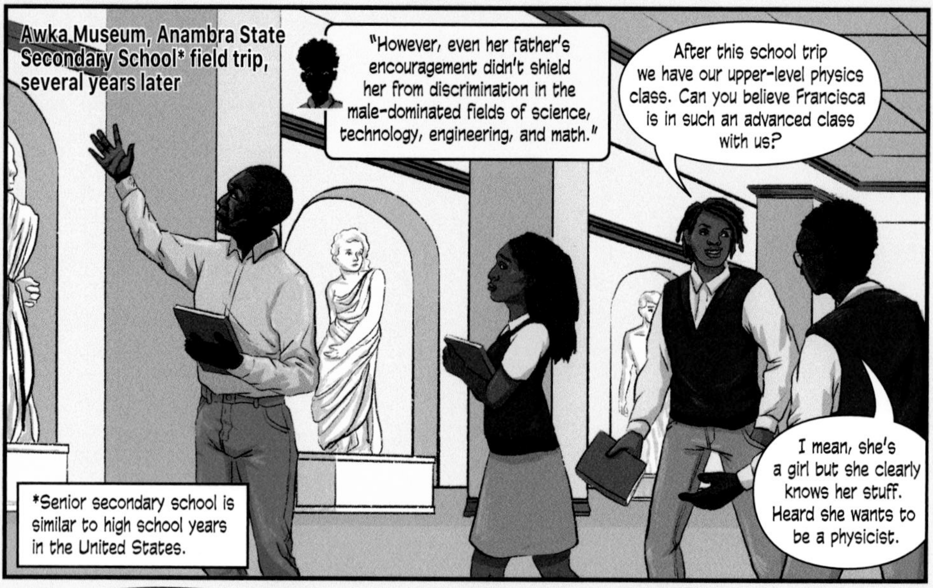
Awka Museum, Anambra State Secondary School* field trip, several years later
"However, even her father's encouragement didn't shield her from discrimination in the male-dominated fields of science, technology, engineering, and math."
After this school trip we have our upper-level physics class. Can you believe Francisca is in such an advanced class with us?
I mean, she's a girl but she clearly knows her stuff. Heard she wants to be a physicist.
*Senior secondary school is similar to high school years in the United States.

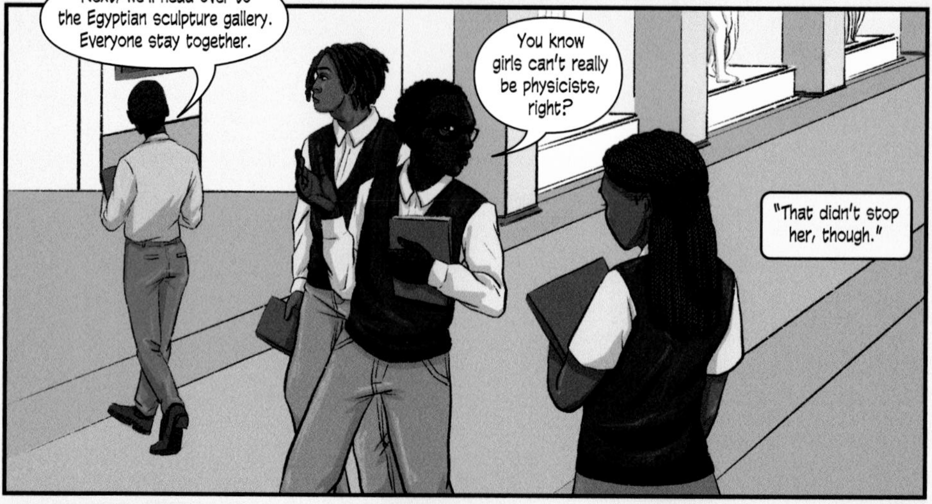
Next, we'll head over to the Egyptian sculpture gallery. Everyone stay together.
You know girls can't really be physicists, right?
"That didn't stop her, though."

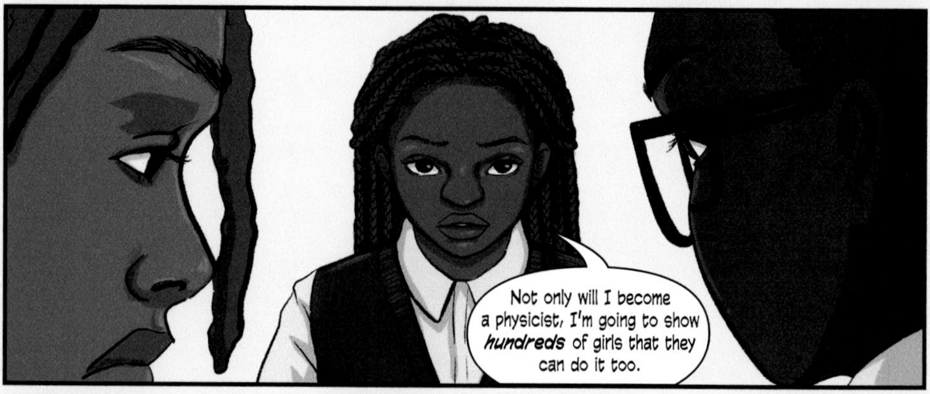
Not only will I become a physicist, I'm going to show *hundreds* of girls that they can do it too.

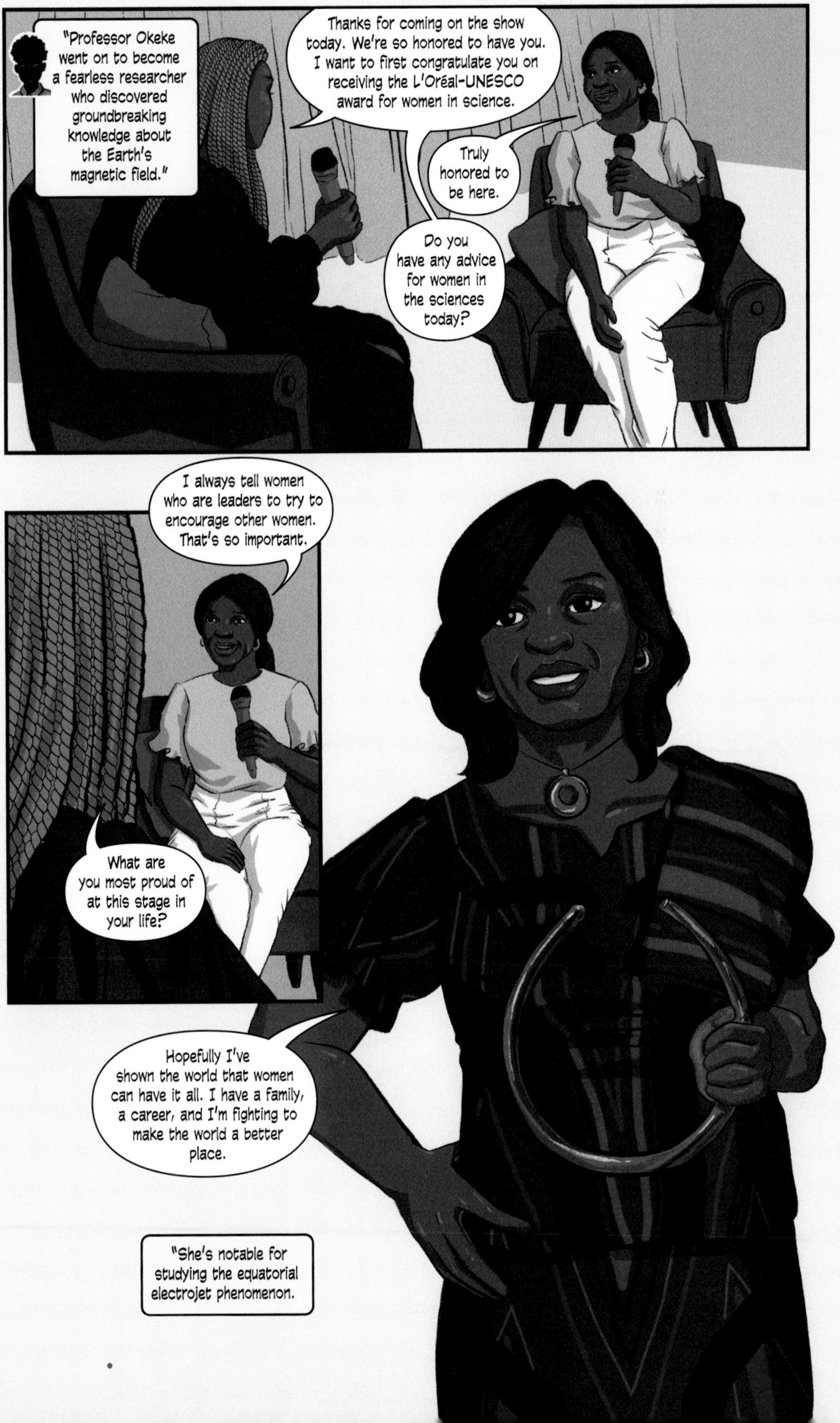
"Professor Okeke went on to become a fearless researcher who discovered groundbreaking knowledge about the Earth's magnetic field."
Thanks for coming on the show today. We're so honored to have you. I want to first congratulate you on receiving the L'Oréal-UNESCO award for women in science.
Truly honored to be here.
Do you have any advice for women in the sciences today?
I always tell women who are leaders to try to encourage other women. That's so important.
What are you most proud of at this stage in your life?
Hopefully I've shown the world that women can have it all. I have a family, a career, and I'm fighting to make the world a better place.
"She's notable for studying the equatorial electrojet phenomenon.

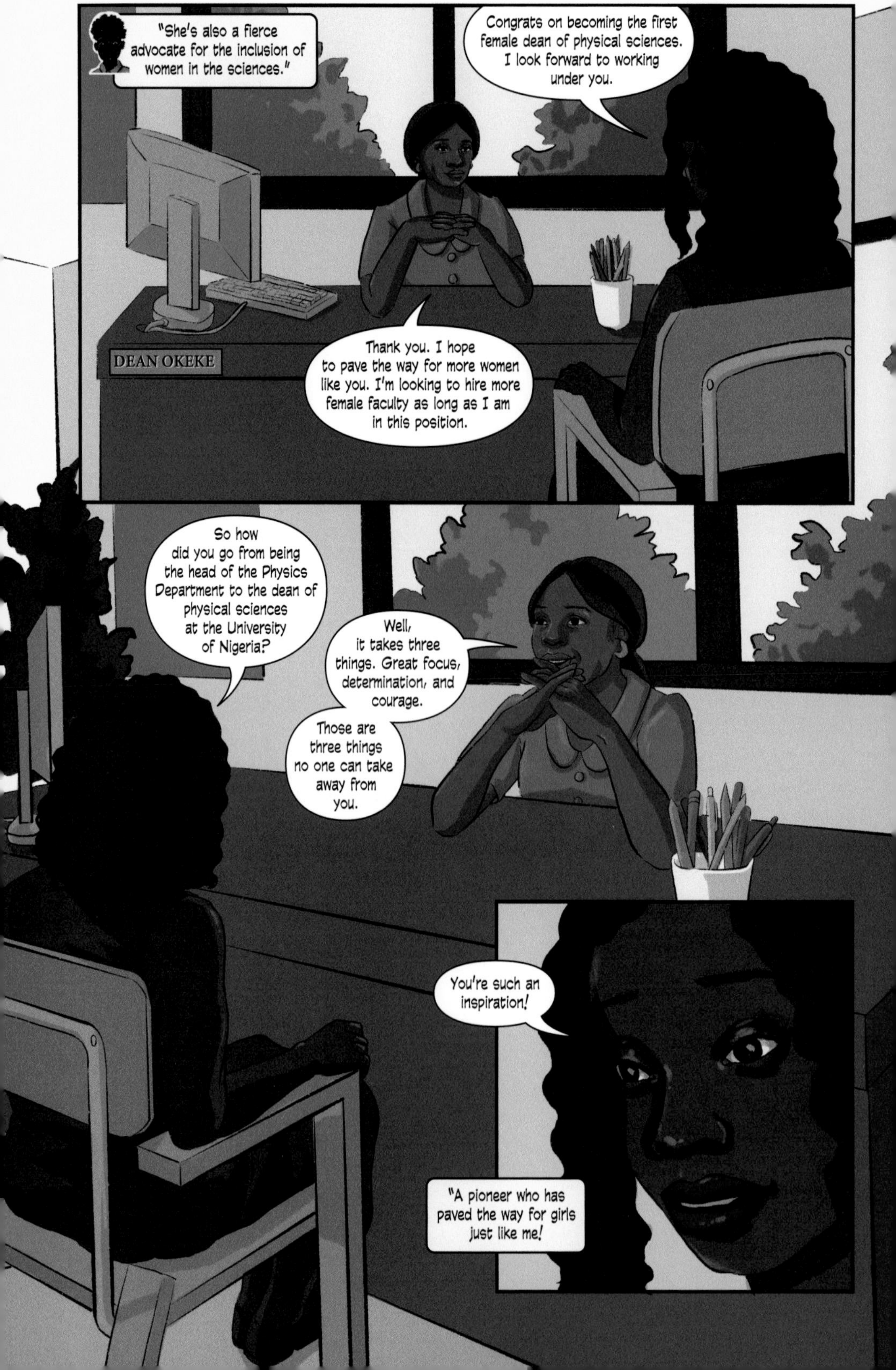
"She's also a fierce advocate for the inclusion of women in the sciences."
Congrats on becoming the first female dean of physical sciences. I look forward to working under you.
DEAN OKEKE
Thank you. I hope to pave the way for more women like you. I'm looking to hire more female faculty as long as I am in this position.
So how did you go from being the head of the Physics Department to the dean of physical sciences at the University of Nigeria?
Well, it takes three things. Great focus, determination, and courage.
Those are three things no one can take away from you.
You're such an inspiration!
"A pioneer who has paved the way for girls just like me!

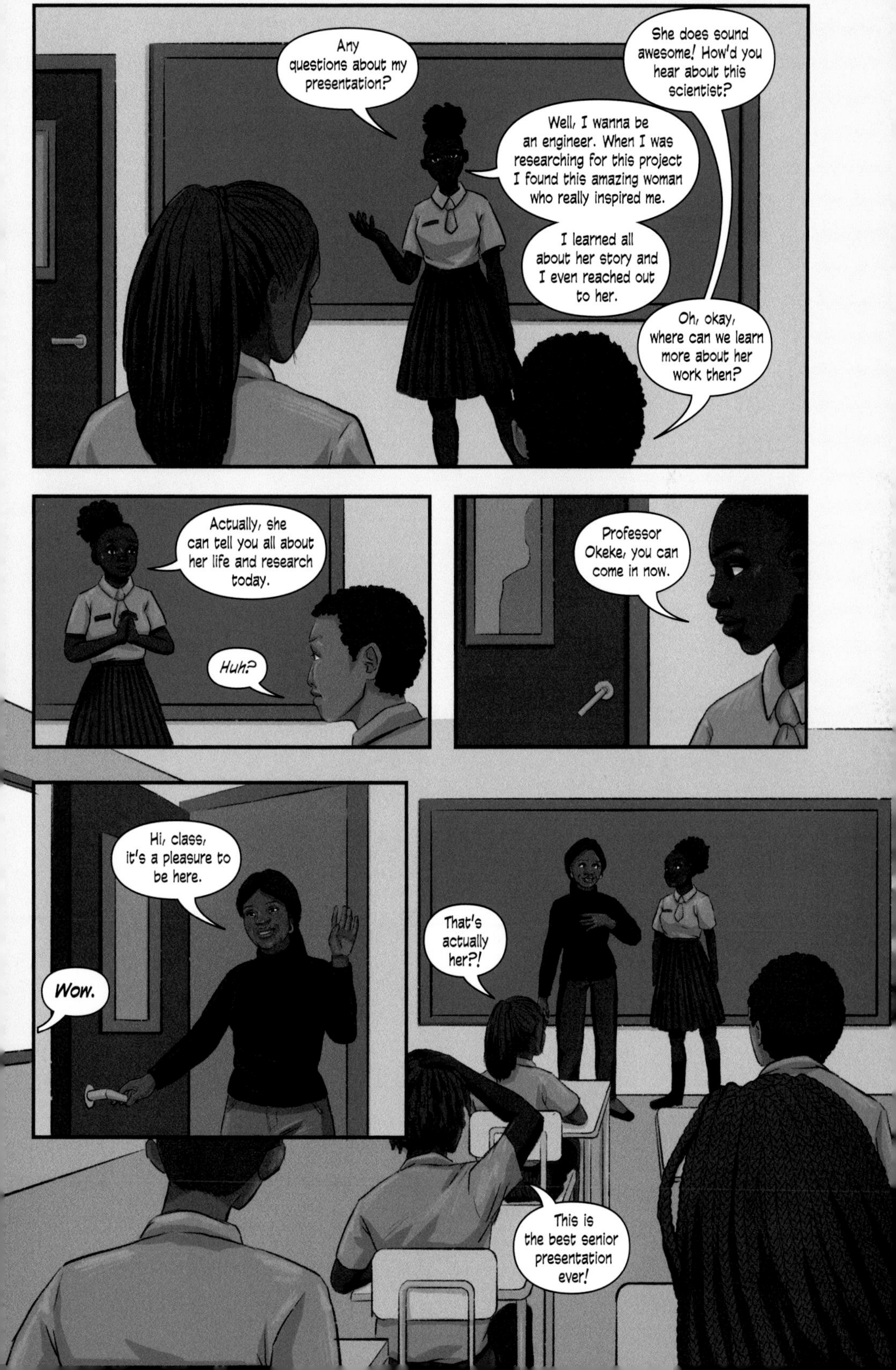
Any questions about my presentation?
She does sound awesome! How'd you hear about this scientist?
Well, I wanna be an engineer. When I was researching for this project I found this amazing woman who really inspired me.
I learned all about her story and I even reached out to her.
Oh, okay, where can we learn more about her work then?
Actually, she can tell you all about her life and research today.
Huh?
Professor Okeke, you can come in now.
Hi, class, it's a pleasure to be here.
Wow.
That's actually her?!
This is the best senior presentation ever!

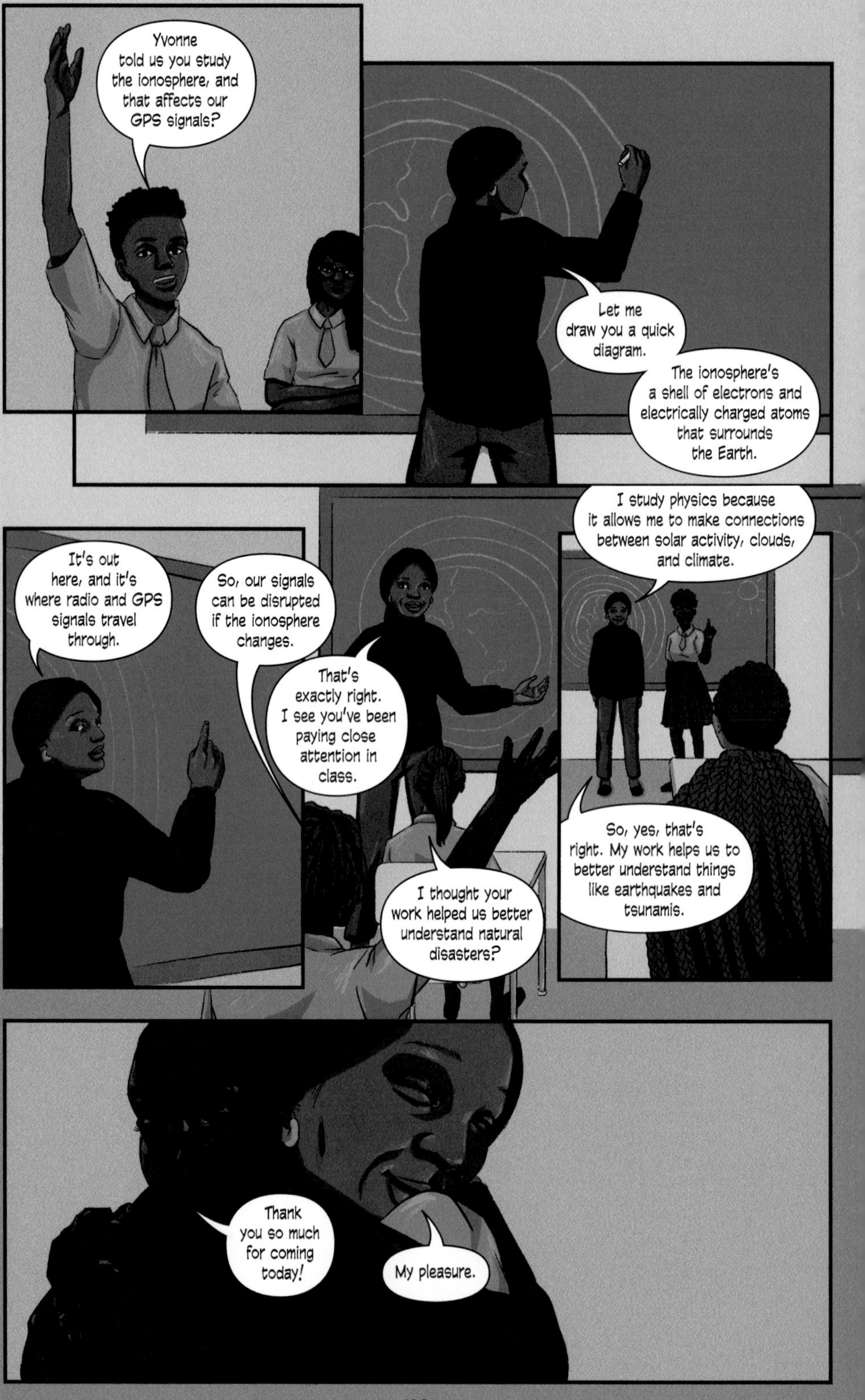
Yvonne told us you study the ionosphere, and that affects our GPS signals?
Let me draw you a quick diagram.
The ionosphere's a shell of electrons and electrically charged atoms that surrounds the Earth.
It's out here, and it's where radio and GPS signals travel through.
So, our signals can be disrupted if the ionosphere changes.
That's exactly right. I see you've been paying close attention in class.
I thought your work helped us better understand natural disasters?
I study physics because it allows me to make connections between solar activity, clouds, and climate.
So, yes, that's right. My work helps us to better understand things like earthquakes and tsunamis.
Thank you so much for coming today!
My pleasure.

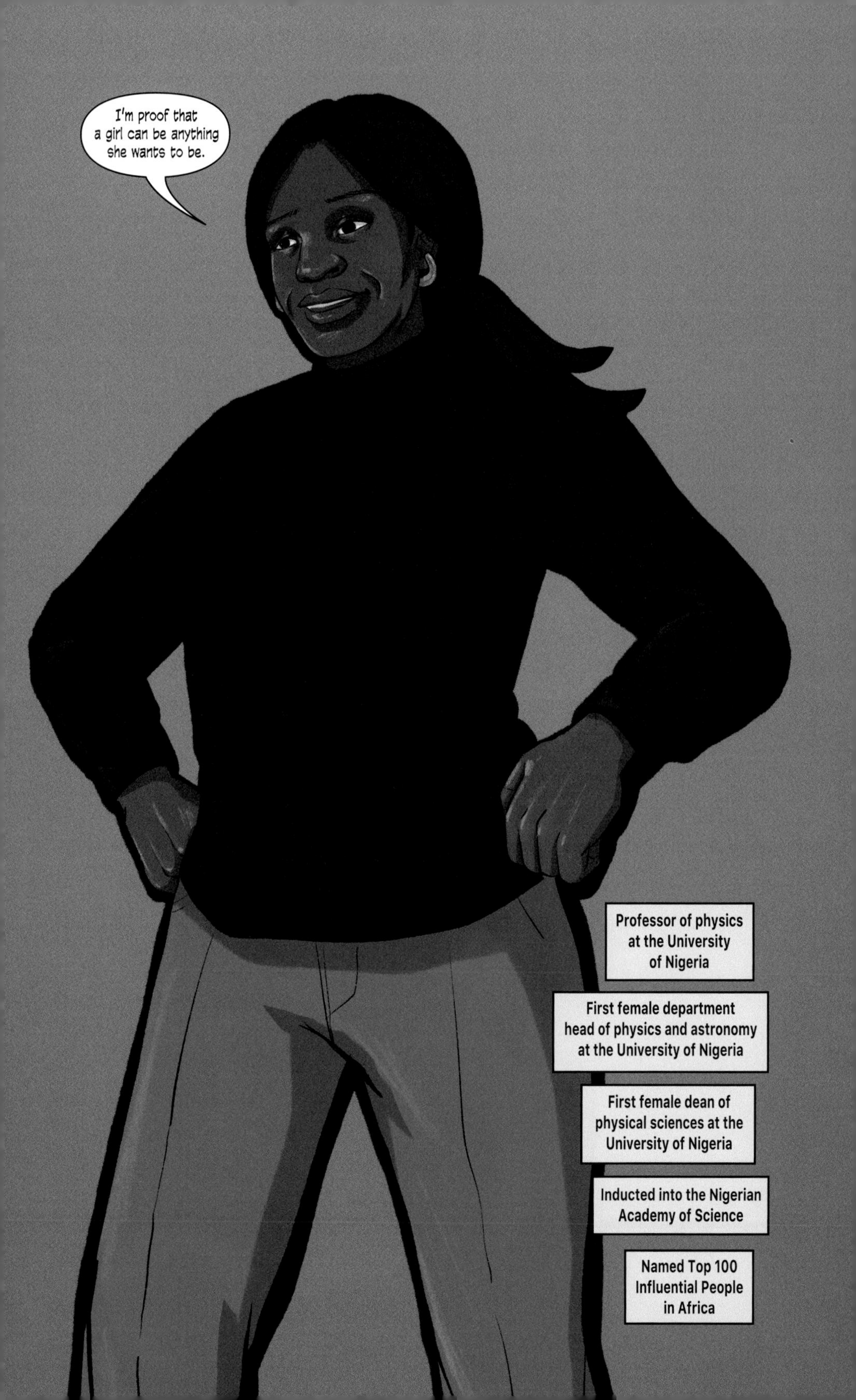
I'm proof that a girl can be anything she wants to be.
Professor of physics at the University of Nigeria
First female department head of physics and astronomy at the University of Nigeria
First female dean of physical sciences at the University of Nigeria
Inducted into the Nigerian Academy of Science
Named Top 100 Influential People in Africa

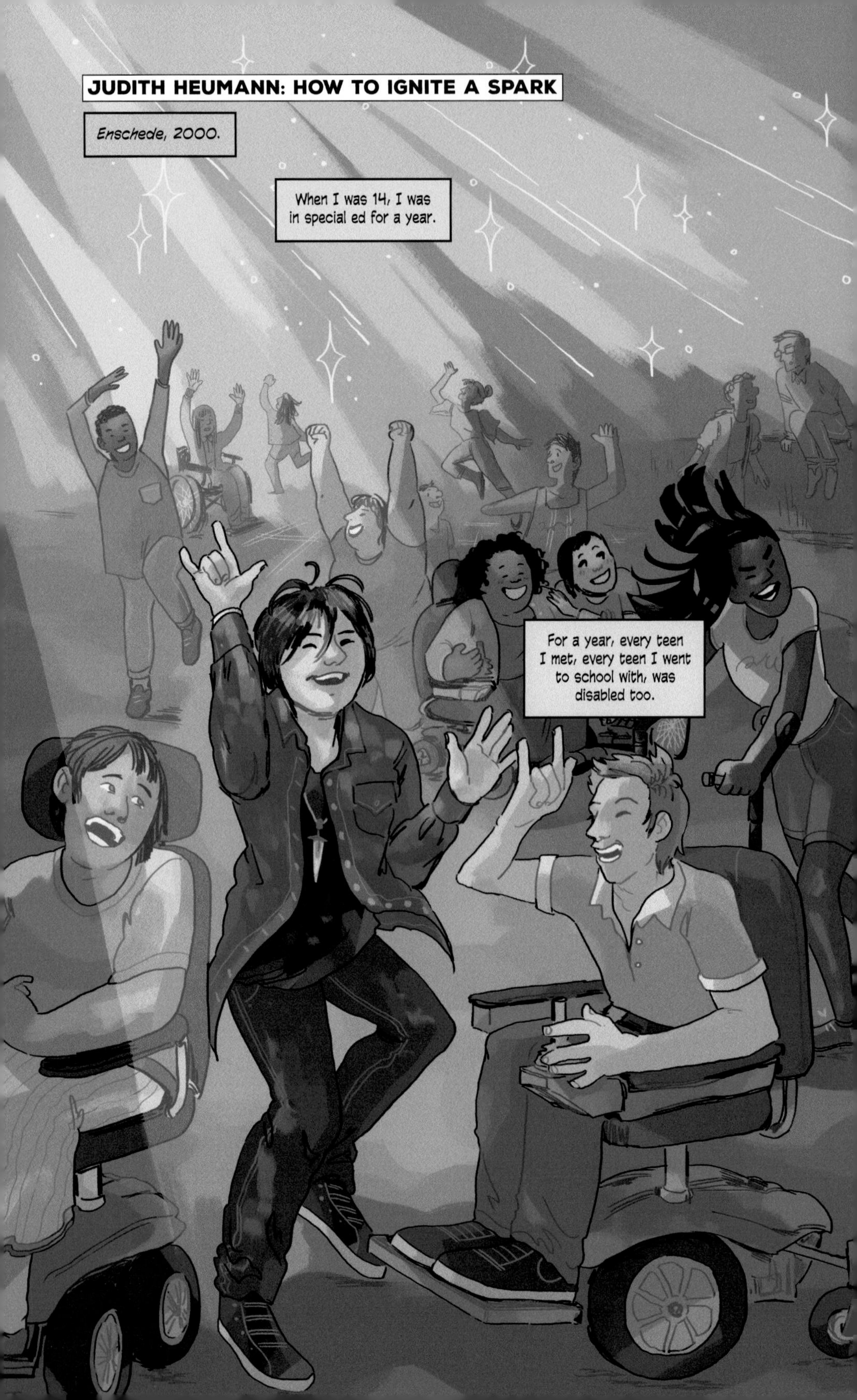
JUDITH HEUMANN: HOW TO IGNITE A SPARK
Enschede, 2000.
When I was 14, I was in special ed for a year.
For a year, every teen I met, every teen I went to school with, was disabled too.

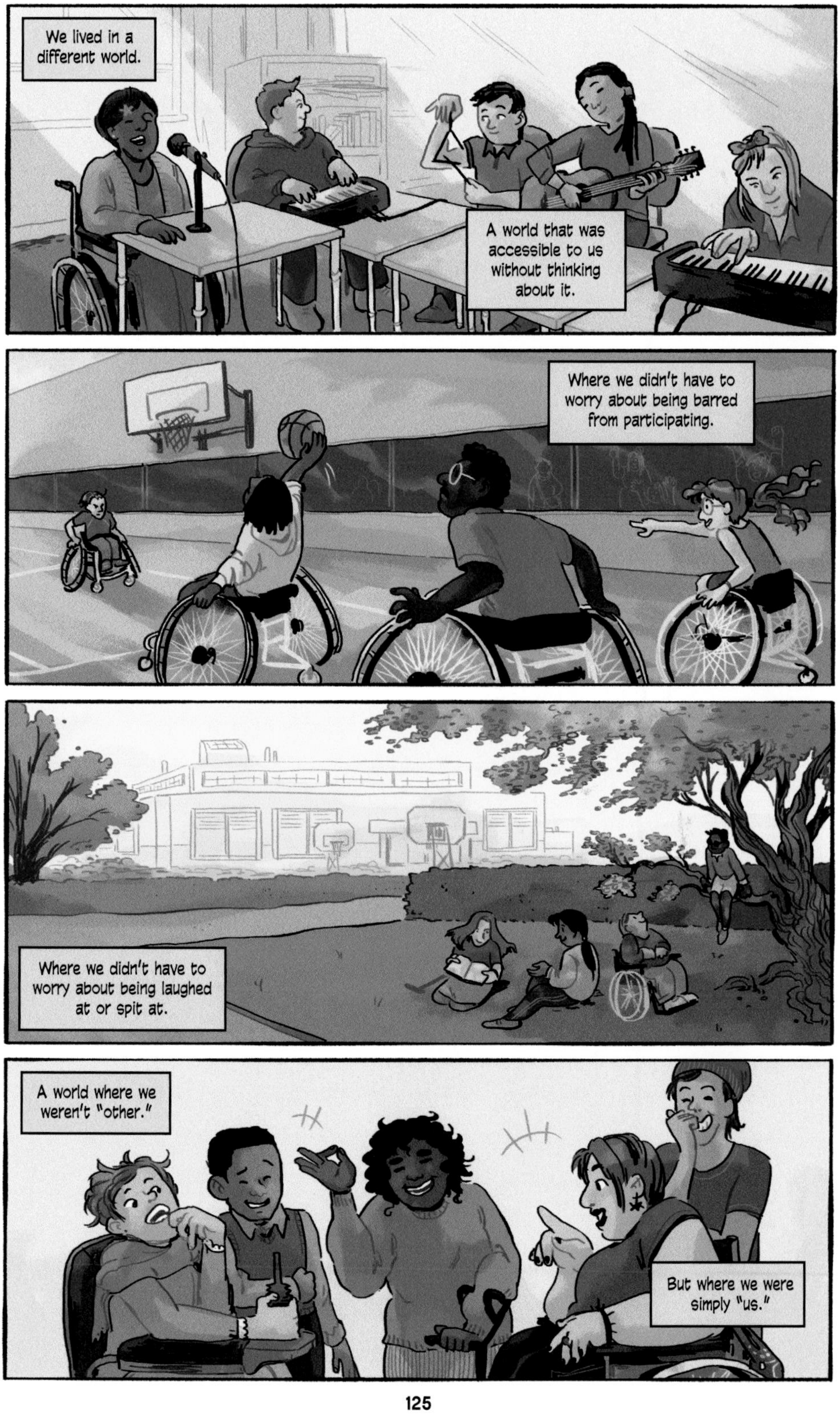
We lived in a different world.
A world that was accessible to us without thinking about it.
Where we didn't have to worry about being barred from participating.
Where we didn't have to worry about being laughed at or spit at.
A world where we weren't "other."
But where we were simply "us."

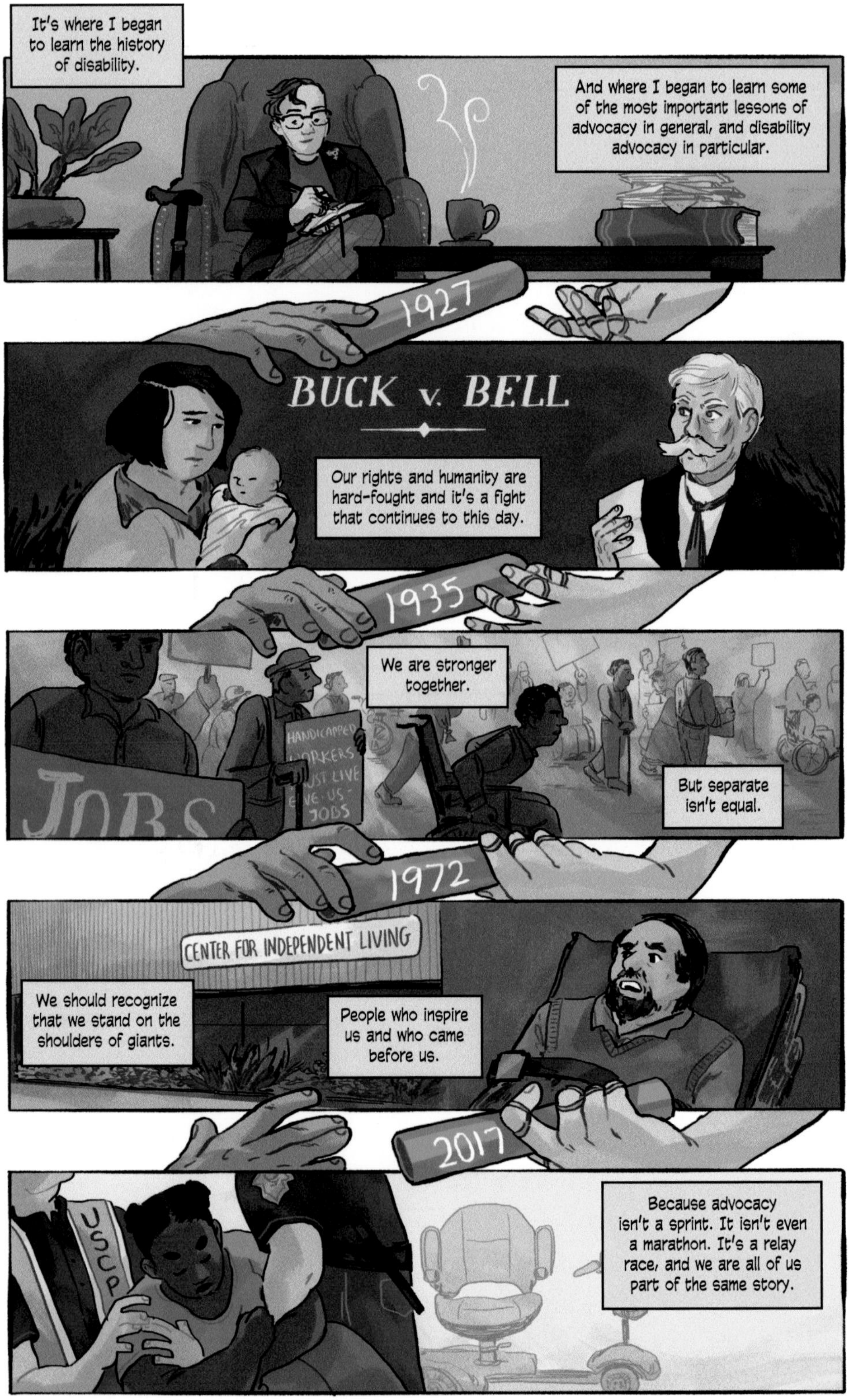

It's where I began to learn the history of disability.
And where I began to learn some of the most important lessons of advocacy in general, and disability advocacy in particular.
1927
BUCK v. BELL
Our rights and humanity are hard-fought and it's a fight that continues to this day.
1935
We are stronger together.
JOBS
HANDICAPPED WORKERS MUST LIVE GIVE US JOBS
But separate isn't equal.
1972
CENTER FOR INDEPENDENT LIVING
We should recognize that we stand on the shoulders of giants.
People who inspire us and who came before us.
2017
USCP
Because advocacy isn't a sprint. It isn't even a marathon. It's a relay race, and we are all of us part of the same story.

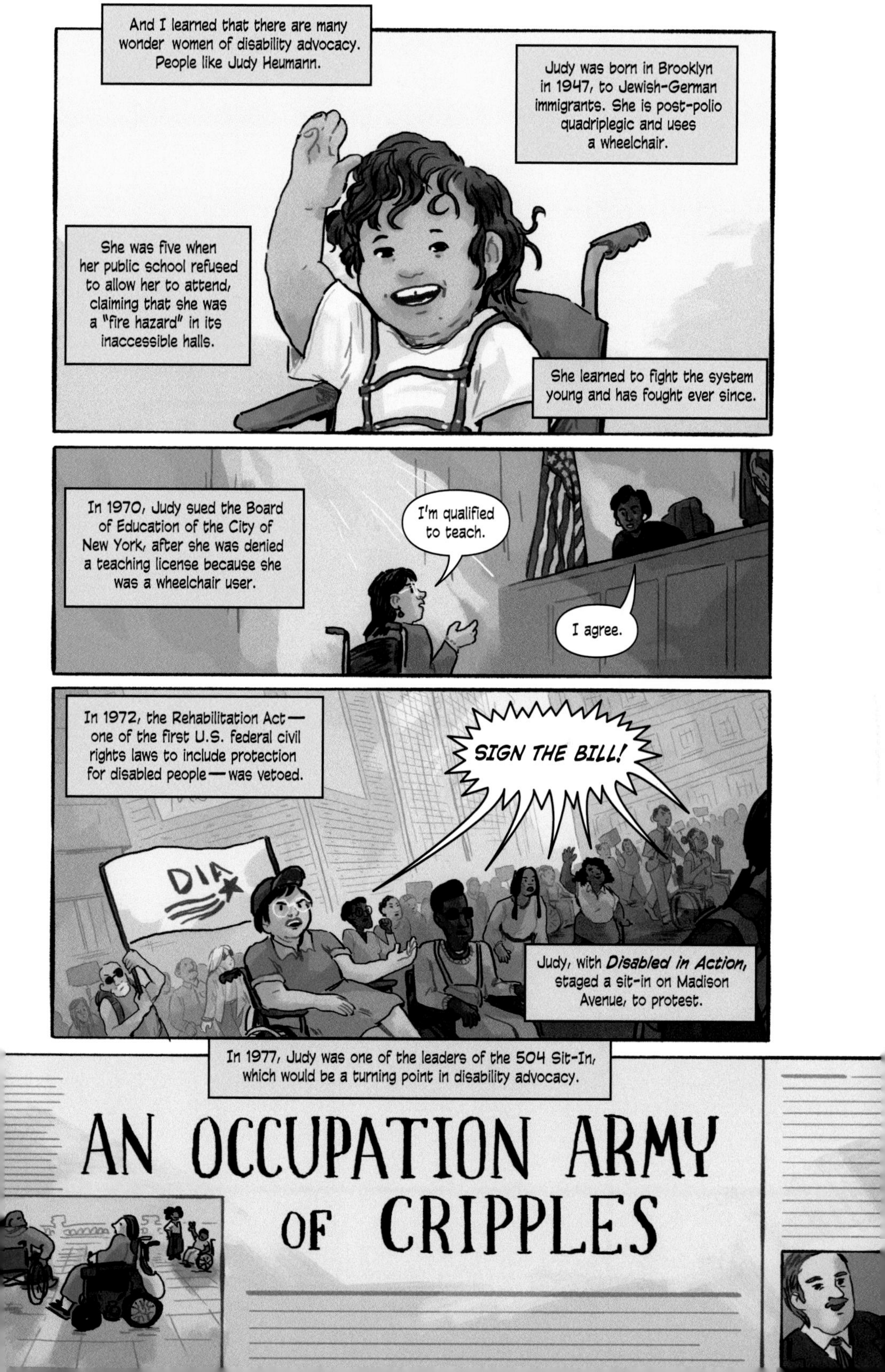
And I learned that there are many wonder women of disability advocacy. People like Judy Heumann.
Judy was born in Brooklyn in 1947, to Jewish-German immigrants. She is post-polio quadriplegic and uses a wheelchair.
She was five when her public school refused to allow her to attend, claiming that she was a "fire hazard" in its inaccessible halls.
She learned to fight the system young and has fought ever since.
In 1970, Judy sued the Board of Education of the City of New York, after she was denied a teaching license because she was a wheelchair user.
I'm qualified to teach.
I agree.
In 1972, the Rehabilitation Act—one of the first U.S. federal civil rights laws to include protection for disabled people—was vetoed.
SIGN THE BILL!
DIA
Judy, with *Disabled in Action*, staged a sit-in on Madison Avenue, to protest.
In 1977, Judy was one of the leaders of the 504 Sit-In, which would be a turning point in disability advocacy.
AN OCCUPATION ARMY OF CRIPPLES

Section 504

The Rehabilitation Act was signed into law in 1973.

No otherwise qualified individual with a disability in the United States (...) shall, solely by reason of his or her disability, be excluded from the participation in, be denied the benefits of, or be subjected to discrimination under any program or activity receiving Federal financial assistance or under any program or activity conducted by any Executive agency or by the United States Postal Service.

And it included Section 504, a major step toward civil rights for disabled people.

But in order for the law to be effective, it required definitions and regulations.

Regulations
"What is disability?"
"What is discrimination?"

To be issued by the Department of Health, Education, and Welfare, or HEW.

But for four years after the signing of the Rehabilitation Act, HEW made no move to act on it.

The Office for Civil Rights drafted regulations, but the HEW Secretary stalled, hesitated, and tried to weaken them.

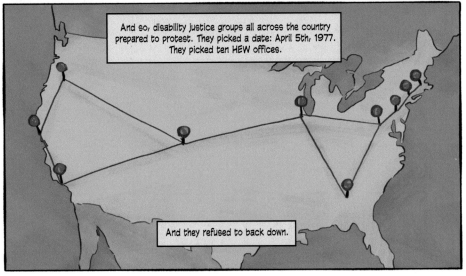

And so, disability justice groups all across the country prepared to protest. They picked a date: April 5th, 1977. They picked ten HEW offices.

And they refused to back down.

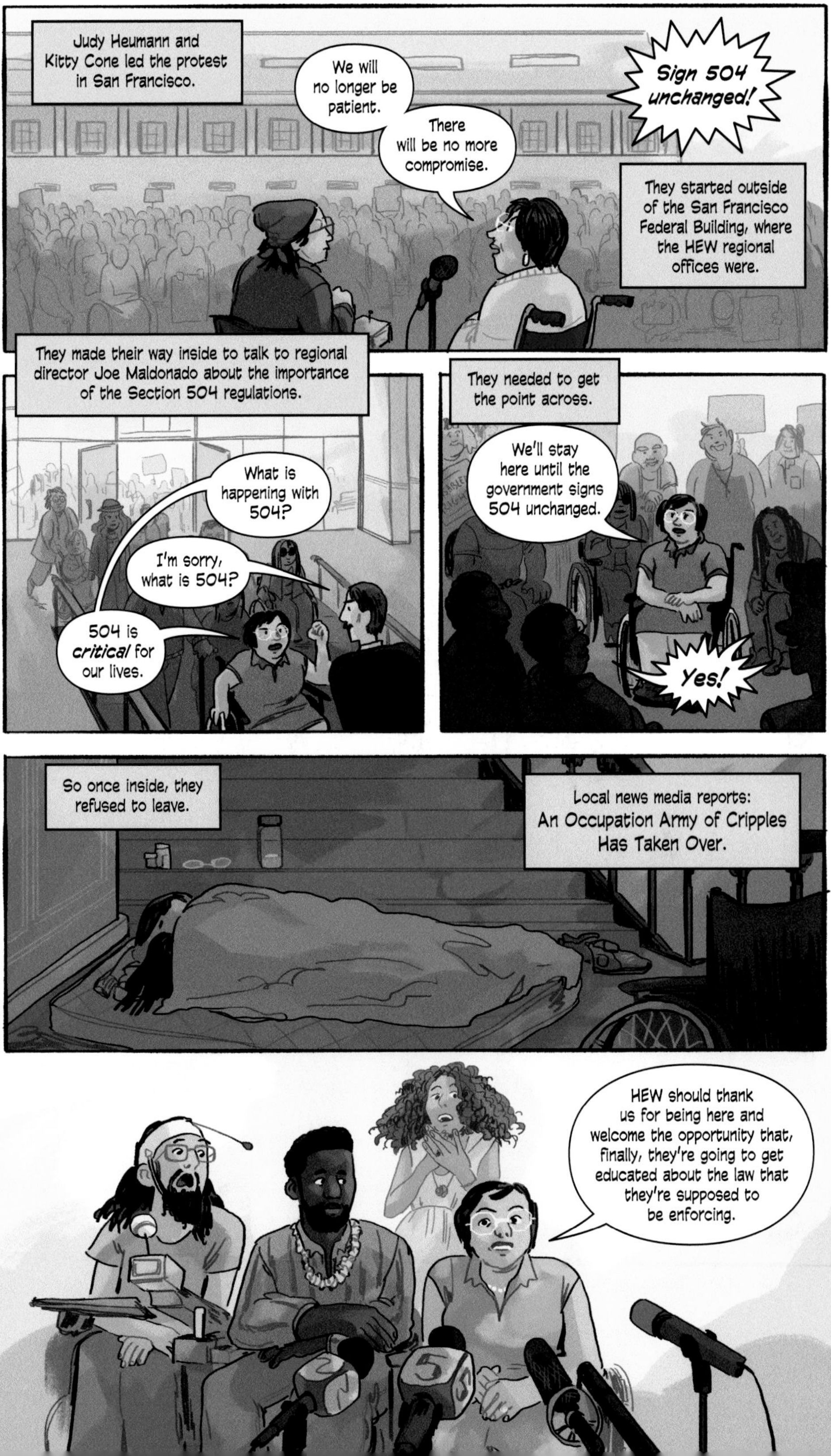
Judy Heumann and Kitty Cone led the protest in San Francisco.
We will no longer be patient.
There will be no more compromise.
Sign 504 unchanged!
They started outside of the San Francisco Federal Building, where the HEW regional offices were.
They made their way inside to talk to regional director Joe Maldonado about the importance of the Section 504 regulations.
What is happening with 504?
I'm sorry, what is 504?
504 is *critical* for our lives.
They needed to get the point across.
We'll stay here until the government signs 504 unchanged.
Yes!
So once inside, they refused to leave.
Local news media reports: An Occupation Army of Cripples Has Taken Over.
HEW should thank us for being here and welcome the opportunity that, finally, they're going to get educated about the law that they're supposed to be enforcing.

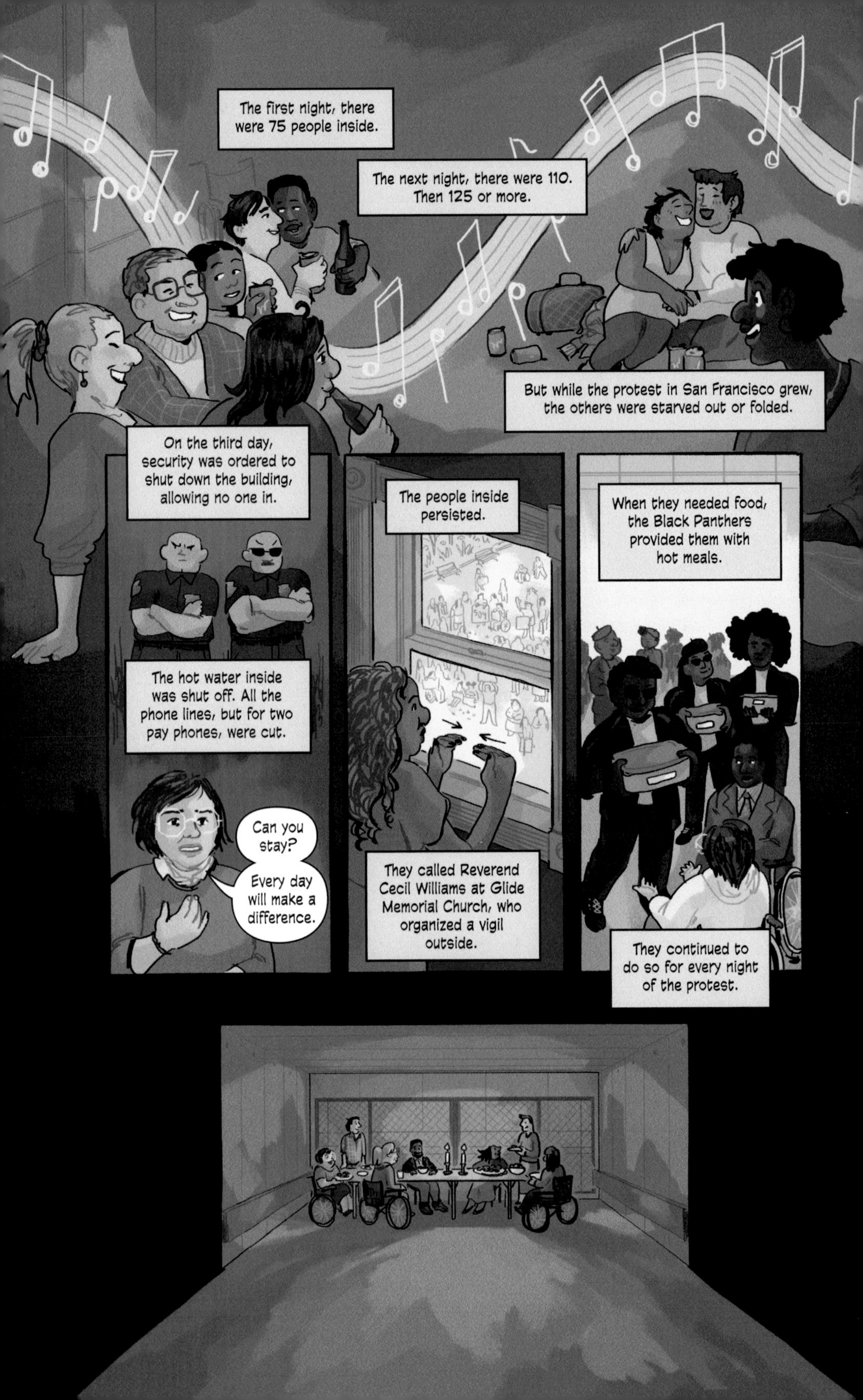
The first night, there were 75 people inside.
The next night, there were 110. Then 125 or more.
But while the protest in San Francisco grew, the others were starved out or folded.
On the third day, security was ordered to shut down the building, allowing no one in.
The hot water inside was shut off. All the phone lines, but for two pay phones, were cut.
Can you stay?
Every day will make a difference.
The people inside persisted.
504
They called Reverend Cecil Williams at Glide Memorial Church, who organized a vigil outside.
When they needed food, the Black Panthers provided them with hot meals.
They continued to do so for every night of the protest.

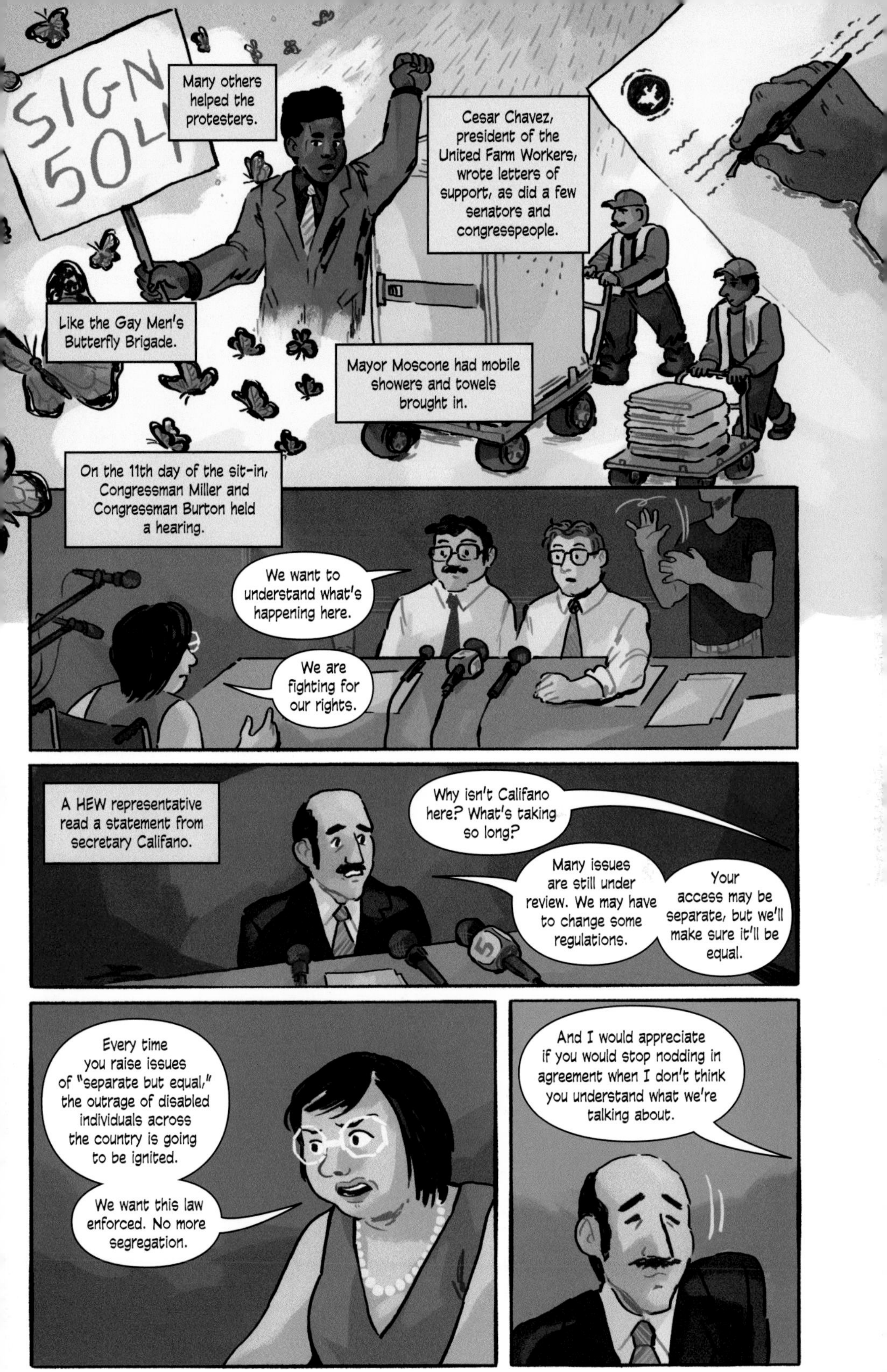
SIGN 504
Many others helped the protesters.
Cesar Chavez, president of the United Farm Workers, wrote letters of support, as did a few senators and congresspeople.
Like the Gay Men's Butterfly Brigade.
Mayor Moscone had mobile showers and towels brought in.
On the 11th day of the sit-in, Congressman Miller and Congressman Burton held a hearing.
We want to understand what's happening here.
We are fighting for our rights.
A HEW representative read a statement from secretary Califano.
Why isn't Califano here? What's taking so long?
Many issues are still under review. We may have to change some regulations.
Your access may be separate, but we'll make sure it'll be equal.
Every time you raise issues of "separate but equal," the outrage of disabled individuals across the country is going to be ignited.
We want this law enforced. No more segregation.
And I would appreciate if you would stop nodding in agreement when I don't think you understand what we're talking about.

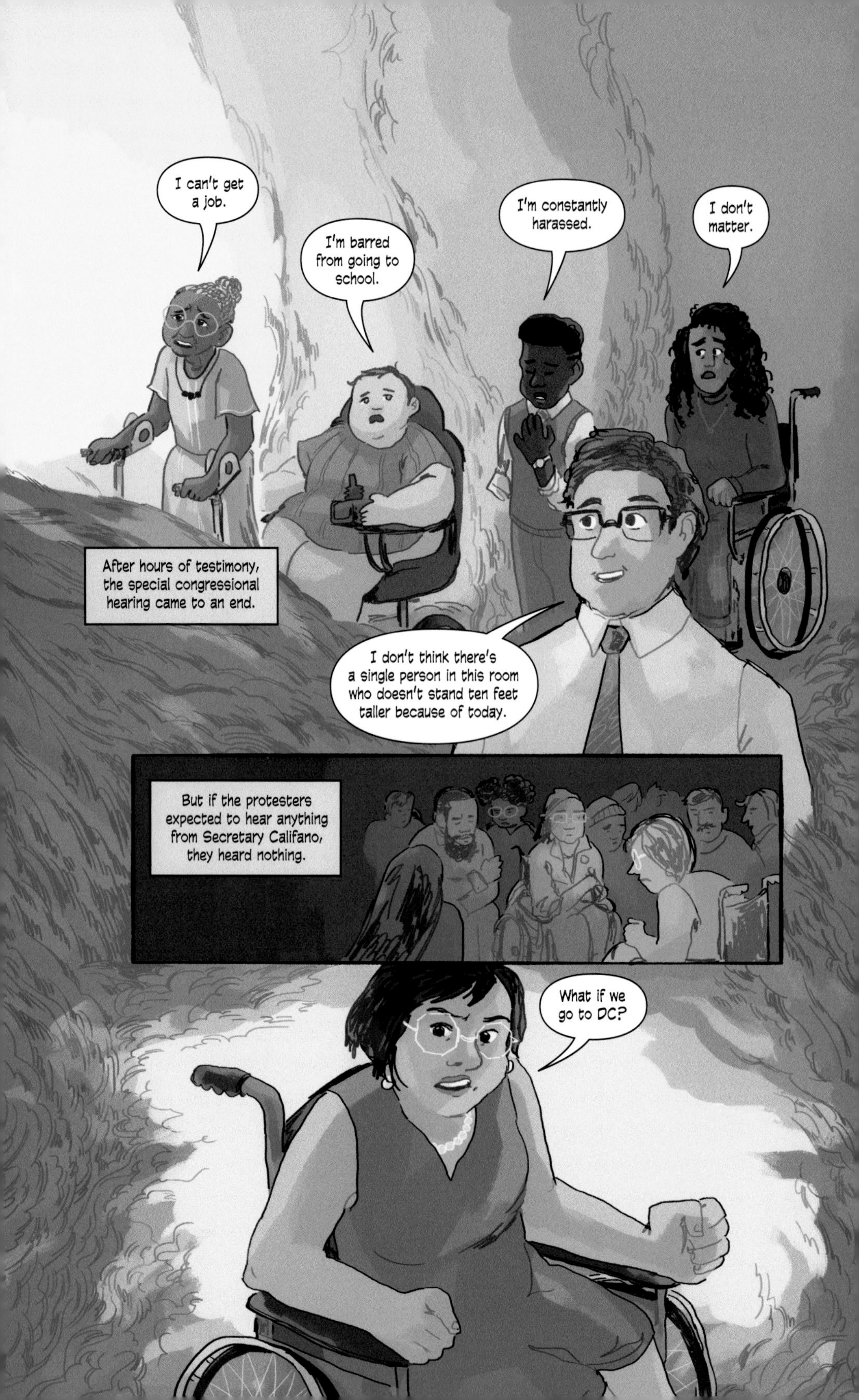
I can't get a job.
I'm barred from going to school.
I'm constantly harassed.
I don't matter.
After hours of testimony, the special congressional hearing came to an end.
I don't think there's a single person in this room who doesn't stand ten feet taller because of today.
But if the protesters expected to hear anything from Secretary Califano, they heard nothing.
What if we go to DC?

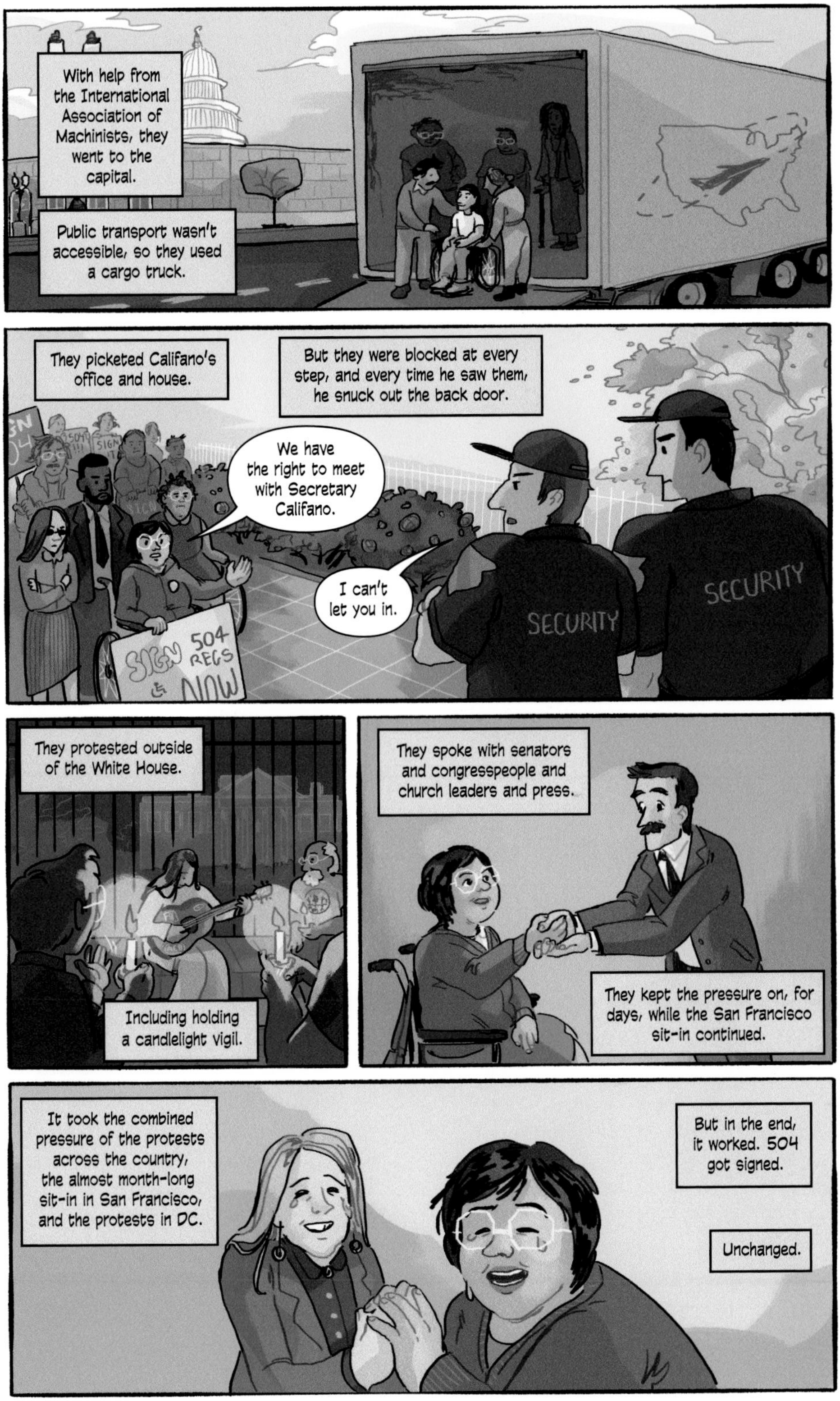

With help from the International Association of Machinists, they went to the capital.
Public transport wasn't accessible, so they used a cargo truck.
They picketed Califano's office and house.
But they were blocked at every step, and every time he saw them, he snuck out the back door.
We have the right to meet with Secretary Califano.
I can't let you in.
SIGN 504 REGS NOW
SECURITY
SECURITY
They protested outside of the White House.
Including holding a candlelight vigil.
They spoke with senators and congresspeople and church leaders and press.
They kept the pressure on, for days, while the San Francisco sit-in continued.
It took the combined pressure of the protests across the country, the almost month-long sit-in in San Francisco, and the protests in DC.
But in the end, it worked. 504 got signed.
Unchanged.

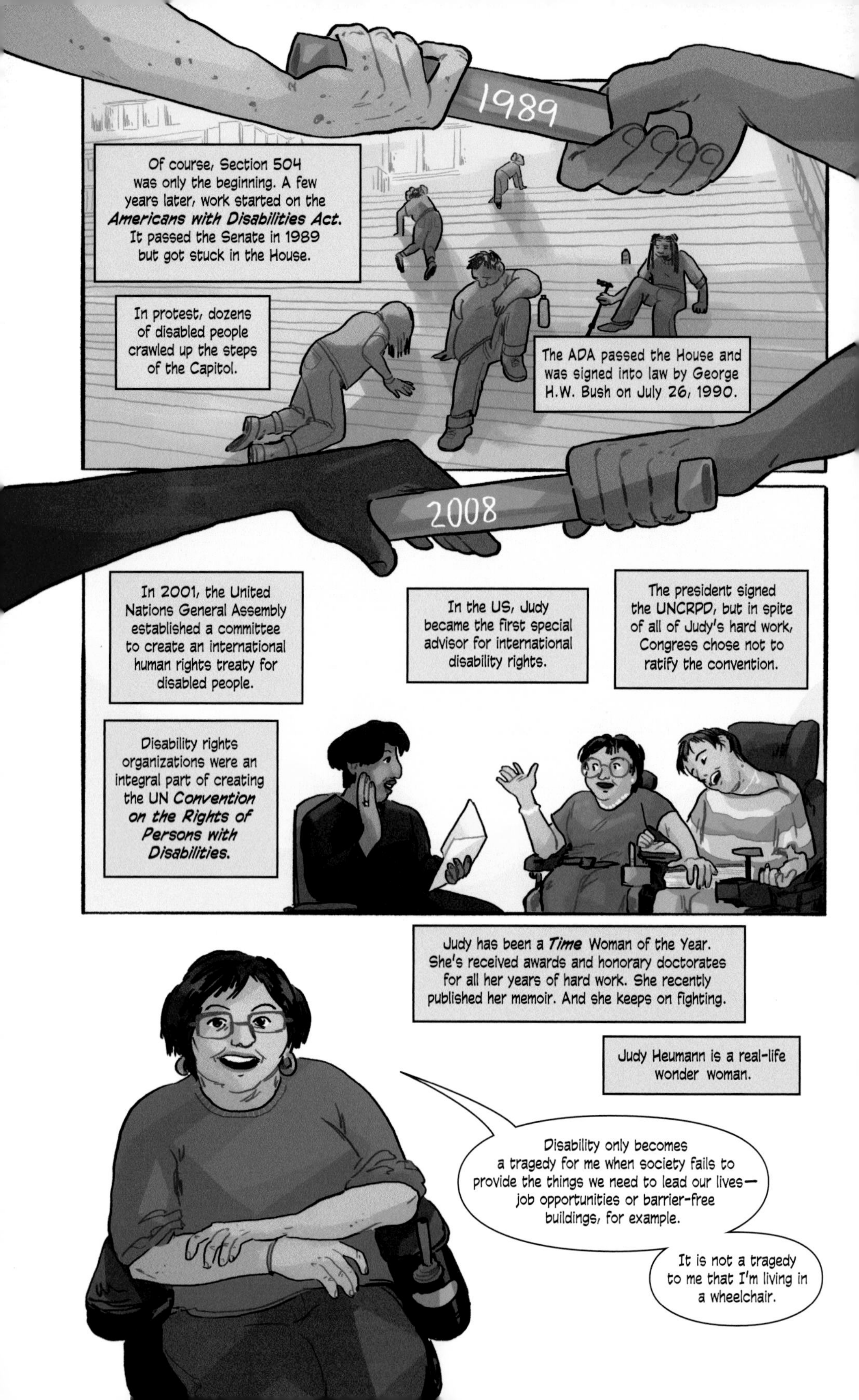
1989
Of course, Section 504 was only the beginning. A few years later, work started on the *Americans with Disabilities Act*. It passed the Senate in 1989 but got stuck in the House.
In protest, dozens of disabled people crawled up the steps of the Capitol.
The ADA passed the House and was signed into law by George H.W. Bush on July 26, 1990.
2008
In 2001, the United Nations General Assembly established a committee to create an international human rights treaty for disabled people.
In the US, Judy became the first special advisor for international disability rights.
The president signed the UNCRPD, but in spite of all of Judy's hard work, Congress chose not to ratify the convention.
Disability rights organizations were an integral part of creating the UN *Convention on the Rights of Persons with Disabilities*.
Judy has been a *Time* Woman of the Year. She's received awards and honorary doctorates for all her years of hard work. She recently published her memoir. And she keeps on fighting.
Judy Heumann is a real-life wonder woman.
Disability only becomes a tragedy for me when society fails to provide the things we need to lead our lives—job opportunities or barrier-free buildings, for example.
It is not a tragedy to me that I'm living in a wheelchair.

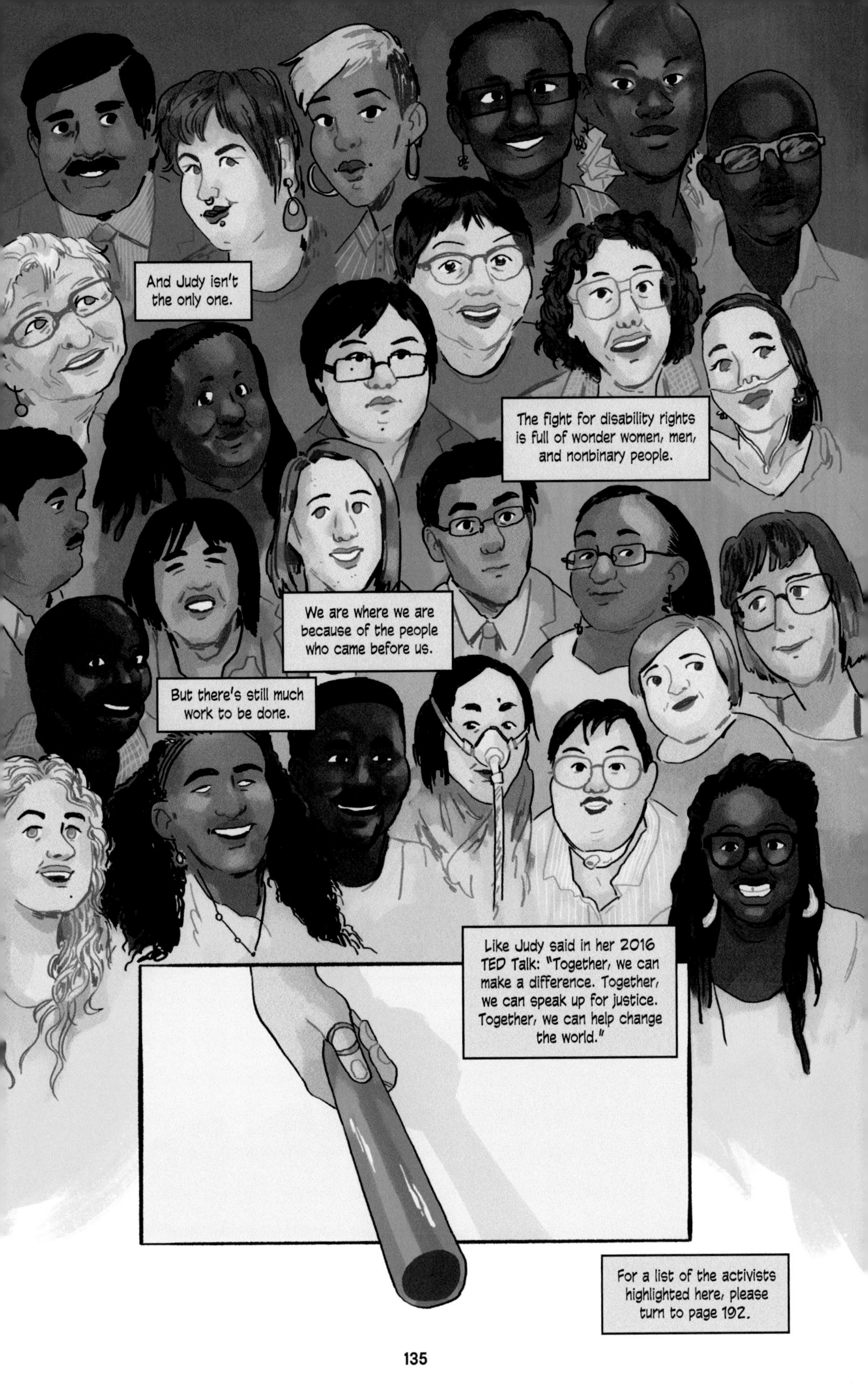

And Judy isn't the only one.
The fight for disability rights is full of wonder women, men, and nonbinary people.
We are where we are because of the people who came before us.
But there's still much work to be done.
Like Judy said in her 2016 TED Talk: "Together, we can make a difference. Together, we can speak up for justice. Together, we can help change the world."
For a list of the activists highlighted here, please turn to page 192.

MÁRCIA BARBOSA: WATER IS WEIRD

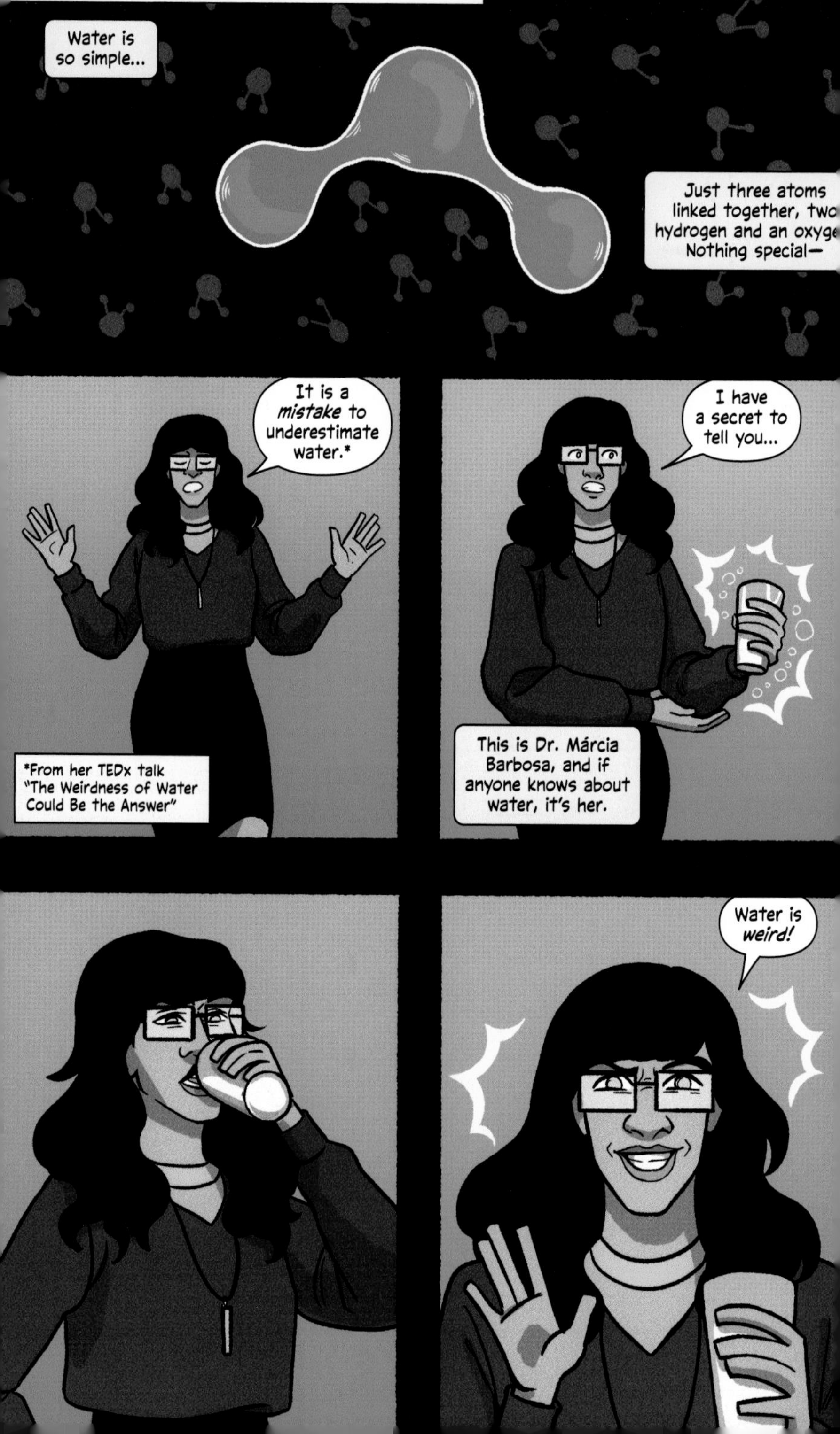

Water is so simple...
Just three atoms linked together, two hydrogen and an oxyge Nothing special—
It is a *mistake* to underestimate water.*
*From her TEDx talk "The Weirdness of Water Could Be the Answer"
I have a secret to tell you...
This is Dr. Márcia Barbosa, and if anyone knows about water, it's her.
Water is *weird!*

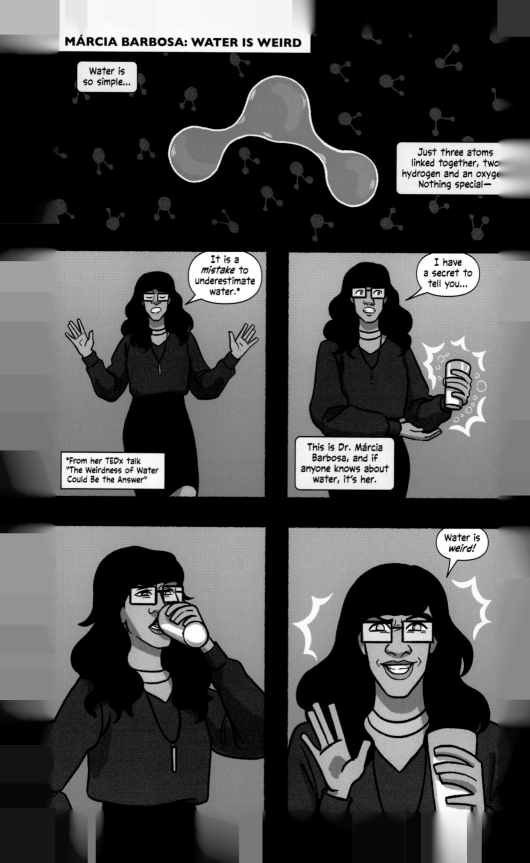

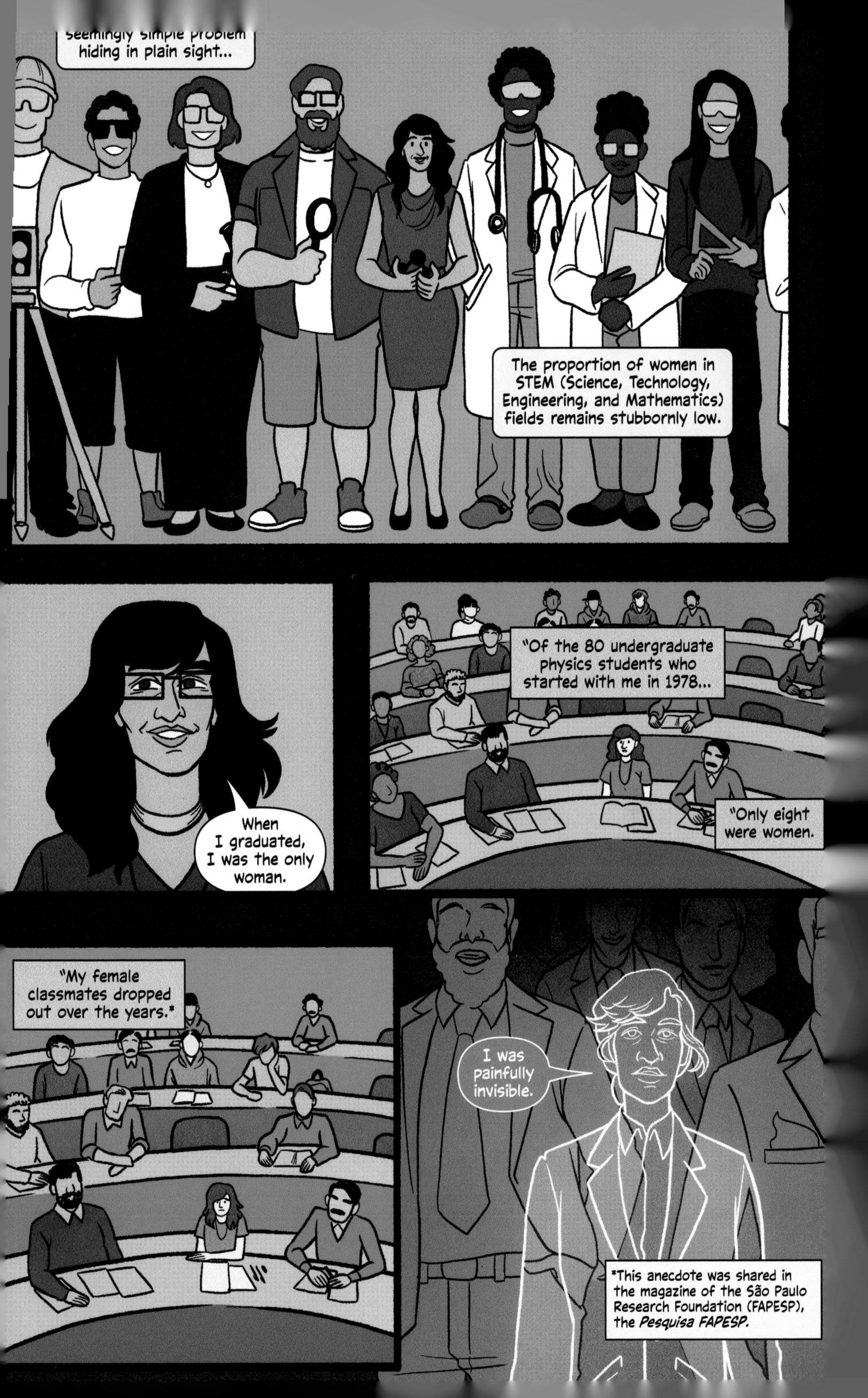
seemingly simple problem hiding in plain sight...
The proportion of women in STEM (Science, Technology, Engineering, and Mathematics) fields remains stubbornly low.
When I graduated, I was the only woman.
"Of the 80 undergraduate physics students who started with me in 1978...
"Only eight were women.
"My female classmates dropped out over the years.*
I was painfully invisible.
*This anecdote was shared in the magazine of the São Paulo Research Foundation (FAPESP), the *Pesquisa FAPESP*.

70% of the cover of the planet is water.

But less than 1% is drinkable.

The need for more fresh water and the need for more women in STEM might not seem related...

By 2050, one out of every two people will lack fresh water.

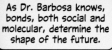

But don't panic!

We can use the weirdness of water to get more fresh water.

In much the same way, we can use the solidarity of women to ensure more women end up in STEM fields.

As Dr. Barbosa knows, bonds, both social and molecular, determine the shape of the future.

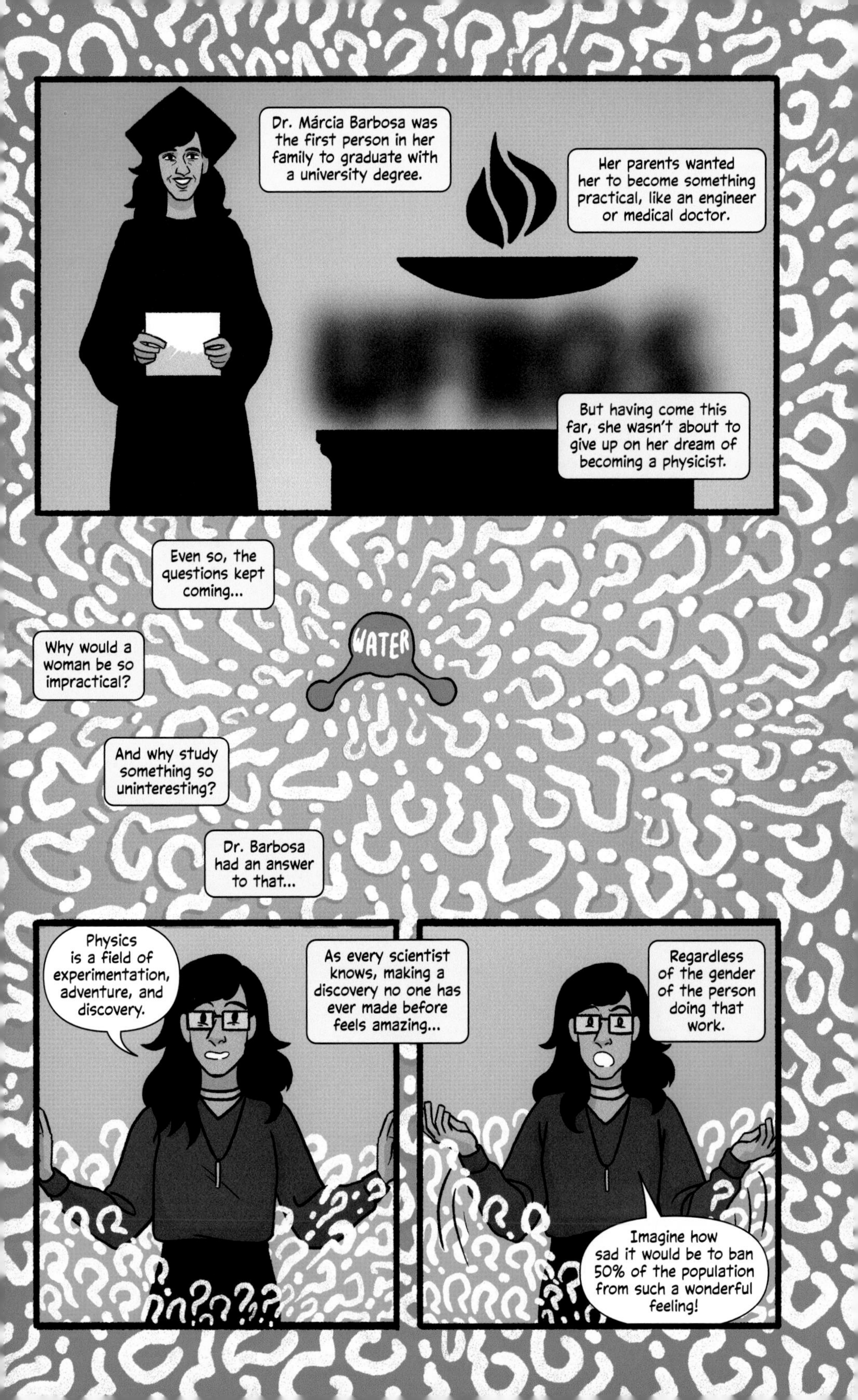
Dr. Márcia Barbosa was the first person in her family to graduate with a university degree.
Her parents wanted her to become something practical, like an engineer or medical doctor.
But having come this far, she wasn't about to give up on her dream of becoming a physicist.
Even so, the questions kept coming...
WATER
Why would a woman be so impractical?
And why study something so uninteresting?
Dr. Barbosa had an answer to that...
Physics is a field of experimentation, adventure, and discovery.
As every scientist knows, making a discovery no one has ever made before feels amazing...
Regardless of the gender of the person doing that work.
Imagine how sad it would be to ban 50% of the population from such a wonderful feeling!

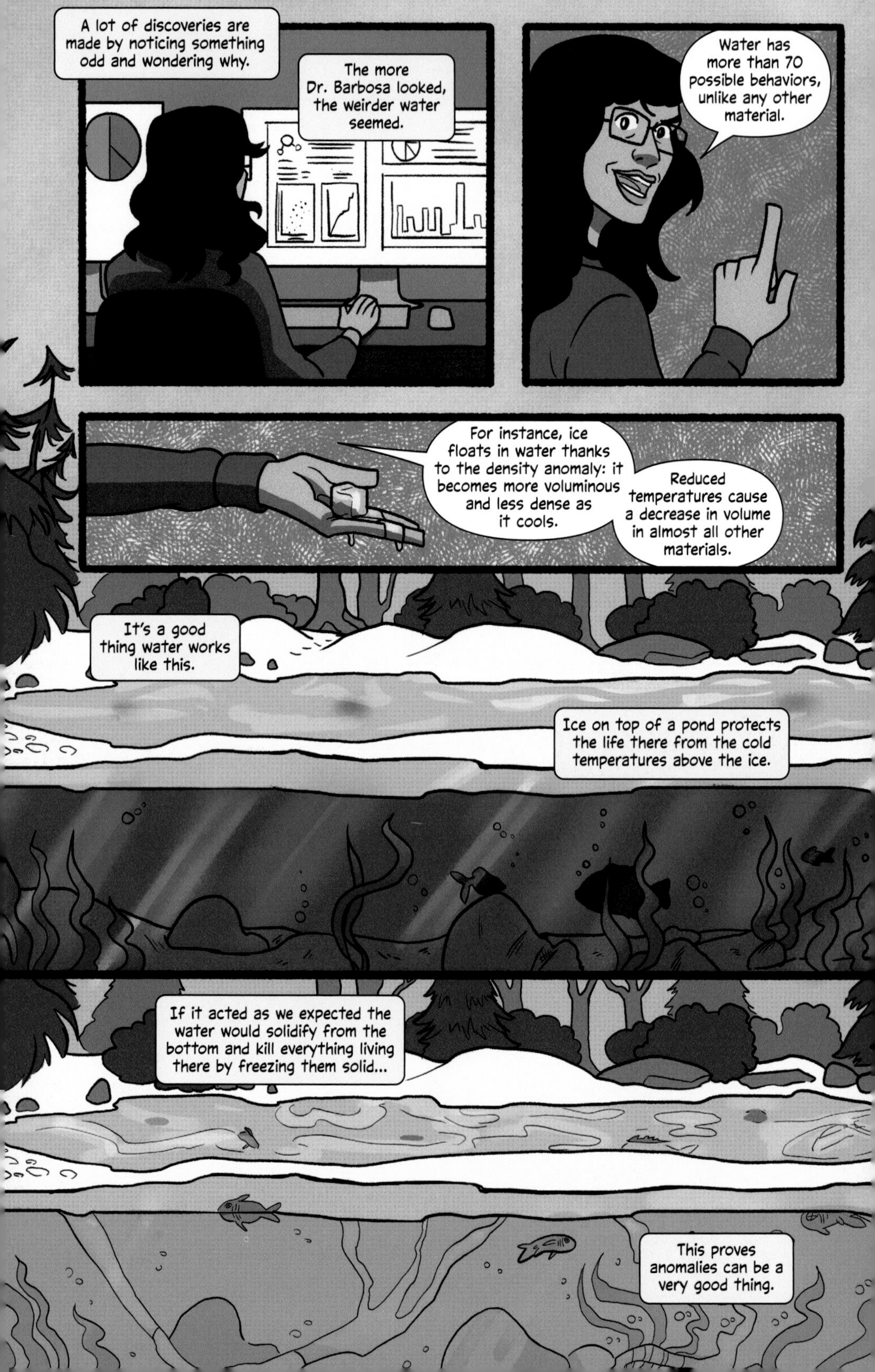
A lot of discoveries are made by noticing something odd and wondering why.
The more Dr. Barbosa looked, the weirder water seemed.
Water has more than 70 possible behaviors, unlike any other material.
For instance, ice floats in water thanks to the density anomaly: it becomes more voluminous and less dense as it cools.
Reduced temperatures cause a decrease in volume in almost all other materials.
It's a good thing water works like this.
Ice on top of a pond protects the life there from the cold temperatures above the ice.
If it acted as we expected the water would solidify from the bottom and kill everything living there by freezing them solid...
This proves anomalies can be a very good thing.

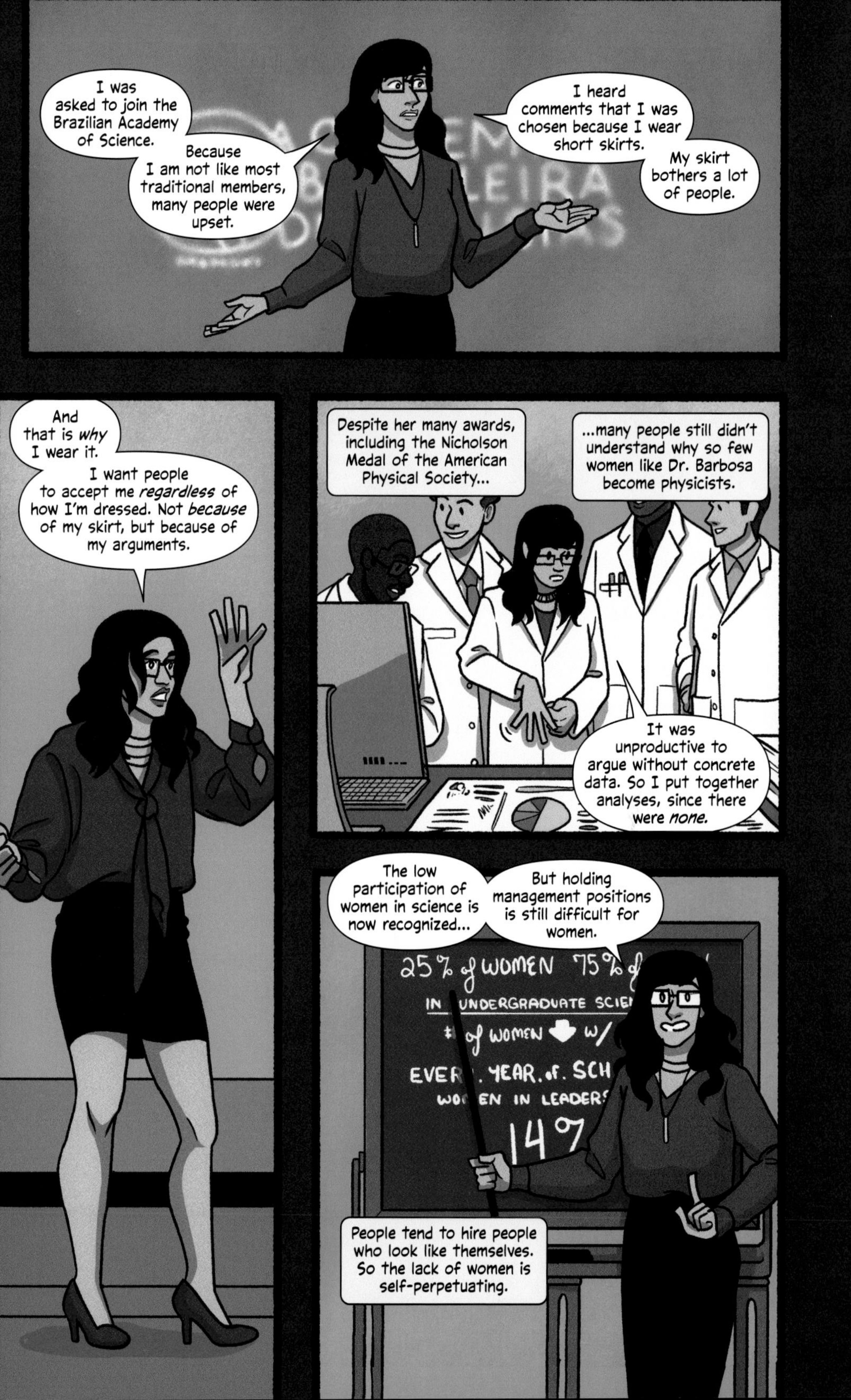
I was asked to join the Brazilian Academy of Science.
Because I am not like most traditional members, many people were upset.
I heard comments that I was chosen because I wear short skirts.
My skirt bothers a lot of people.
And that is *why* I wear it.
I want people to accept me *regardless* of how I'm dressed. Not *because* of my skirt, but because of my arguments.
Despite her many awards, including the Nicholson Medal of the American Physical Society...
...many people still didn't understand why so few women like Dr. Barbosa become physicists.
It was unproductive to argue without concrete data. So I put together analyses, since there were *none.*
The low participation of women in science is now recognized...
But holding management positions is still difficult for women.
25% of WOMEN 75%
IN UNDERGRADUATE SCIE
# of WOMEN w/
EVER . YEAR . of . SCH
EN IN LEADERS
14%
People tend to hire people who look like themselves. So the lack of women is self-perpetuating.

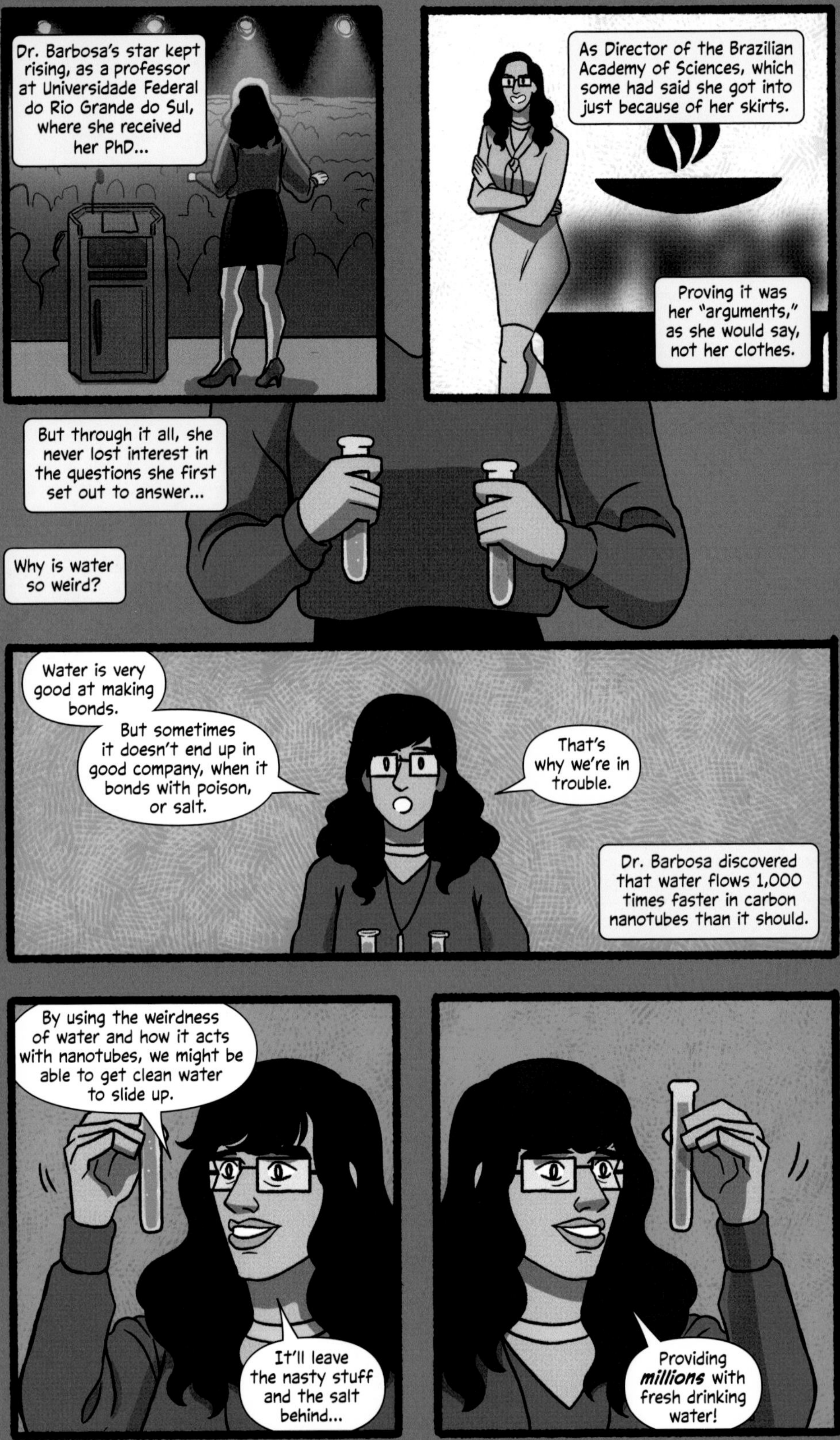
Dr. Barbosa's star kept rising, as a professor at Universidade Federal do Rio Grande do Sul, where she received her PhD...
As Director of the Brazilian Academy of Sciences, which some had said she got into just because of her skirts.
Proving it was her "arguments," as she would say, not her clothes.
But through it all, she never lost interest in the questions she first set out to answer...
Why is water so weird?
Water is very good at making bonds.
But sometimes it doesn't end up in good company, when it bonds with poison, or salt.
That's why we're in trouble.
Dr. Barbosa discovered that water flows 1,000 times faster in carbon nanotubes than it should.
By using the weirdness of water and how it acts with nanotubes, we might be able to get clean water to slide up.
It'll leave the nasty stuff and the salt behind...
Providing *millions* with fresh drinking water!

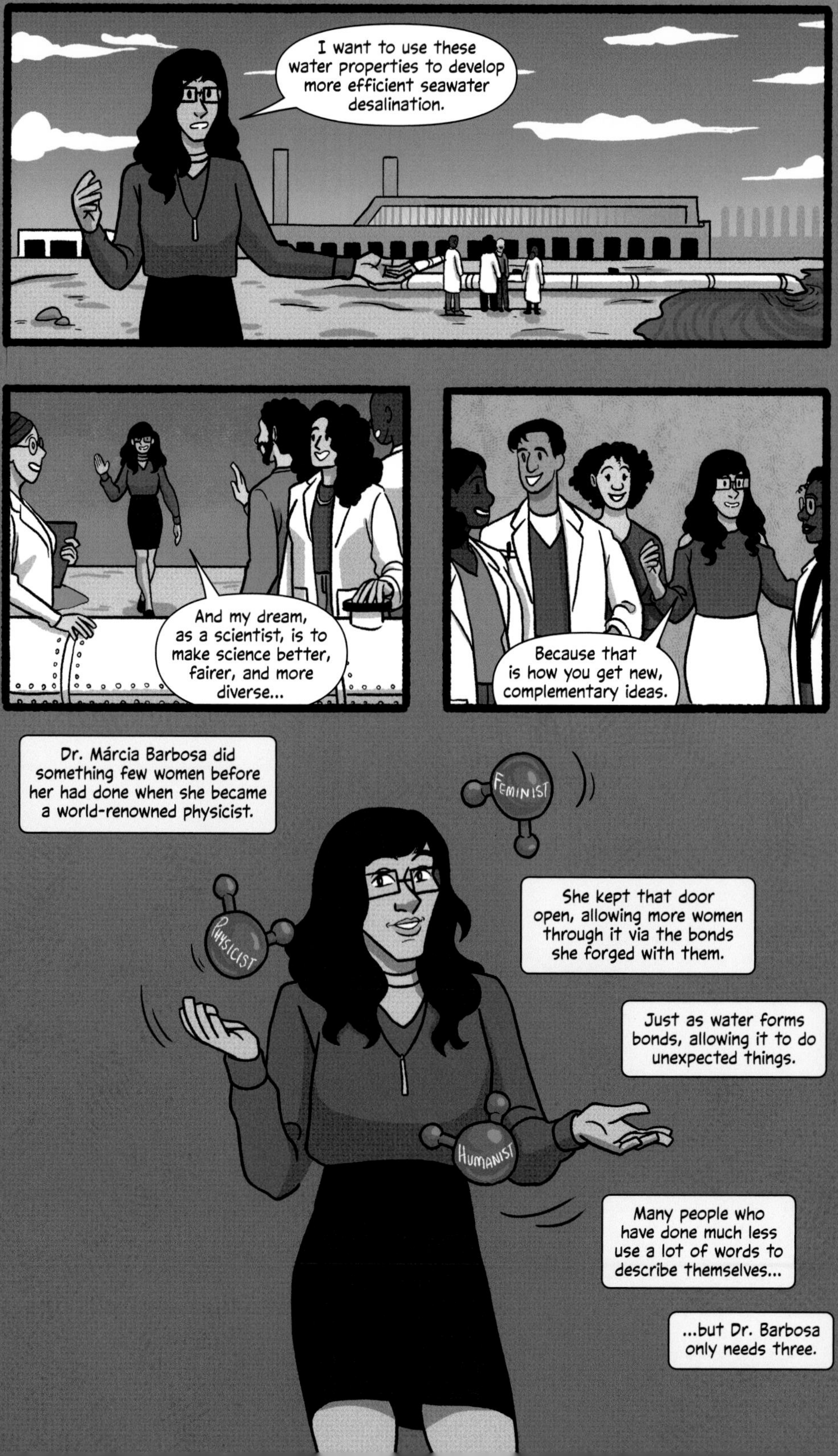
I want to use these water properties to develop more efficient seawater desalination.
And my dream, as a scientist, is to make science better, fairer, and more diverse...
Because that is how you get new, complementary ideas.
Dr. Márcia Barbosa did something few women before her had done when she became a world-renowned physicist.
Feminist
Physicist
She kept that door open, allowing more women through it via the bonds she forged with them.
Just as water forms bonds, allowing it to do unexpected things.
Humanist
Many people who have done much less use a lot of words to describe themselves...
...but Dr. Barbosa only needs three.

part five

EQUALITY

Venus Williams has long represented the dichotomy of equality in the United States—a truth we claim as self-evident that isn't experienced by many members of our society. As she strives for greatness, she pushes us to look for closed doors in our own communities that should be held open for others.

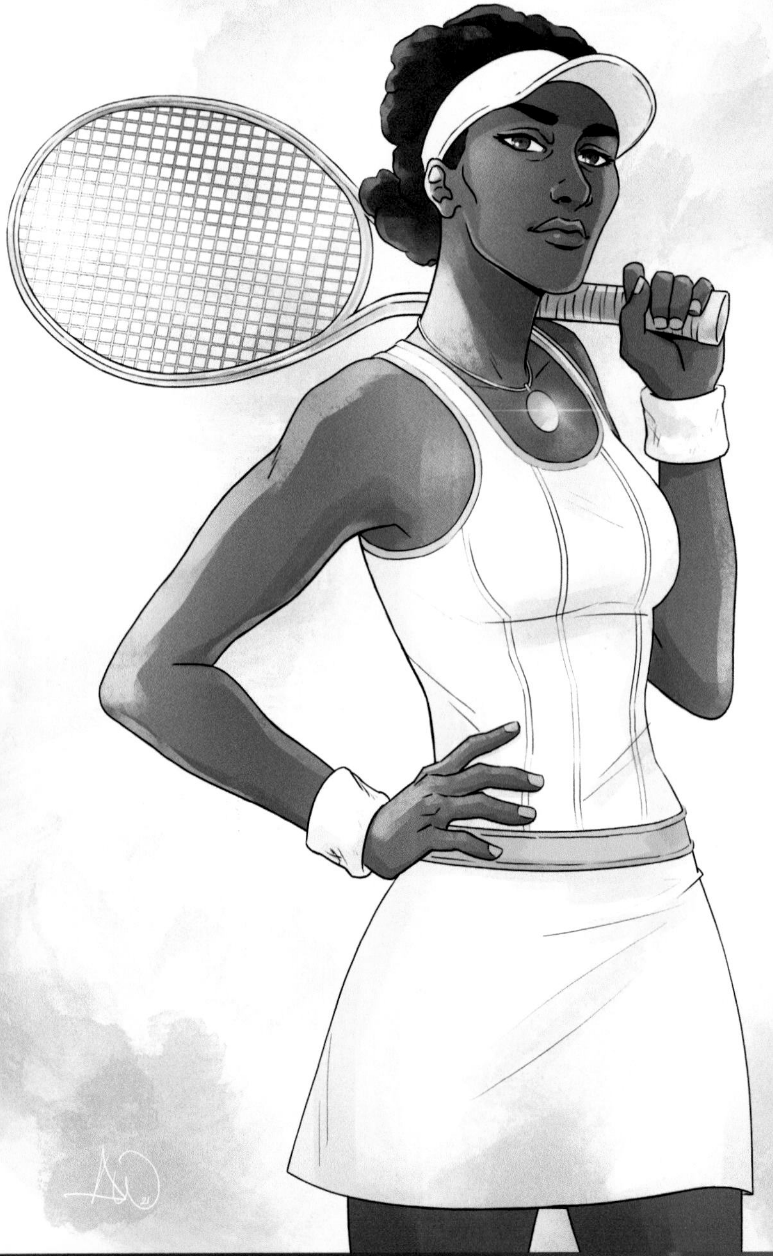

ELLEN OCHOA: DESTINATION—SPACE!

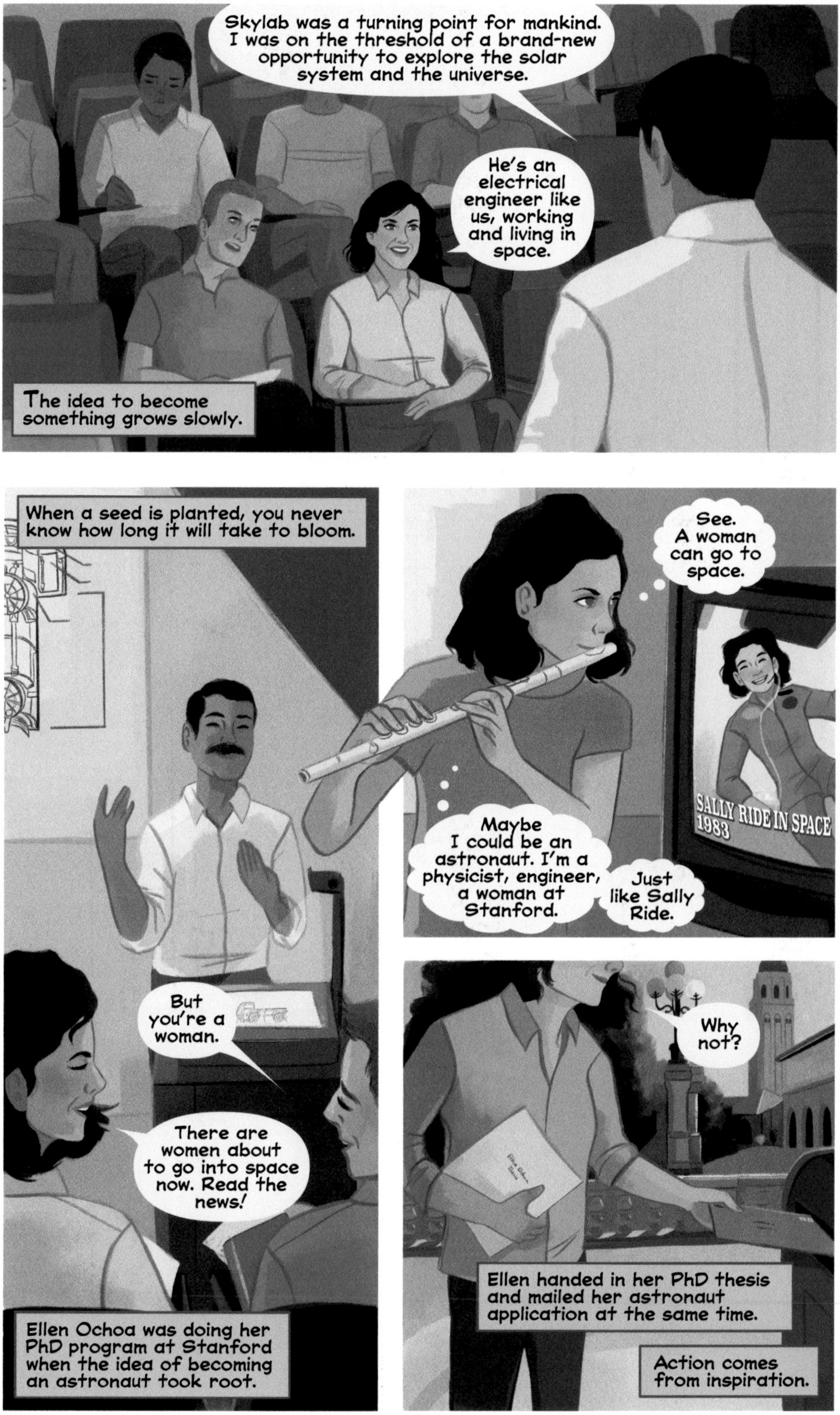
Skylab was a turning point for mankind. I was on the threshold of a brand-new opportunity to explore the solar system and the universe.
He's an electrical engineer like us, working and living in space.
The idea to become something grows slowly.
When a seed is planted, you never know how long it will take to bloom.
But you're a woman.
There are women about to go into space now. Read the news!
Ellen Ochoa was doing her PhD program at Stanford when the idea of becoming an astronaut took root.
See. A woman can go to space.
SALLY RIDE IN SPACE 1983
Maybe I could be an astronaut. I'm a physicist, engineer, a woman at Stanford.
Just like Sally Ride.
Why not?
Ellen handed in her PhD thesis and mailed her astronaut application at the same time.
Action comes from inspiration.

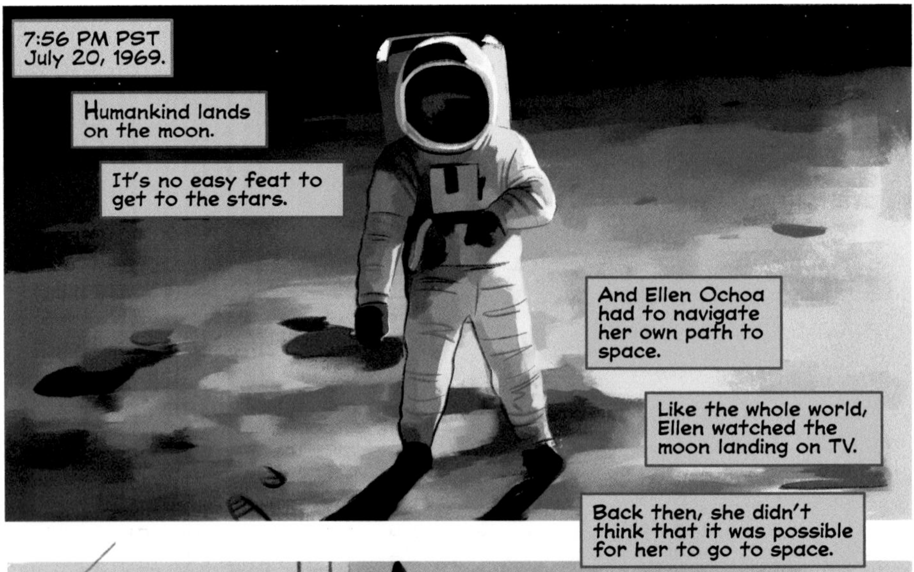
7:56 PM PST
July 20, 1969.
Humankind lands on the moon.
It's no easy feat to get to the stars.
And Ellen Ochoa had to navigate her own path to space.
Like the whole world, Ellen watched the moon landing on TV.
Back then, she didn't think that it was possible for her to go to space.

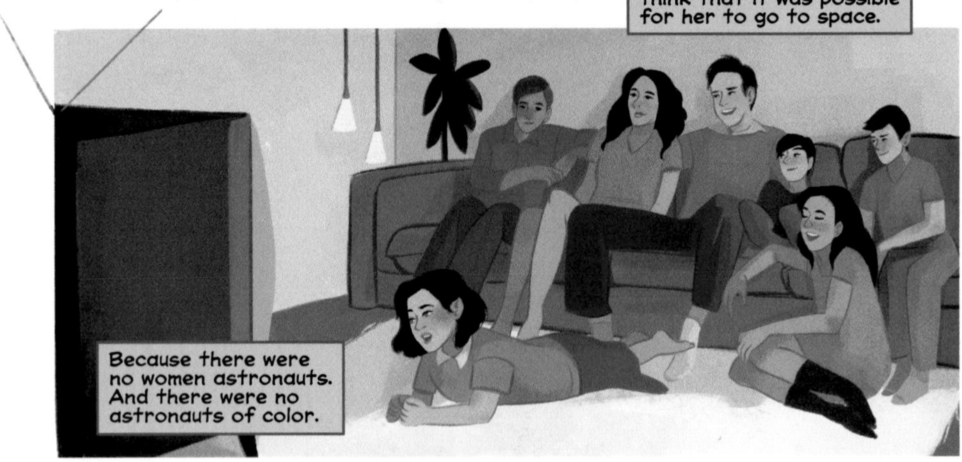
Because there were no women astronauts. And there were no astronauts of color.

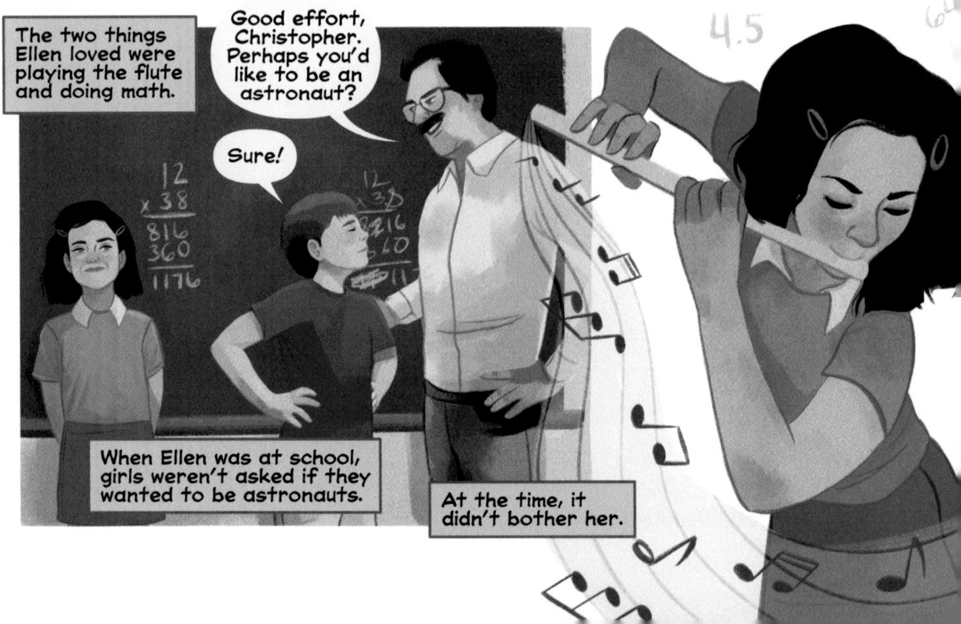
The two things Ellen loved were playing the flute and doing math.
Good effort, Christopher. Perhaps you'd like to be an astronaut?
Sure!
12
x 38
816
360
1176
When Ellen was at school, girls weren't asked if they wanted to be astronauts.
At the time, it didn't bother her.

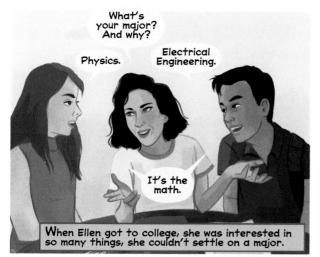

What's your major? And why?

Physics.

Electrical Engineering.

It's the math.

When Ellen got to college, she was interested in so many things, she couldn't settle on a major.

I'll check them both out.

DAILY PLANET

NEW ASTRONAUTS SELECTED!

Group 8 includes women and minorities

Electrical Engineering

OFFICE HOURS 11-2

Oh, we had a woman come through here once. Can you handle working with dirty electronics?

But not everyone welcomed new competition.

The Physics department was more welcoming.

I've done all the calculus courses. I really like math.

Great! You'll be ahead of students who'll be taking math classes concurrently. I think you'll do really well in the Physics department.

In the end, Ellen ended up doing both! Her undergrad Physics degree led her to Stanford and Electrical Engineering.

I love how everyone's story has twists and turns and surprises. Ellen's has many.

I bet you're wondering why I care so much about Ellen Ochoa's story?

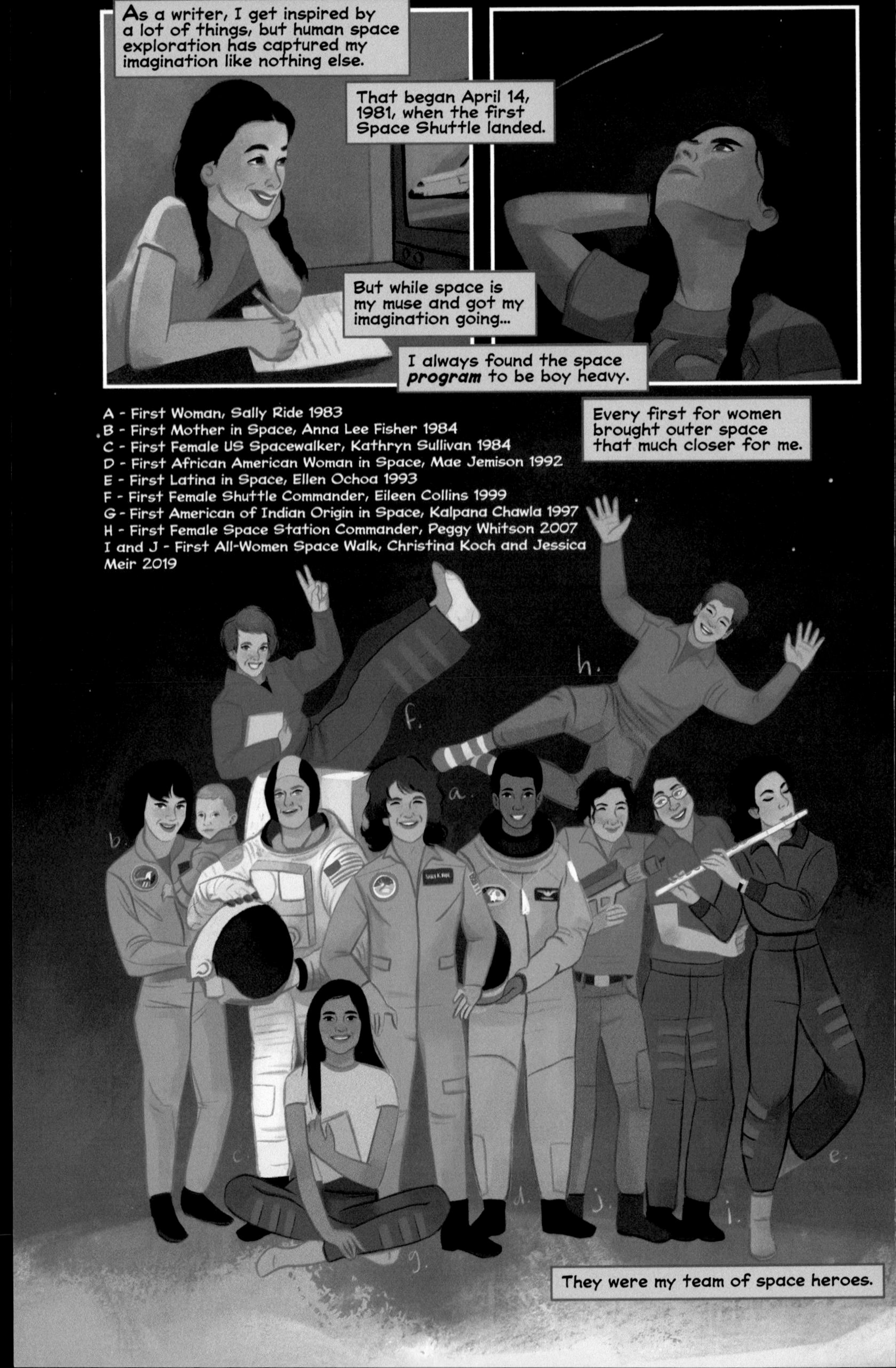
As a writer, I get inspired by a lot of things, but human space exploration has captured my imagination like nothing else.
That began April 14, 1981, when the first Space Shuttle landed.
But while space is my muse and got my imagination going...
I always found the space ***program*** to be boy heavy.
A - First Woman, Sally Ride 1983
B - First Mother in Space, Anna Lee Fisher 1984
C - First Female US Spacewalker, Kathryn Sullivan 1984
D - First African American Woman in Space, Mae Jemison 1992
E - First Latina in Space, Ellen Ochoa 1993
F - First Female Shuttle Commander, Eileen Collins 1999
G - First American of Indian Origin in Space, Kalpana Chawla 1997
H - First Female Space Station Commander, Peggy Whitson 2007
I and J - First All-Women Space Walk, Christina Koch and Jessica Meir 2019
Every first for women brought outer space that much closer for me.
They were my team of space heroes.

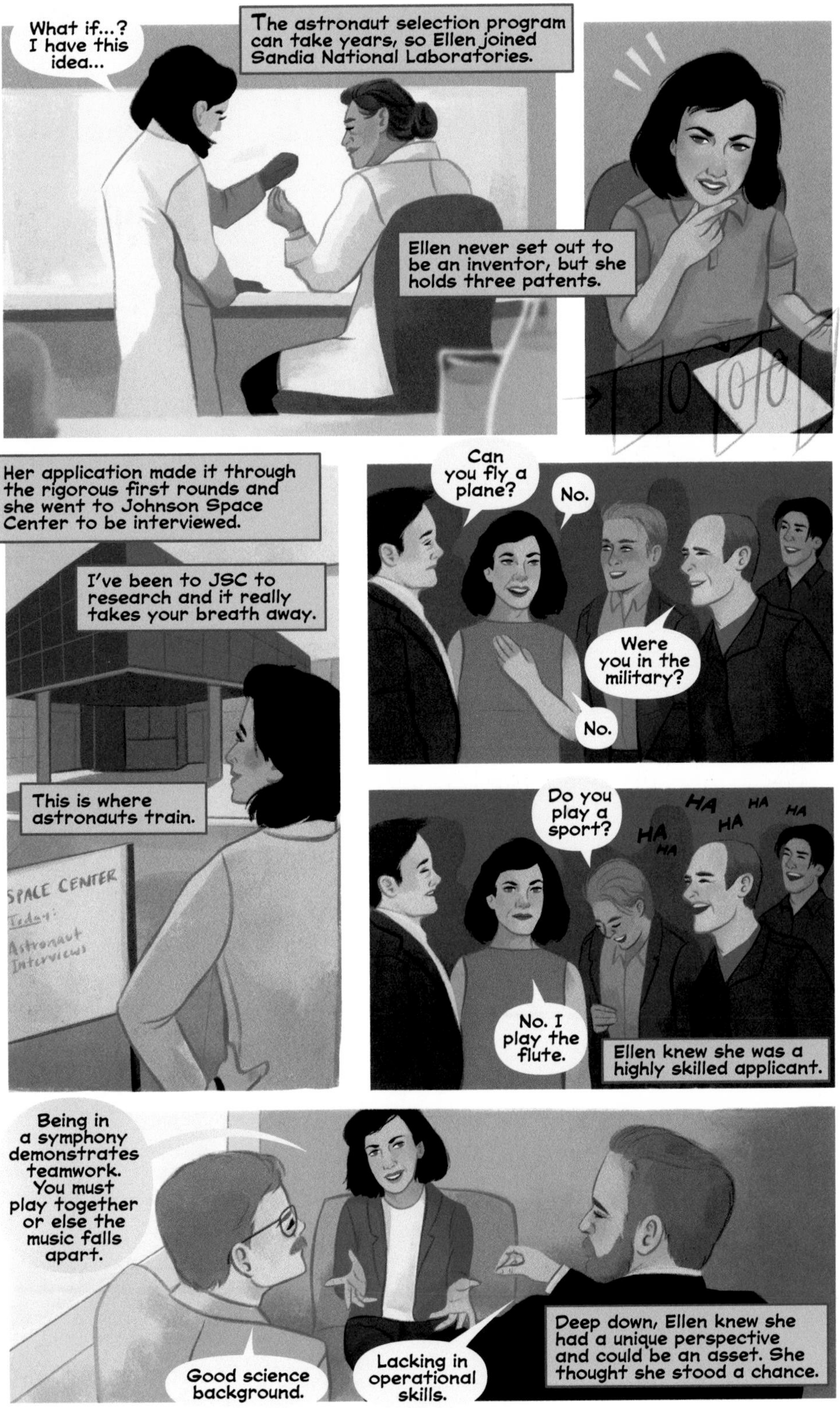
What if...? I have this idea...
The astronaut selection program can take years, so Ellen joined Sandia National Laboratories.
Ellen never set out to be an inventor, but she holds three patents.
Her application made it through the rigorous first rounds and she went to Johnson Space Center to be interviewed.
I've been to JSC to research and it really takes your breath away.
This is where astronauts train.
SPACE CENTER
Today:
Astronaut Interviews
Can you fly a plane?
No.
Were you in the military?
No.
Do you play a sport?
HA HA HA HA HA HA
No. I play the flute.
Ellen knew she was a highly skilled applicant.
Being in a symphony demonstrates teamwork. You must play together or else the music falls apart.
Good science background.
Lacking in operational skills.
Deep down, Ellen knew she had a unique perspective and could be an asset. She thought she stood a chance.

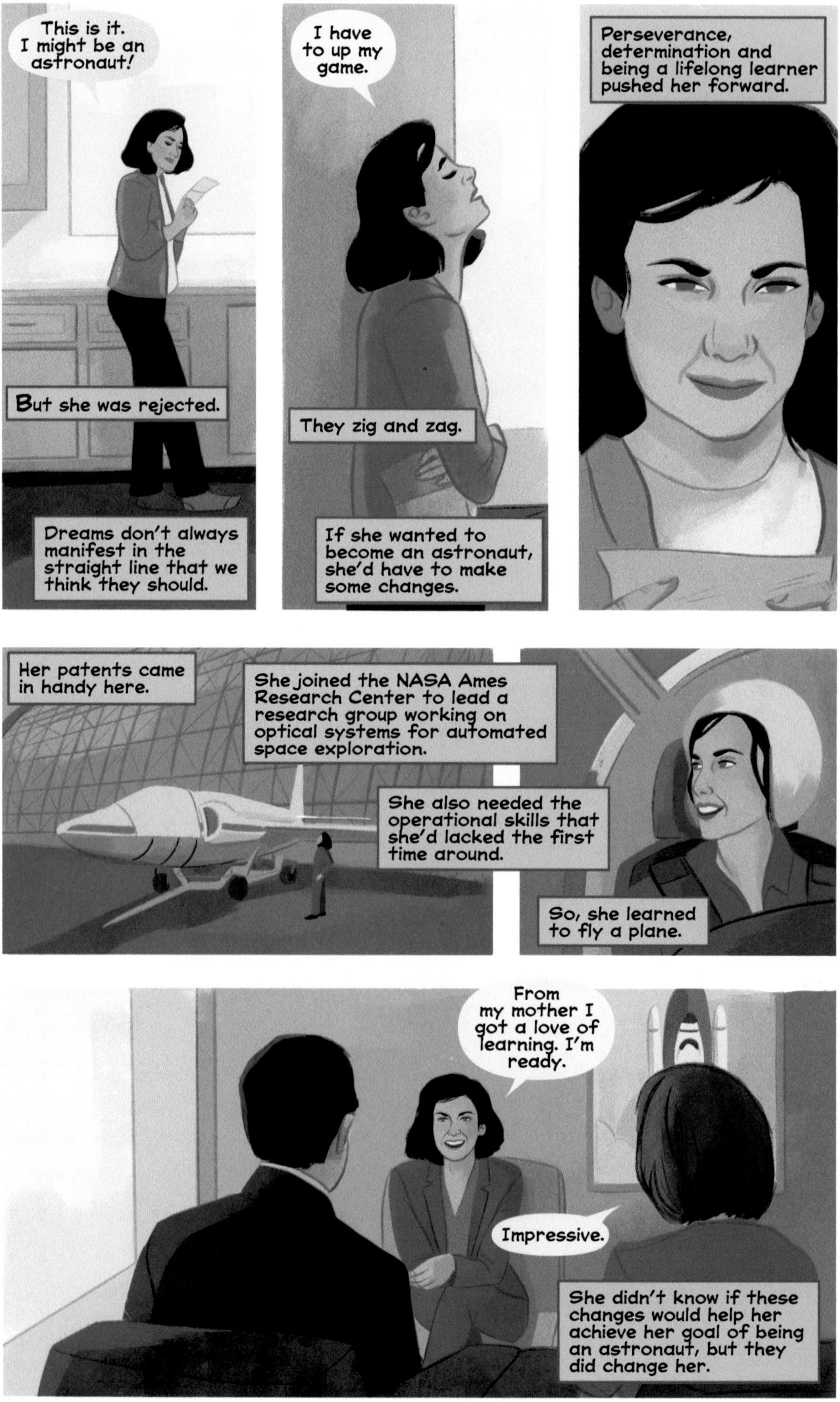
This is it. I might be an astronaut!
But she was rejected.
Dreams don't always manifest in the straight line that we think they should.
I have to up my game.
They zig and zag.
If she wanted to become an astronaut, she'd have to make some changes.
Perseverance, determination and being a lifelong learner pushed her forward.
Her patents came in handy here.
She joined the NASA Ames Research Center to lead a research group working on optical systems for automated space exploration.
She also needed the operational skills that she'd lacked the first time around.
So, she learned to fly a plane.
From my mother I got a love of learning. I'm ready.
Impressive.
She didn't know if these changes would help her achieve her goal of being an astronaut, but they did change her.

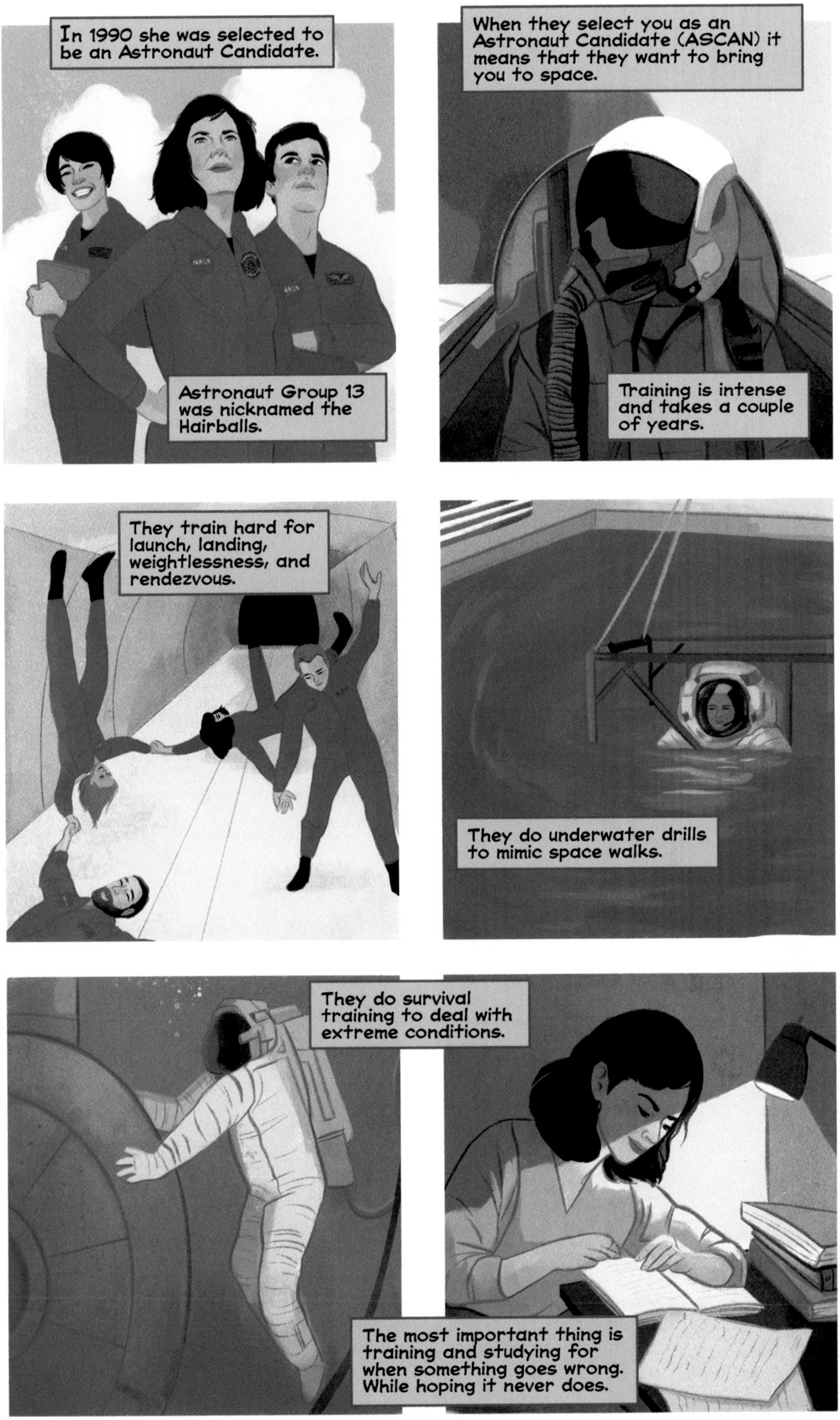
In 1990 she was selected to be an Astronaut Candidate.
Astronaut Group 13 was nicknamed the Hairballs.
When they select you as an Astronaut Candidate (ASCAN) it means that they want to bring you to space.
Training is intense and takes a couple of years.
They train hard for launch, landing, weightlessness, and rendezvous.
They do underwater drills to mimic space walks.
They do survival training to deal with extreme conditions.
The most important thing is training and studying for when something goes wrong. While hoping it never does.

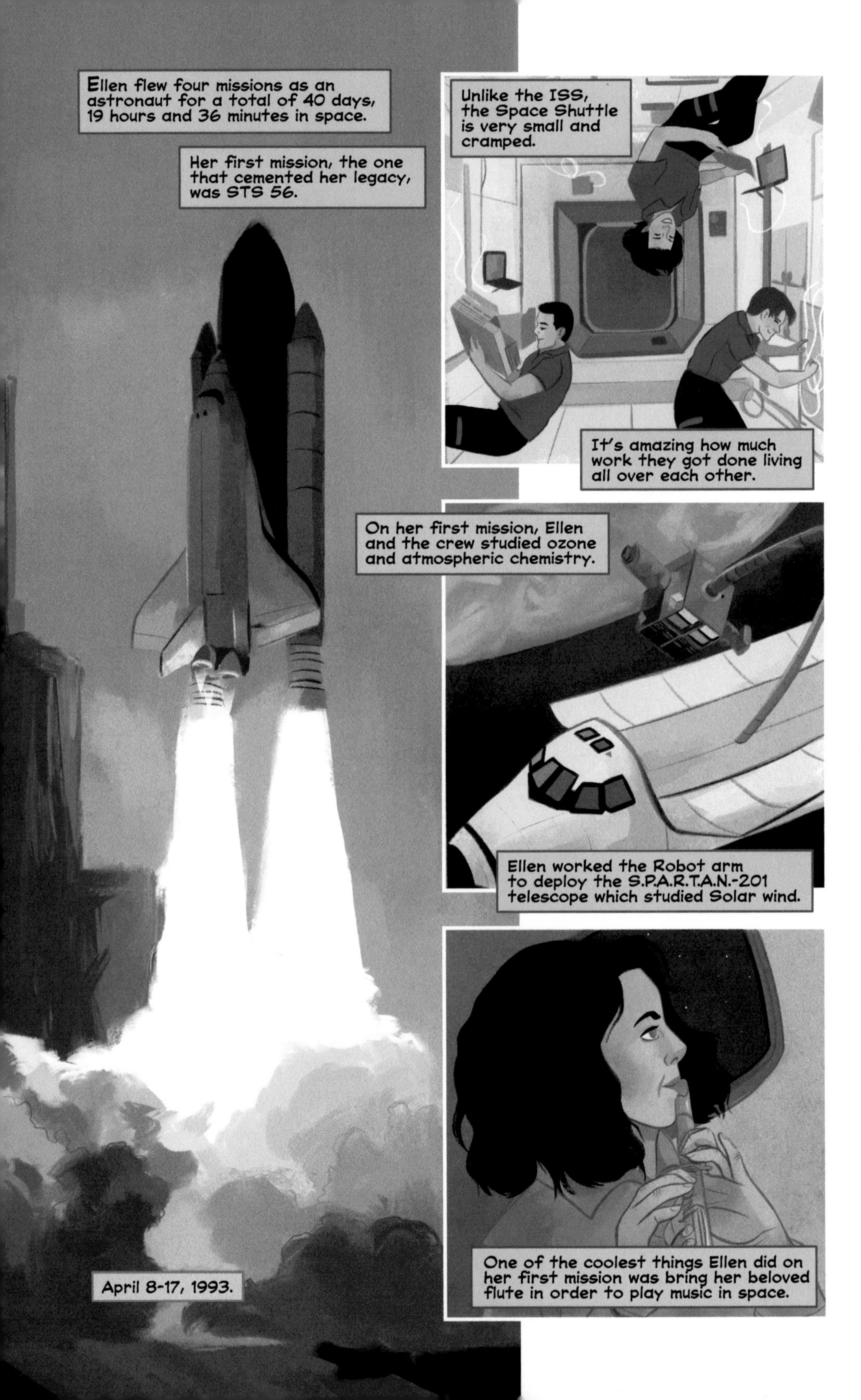
Ellen flew four missions as an astronaut for a total of 40 days, 19 hours and 36 minutes in space.
Her first mission, the one that cemented her legacy, was STS 56.
April 8-17, 1993.
Unlike the ISS, the Space Shuttle is very small and cramped.
It's amazing how much work they got done living all over each other.
On her first mission, Ellen and the crew studied ozone and atmospheric chemistry.
Ellen worked the Robot arm to deploy the S.P.A.R.T.A.N.-201 telescope which studied Solar wind.
One of the coolest things Ellen did on her first mission was bring her beloved flute in order to play music in space.

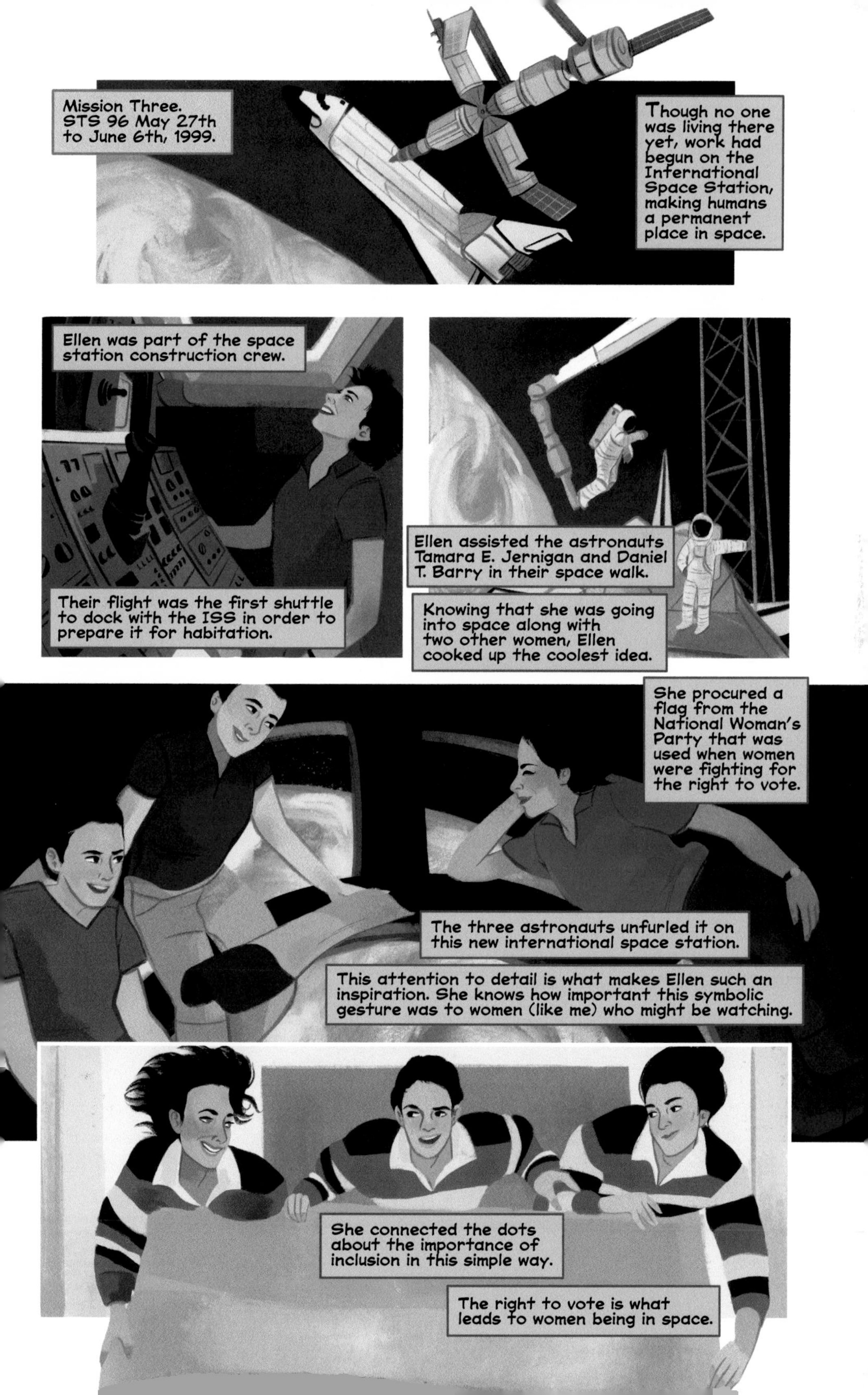
Mission Three.
STS 96 May 27th to June 6th, 1999.
Though no one was living there yet, work had begun on the International Space Station, making humans a permanent place in space.
Ellen was part of the space station construction crew.
Their flight was the first shuttle to dock with the ISS in order to prepare it for habitation.
Ellen assisted the astronauts Tamara E. Jernigan and Daniel T. Barry in their space walk.
Knowing that she was going into space along with two other women, Ellen cooked up the coolest idea.
She procured a flag from the National Woman's Party that was used when women were fighting for the right to vote.
The three astronauts unfurled it on this new international space station.
This attention to detail is what makes Ellen such an inspiration. She knows how important this symbolic gesture was to women (like me) who might be watching.
She connected the dots about the importance of inclusion in this simple way.
The right to vote is what leads to women being in space.

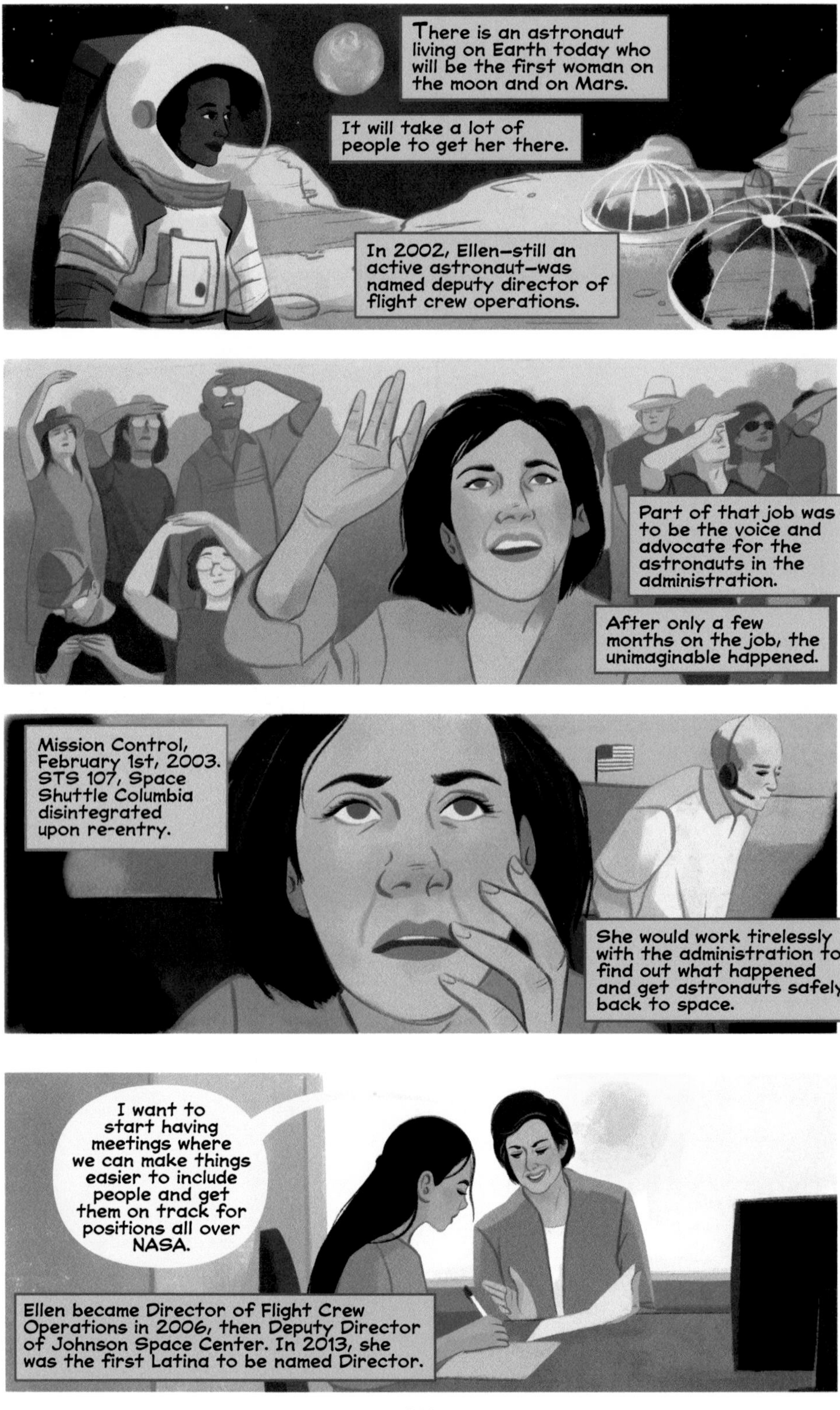
There is an astronaut living on Earth today who will be the first woman on the moon and on Mars.
It will take a lot of people to get her there.
In 2002, Ellen—still an active astronaut—was named deputy director of flight crew operations.
Part of that job was to be the voice and advocate for the astronauts in the administration.
After only a few months on the job, the unimaginable happened.
Mission Control, February 1st, 2003. STS 107, Space Shuttle Columbia disintegrated upon re-entry.
She would work tirelessly with the administration to find out what happened and get astronauts safely back to space.
I want to start having meetings where we can make things easier to include people and get them on track for positions all over NASA.
Ellen became Director of Flight Crew Operations in 2006, then Deputy Director of Johnson Space Center. In 2013, she was the first Latina to be named Director.

May 30, 2020.
Dragon launch.

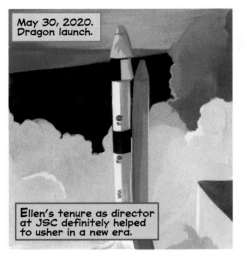

Ellen's tenure as director at JSC definitely helped to usher in a new era.

The goal is to be self-dependent and launch from American soil. Then we can start thinking about how to get past low Earth orbit and to the moon and beyond.

She partnered with commercial space partners to help move launches back to the US.

Wow, I heard we were getting new tech faster, but in only 10 months?!

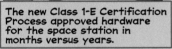

The new Class 1-E Certification Process approved hardware for the space station in months versus years.

How you feeling?

I'm going to come down there taller than Mark.

There are a lot of real Earth benefits to these technologies and experiments, such as telemedicine.

Ellen oversaw missions on the long-term effects of space on the human body, such as the twin study on the Kelly brothers.

I liked the way the book depicted the business of space travel.

They must have talked to a bunch of space scientists.

She fostered inclusivity and diversity by initiating many different kinds of programs to start dialogues.

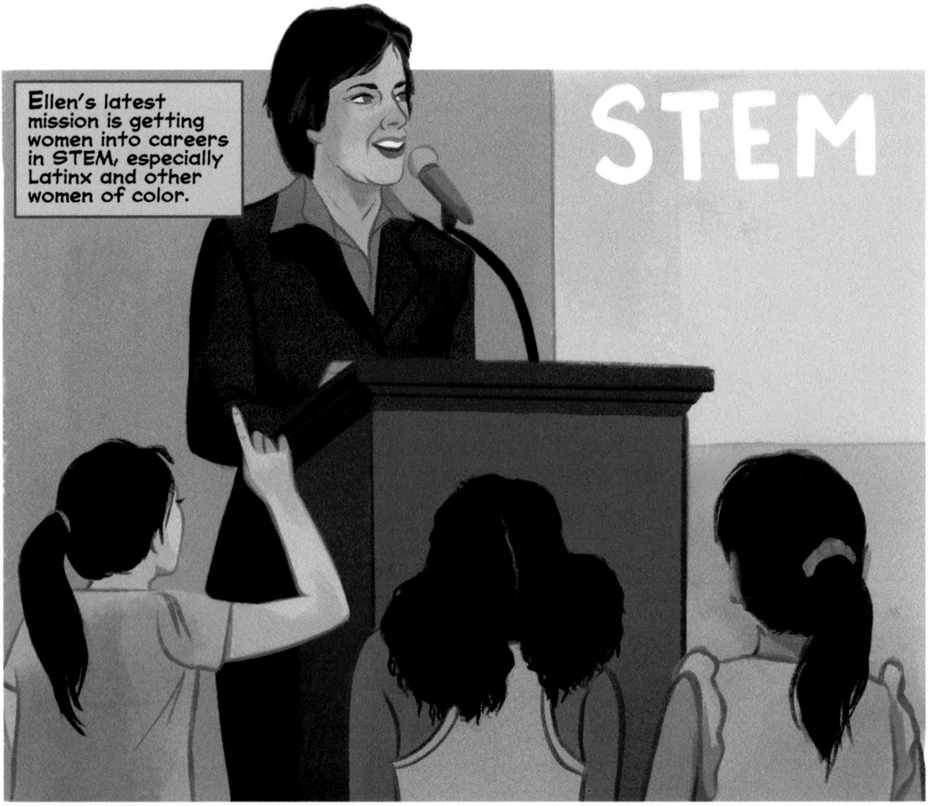
Ellen's latest mission is getting women into careers in STEM, especially Latinx and other women of color.
STEM

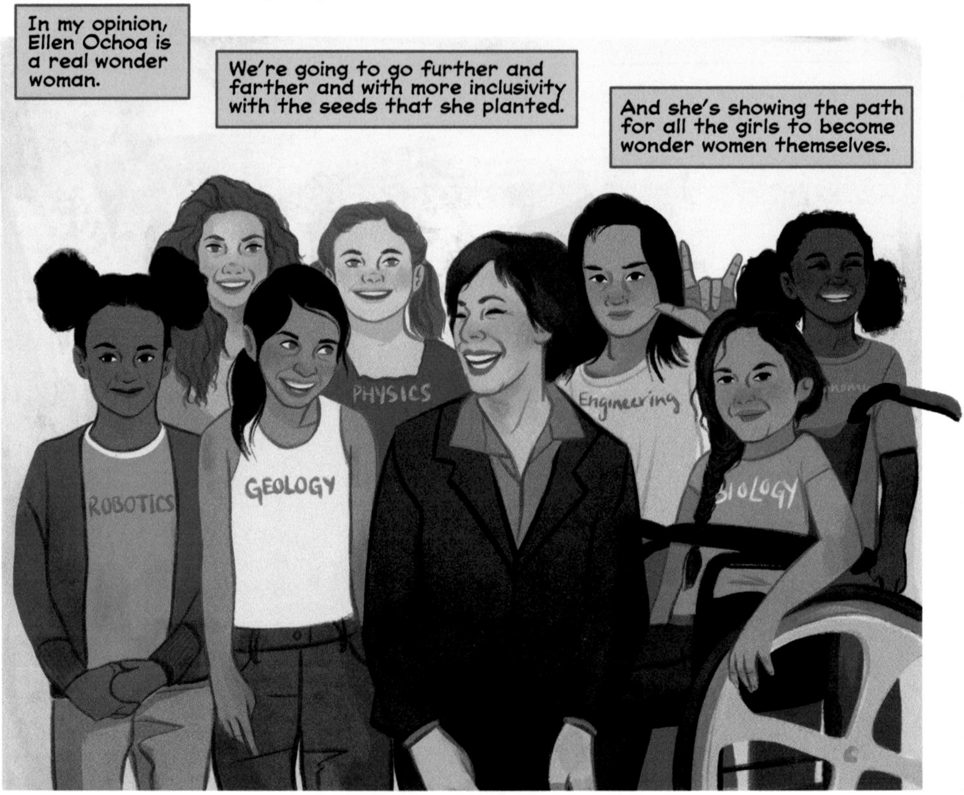
In my opinion, Ellen Ochoa is a real wonder woman.
We're going to go further and farther and with more inclusivity with the seeds that she planted.
And she's showing the path for all the girls to become wonder women themselves.
PHYSICS
Engineering
ROBOTICS
GEOLOGY

NAOMI WATANABE: FINDING YOUR FIT

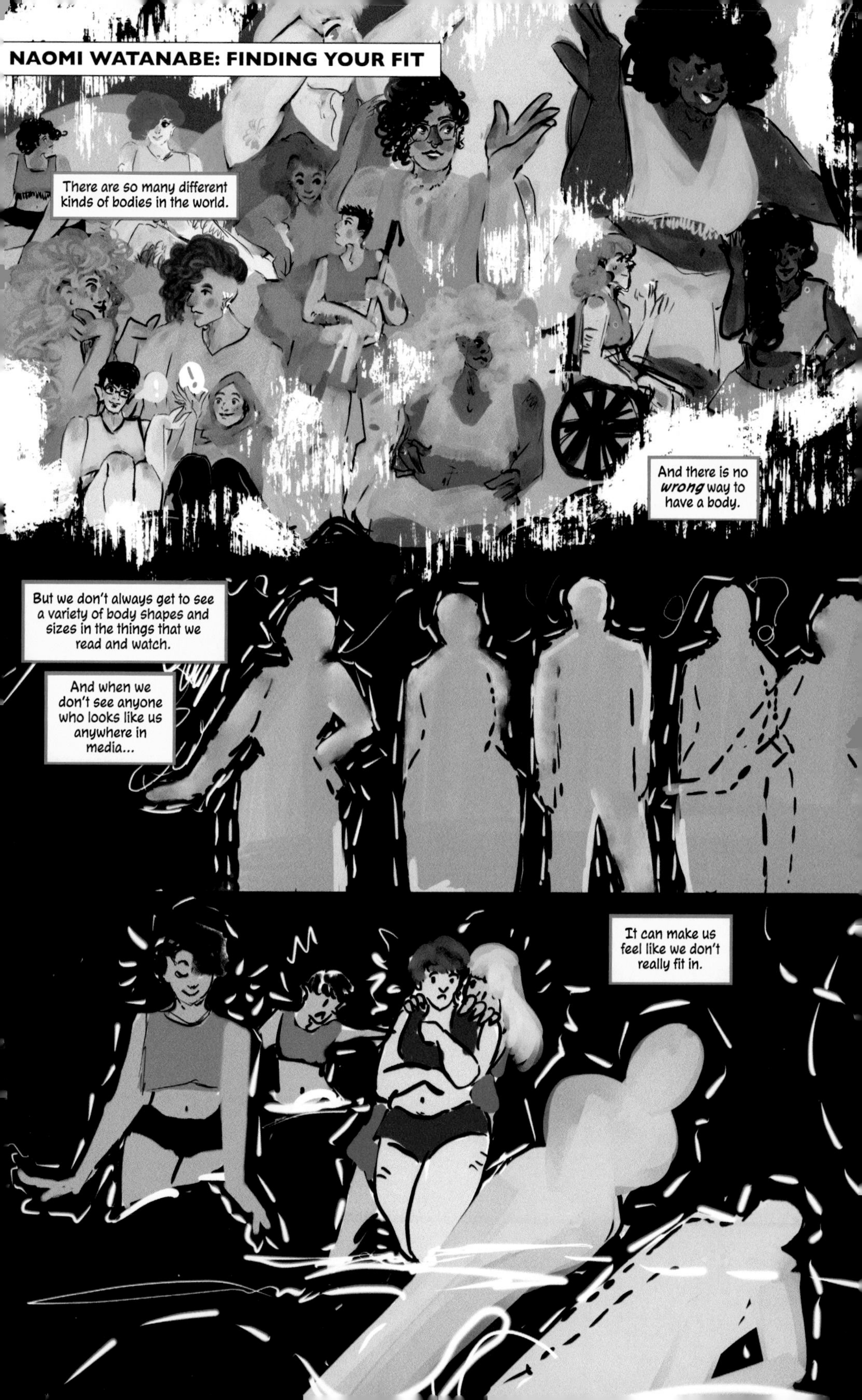
There are so many different kinds of bodies in the world.
And there is no *wrong* way to have a body.
But we don't always get to see a variety of body shapes and sizes in the things that we read and watch.
And when we don't see anyone who looks like us anywhere in media...
It can make us feel like we don't really fit in.

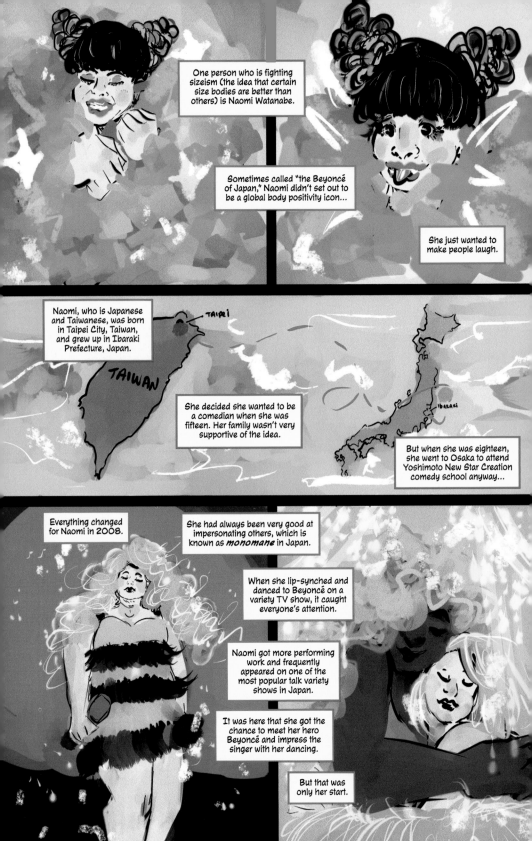

One person who is fighting sizeism (the idea that certain size bodies are better than others) is Naomi Watanabe.

Sometimes called "the Beyoncé of Japan," Naomi didn't set out to be a global body positivity icon...

She just wanted to make people laugh.

Naomi, who is Japanese and Taiwanese, was born in Taipei City, Taiwan, and grew up in Ibaraki Prefecture, Japan.

TAIPEI

TAIWAN

IBARAKI

She decided she wanted to be a comedian when she was fifteen. Her family wasn't very supportive of the idea.

But when she was eighteen, she went to Osaka to attend Yoshimoto New Star Creation comedy school anyway...

Everything changed for Naomi in 2008.

She had always been very good at impersonating others, which is known as *monomane* in Japan.

When she lip-synched and danced to Beyoncé on a variety TV show, it caught everyone's attention.

Naomi got more performing work and frequently appeared on one of the most popular talk variety shows in Japan.

It was here that she got the chance to meet her hero Beyoncé and impress the singer with her dancing.

But that was only her start.

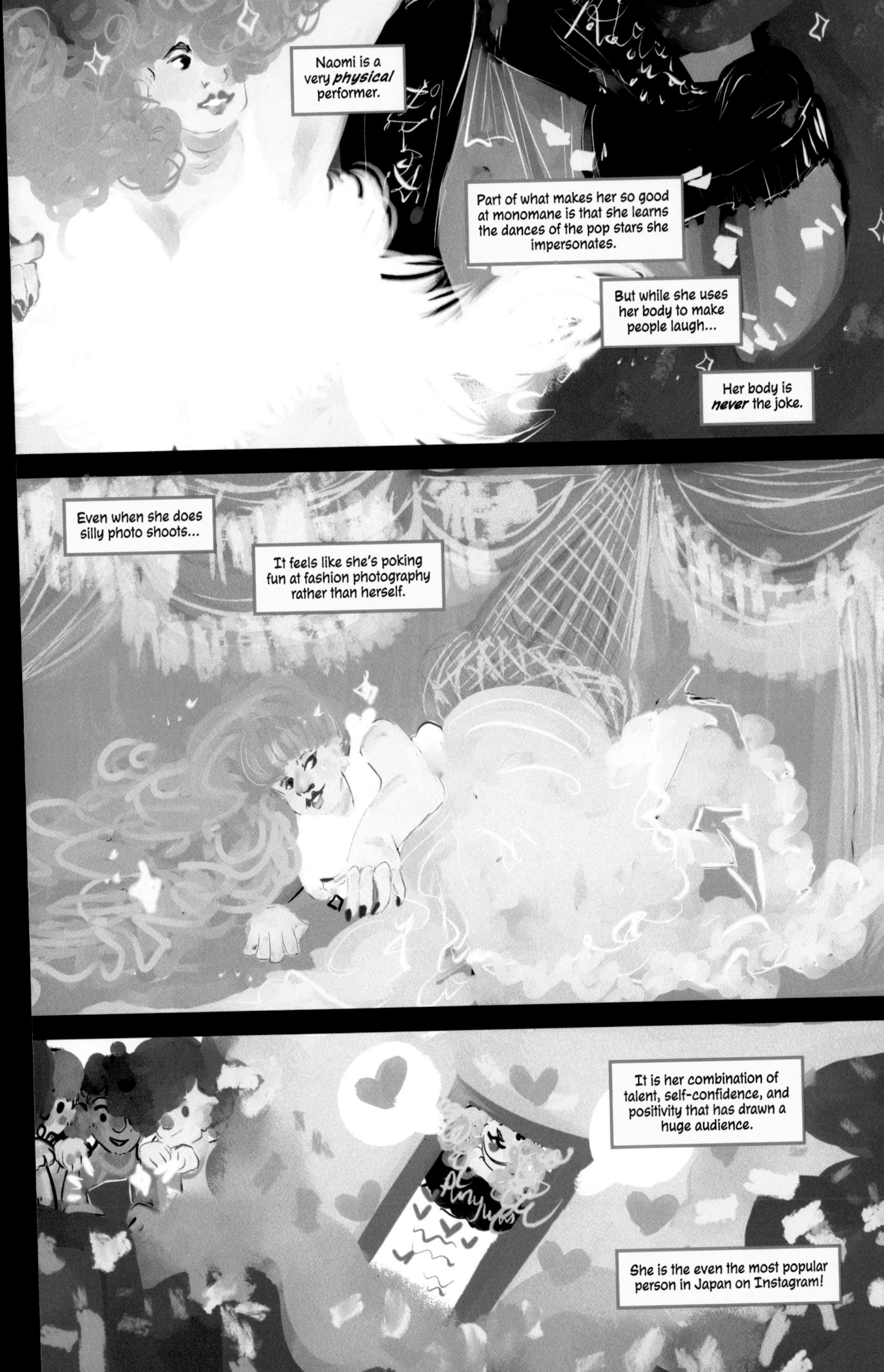
Naomi is a very *physical* performer.
Part of what makes her so good at monomane is that she learns the dances of the pop stars she impersonates.
But while she uses her body to make people laugh...
Her body is *never* the joke.
Even when she does silly photo shoots...
It feels like she's poking fun at fashion photography rather than herself.
It is her combination of talent, self-confidence, and positivity that has drawn a huge audience.
She is the even the most popular person in Japan on Instagram!

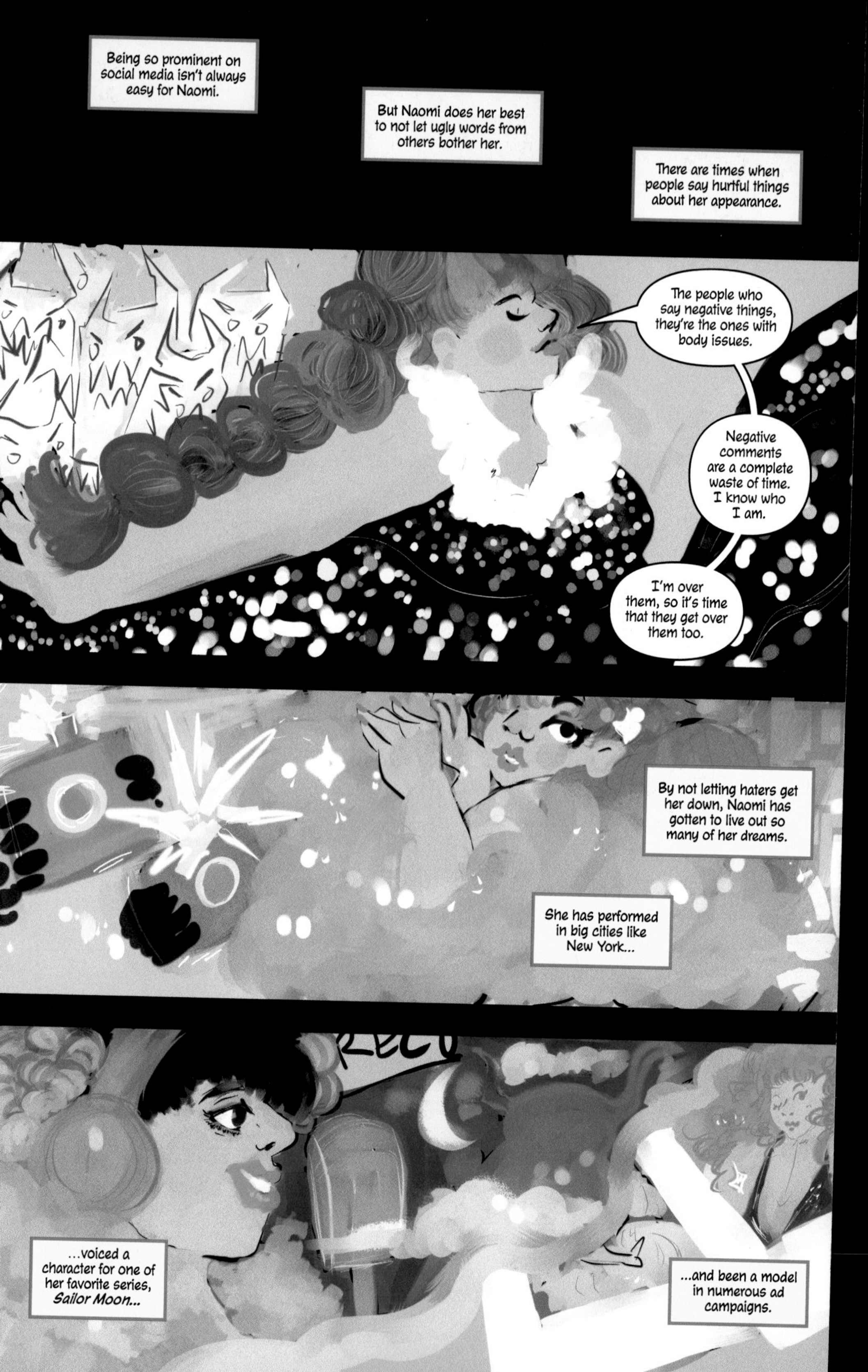
Being so prominent on social media isn't always easy for Naomi.
But Naomi does her best to not let ugly words from others bother her.
There are times when people say hurtful things about her appearance.
The people who say negative things, they're the ones with body issues.
Negative comments are a complete waste of time. I know who I am.
I'm over them, so it's time that they get over them too.
By not letting haters get her down, Naomi has gotten to live out so many of her dreams.
She has performed in big cities like New York...
...voiced a character for one of her favorite series, *Sailor Moon*...
...and been a model in numerous ad campaigns.

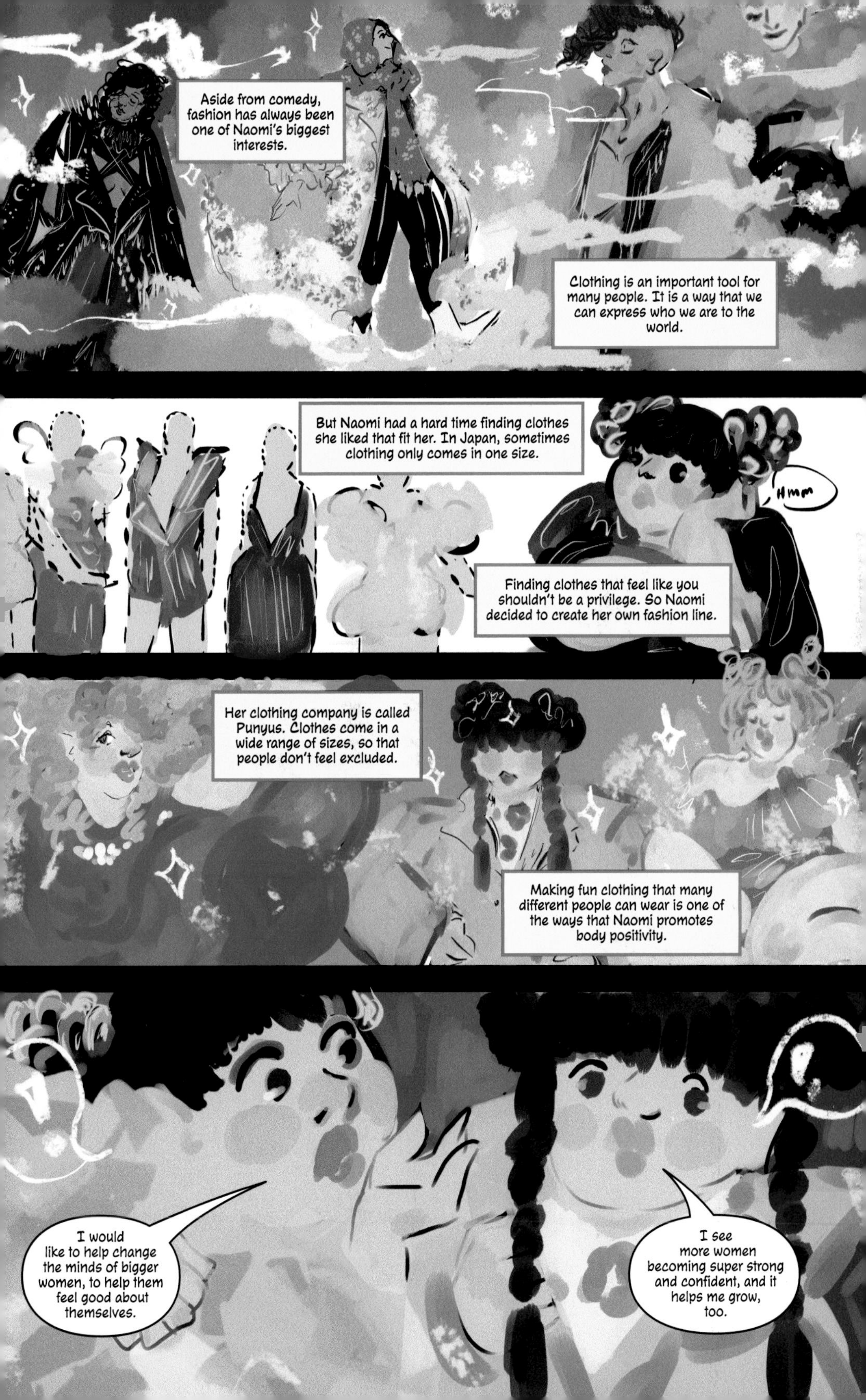

Aside from comedy, fashion has always been one of Naomi's biggest interests.
Clothing is an important tool for many people. It is a way that we can express who we are to the world.
But Naomi had a hard time finding clothes she liked that fit her. In Japan, sometimes clothing only comes in one size.
Hmm
Finding clothes that feel like you shouldn't be a privilege. So Naomi decided to create her own fashion line.
Her clothing company is called Punyus. Clothes come in a wide range of sizes, so that people don't feel excluded.
Making fun clothing that many different people can wear is one of the ways that Naomi promotes body positivity.
I would like to help change the minds of bigger women, to help them feel good about themselves.
I see more women becoming super strong and confident, and it helps me grow, too.

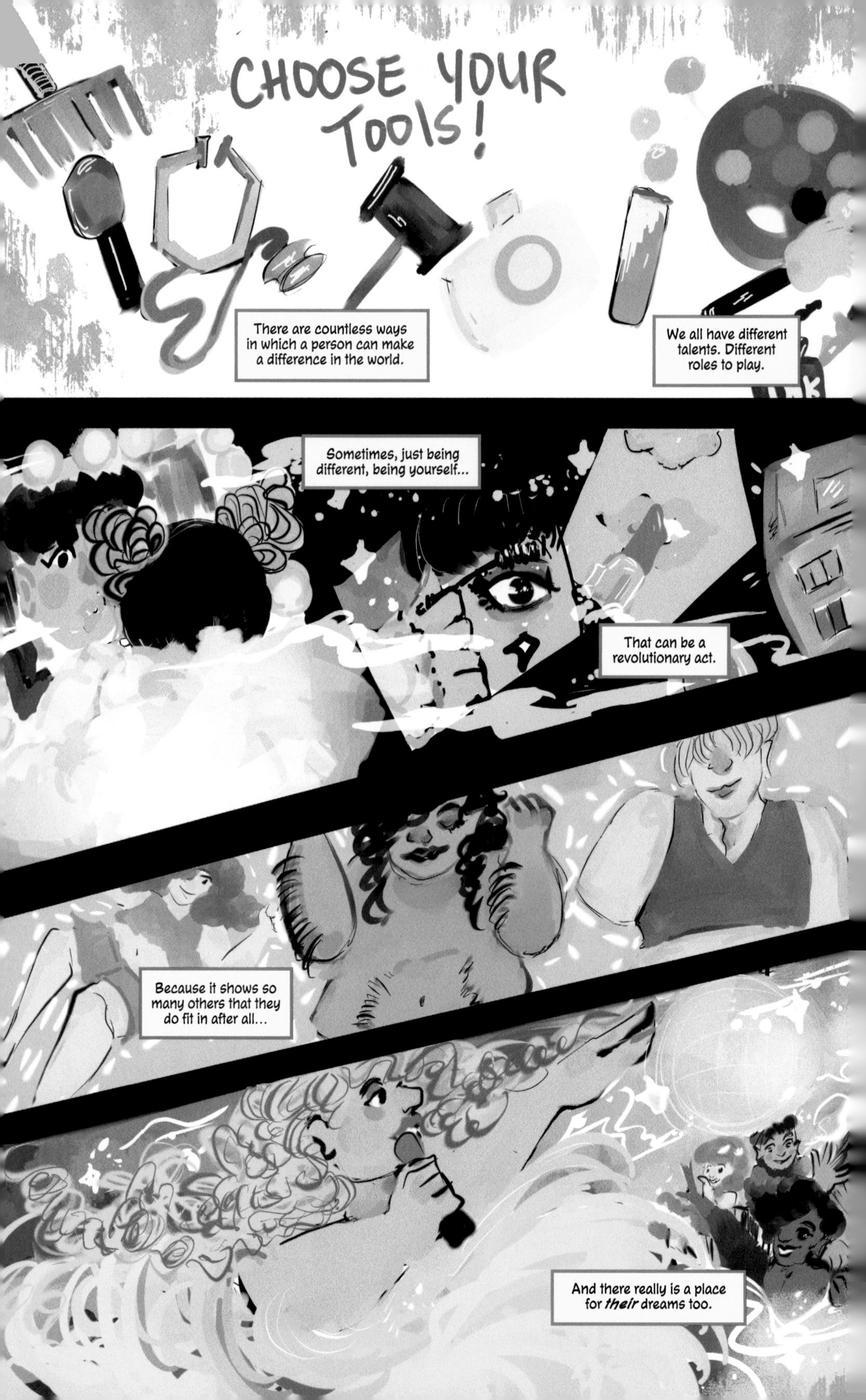
CHOOSE YOUR TOOLS!
There are countless ways in which a person can make a difference in the world.
We all have different talents. Different roles to play.
Sometimes, just being different, being yourself...
That can be a revolutionary act.
Because it shows so many others that they do fit in after all...
And there really is a place for *their* dreams too.

MARSHA P. JOHNSON: THE BEAUTY OF A BRICK

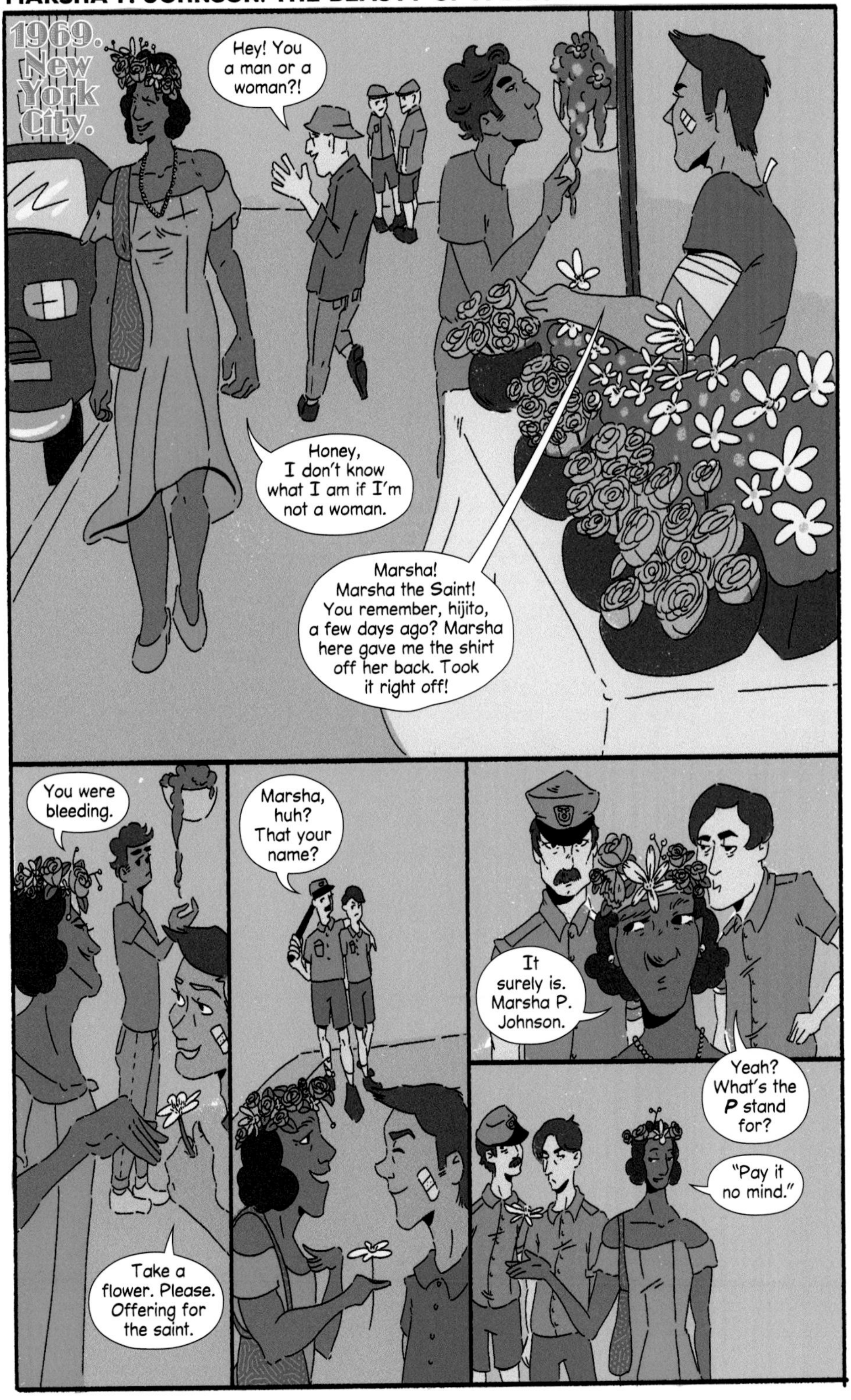
1969. New York City.
Hey! You a man or a woman?!
Honey, I don't know what I am if I'm not a woman.
Marsha! Marsha the Saint! You remember, hijito, a few days ago? Marsha here gave me the shirt off her back. Took it right off!
You were bleeding.
Take a flower. Please. Offering for the saint.
Marsha, huh? That your name?
It surely is. Marsha P. Johnson.
Yeah? What's the **P** stand for?
"Pay it no mind."

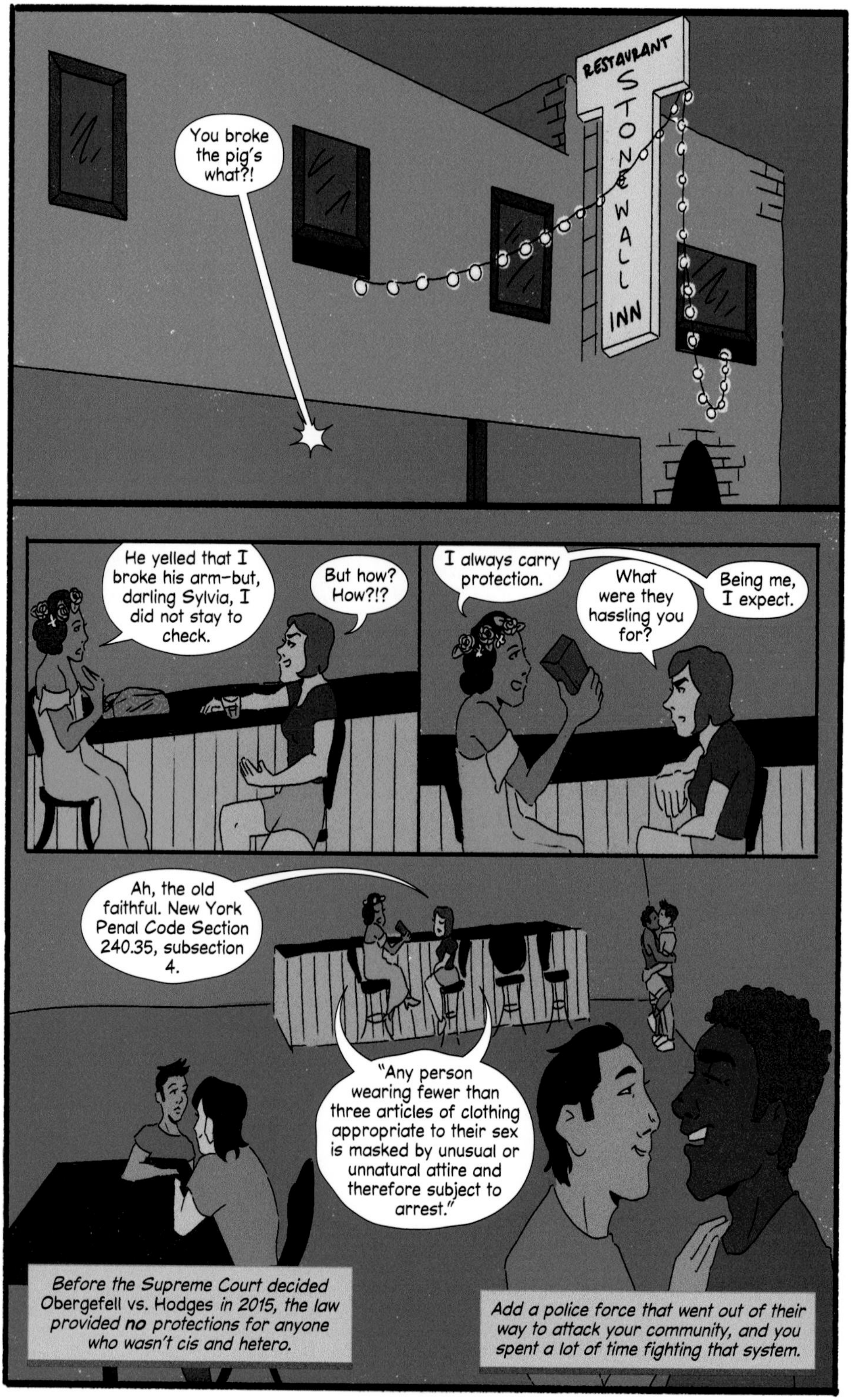
RESTAURANT
STONEWALL INN
You broke the pig's what?!
He yelled that I broke his arm—but, darling Sylvia, I did not stay to check.
But how? How?!?
I always carry protection.
What were they hassling you for?
Being me, I expect.
Ah, the old faithful. New York Penal Code Section 240.35, subsection 4.
"Any person wearing fewer than three articles of clothing appropriate to their sex is masked by unusual or unnatural attire and therefore subject to arrest."
Before the Supreme Court decided Obergefell vs. Hodges *in 2015, the law provided* **no** *protections for anyone who wasn't cis and hetero.*
Add a police force that went out of their way to attack your community, and you spent a lot of time fighting that system.

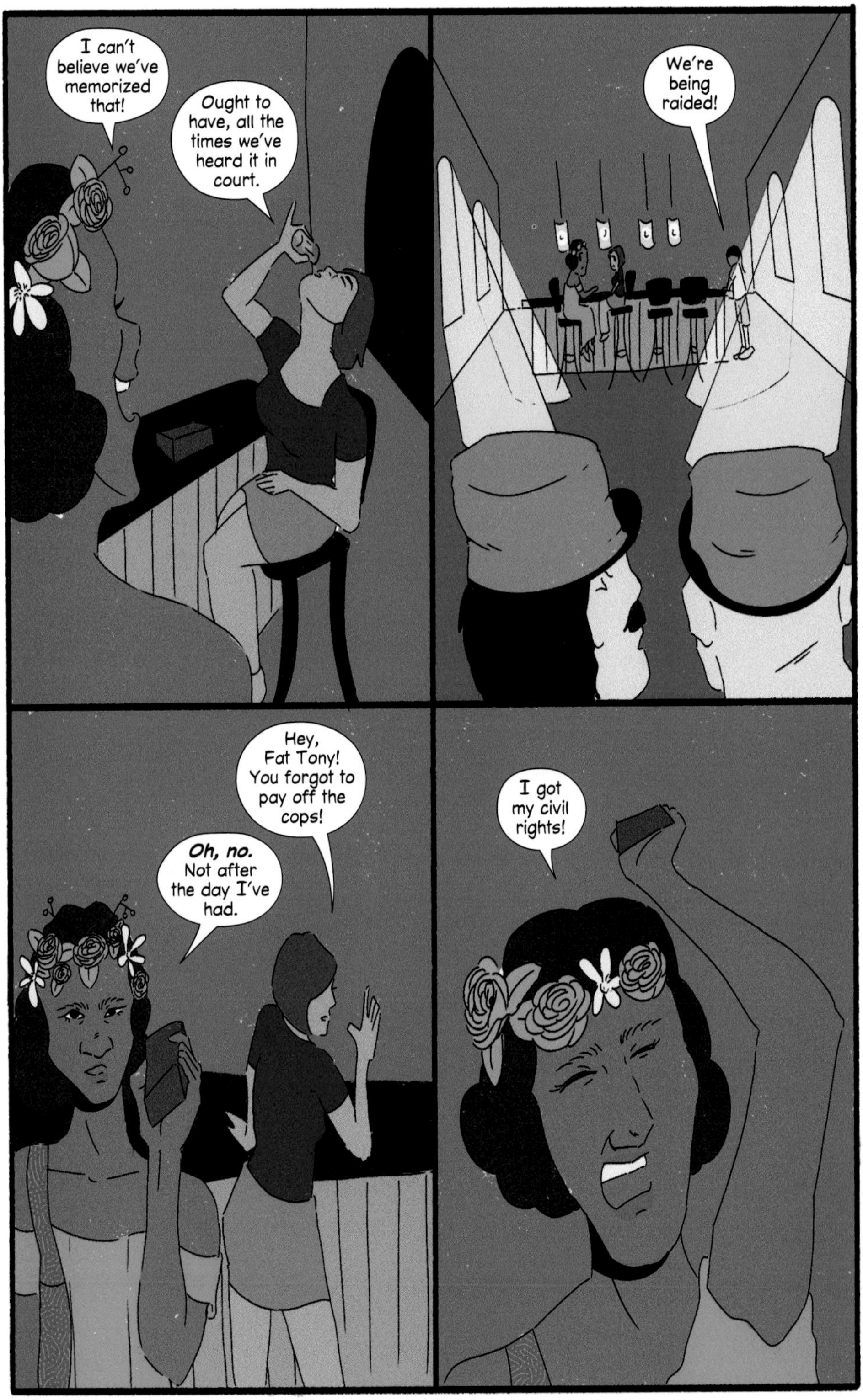
I can't believe we've memorized that!
Ought to have, all the times we've heard it in court.
We're being raided!
Hey, Fat Tony! You forgot to pay off the cops!
Oh, no. Not after the day I've had.
I got my civil rights!

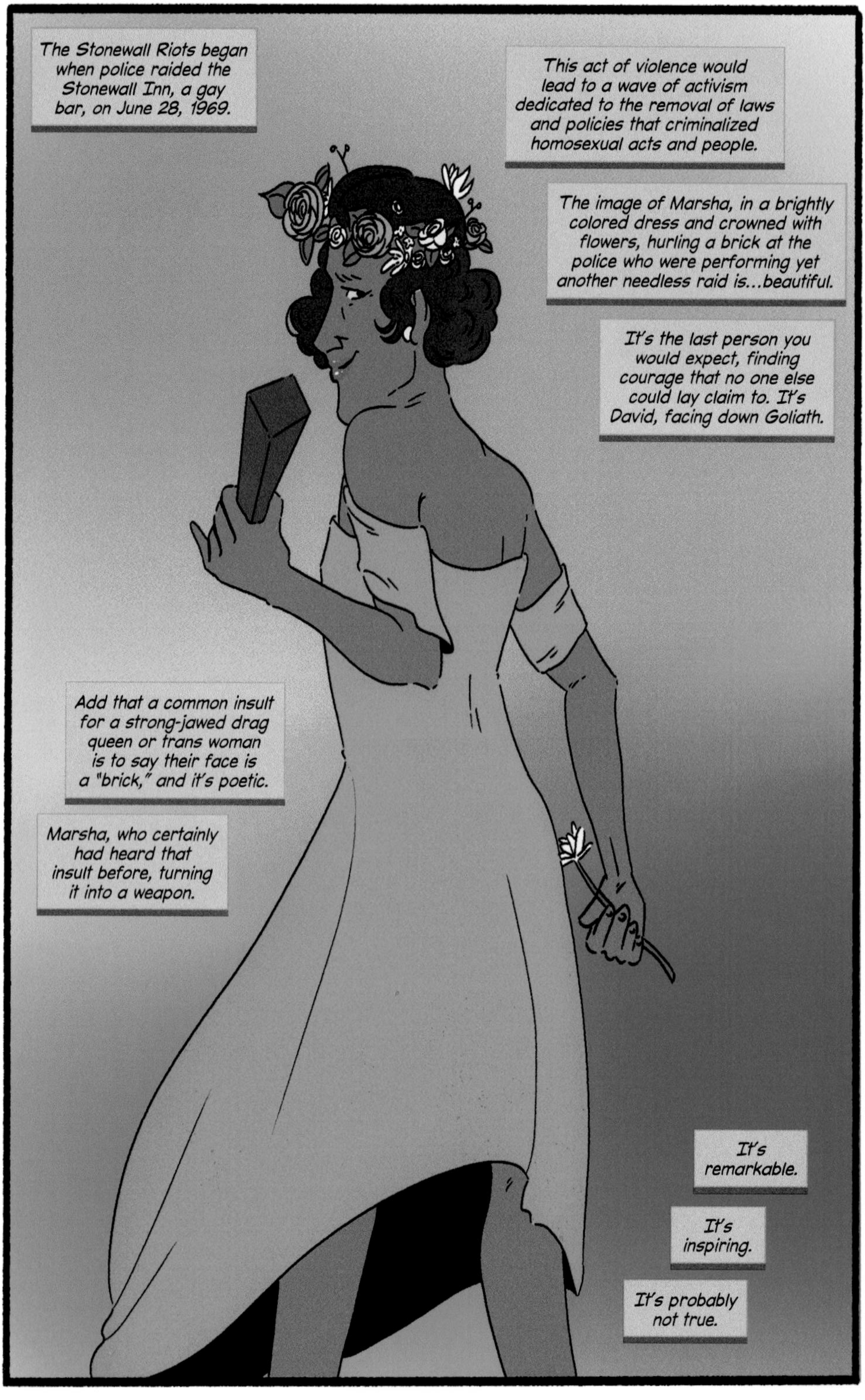
The Stonewall Riots began when police raided the Stonewall Inn, a gay bar, on June 28, 1969.
This act of violence would lead to a wave of activism dedicated to the removal of laws and policies that criminalized homosexual acts and people.
The image of Marsha, in a brightly colored dress and crowned with flowers, hurling a brick at the police who were performing yet another needless raid is...beautiful.
It's the last person you would expect, finding courage that no one else could lay claim to. It's David, facing down Goliath.
Add that a common insult for a strong-jawed drag queen or trans woman is to say their face is a "brick," and it's poetic.
Marsha, who certainly had heard that insult before, turning it into a weapon.
It's remarkable.
It's inspiring.
It's probably not true.

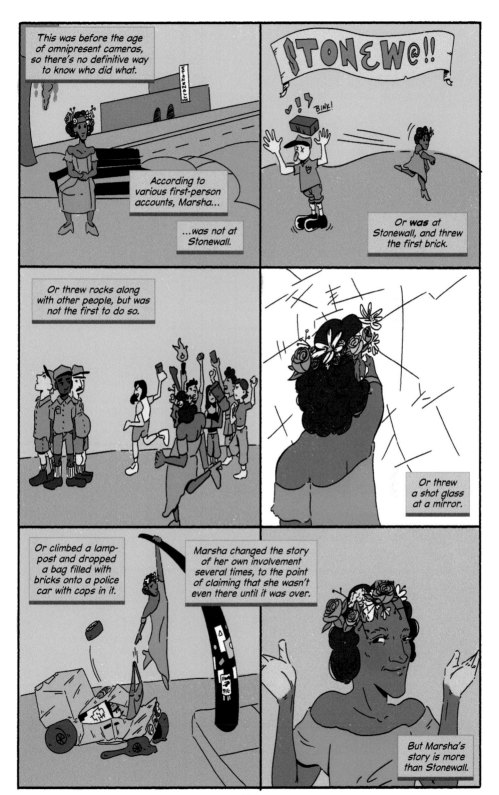

This was before the age of omnipresent cameras, so there's no definitive way to know who did what.

STONEW@!!

BINK!

According to various first-person accounts, Marsha...

...was not at Stonewall.

Or **was** at Stonewall, and threw the first brick.

Or threw rocks along with other people, but was not the first to do so.

Or threw a shot glass at a mirror.

Or climbed a lamp-post and dropped a bag filled with bricks onto a police car with cops in it.

Marsha changed the story of her own involvement several times, to the point of claiming that she wasn't even there until it was over.

But Marsha's story is more than Stonewall.

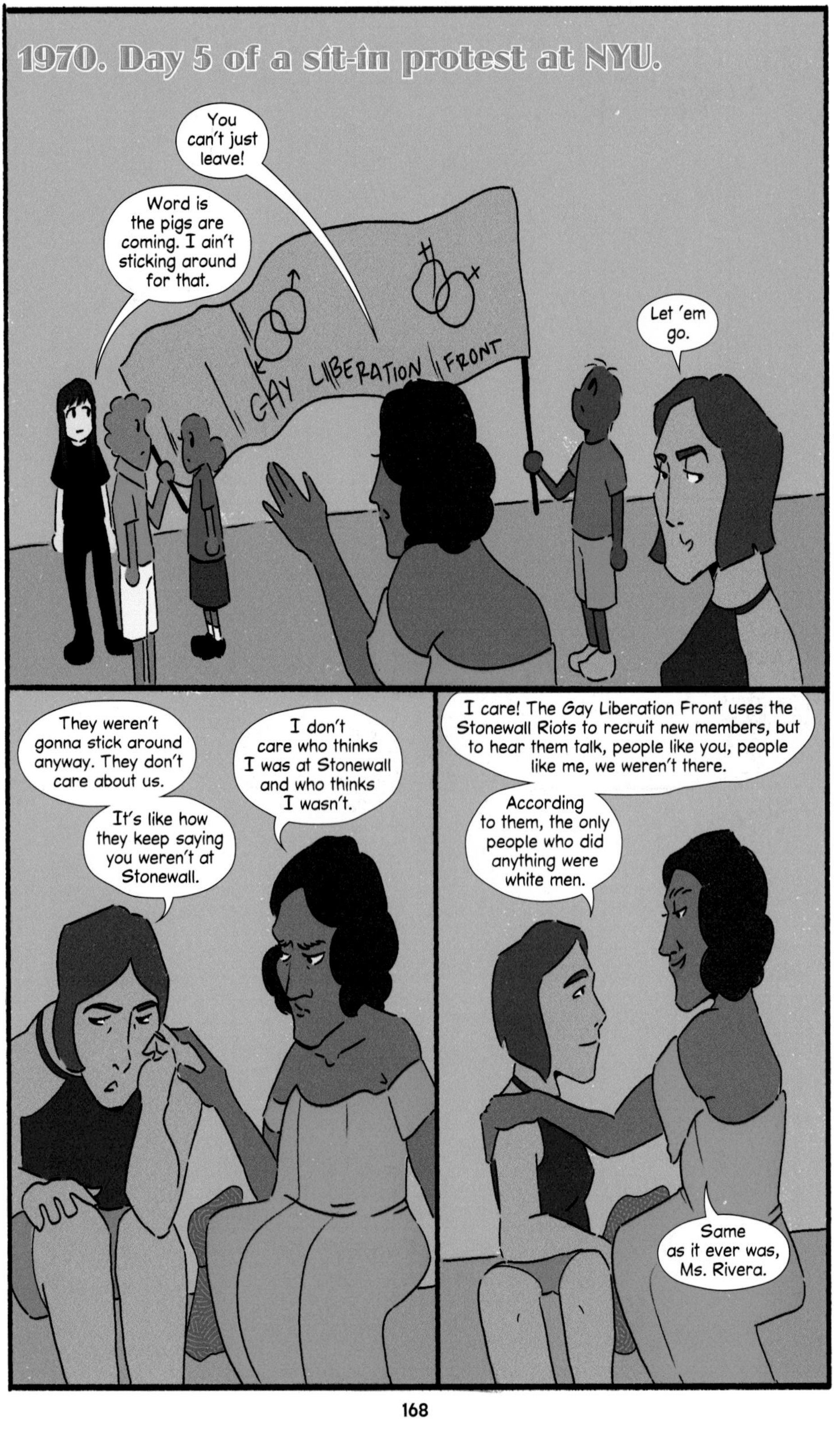
1970. Day 5 of a sit-in protest at NYU.
Word is the pigs are coming. I ain't sticking around for that.
You can't just leave!
GAY LIBERATION FRONT
Let 'em go.
They weren't gonna stick around anyway. They don't care about us.
It's like how they keep saying you weren't at Stonewall.
I don't care who thinks I was at Stonewall and who thinks I wasn't.
I care! The *Gay Liberation Front* uses the Stonewall Riots to recruit new members, but to hear them talk, people like you, people like me, we weren't there.
According to them, the only people who did anything were white men.
Same as it ever was, Ms. Rivera.

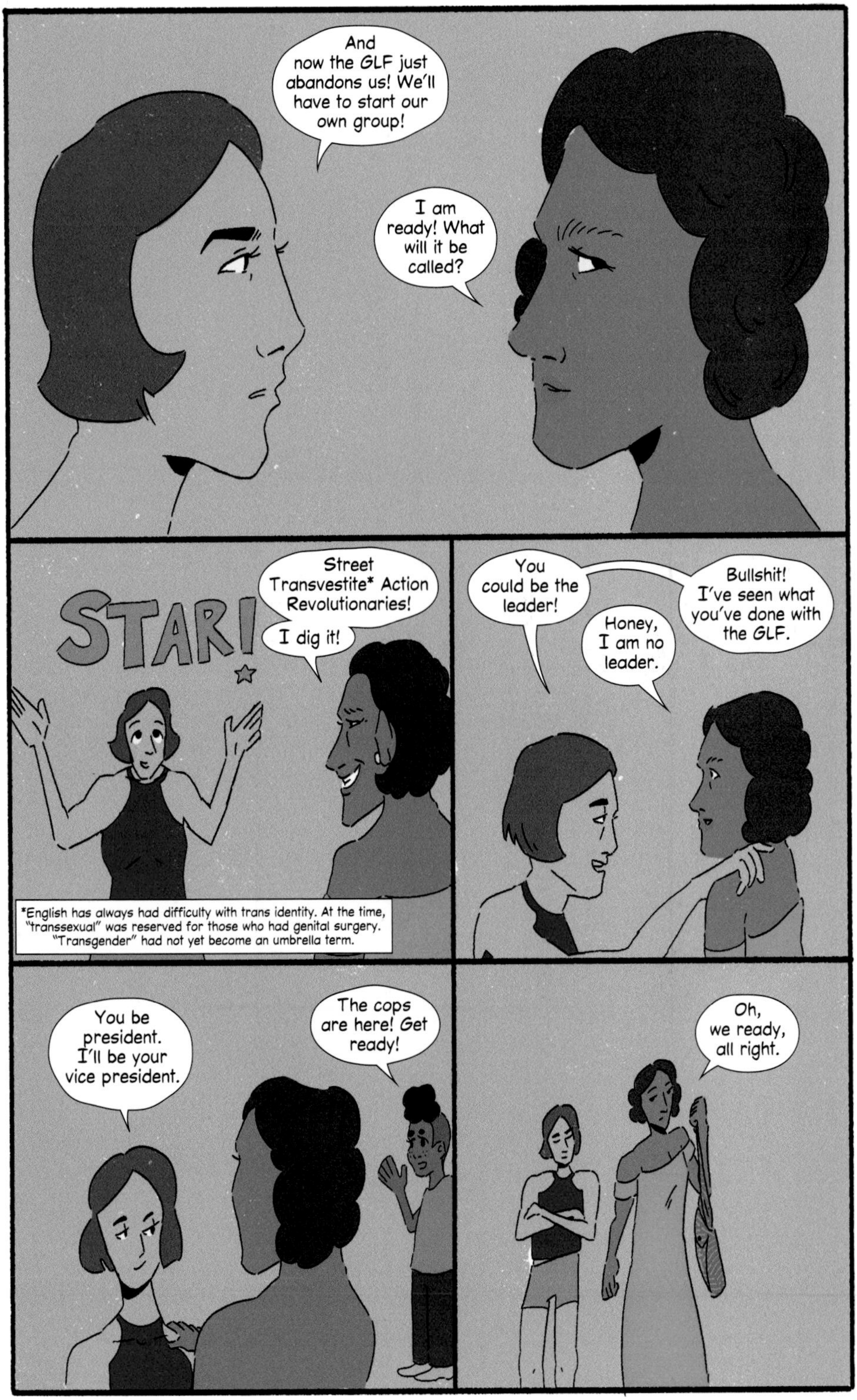
And now the GLF just abandons us! We'll have to start our own group!
I am ready! What will it be called?
Street Transvestite* Action Revolutionaries!
STAR!
I dig it!
*English has always had difficulty with trans identity. At the time, "transsexual" was reserved for those who had genital surgery. "Transgender" had not yet become an umbrella term.
You could be the leader!
Honey, I am no leader.
Bullshit! I've seen what you've done with the GLF.
You be president. I'll be your vice president.
The cops are here! Get ready!
Oh, we ready, all right.

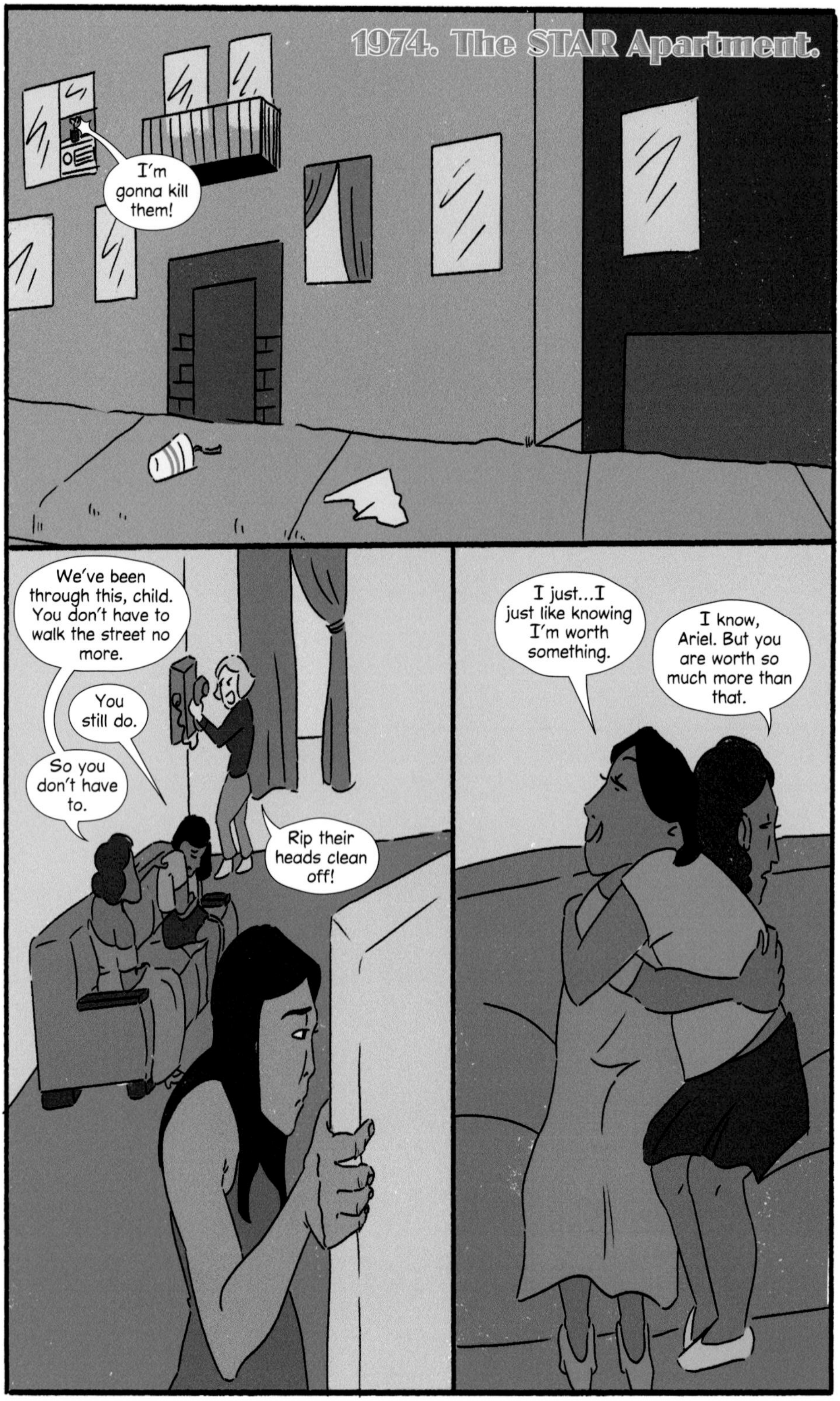
1974. The STAR Apartment.
I'm gonna kill them!
We've been through this, child. You don't have to walk the street no more.
You still do.
So you don't have to.
Rip their heads clean off!
I just...I just like knowing I'm worth something.
I know, Ariel. But you are worth so much more than that.

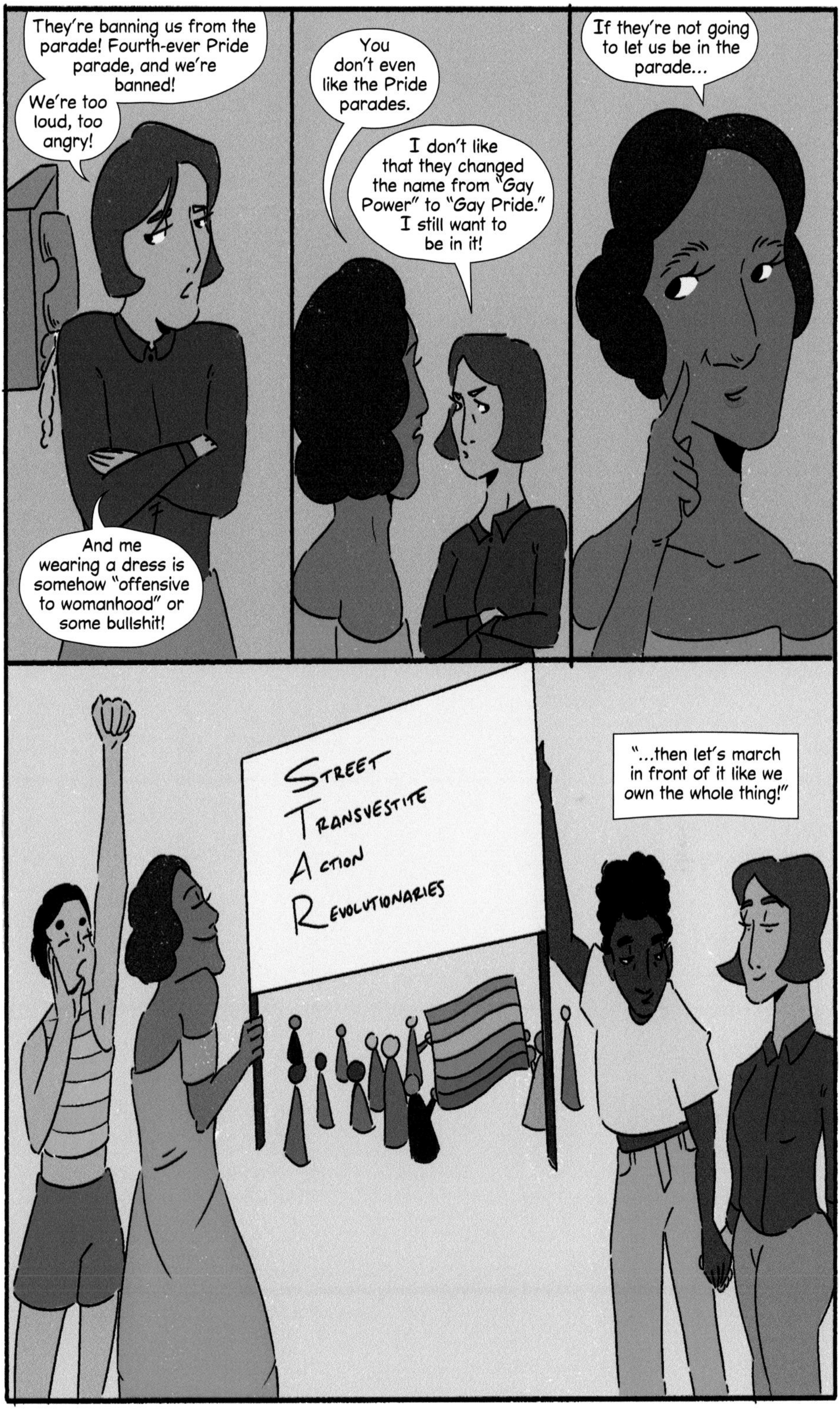
They're banning us from the parade! Fourth-ever Pride parade, and we're banned!
We're too loud, too angry!
And me wearing a dress is somehow "offensive to womanhood" or some bullshit!
You don't even like the Pride parades.
I don't like that they changed the name from "Gay Power" to "Gay Pride." I still want to be in it!
If they're not going to let us be in the parade...
STREET TRANSVESTITE ACTION REVOLUTIONARIES
"...then let's march in front of it like we own the whole thing!"

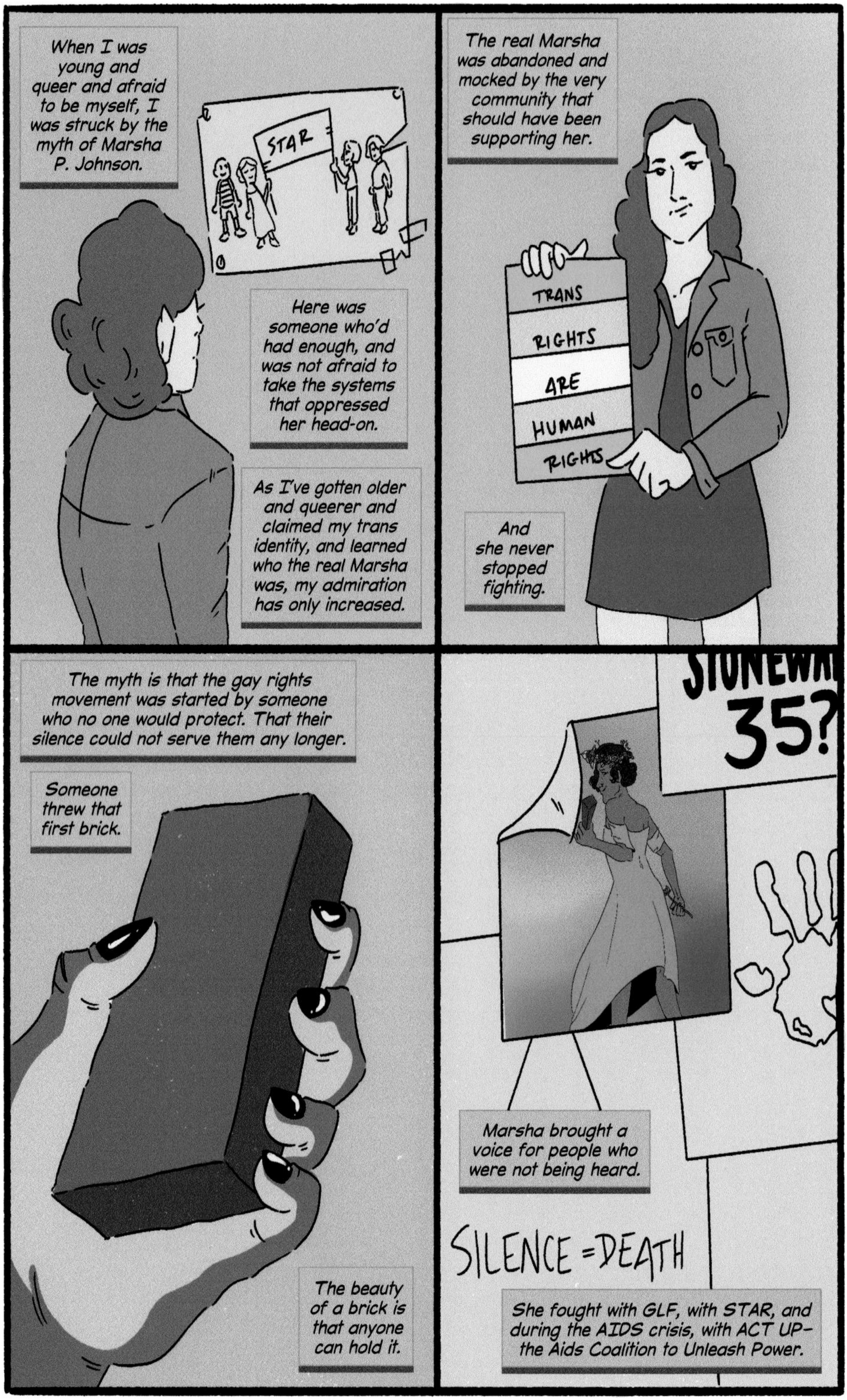

When I was young and queer and afraid to be myself, I was struck by the myth of Marsha P. Johnson.
STAR
Here was someone who'd had enough, and was not afraid to take the systems that oppressed her head-on.
As I've gotten older and queerer and claimed my trans identity, and learned who the real Marsha was, my admiration has only increased.
The real Marsha was abandoned and mocked by the very community that should have been supporting her.
TRANS
RIGHTS
ARE
HUMAN
RIGHTS
And she never stopped fighting.
The myth is that the gay rights movement was started by someone who no one would protect. That their silence could not serve them any longer.
Someone threw that first brick.
The beauty of a brick is that anyone can hold it.
35?
Marsha brought a voice for people who were not being heard.
SILENCE =DEATH
She fought with GLF, with STAR, and during the AIDS crisis, with ACT UP— the Aids Coalition to Unleash Power.

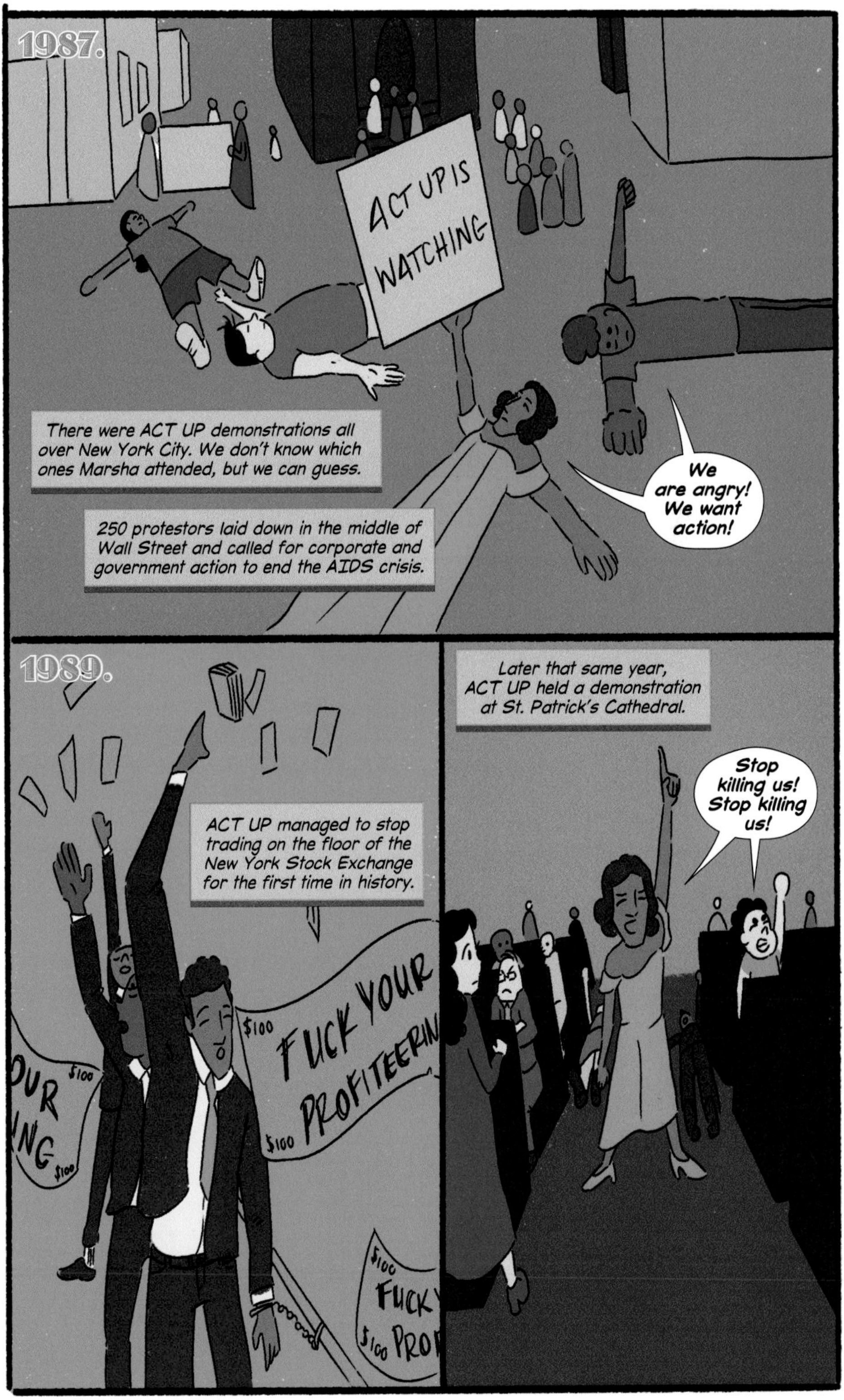
1987.
ACT UP IS WATCHING
There were ACT UP demonstrations all over New York City. We don't know which ones Marsha attended, but we can guess.
250 protestors laid down in the middle of Wall Street and called for corporate and government action to end the AIDS crisis.
We are angry! We want action!
1989.
ACT UP managed to stop trading on the floor of the New York Stock Exchange for the first time in history.
FUCK YOUR PROFITEERIN
$100
Later that same year, ACT UP held a demonstration at St. Patrick's Cathedral.
Stop killing us! Stop killing us!

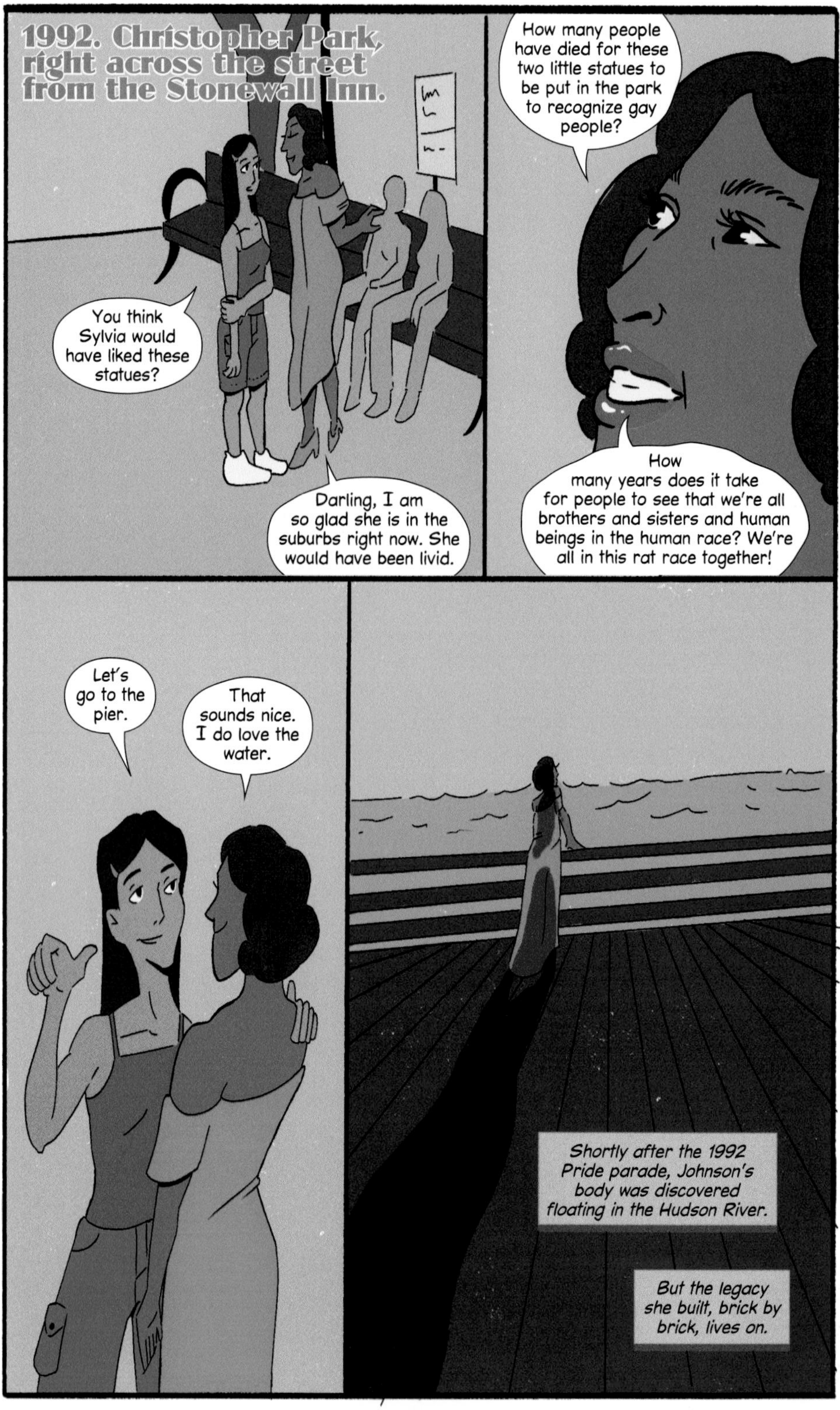
1992. Christopher Park, right across the street from the Stonewall Inn.
You think Sylvia would have liked these statues?
Darling, I am so glad she is in the suburbs right now. She would have been livid.
How many people have died for these two little statues to be put in the park to recognize gay people?
How many years does it take for people to see that we're all brothers and sisters and human beings in the human race? We're all in this rat race together!
Let's go to the pier.
That sounds nice. I do love the water.
Shortly after the 1992 Pride parade, Johnson's body was discovered floating in the Hudson River.
But the legacy she built, brick by brick, lives on.

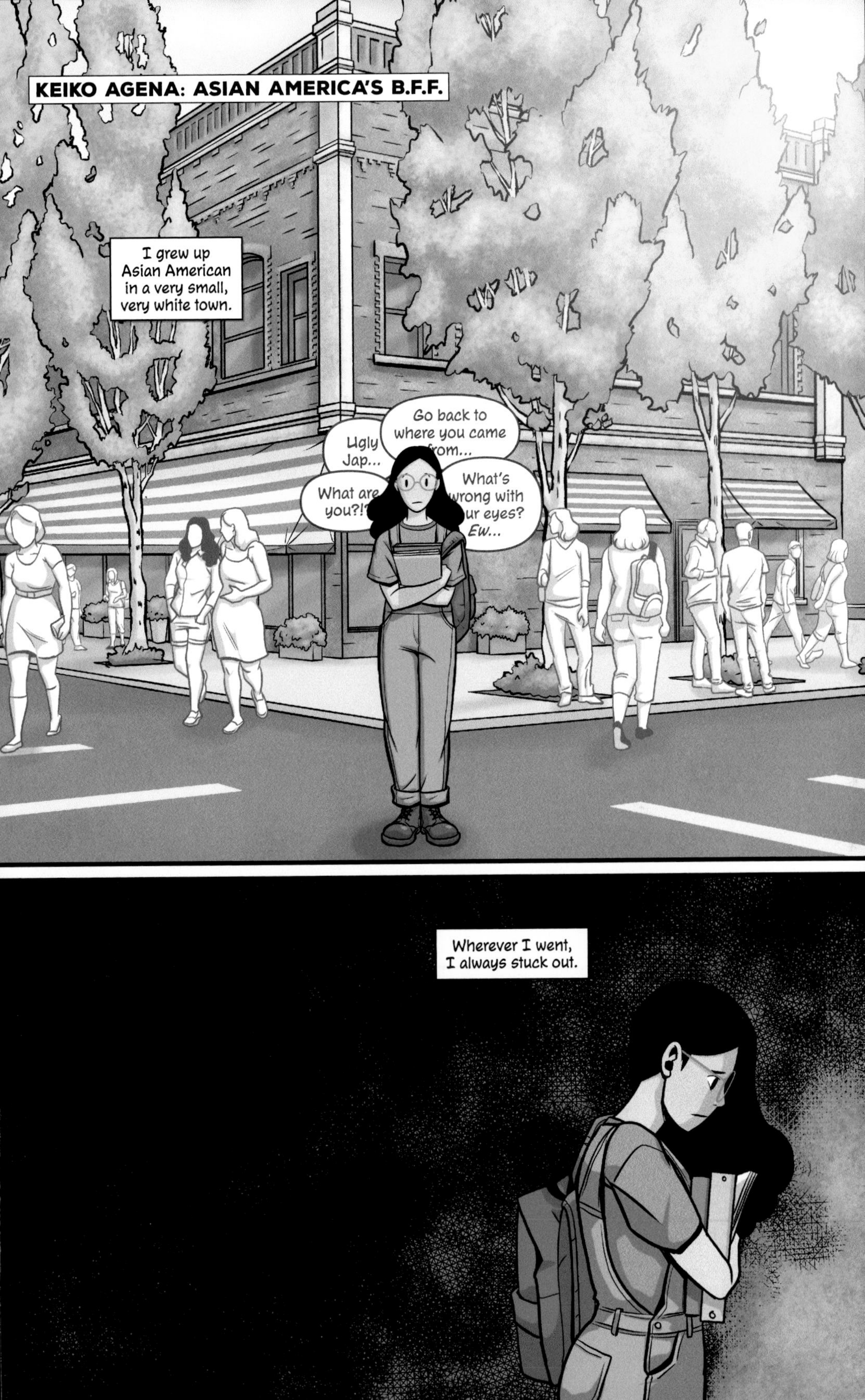
KEIKO AGENA: ASIAN AMERICA'S B.F.F.
I grew up Asian American in a very small, very white town.
Ugly Jap...
Go back to where you came from...
What are you?!
What's wrong with ur eyes? Ew...
Wherever I went, I always stuck out.

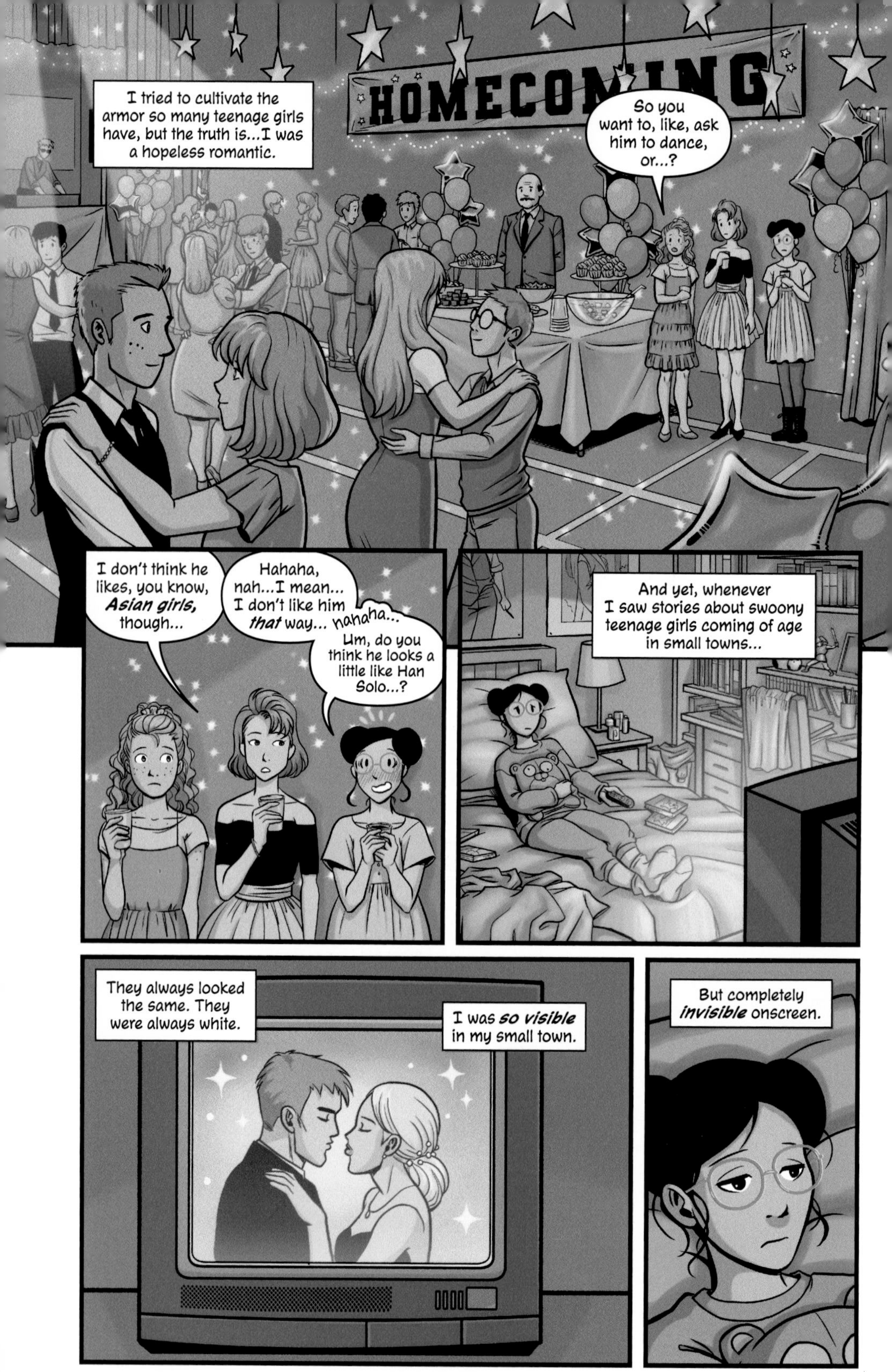
HOMECOMING
I tried to cultivate the armor so many teenage girls have, but the truth is...I was a hopeless romantic.
So you want to, like, ask him to dance, or...?
I don't think he likes, you know, ***Asian girls,*** though...
Hahaha, nah...I mean... I don't like him ***that*** way... hahaha...
Um, do you think he looks a little like Han Solo...?
And yet, whenever I saw stories about swoony teenage girls coming of age in small towns...
They always looked the same. They were always white.
I was ***so visible*** in my small town.
But completely ***invisible*** onscreen.

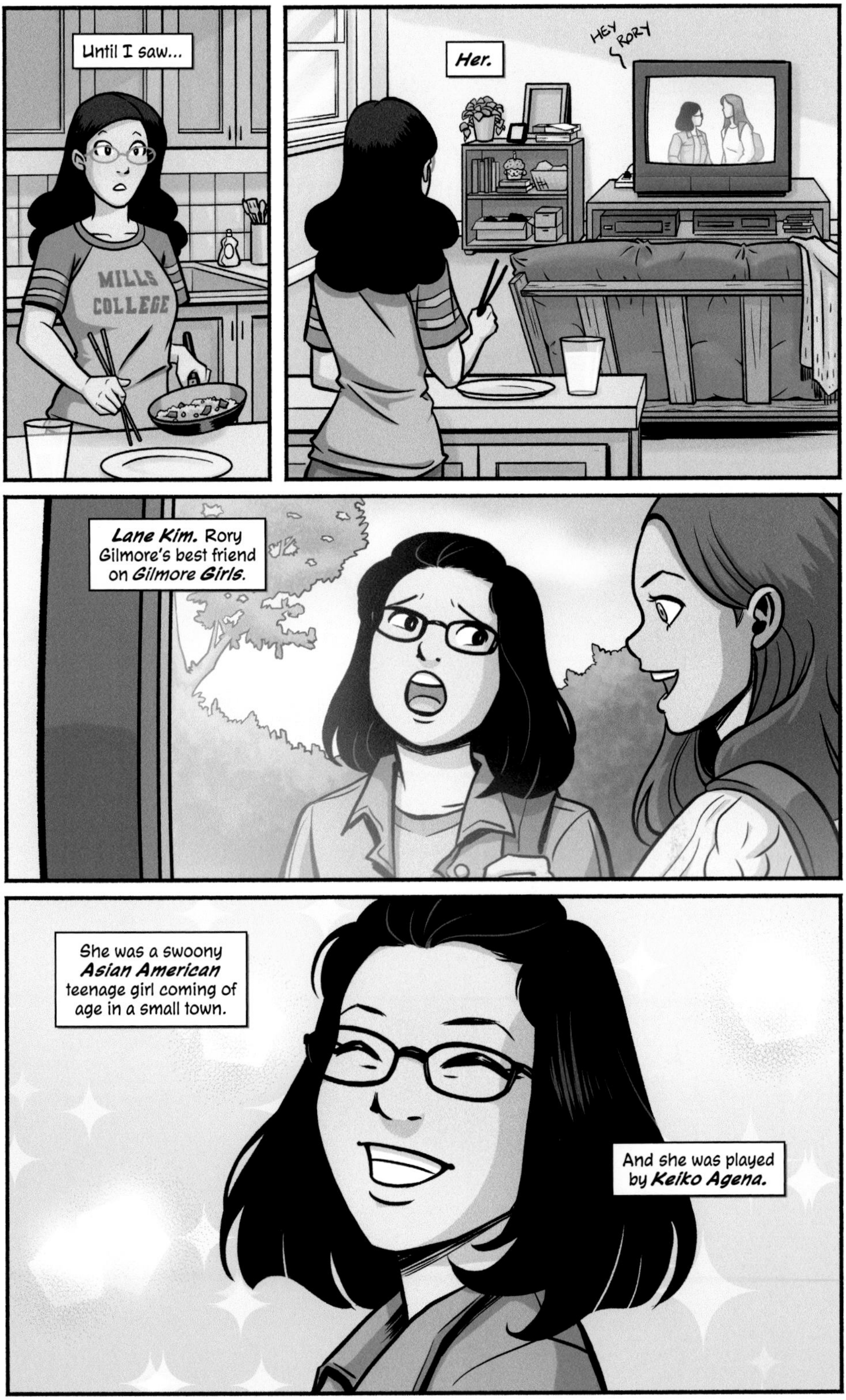
Until I saw...
Her.
HEY RORY
MILLS COLLEGE
Lane Kim. Rory Gilmore's best friend on Gilmore Girls.
She was a swoony Asian American teenage girl coming of age in a small town.
And she was played by Keiko Agena.

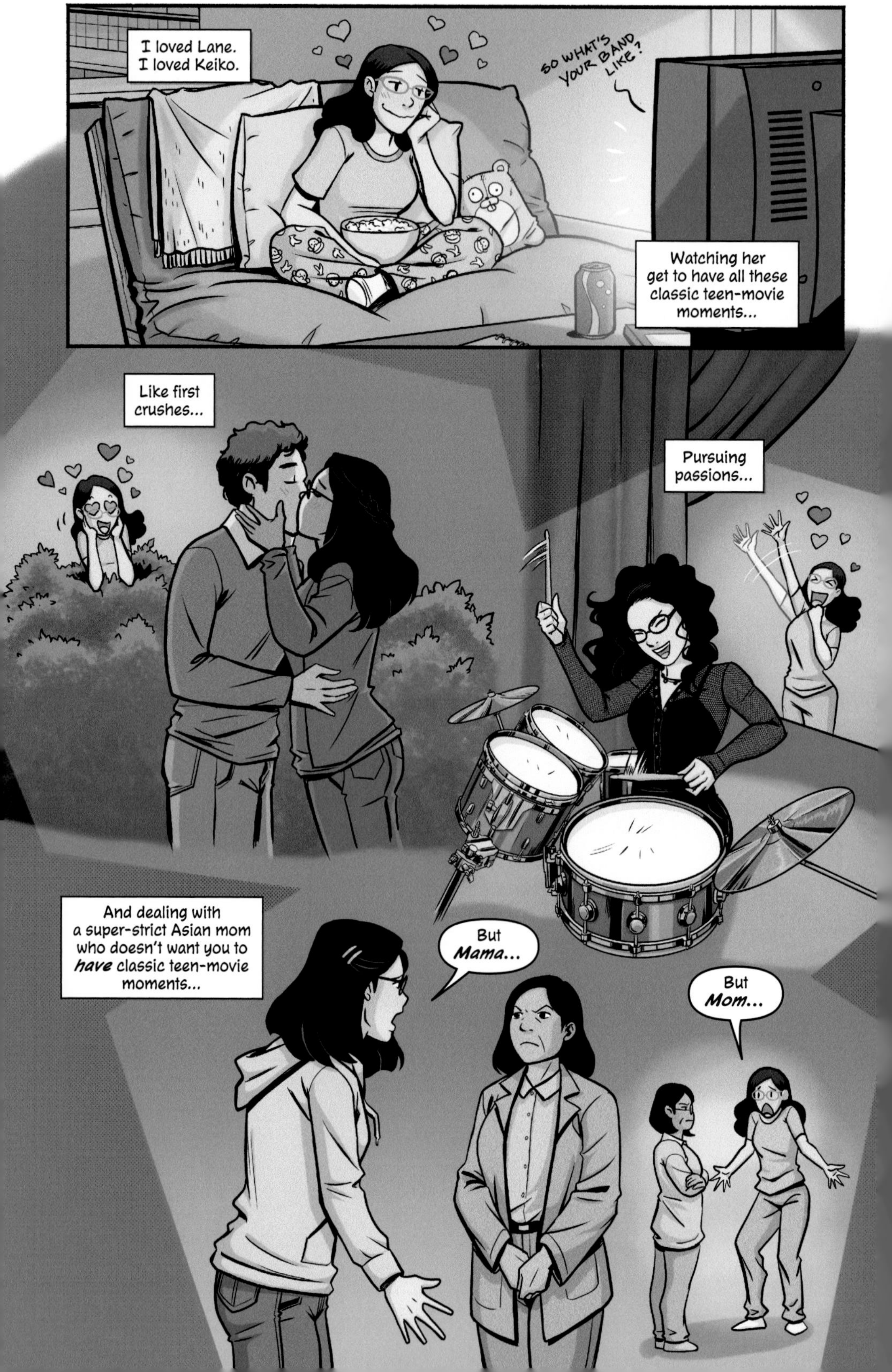
I loved Lane.
I loved Keiko.
SO WHAT'S YOUR BAND LIKE?
Watching her get to have all these classic teen-movie moments...
Like first crushes...
Pursuing passions...
And dealing with a super-strict Asian mom who doesn't want you to *have* classic teen-movie moments...
But *Mama...*
But *Mom...*

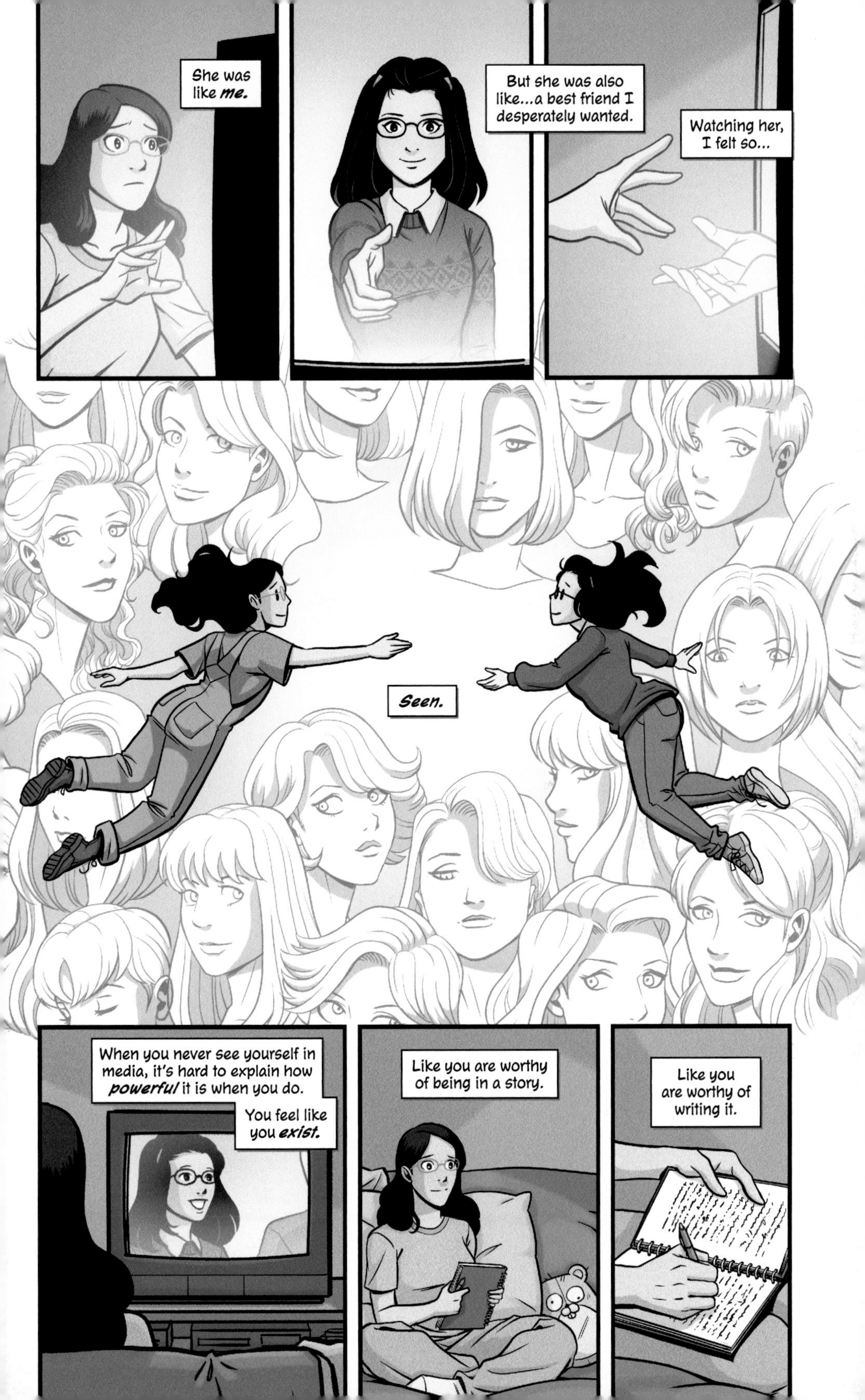
She was like *me.*
But she was also like...a best friend I desperately wanted.
Watching her, I felt so...
Seen.
When you never see yourself in media, it's hard to explain how *powerful* it is when you do.
You feel like you *exist.*
Like you are worthy of being in a story.
Like you are worthy of writing it.

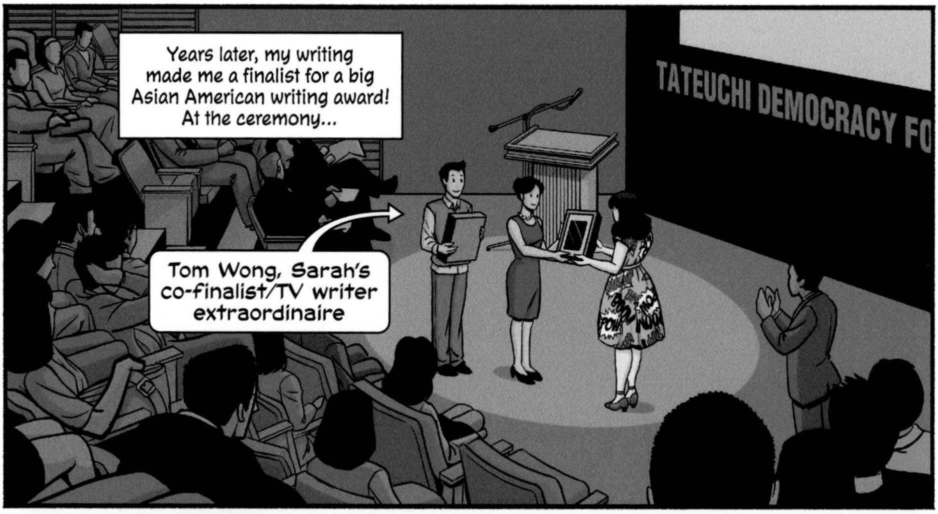
Years later, my writing made me a finalist for a big Asian American writing award! At the ceremony...
TATEUCHI DEMOCRACY FO
Tom Wong, Sarah's co-finalist/TV writer extraordinaire

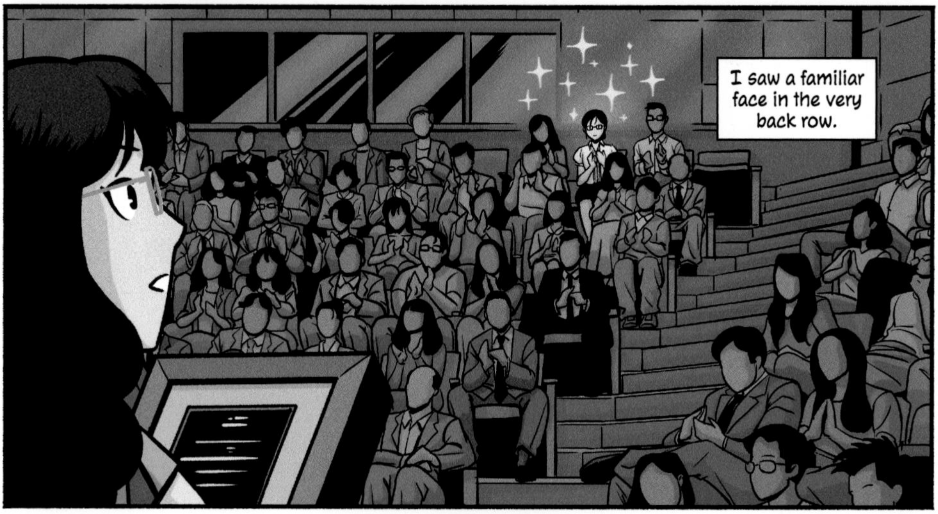
I saw a familiar face in the very back row.

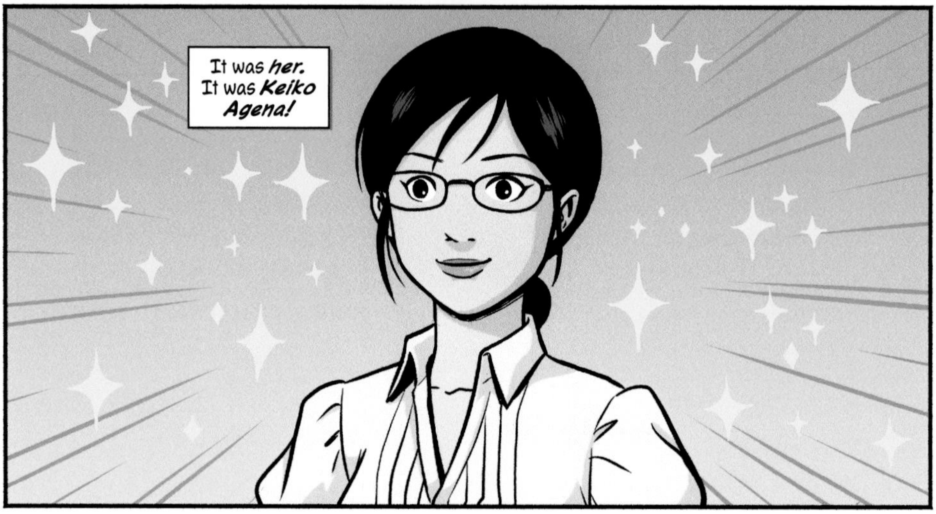
It was *her.* It was *Keiko Agena!*

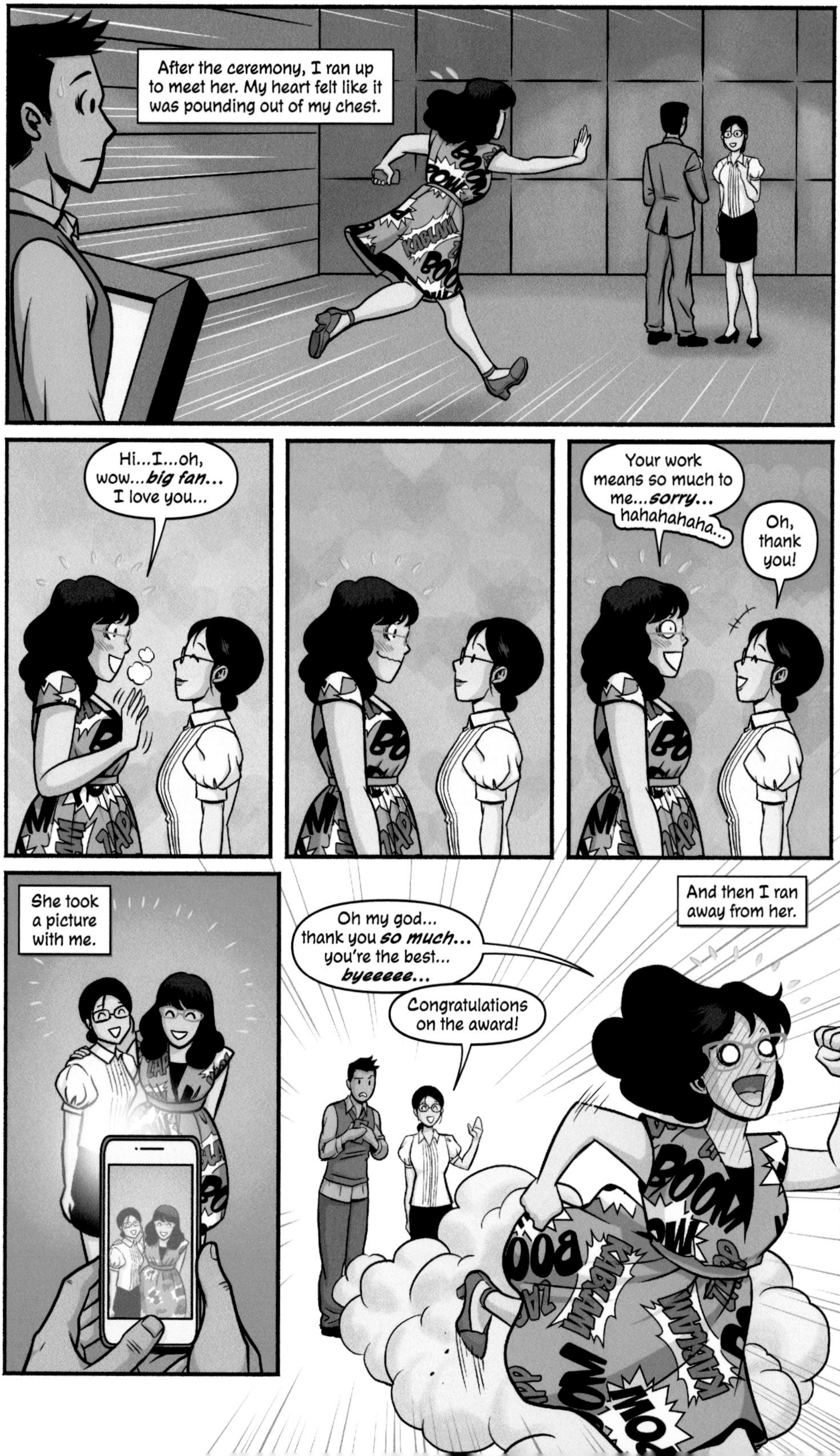

After the ceremony, I ran up to meet her. My heart felt like it was pounding out of my chest.
Hi...I...oh, wow...*big fan...* I love you...
Your work means so much to me...*sorry...* hahahahaha...
Oh, thank you!
She took a picture with me.
And then I ran away from her.
Oh my god... thank you *so much...* you're the best... *byeeeee...*
Congratulations on the award!

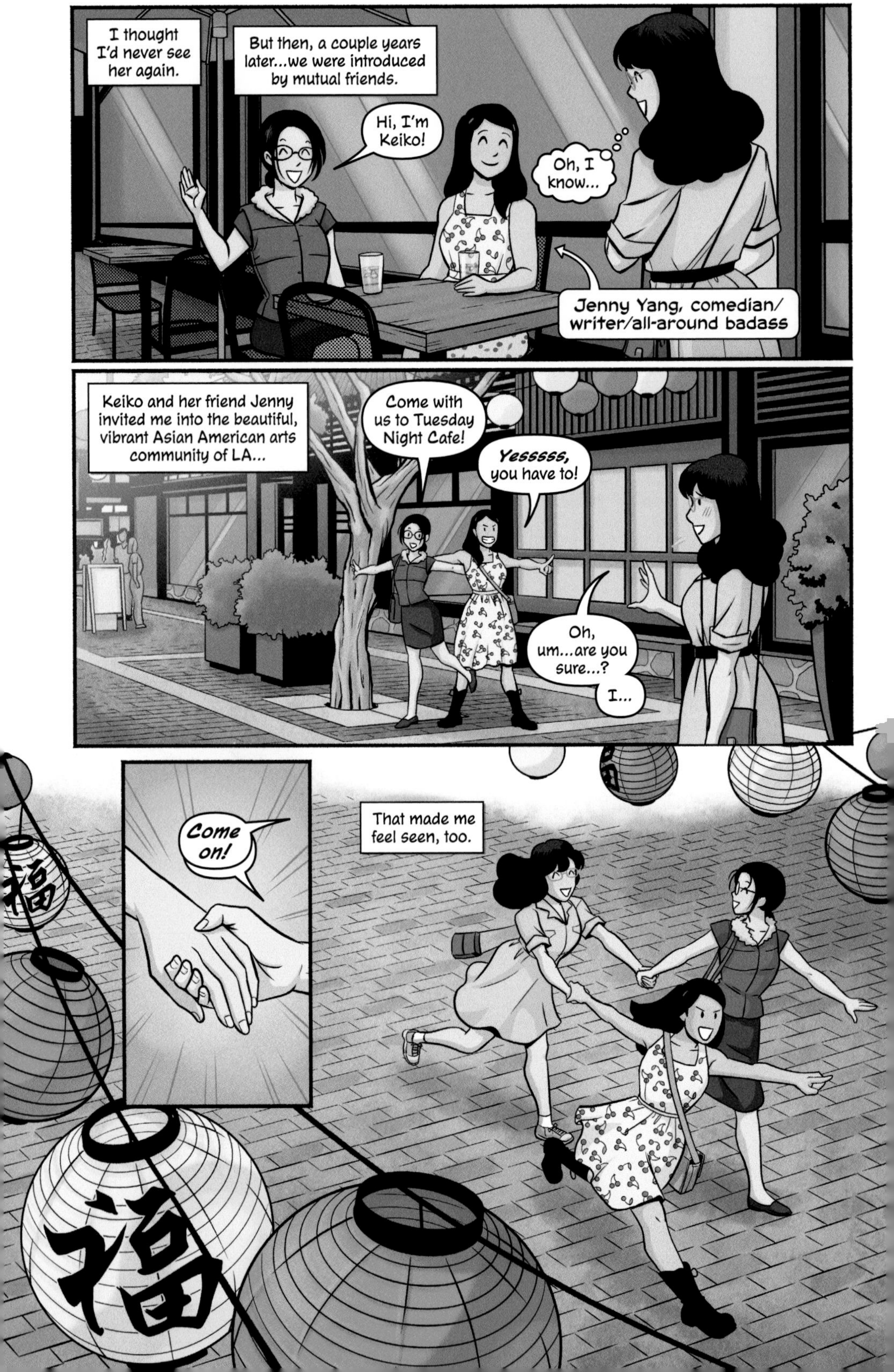
I thought I'd never see her again.
But then, a couple years later...we were introduced by mutual friends.
Hi, I'm Keiko!
Oh, I know...
Jenny Yang, comedian/ writer/all-around badass
Keiko and her friend Jenny invited me into the beautiful, vibrant Asian American arts community of LA...
Come with us to Tuesday Night Cafe!
Yesssss, you have to!
Oh, um...are you sure...?
I...
Come on!
That made me feel seen, too.
福
福

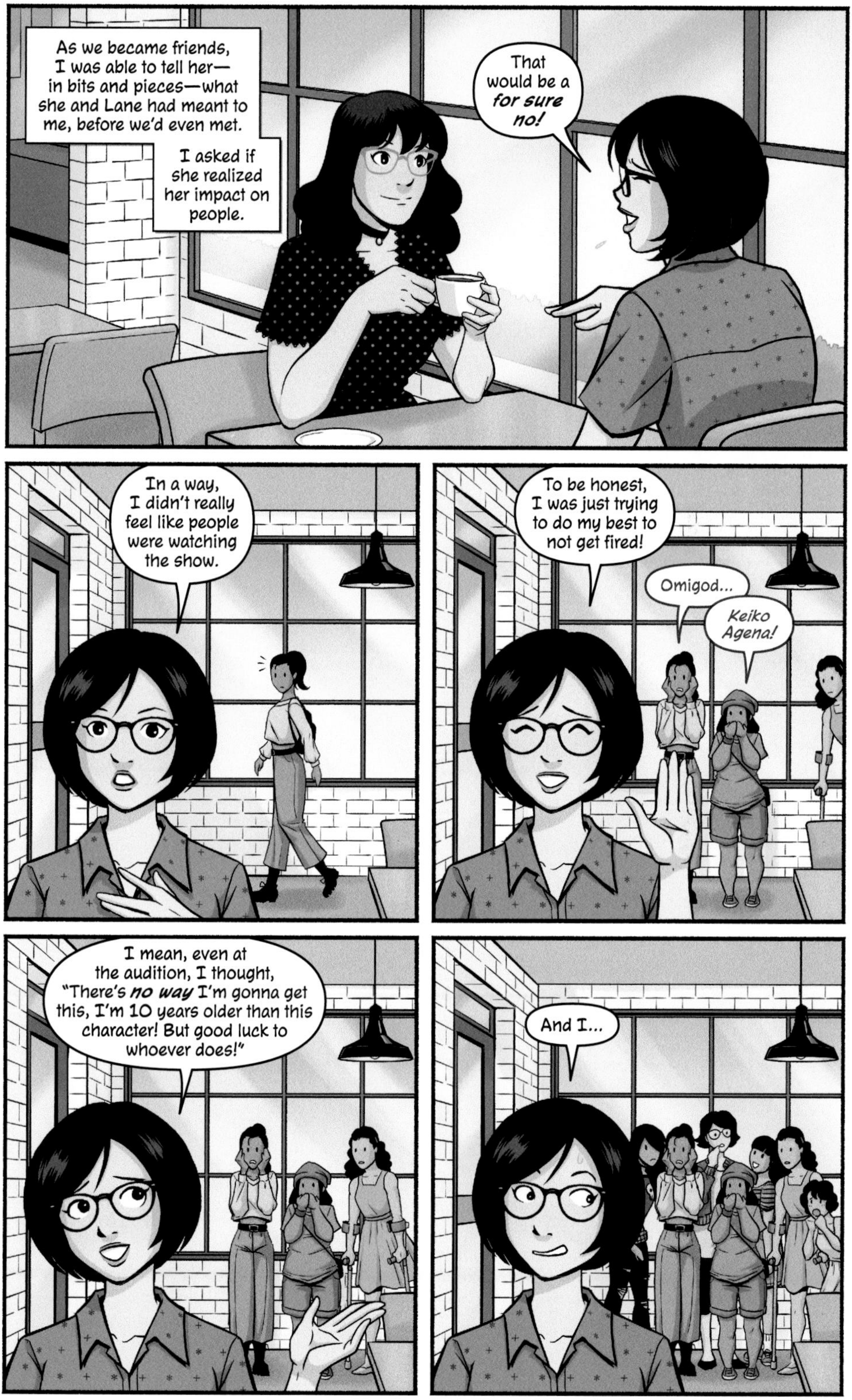
As we became friends, I was able to tell her—in bits and pieces—what she and Lane had meant to me, before we'd even met.
I asked if she realized her impact on people.
That would be a *for sure no!*
In a way, I didn't really feel like people were watching the show.
To be honest, I was just trying to do my best to not get fired!
Omigod...
Keiko Agena!
I mean, even at the audition, I thought, "There's *no way* I'm gonna get this, I'm 10 years older than this character! But good luck to whoever does!"
And I...

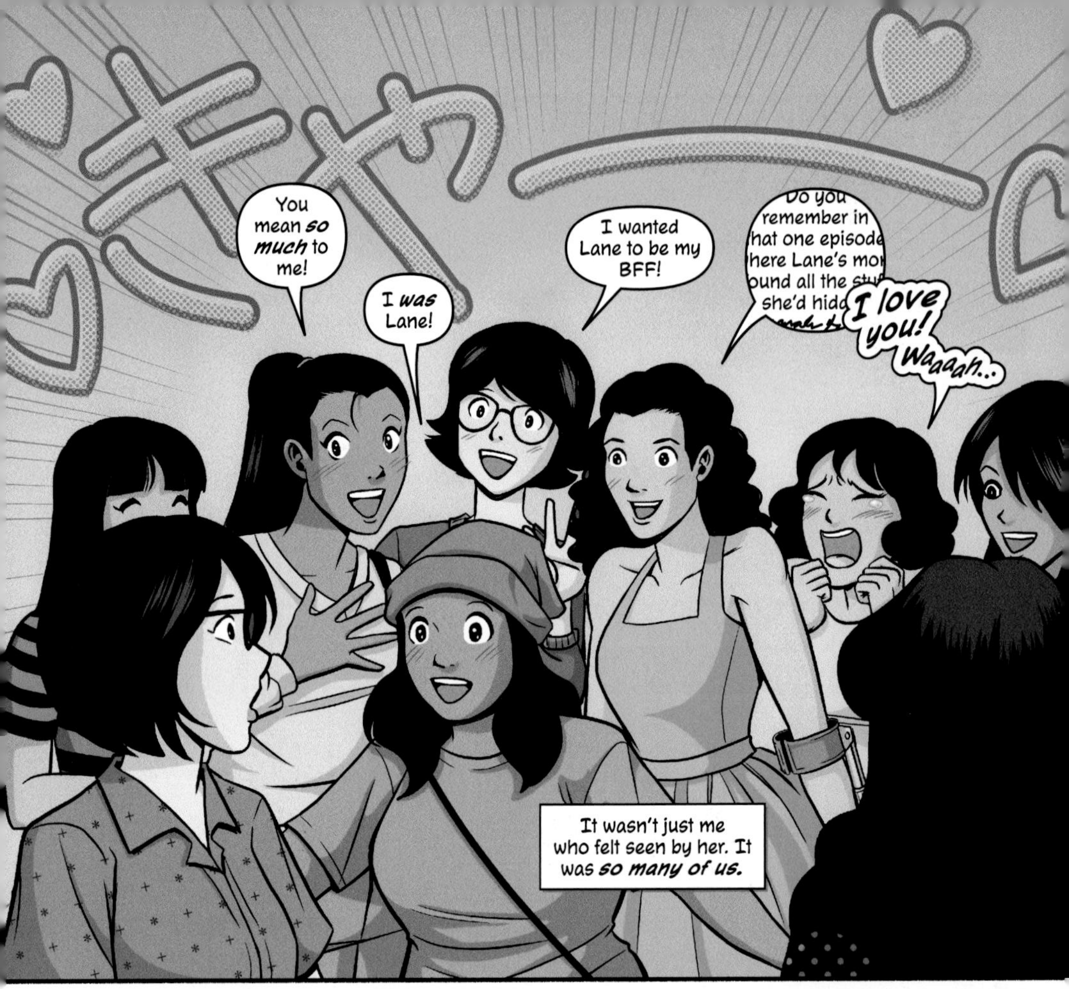
きゃー
You mean *so much* to me!
I *was* Lane!
I wanted Lane to be my BFF!
Do you remember in hat one episode here Lane's mo ound all the stu she'd hidd
I love you! Waaaah...
It wasn't just me who felt seen by her. It was *so many of us.*

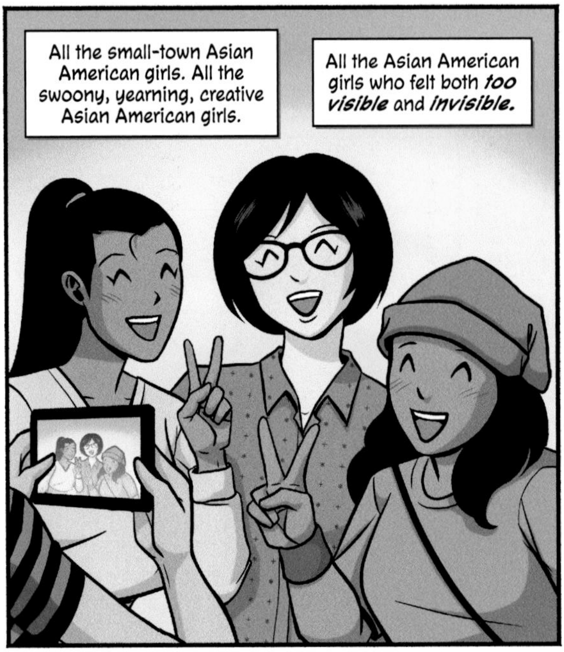
All the small-town Asian American girls. All the swoony, yearning, creative Asian American girls.
All the Asian American girls who felt both *too visible* and *invisible.*

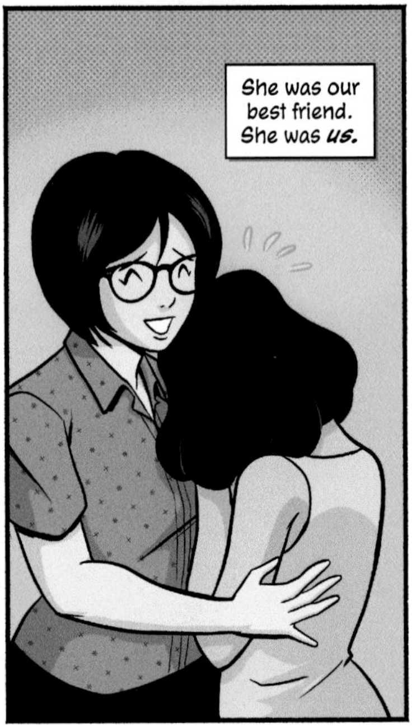
She was our best friend. She was *us.*

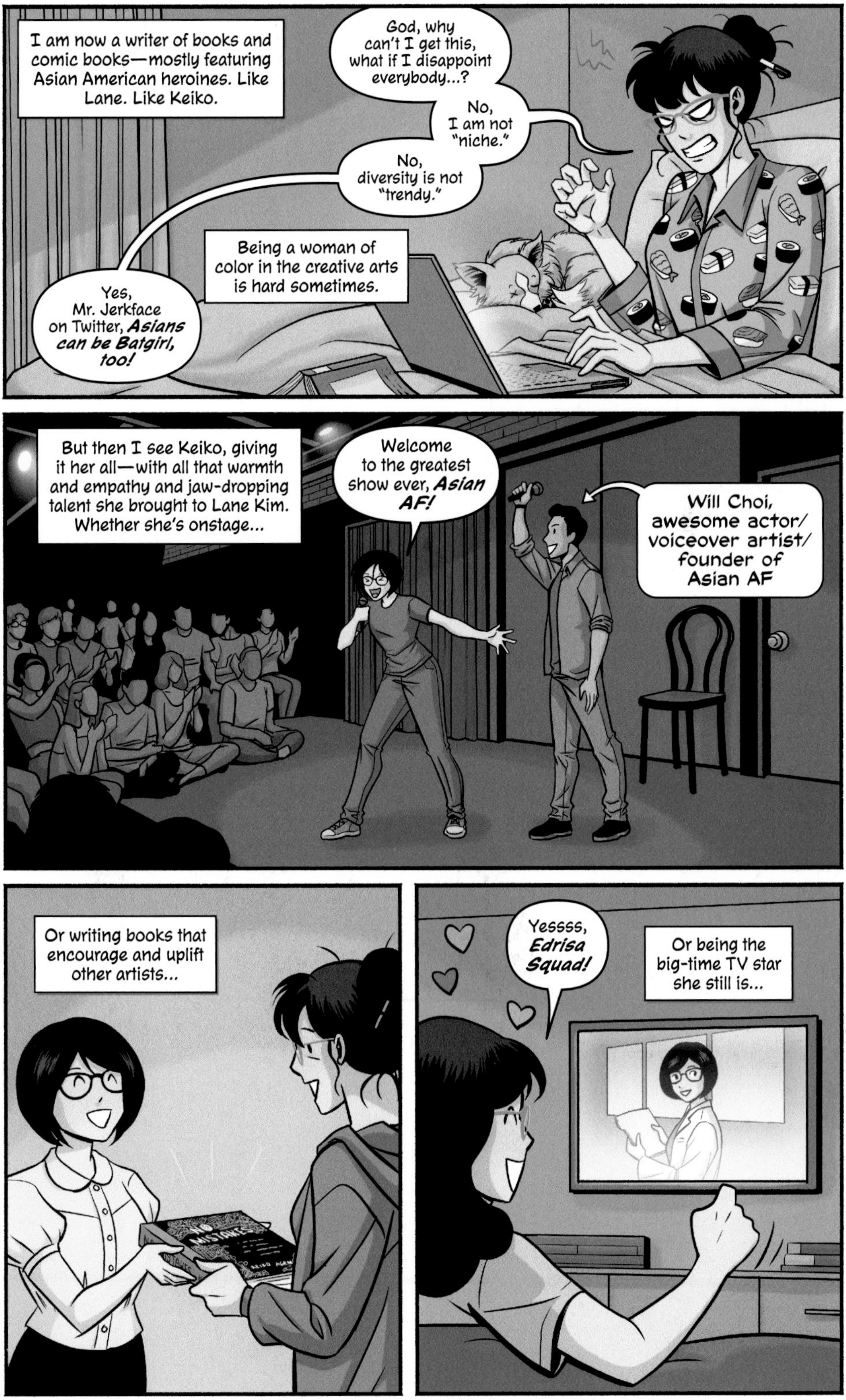

I am now a writer of books and comic books—mostly featuring Asian American heroines. Like Lane. Like Keiko.
God, why can't I get this, what if I disappoint everybody...?
No, I am not "niche."
No, diversity is not "trendy."
Being a woman of color in the creative arts is hard sometimes.
Yes, Mr. Jerkface on Twitter, ***Asians can be Batgirl, too!***
But then I see Keiko, giving it her all—with all that warmth and empathy and jaw-dropping talent she brought to Lane Kim. Whether she's onstage...
Welcome to the greatest show ever, ***Asian AF!***
Will Choi, awesome actor/ voiceover artist/ founder of Asian AF
Or writing books that encourage and uplift other artists...
NO MISTAKES
Or being the big-time TV star she still is...
Yessss, ***Edrisa Squad!***

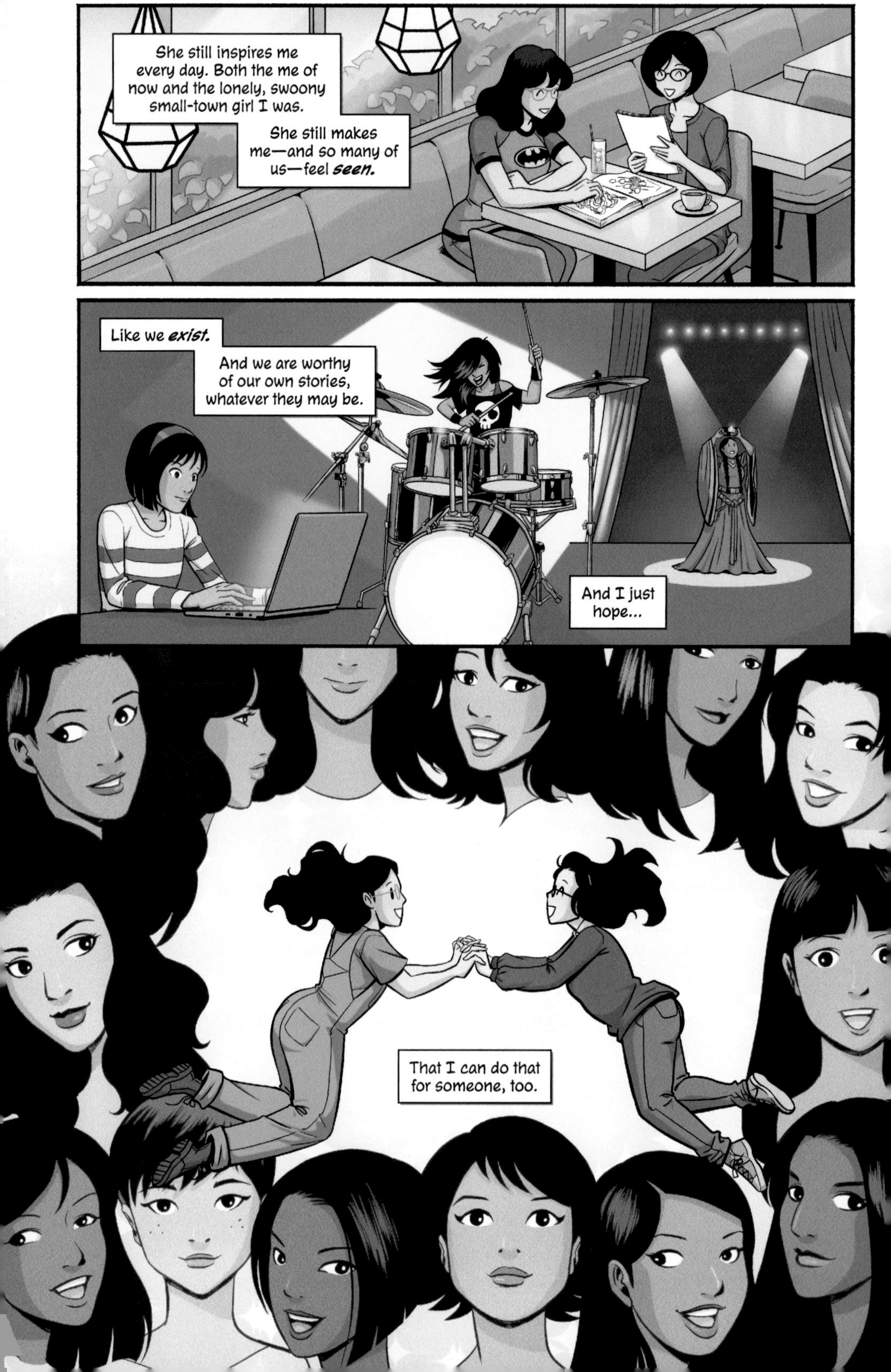
She still inspires me every day. Both the me of now and the lonely, swoony small-town girl I was.
She still makes me—and so many of us—feel *seen.*
Like we *exist.*
And we are worthy of our own stories, whatever they may be.
And I just hope...
That I can do that for someone, too.

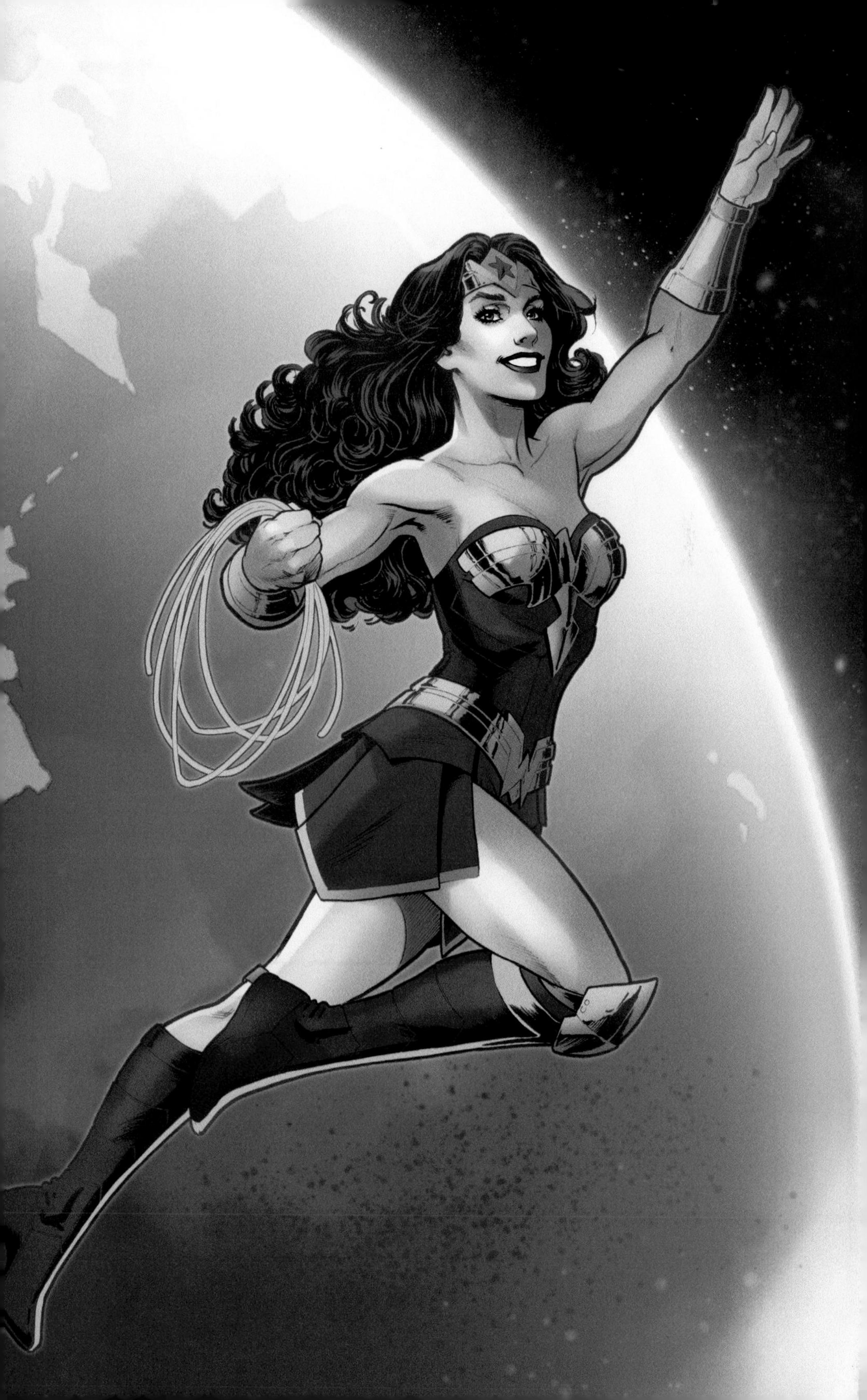

TEAM BIOGRAPHIES
and RESULTS RESOURCES *to learn more about these icons!*

BEYONCÉ: A DIVA WHO MEANS BUSINESS
Visit beyonce.com/beygood to discover the many ways Beyoncé is making our world a more just place.

MIKKI KENDALL (she/her) is the author of the *New York Times* bestseller *Hood Feminism* and the graphic novel *Amazons, Abolitionists, and Activists: A Graphic History of Women's Fight for Their Rights* (also with A. D'Amico). Her essays have appeared in *Time*, the *New York Times*, the *Washington Post*, and the *Guardian*, among others; her appearances as a commentator include *The Daily Show*, BBC radio, NPR, PBS, and *Good Morning America*.

A. D'AMICO is a queer comics artist and illustrator who loves all things tea, historical fashion, and horror. Her works include *Amazons, Abolitionists, and Activists*, written by Mikki Kendall; several anthologies including *True War Stories*, *Spitball*, and 2018 Prism Award winner *Dates!*; and many self-published works like *Dreamscapes*, *Hair Dye*, and *Dark Eyed Girl*. She also publishes a weekly journal webcomic, *Kid the Adult*, about the inner thoughts and daily goings-on of a 20-something weirdo navigating modern life.

KEIKO AGENA: ASIAN AMERICA'S B.F.F.
No Mistakes is a philosophy that improv artists follow, reframing missteps as opportunities. It's also a workbook Keiko wrote "for imperfect artists" — and aren't we all?

SARAH KUHN (she/her) is the author of the popular Heroine Complex novels — a series starring Asian American superheroines. Her YA debut, the Japan-set romantic comedy *I Love You So Mochi*, is a Junior Library Guild selection and a nominee for YALSA's Best Fiction for Young Adults. She's penned a variety of short fiction and comics, including the critically acclaimed graphic novel *Shadow of the Batgirl*, drawn by Nicole Goux, and the Star Wars audiobook original *Doctor Aphra*. A third-generation Japanese American, she lives in Los Angeles with her husband and an overflowing closet of vintage treasures.

LYNNE YOSHII is an alumna of DC Comics' 2016 Talent Development Workshop and a graduate of the School of Visual Arts in New York. Her works include DC's *New Talent Showcase 2017*, DC's *Gotham City Garage*, and cover illustrations for Boom! Studios and Dark Horse. She is currently working on the graphic novel *Nuclear Power* with Fanbase Press.

We shared some key moments from Marcia's talk, but you can watch the rest at: tedxcern.web.cern.ch/video/2014/weirdness-water-could-be-answer.

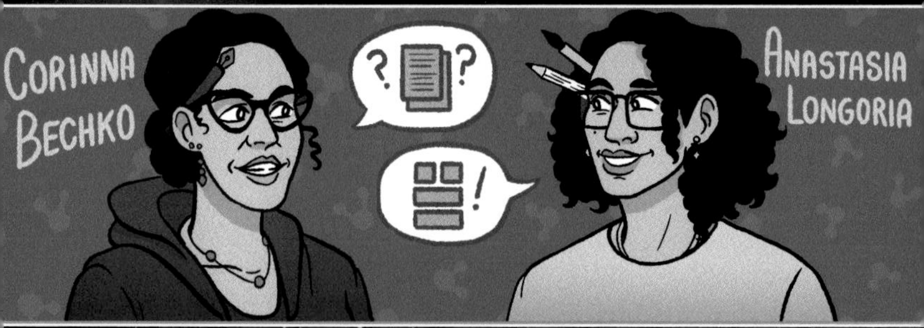
CORINNA BECHKO
? ?
!
ANASTASIA LONGORIA

CORINNA BECHKO is a Hugo- and Eisner-nominated, *New York Times* bestselling author who has worked for numerous publishers including DC, Marvel, Dark Horse, and Boom! on titles such as *Star Wars: Legacy*, *Savage Hulk*, *Angel*, *Once Upon a Time*, *The Expanse*, *Green Lantern: Earth One*, and *Invisible Republic* (co-written with Gabriel Hardman). She loves to work on science books for young readers, too, including *Smithsonian Dig It: Dinosaurs and Other Prehistoric Creatures* and *Smithsonian 1,000 Super Space Facts*. When not writing, Corinna works as a fossil preparator and volunteers with a naturalized parrot rescue.

ANASTASIA LONGORIA is a Latinx illustrator, focusing on creating comics about LGBTQ+ characters of color. Alongside the writers she collaborated with, Anastasia has been published in *Local Haunts Anthology*, *Bi Pride*, *Dates III Anthology*, and most recently *Mañana*, the Latinx science fiction comics anthology. She partnered with Dillon Gilbertson on their science fiction comic *Anew*, which tackles grief from a cosmic viewpoint. On her own, Anastasia has made several short comics, including *Autumn Leaves*, about lost love, and *Canciones de La Noche*, which covers childhood dreams. Anastasia currently lives in Maryland with her partner and is learning how to roller skate.

BRENÉ BROWN: BRAVING

We're big fans of all of Brené's work, which you can find at DareToLead.BreneBrown.com. The world needs bravery and trust, and we're looking forward to the next generation's courageous leaders.

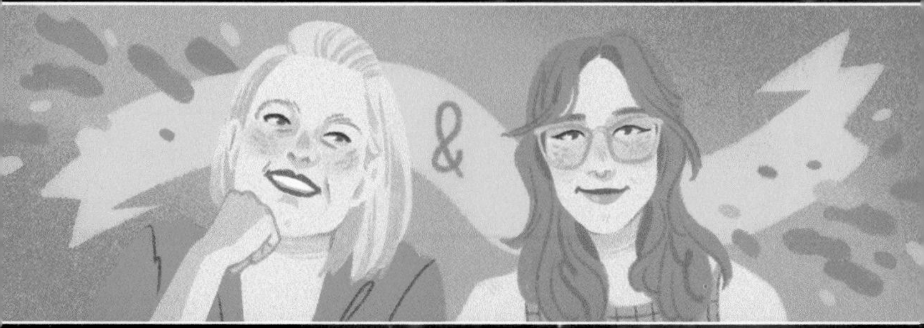
&

LOUISE SIMONSON has written comics, books, and animation for superhero, science fiction, horror, and fantasy universes. For Marvel, she created and wrote the award-winning *Power Pack*, *X-Factor*, *The New Mutants*, *Web of Spider-Man*, and *Wolverine: Meltdown*, with her husband, Walter Simonson. Her DC Comics works include *Superman: Man of Steel*, featuring the Death and Return of Superman; *Steel*; *World of Warcraft*; and comics adaptions of the YA novels *Wonder Woman: Warbringer* and *Catwoman: Soulstealer*. Her co-creations Apocalypse, Cable, Steel, and Doomsday are featured in movies and on TV. She lives with her husband, Walter, and dog, Loki, in the suburbs of New York City.

NICOLE GOUX is an illustrator and cartoonist from Los Angeles. She's the artist of DC's *Shadow of the Batgirl* and the co-creator of *F*ck Off Squad* from Silver Sprocket Bicycle Club and *Everyone is Tulip* from Dark Horse. She has an upcoming comic, *Forest Hills Bootleg Society*, debuting from Simon and Schuster in 2022. Her work often explores the themes of coming of age, interpersonal drama, and learning how to be a human. Lately she's spent a lot of time in the house (like, *a lot* a lot), but she loves traveling the country selling her

MARIANA COSTA CHECA: LABORATORIA OF CHANGE

To learn more about Laboratoria's mission to develop skills for the digital age, visit laboratoria.la/en.

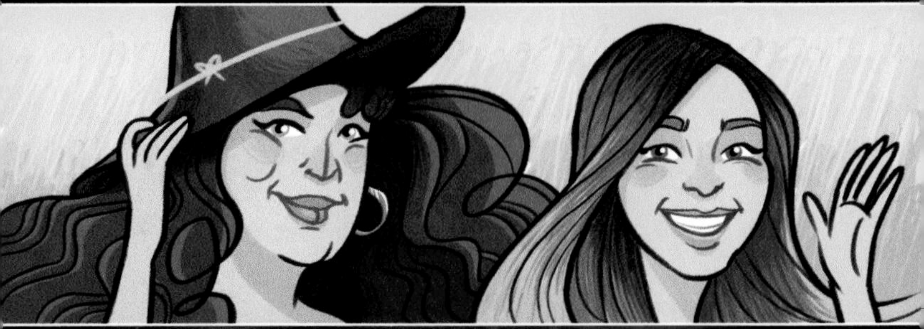

MELISSA MARR writes fiction for adults, teens, and children. Her novels and picture books have won awards, been translated into 28 languages, and been bestsellers in the *New York Times*, *Los Angeles Times*, *USA Today*, and more. Previously, she taught literature and gender studies, worked an archaeology dig, and taught historical sword-fighting. Currently, when not writing, Melissa can be found in her kayak or with her partner and kids.

MARCELA "MACE" CESPEDES has always been a huge bookworm with an adventurous spirit. Born in Colombia, her journey has taken her from a career in advertising to her true passion, telling stories through pictures. She has illustrated the wonderful worlds of clients such as Nickelodeon, Penguin Random House, and Disney Jr., among others, and she is eager to tell many more stories, especially her own. You can always find her reading the most recent graphic novel in a park, learning yet another language, or traveling around the world with her husband, Sam.

MARI COPENY: FIGHTING FOR FLINT

To support the children of Flint, visit the Community Foundation of Greater Flint at cfgf.org to learn about their programs on food access and literacy.

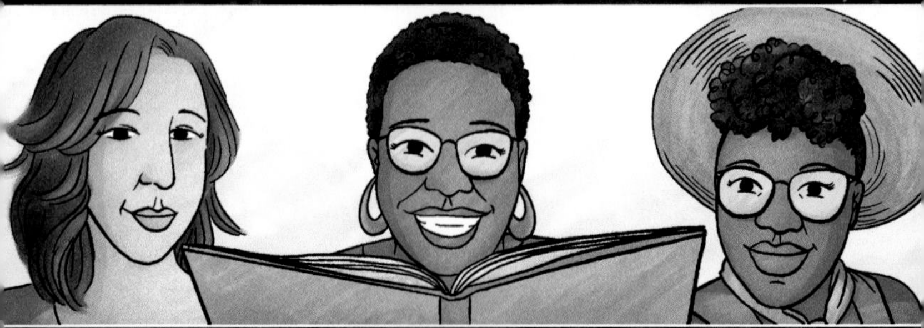

OLUGBEMISOLA RHUDAY-PERKOVICH is the author of *8th Grade Superzero*, the adapted *Alice's Adventures in Wonderland*, and the forthcoming *Operation Sisterhood*. She co-authored the NAACP Image Award–nominated *Two Naomis* and its sequel, *Naomis Too*. She has written a number of nonfiction titles and was the editor of *The Hero Next Door* from We Need Diverse Books. She lives with her family (including the very cool cat Batman) in NYC, where she loves to bake, eat cake, and take walks, and she needs to get more sleep.

SHAREE MILLER is an acclaimed illustrator and author of many picture books, including *Don't Touch My Hair!* She loves sharing the stories of strong women that will inspire the next generation of strong women. She lives and works in Jersey City with her husband and their two cats, Pumpkin and Spice.

SILVANA BRYS is an expert digital colorist who has colored numerous (and brave) comic book characters and children's stories since 2002. She has so much fun painting stories of incredible gangs like Scooby-Doo, Looney Tunes, the DC Super Hero Girls, the Teen Titans, and others. When she is not busy with her digital brushes, she loves to take photos as her family documents everything in their path walking through the colorful forest and

TEARA FRASER: HELPING OTHERS SOAR

Samuel's story was based on a real teen! GiveThemWings.ca has a mission to reveal to Indigenous youth the possibilities of flight and map ways to navigate the journey.

TRACI SORELL is the award-winning poet and author of *We Are Grateful: Otsaliheliga*, which received a Sibert honor, a Boston Globe–Horn Book honor, an American Indian Youth Literature Award (AIYLA) honor, and an Orbis Pictus honor. She also wrote *At the Mountain's Base*, an AIYLA-honor book, and co-authored *Indian No More*, an AIYLA winner, with Charlene Willing McManis. In addition to Teara's story, Traci and Natasha Donovan are also co-creators of *Classified: The Secret Career of Mary Golda Ross, Cherokee Aerospace Engineer*. Traci is an enrolled citizen of the Cherokee Nation and lives with her family in northeastern Oklahoma, where her tribe is located.

NATASHA DONOVAN is the illustrator of the award-winning picture book series Mothers of Xsan (written by Brett Huson) and the Surviving the City graphic novel series, written by Tasha Spillett. Natasha is Métis and grew up in Canada, and currently lives in an intentional community on a farm in Washington State. She is married to Sky, an artist/mad scientist, and together they attempt to keep up with their almost-wild dog, Luna.

RUTH BADER GINSBURG: DISSENT

To learn more about RBG, read *Notorious RBG: The Life and Times of Ruth Bader Ginsburg* by Irin Carmon and Shana Knizhnik.

LILAH STURGES (she/her/hers) has been writing comics for a very long time, and she thinks she is starting to get the hang of it. Her works have been nominated for the Eisner, Ignatz, and GLAAD Media awards (which she lost) and the PRISM Award (which she won!). These days she's best known for her work on the *Lumberjanes* graphic novels and *The Magicians* comics. She once wrote a story where Blue Beetle plays mini golf. She lives in Austin, Texas, with her two daughters and her cat, Greg.

DEVAKI NEOGI, a comic book artist from Bengaluru, India, has been working in the U.S. industry for the past seven years. She's worked for Archie Comics on *Josie and the Pussycats in Space* and for Dynamite Comics on a *Sweet Valley High* graphic novel adaptation. She is one half of the creator team for *Curb Stomp* (at Boom! Studios) and *The Skeptics* (at Black Mask Studios), as well as a contributor to many anthologies, most recently *Insider Art*. Before drawing comics, she worked as a fashion designer after graduating from NIFT Bengaluru. She lives with a bunch of four-legged beasts and her husband. When she's not drawing, she's either cooking or baking.

JUDITH HEUMANN: HOW TO IGNITE A SPARK

To hear from more intersectional voices in disability justice, we recommend *Disability Visibility: First-Person Stories from the 21st Century*, edited by Alice Wong.

MARIEKE NIJKAMP (she/they) is a #1 *New York Times* bestselling author of YA novels, graphic novels, and comics. Her work includes *This Is Where It Ends*, *Even If We Break*, and *The Oracle Code*. She also edited the anthology *Unbroken: 13 Stories Starring Disabled Teens*. Marieke is a nonbinary, disabled storyteller, globe-trotter, and geek.

ASHANTI FORTSON is an award-nominated cartoonist and illustrator whose work explores transience and reflection through a tenderhearted lens. They've worked with Abrams Books, Bitch Media, the *New York Times*, My Kid Is Gay, Sterling Publishing, Medium, Zeal, Power & Magic Press, and more. They're currently working on their debut graphic novel, *Cress & Petra* (HarperCollins, 2023). Ashanti also does freelance comics editing on the side, and they were an assistant editor on TO Comix's anthology *Wayward Kindred*. They teach illustration and comics in Baltimore and live happily with their wife, their cat, and their two pet rats.

DISABILITY ACTIVISTS ON PAGE 135

1: Mosharraf Hossain
2: Danika Ransome
3: Jillian Mercado
4: Gertrude Oforiwa Fefoame
5: Mama Càx
6: Bahati Satir Omar
7: Mary Jane Owen
8: Imani Barbarin
9: Lydia X.Z. Brown
10: Judith Heumann
11: Kitty Cone
12: Madison Lawson
13: Zamir Dhale
14: Fredrick Ouko
15: Silvia Quan
16: Rebecca Cokley
17: Firoz Alizada
18: Vilissa Thompson
19: Stella Young
20: Rebekah Taussig
21: Ali Stroker
22: Yetnebersh Nigussie
23: Emmanuel Ofosu Yeboah
24: Alice Wong
25: Stacey Park Milbern
26: Keah Brown

LEIOMY MALDONADO: GENERATIONAL

You can check Leiomy's style out on HBO Max's *Legendary*, where she's a judge.

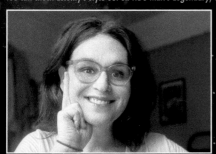

MAGDALENE VISAGGIO is the Eisner- and GLAAD Media award-nominated writer of *Kim & Kim*, *Eternity Girl*, *Doctor Mirage*, *Jinny Hex*, and *Vagrant Queen*, which was adapted for television on Syfy in 2020. She is also the writer of the young adult adventure horror graphic novel *The Ojja-Wojja*, due out from Balzer + Bray (an imprint of HarperCollins) in 2022, and she's a decent rhythm guitarist to boot. Born in Long Island and raised in central Virginia, she currently lives in Manhattan with her wife and cat.

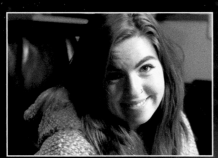

EMMA KUBERT has worked for various companies including Image Comics, Dynamite Entertainment, and, of course, DC Comics, where she's contributed to *DC Super Hero Girls: Weird Science* and *Teen Titans Go!* She is drawn to stories with funny, strong female characters, which made working on this story a dream come true. She is currently working with fellow artist Rusty Gladd on their creator-owned project *Inkblot* for Image Comics.

ALEXIS WILLIAMS began drawing Leiomy's story but had to withdraw. We're extremely grateful for her contribution, and we think you should check out her art at jokeboi.carrd.co.

As promised on page 45, here's the English translation of the scene in the bodega!

mid-
2019
Did you see that pervert walk in?
Uh, I think she can hear—
I just don't understand how anyone can do that to themselves.
It makes me want to vomit.
HEY!
You didn't pay for that!
I'm not kicking your ass, sweetie. Consider that payment in full.

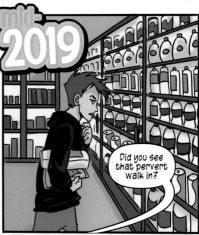

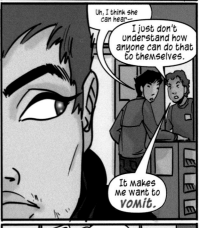

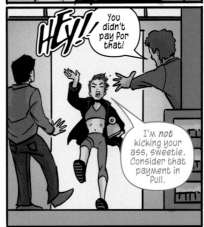

MARSHA P. JOHNSON: THE BEAUTY OF A BRICK

While TheOkraProject.com wasn't around in Marsha's day, she'd approve of their mission to extend free, delicious, and nutritious meals to Black trans people experiencing food insecurity.

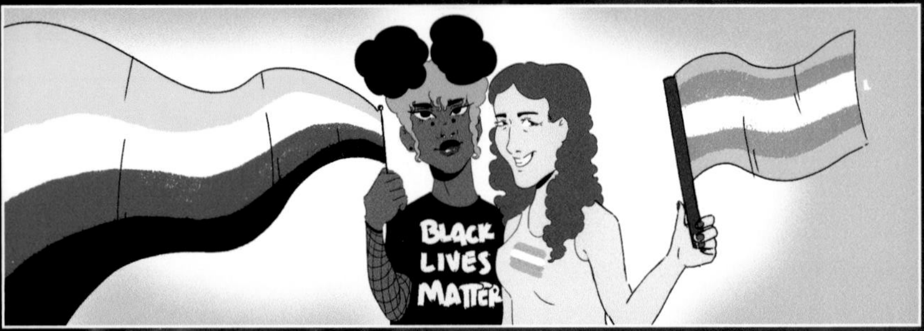
BLACK LIVES MATTER

JADZIA AXELROD (she/her) is an award-winning author, illustrator, activist, gadabout, style maven, and circus performer. She is the writer of an upcoming graphic novel for DC Books for Young Readers, as well as comics for Tor, Quirk Books, and Epic Books. She is the writer and producer of the popular fiction podcasts *The Voice of Free Planet X*, *Aliens You Will Meet*, and *Fables of the Flying City*. She lives in Philadelphia, where she cooks overly elaborate meals for her wonderful wife and delightful child.

MICHAELA WASHINGTON is a 23-year-old nonbinary comics artist and writer from Dallas, Texas. They enjoy anime, concerts, and watching *The Matrix*. Some comics they've written include *The Devil Stole a Shooting Star*, *This Is My First Diary Comic*, and *The Last Day on Earth*. They are currently being held captive in Chicago by an evil cat named Ashley.

ELLEN OCHOA: DESTINATION — SPACE!

For more info about how the United States prepares future astronauts, check out nasa.gov/stem.

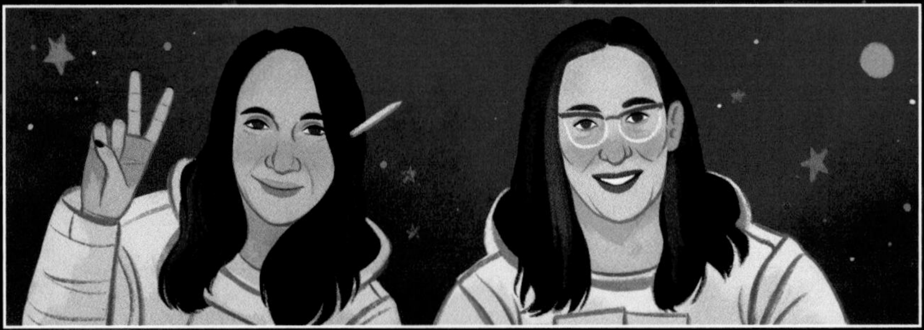

CECIL CASTELLUCCI (she/her) is the award-winning and *New York Times* bestselling author of novels and comics for young adults including *Batgirl*; *Shade, the Changing Girl*; *Female Furies*; *Soupy Leaves Home*; and *The Plain Janes*. She is the daughter of two scientists and is a huge space enthusiast. She follows all things astronaut- and space-related and always has her eyes and heart pointed toward the stars. She lives in Los Angeles.

CARINA GUEVARA is a Latinx illustrator and comics artist, and *Wonderful Women of the World* marks her debut. She got her start as an illustrator freelancing in editorial and commercial illustration. Carina lives in Austin, Texas, with her husband. When she's not drawing, she likes to roller-skate, play elaborate RPGs with her friends, and read good books late into the night. Carina also drew portraits of team members who couldn't send their own: Laurie Halse Anderson, Janice Chiang, Agnes Garbowska, Ariana Maher, Carrie Strachan, Saida Temofonte, and Ashley A. Woods.

FRANCISCA NNEKA OKEKE: CLIMATE CHANGE ACTIVIST AND SHERO

Visit nsesafoundation.org, a nonprofit based in Ghana that is fostering a culture of innovation focused on STEM research, coaching African youths to develop solutions to problems in their communities.

DR. SHEENA C. HOWARD is an award-winning author, scholar, and filmmaker. Sheena is the first Black woman to win an Eisner Award, and she's the author of several critically acclaimed books and comics on a range of social justice topics. Sheena is an image activist with a passion for telling stories, through various mediums, that encourage audiences to consider narratives that are different from their own. She especially enjoys writing graphic novel adaptations in the academic space. In her free time, she enjoys kickboxing.

LAYLIE FRAZIER is a digital illustrator from Houston, Texas. She began drawing when she was ten years old and has been drawing ever since. She combines texture, color, and pattern to create warm and expressive portraits, pulling inspiration from nature and utilizing abstract plant, mountain, and sun motifs in her backgrounds. She has worked with Coca-Cola, Disney+, Home Depot, and Ulta Beauty to create illustrated content for their social media feeds. Her household is run by a dog named Pippin, a cat named Costello, and a snake named Dr. Squiggles.

GRETA THUNBERG: CLIMATE JUSTICE

We must all #FaceTheClimateEmergency. Sign the petition at ClimateEmergencyEU.org.

KAMI GARCIA is a #1 *New York Times*, *USA Today*, and international bestselling author and comic book writer with 13 novels and graphic novels published in 51 countries and 38 languages. Her books have sold more than 10 million copies worldwide. Kami's best-known works include *Beautiful Creatures*, the Bram Stoker Award-nominated novels *Unbreakable* and *Unmarked*, and the *New York Times* bestselling graphic novels *Teen Titans: Raven*, *Teen Titans: Beast Boy*, and *Teen Titans: Beast Boy Loves Raven*. She co-founded YALLFest, one of the largest kid-lit book festivals in the United States.

IGZELL is a Mexican illustrator. *Wonderful Women of the World* is her first U.S. publication, but she hopes for a long career as a storyteller, creating images and stories that inspire young people to act on important issues in their lives.

NAOMI WATANABE: FINDING YOUR FIT

To follow Naomi's inspiring (and hilarious) journey, check out instagram.com/watanabenaomi703/.

JODY HOUSER is an award-nominated writer of comics. She has written for *Mother Panic, Harley & Ivy, Supergirl,* and many, many more. When she's not scripting comics, she's rolling dice in one of several RPGs or singing karaoke with her friends. Honestly, she's probably also writing comics on her phone at the same time.

MICHIUMS is a nonbinary illustrator and comics- and merch-maker based in New York City whose work can be found in various indie comic publications such as *Lilies Anthology* (vol. 4-7); Arledge Comics' *My Kingdom for a Panel;* the *Strange Waters* and *What's Left?* Anthologies; *A-Ok!* (April/May 2021 issue); and *Sensory: Life on the Spectrum, an Autistic Comic Anthology* (2021), along with King Features' *Flash Forward!* comic series. When not self-publishing and helping run fan anthology projects, you can find them drinking too much coffee, watching far too many movies and animated series, and thinking about comics.

SERENA WILLIAMS: SUPER SERENA — G.O.A.T.

Serena and Venus support the future of tennis with their academy. To learn more, visit VenusSerenaTennisAcademy.org and see how mentoring students to excel in school is a key focus!

DANIELLE PAIGE is the *New York Times* bestselling author of the Dorothy Must Die series, the Stealing Snow series, and the Ravens series with Kass Morgan. She wrote the *Betty Cooper: Superteen* comic, drawn by Brittney Williams, and the graphic novel *Mera: Tidebreaker,* drawn by Stephen Byrne. She also works in the television industry, where she's received a Writers Guild of America Award and was nominated for several Daytime Emmys. Danielle wrote this story for all her favorite superheroes, her family, but especially her mom and dad, who gave her a love of books and tennis. Danielle's engaged to her very own Batman, Chris Albers.

BRITTNEY WILLIAMS (she/her) is a new plant mom and a storyboard and comic book artist who draws way too much. From Walt Disney Animation to DC Comics, she's worked for a variety of animation studios and publishers. A two-time GLAAD Media Award nominee, she exists to create things for kids and the queer community.

EDITH WINDSOR:
HOW ONE WOMAN'S LOVE CHANGED A NATION

Looking for ways to honor Edie's struggle? SAGE (SageUSA.org) was near and dear to her heart as an advocacy and services organization for elderly LGBTQ+ people.

AMANDA DEIBERT (she/her) is an award-winning television and comic book writer. Her works include *DC Super Hero Girls*, *Teen Titans Go!*, *Wonder Woman '77*, *Sensation Comics Featuring Wonder Woman*, and a story in *Love Is Love* (a *New York Times* #1 bestseller) along with comics for IDW, Dark Horse, Bedside Press, and Storm King). She's written TV shows for CBS, Syfy, OWN, Hulu, and Quibi, and for former vice president Al Gore's international climate broadcast, *24 Hours of Reality*. She lives in Los Angeles with her wife, Cat Staggs, adorable daughter, Vivienne, and kitty, Raven.

CAT STAGGS is best known for her work on the *New York Times* bestselling title *Smallville Season 11* and *Crosswind* with Gail Simone. She's currently working on *John Carpenter's Tales for a HalloweeNight* after many years of superhero comics like *The Death of Superman*, *Adventures of Supergirl*, and *Wonder Woman '77* (DC Comics); other adventures like *The X-Files*, *Orphan Black*, and *Star Trek* (IDW); and over 10 years in the *Star Wars* universe with Lucasfilm. In 2017 a one-of-a-kind original Wonder Woman piece was inducted into the Library of Congress by Lynda Carter along with *Wonder Woman '77 Vol. 1*.

MALALA YOUSAFZAI: ONE FOR ALL

The Malala Fund is working for a world where every girl can learn and lead. Discover their mission at malala.org.

SON M. is an Algerian Muslim writer with a penchant for the bold, the beautiful, and the horrific. Known for their webcomic series *Animalheads* and upcoming graphic novel *Thief of the Heights*, Son works to bring new perspectives into well-loved and established genres. They are very passionate about comics, games, and animation, leading them to create stories in all three mediums. They are afraid of heights and non-productivity. Son draws their power from the sun.

SAFIYA ZERROUGUI started as a freelance illustrator in 2017 and since then has contributed to numerous fan-driven zines and art anthologies, including Bad Co Press's *My Girlfriend: From the Legends*. She's known for stylized pieces borrowing from medieval imagery as well as her passion for the fashion of past eras. If you happen to get into a conversation with her about the intricacies of Renaissance fashion or the highly glamorous 1970s, she'll talk your ears off!

KHATIJAH MOHAMAD YUSOFF: CREATING HEROES FROM VILLAINS

Professor Khatijah was once the vice president of an organization of Islamic scientists, and you can learn more at iasworld.org/what-is-ias.

AMANDA DEIBERT also wrote our Edith Windsor profile. Check out her bio on the previous page!

HANIE MOHD, after being told at an early age that being a jewelry maker was a no-go, decided to pursue art in both studies and as a career. She dabbles in an eclectic range of works (comics, sketch cards, illustrations, and wearable crafts) in both digital and traditional media, using the vast landscape of pop culture and the unassuming beauty of everyday life as inspiration. In her free time, she likes to bake, explore new places, hang out with her husband, watch figure skating and movies that make her cry, read books at least halfway through, and travel vicariously through YouTube food shows around the world. She hopes to one day publish her own book — one that is either about food, travel, figure skating...or all three together.

SHARI CHANKHAMMA is a comics artist, illustrator, colorist, flatter, game assets maker (she did it once, still counts), and general artist for hire. Notable work includes *Codename Baboushka*, *Sheltered*, *The Fuse*, and *Kill Shakespeare*. She was born and lives in Thailand, where the average temperature is 90 degrees Fahrenheit. It's very hot. Shari also colored our beautiful cover!

COVER ART NICOLA SCOTT is an Australian comic book artist with a history in theater and in costume design. Nicola started pursuing a comics career in 2001 and by 2006 she'd become a staple of the U.S. mainstream, working exclusively for DC Comics on iconic characters and team books. 2016 saw the launch of her critically acclaimed Image Comics series *Black Magick* and DC's *Wonder Woman: Year One* to celebrate the character's 75th anniversary, both in collaboration with writer Greg Rucka. She lives in the Blue Mountains with her husband and their cat. Nicola's avatar was drawn by her niece, Ella Brennan.

JENETTE KAHN PORTRAIT AGNES GARBOWSKA has made her name in comics illustrating such titles as the *New York Times* bestselling and award-winning *DC Super Hero Girls* for DC Comics, as well as *Teen Titans Go!* Agnes is a Polish immigrant with a love for comics and animation, since it is thanks to them that she was able to learn to read and speak English.

MARY SEACOLE PORTRAIT BEX GLENDINING (they/she) is a biracial, queer, UK-based illustrator, comics artist, and colorist. Bex has worked as a cover artist, colorist, and interior artist on projects such as *Seen: Edmonia Lewis*, Lars Brown's *Penultimate Quest*, *Rolled & Told*, *Lupina*, and on multiple covers for Penguin Random House. When not working they can usually be found building Gundams, playing video games with friends, or buying new plants.

WILMA MANKILLER PORTRAIT WESHOYOT ALVITRE is a Native comic book illustrator who has worked on video games, graphic novels, and her own self-written projects. She prefers doing things the old-fashioned way and utilizes her antiquing hobby to find antiquarian art supplies, which she uses in her art. Her hobbies outside drawing include yarn spinning, banjo collecting, and other strange skills to survive the zombie apocalypse.

ADA LOVELACE PORTRAIT COLLEEN DORAN has drawn/written/painted many comics and graphic novels with wonderful creators like Neil Gaiman and J. Michael Straczynski. She has some shiny knickknacks like the Eisner Award and the Bram Stoker Award. She lives on a mountain in the middle of nowhere, which is a great place for riding out the zombie apocalypse, though the cell phone reception is terrible.

VENUS WILLIAMS PORTRAIT ASHLEY A. WOODS is a comic book artist, writer, and creator from Chicago known for her work on *Niobe*, *Ladycastle*, and the Tomb Raider series. She got her start self-publishing her action-fantasy comics series *Millennia War*, which led to her career in comics and TV. Recognized for her illustrations and designs for female characters, her most prominent work is *Niobe: She Is Life* with Stranger Comics. Her latest projects include *Heathen* from Vault Comics and *Lovecraft Country* on HBO.

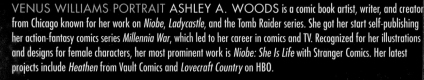

ADDITIONAL COLORISTS AND LETTERERS

BECCA CAREY is a graphic designer and letterer who has worked on books like *Redlands*, *Vampirella/Red Sonja*, *Buffy the Vampire Slayer*, and more super-secret fun projects to watch out for. She loves terrible horror movies and having conversations with her dog and has proudly read *War and Peace*, but couldn't tell you a thing about it.

JANICE CHIANG began hand-lettering comic books in 1974, learning the skills from Larry Hama and Ralph Reese. Her first published work was a Black Panther story for Marvel's *Jungle Action* series. When asked, "What has been your favorite story to letter?" she always replies, "The one I'm presently working on." She's been baking bread, cookies, cakes, brownies, and apple pies since she was eight years old and weight training for over 40 years.

GABRIELA DOWNIE was born and raised in Los Angeles, the daughter of Central American refugees. Gabriela is at the forefront of diversity and inclusion when it comes to the entertainment industry. Self-taught and inspired to keep climbing, along the way she's made friends and family and paved the way for more Latinx artists.

TRÍONA FARRELL is a colorist in Dublin, Ireland, who has worked with many different companies on books such as *Crowded*, *Blackbird*, *West Coast Avengers*, and *Lords of Empyre: Emperor Hulkling*. She loves cats and nerd things and can generally be found wandering the wilds when she isn't coloring.

ARIANA MAHER is a Brazilian American letterer who recently worked on *Green Lantern: Legacy* and *Zatanna and the House of Secrets*. Ten years ago, bored by her day job, she started to teach herself how to letter comics using online tutorials as a hobby. This year, she quit her day job to become a full-time comic book letterer for Marvel and DC Comics. She's fluent in Japanese and used to work at a major corporation but interpreting at business meetings was a headache—comics are way more fun!

MORGAN MARTINEZ has worked in comics since 2011 and lettered acclaimed books such as Natasha Alterici's *Heathen*, John Leguizamo's *Freak*, Cullen Bunn and J.B. Bastos's *Night Trap*, and Brandon Easton and Denis Medri's *Andre the Giant: Closer to Heaven*. When she isn't working on comics or graphic design, Morgan's interests include writing, drawing, computers, intersectional feminism and trans rights, Nintendo Switch, and being as unserious as circumstances allow. She lives in the South Bronx with her wife and their cat, Darcy.

CAITLIN QUIRK has been coloring comics since fall 2017 and has worked on several DC titles such as *Black Canary: Ignite* and *Lois Lane and the Friendship Challenge*. She is also the main colorist on Image Comics' *Moonstruck*. In addition to YA comics, Caitlin loves to illustrate fashion portraits, anime fan art, and K-pop idols. When she's not drawing for a living, she loves to sit on the couch, play *Animal Crossing*, and rewatch her favorite feel-good movies for the 100th time.

CHRISTY SAWYER joined DC Comics as a production administrator in the collected editions department in 2017, but still occasionally revisits her past career as a letterer. She's lettered various titles from DC, Zenescope, Dark Horse, Papercutz, and more. She has an identical twin sister named Megan and has promised her coworkers that they would never trade places. Or would they?

CARRIE STRACHAN is an award-awaiting colorist from San Diego, California. Her work has appeared in such titles as *DC Super Hero Girls*, *Hellblazer*, *MAD*, and *Suicide Squad Most Wanted: Deadshot & Katana*. When she's not trying to meet her deadlines, Carrie enjoys reading, playing video games, and watching old movies.

SAIDA TEMOFONTE is a Los Angelina by heart currently based in Florida. She's been lettering and designing since 1997 with all major comic book players. When she's not missing California mountains, she can be found fishing in Florida.

JODI TONG is currently the pre-press manager at DC Comics and has been ensuring every comics page goes out looking its best since 2013. A cartoonist in her own right with a healthy-ish obsession with bunnies, she creates and publishes her ongoing comic, *Bunny Mom*, and is working on *Chubbeh Bunnehs*. She also loves to bake—especially desserts—honing new techniques and recipes to delight the palate...and unfortunately expand people's waistlines.

LOOKING FOR FANTASTIC FICTION FROM OUR WRITERS AND ARTISTS? CHECK OUT THESE TITLES!

MERA: TIDEBREAKER

Danielle Paige,
Stephen Byrne

A powerful story that explores duty, love, heroism, and freedom... told through the eyes of an independent undersea princess.

ISBN: 978-1-4012-8339-1

CATWOMAN: SOULSTEALER

Sarah J. Maas
Louise Simonson
Samantha Dodge

When the Bat's away, the Cat returns to Gotham City, where she must fight Batwing and the League of Assassins!

ISBN: 978-1-4012-9641-4

THE ORACLE CODE

Marieke Nijkamp,
Manuel Preitano

A haunting mystery in a rehabilitation center where Barbara Gordon must battle the phantoms of her past before they consume her future.

ISBN: 978-1-4012-9066-5

SHADOW OF THE BATGIRL

Sarah Kuhn,
Nicole Goux

The harrowing story of a girl who overcomes the odds to find her unique identity.

ISBN: 978-1-4012-8978-2

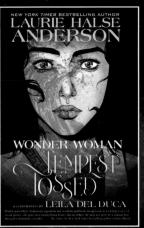

WONDER WOMAN: TEMPEST TOSSED

Laurie Halse Anderson,
Leila Del Duca

Cut off from her island home and fellow Amazons, Princess Diana of Themyscira finds herself a refugee in an unfamiliar land.

ISBN: 978-1-4012-8645-3

TEEN TITANS: RAVEN
ISBN: 978-1-4012-8623-1

TEEN TITANS: BEAST BOY
ISBN: 978-1-4012-8719-1

TEEN TITANS: BEAST BOY LOVES RAVEN
ISBN: 978-1-4012-8719-1

Kami Garcia, Gabriel Picolo
The New York Times bestselling series about first loves, faithful friendships, family secrets, and finding your true self.